ONE WEEK LOAN
UNIVERSITY OF GLAMORGAN
TREFOREST LEARNING RESOURCES CENTRE
Pontypridd, CF37 1DL
Telephone: (01443) 482626
Books are to be returned on or before the last date below

NAFTA
IN TRANSITION

Edited by

Stephen J. Randall
and
Herman W. Konrad

UNIVERSITY OF CALGARY PRESS

Canadian Cataloguing in Publication Data

Main entry under title:
NAFTA in transition

Includes bibliographical references and index.
ISBN 1-895176-63-8

1. Free trade – Social aspects – North America. 2. Free trade –
Political aspects – North America. 3. North America – Economic
integration. I. Randall, Stephen J., 1944– II. Konrad, Herman W.
HF1746.N33 1995   382'.917   C95-911147-6

COMMITTED TO THE DEVELOPMENT OF CULTURE AND THE ARTS

Printed and bound in Canada by DWFriesen.
Front cover illustration: © Tony Stone Images.

∞ This book is printed on acid-free paper.

Table of Contents

III. Borderlands, Industry, Labour, and Immigration

IV. Energy and the Environment

V. Public Policy and Culture

Acknowledgements

As with any joint effort, this book embodies the skills, knowledge and contributions of many people. The editors would especially like to express their appreciation to those who contributed chapters to the volume and, in so doing, have furthered our understanding of the ways in which the North American political, economic and social landscapes are changing in the age of NAFTA.

A number of individuals have made particularly important contributions to the technical preparation of the manuscript. Copy-editing was the work of Eileen Delman at an early stage, followed by Windsor Viney, Terry Teskey, and Eileen Eckert. Cliff Kadatz prepared the cover design, and John King, production editor of the University of Calgary Press, as on so many occasions added remarkable expertise and insight into every stage of the production process. Shirley Onn, director of the Press, encouraged us in this project from its inception.

We acknowledge the Canadian–American Center at the University of Maine for granting permission to quote material from the Borderlands Monograph Series (pp. 179–192). We thank McClelland and Stewart and the authors for permission to quote Pierre Berton and Rick Salutin (pp. 393 and 395). Telefilm Canada is acknowledged for granting permission to quote from their *Co-production: Policies and Procedures* (Montreal: Telefilm Canada, 1989). We acknowledge Tony Stone Images/Vancouver for supplying the image of North America that appears on the front cover. Publication has been made possible, in part, by a grant from the Endowment Fund of The University of Calgary and by a grant from the Imperial Oil–Lincoln McKay Chair in American Studies of The University of Calgary.

To all of the above we extend our appreciation, although we assume responsibility for whatever technical or factual errors might remain.

HK
SJR

Stephen J. Randall, Chair in American Studies
Herman W. Konrad, History and Anthropology
University of Calgary

1

Introduction

The political and economic landscape of North America has undergone dramatic changes since *North America Without Borders* was published in 1992 (now out of print). The book reflected the insights of a broad collection of scholars in 1991, shortly after the implementation of the Canada–United States Free Trade Agreement (FTA) and when the inclusion of Mexico in a trinational agreement was still very much in doubt. Three years later, and over a year after the implementation of the North American Free Trade Agreement (NAFTA), all three countries not only have changed governments but also political agendas, in response to intervening economic and political forces. NAFTA is now an accomplished reality and one has to address the impact of the agreement as well as the past. NAFTA, as the title of this volume suggests, is truly "in transition." The evolving nature of a North America 'without borders' is clearly reflected in the pages of this new volume, although the editors and authors have chosen not to examine the increasingly important question of the extension of NAFTA to other countries in Latin America. Nonetheless, the new chapters in this volume reflect the preoccupation of both supporters and critics of free trade and of NAFTA. There are expanded sections on energy and the environment as well as new material treating the automobile industry and the *maquiladora* sector; agricultural trade; women in industry and Mexican labour in general; poverty and income distribution in Mexico. There is also an expanded section on the U.S.–Mexico border region, along with several chapters which examine the academic, cultural and institutional implications and developments that have occurred as part of continued trilateralism.

In 1989, Canada and the United States concluded a bilateral free trade agreement (FTA), following one of the most intense political debates in Canadian history over relations with the United States and the nature of the Canadian political economy. The Canadian federal election of 1988, in which the FTA featured as the single most important issue, and the subsequent conclusion of the agreement have not ended that debate.

The vitality of the issue derived from several factors. The first was the continuing evolution of Canada–United States economic, political, and cultural relations. A second factor was the discontent fostered by the international economic recession in 1990–92, and the widespread impression in Canada that the high loss of jobs in industrial Canada to the United States and Mexico was a result of the FTA. A third factor was the high current level of political conflict in Canada over a wide range of issues, from the FTA to federal-provincial relations, the constitutional crisis, and the controversial economic policies of the Conservative government.

With the Salinas turnabout, in favour of a Mexico–United States FTA, and Canada's entry into the negotiations, resulting in the NAFTA agreement inked by Brian Mulroney, Carlos Salinas, and George Bush in Texas in late 1992, the free trade debate took on new dimensions. Opposition parties in all three countries—the Canadian Liberal Party led by Jean Chrétien, the Mexican Party of the Democratic Revolution (PRD) under Cuauhtémoc Cardenas, and the U.S. Democratic Party led by Bill Clinton—provided political platforms for intensive scrutiny and debate. Clinton, once elected, became a staunch advocate of NAFTA provided that side-agreements were negotiated on labour and environmental issues. The rich and eccentric H. Ross Perot, with Republican (for example, Robert Torricelli) and Democratic (the AFL-CIO) bedfellows, campaigned vigorously against it. For this 'unholy' alliance, which included a broad spectrum of concerned U.S. citizens, NAFTA represented massive job losses, environmental degradation, and an attack on the 'American Dream.' Buttressed by Big Business, a lot of arm twisting, and the hastily negotiated side-agreements, the Clinton forces won sufficient congressional votes to allow the mandated 1 January 1994 NAFTA start-up date to become a reality.

Jean Chrétien, having decimated the governing Conservatives and routed the New Democrats in the 1993 elections, made the traditional Liberal Party adjustments to expediency. Now comfortably again in power, the Canadian Liberals were free to adopt policies previously opposed while in opposition. Faced with the realities of the economic agendas of Canada's new political alignment—the western-based Reform Party and the separatist Bloc Québecois, both pro-NAFTA—Chrétien has become a national and hemisphere sponsor of not only North American but also hemisphere free trade. He has led significant trade delegations to Mexico and South America and, at the Hemisphere heads-of-state meetings in Miami (December 1994), was actively lobbying for Chile's entry into NAFTA. Meanwhile, in Canada, the Canadian Labour Congress and the Canadian Auto Workers have led the critique of bilateral and trilateral free trade, insisting that the agenda is to exploit Mexico's cheap labour at the expense of Canadian labour and investment in Canada.

In Mexico, with the all-powerful PRI party behind him and most of the public media onside, Carlos Salinas's economic and constitutional adjustments to meet his neoliberal economic agenda and its free trade implications were easily implemented. His acquiescent Congress and Senate, despite strident opposition from the PRD, quickly approved presidential initiatives. Ratification of the NAFTA, requiring only Senate approval, took place almost immediately after the bill's passage in the United States. Mexicans were led to believe, and the majority appeared ready to believe, that a brighter, more prosperous future would be forthcoming with Mexico as a formal economic partner with its richer U.S. and Canadian neighbours. The business at hand now, in late 1993, was the forthcoming national elections for which Salinas unveiled Luis Donaldo Colosio as the PRI standard-bearer. Like the earlier López Portillo forecast of Mexico needing to think in terms of coming to terms with the management of prosperity, based on projected petroleum revenues, the Salinas forecast was framed in terms of Mexico moving from third to first world status.

Unforeseen events shattered both optimistic forecasts. The 1982 collapse of oil prices unraveled the López Portillo vision of the future, plunging Mexico into a decade of belt-tightening economic adjustments. For Salinas, the shot that undermined his first world future came from marginalized, mostly indigenous and economically depressed Chiapas in the form of the masked Zapatista Army of National Liberation (EZLN). Led by the charismatic *subcomandante*, Marcos, who claimed only to be the voice of the General Command of the Clandestine Revolutionary Indigenous Committee (CCRI), this jungle-trained group of insurgents declared war on the Mexican Federal Army. The declaration, symbolized by the armed occupation of San Cristobal de las Casas, in the first hour of 1 January 1994, was purposely timed to coincide with the official start-up of NAFTA. It, claimed the rebels, represented the death-knoll of Mexico's rural indigenous peasantry. Echoing the rallying call of revolutionary Mexico's Emiliano Zapata, whose ideals they identified with, the EZLN demanded "Work, Land, Housing, Food, Health, Education, Democracy, Liberty, Peace, Independence, and Justice" (*trabajo, tierra, techo, pan, salud, educación, democracia, libertad, paz, independencia, y justicia*). The immediate response of the national and international media, and the Mexican army, quickly focused attention on the 'other face' of Salinas's Mexican 'miracle'—the lag between social/political/economic progress, and economic and constitutional restructuring—for Mexico's rural and urban underclasses.

Although shaken, the Salinas agenda was not derailed by the upstart EZLN, more skilled in attracting media attention than military actions. This attention, and increased scrutiny by the NAFTA partners, resulted in electoral reforms and uneven foreign investment in Mexico. The March 23rd assassination of the PRI presidential candidate and the failure to reach a negotiated settlement with the Zapatistas heightened national tensions, increased international concerns regarding Mexican stability and the outcome of the August 21st national elections, and stimulated the flight of capital—both national and foreign speculative—but did not alter the PRI tradition of an almost clean sweep, or *carro completo*, in election results. Salinas's hastily designated Colosio substitute, Ernesto Zedillo, backed by official and unofficial financing, the organizing skills of the PRI conservative wing (known as the 'dinosaurs'), and a flood of funds channeled to rural sectors through government programs (*Procampo* and *Pronasol*), brought out unprecedented numbers of voters on August 21st.

For the first time in Mexico's history its election run-up and voting was accompanied by a presidential candidates' televised national debate, numerous polls, international observers, and exit polls. Despite vigorous campaigning, large crowds in public meetings but little media exposure, Cuauhtémoc Cardenas' anti-NAFTA forces suffered a resounding defeat. The pro-NAFTA conservative National Action Party (PAN) replaced the PRD as the main opposition party. The PRI, in sharp contrast to the 1988 disputed electoral results, this time appeared to be firmly in control, following an election internationally recognized as the cleanest in Mexican memory. Salinas's restructuring program, under Zedillo, would continue, with sighs of relief coming from Washington and Ottawa. North America's future, as the world's largest free-trade block, appeared to be moving in the right direction. The assassination of José Francisco Ruis Massieu, designated leader of the PRI-dominated Chamber of Deputies, in October 1994, raised questions about political stability but not about economic directions. Salinas finished his six-year term inaugurating countless public and private economic projects, including many foreign-financed business ventures looking to take advantage of Mexican opportunities under NAFTA. Attention now turned to the optimistic forecasts of the Zedillo term of office (1994–2000) and its impact. The Zapatista 'problem' had been overtaken by voter confidence in continuity under a political party in power since 1929.

Yet no sooner was Zedillo installed as president (1 December 1994), with an administration replete with Salinas hold-overs, than the wheels began to fall off the restructured Mexico, built to meet the challenges of the future. The Zapatista revoking of the military truce which had held up for most of the year, and the draining of Mexico's financial reserves by anxious Mexicans and nervous investors, quickly resulted in a run on, and collapse of, the Mexican peso. Jaime Serra Puche, under Salinas Mexico's NAFTA negotiator, and now finance minister, was forced to resign in disgrace. Public anger directed at Salinas and his cabinet, for not having made earlier adjustments which might have avoided the economic collapse, resulted in public and opposition parties' calling for a public accounting and judicial penalties against the former president. Zedillo was forced to turn to foreign banks and the International Monetary Fund for a financial bail-out in an attempt to halt the run on Mexican currency which was having a ripple effect (*efecto tequila*) on all hemisphere financial institutions. Mexico, within a matter of a few months, according to national and international commentators, had been transformed from the 'model third world economy' on the road to prosperity to a 'basket-case.' By March 1995, President Zedillo had been forced to make a series of cabinet changes, issue a stream of economic stabilization plans, and accept externally-conditioned financial rescue packages. Carlos Salinas, like Luís Echevarria (in 1977) and José López Portillo (in 1983), was forced to leave Mexico after the arrest of his brother Raul as the intellectual co-author of the Ruis Massieu assassination. Mexico, once again, faced the trauma of the belt-tightening hard times and an uncertain economic future.

By the beginning of spring 1995 the political and economic face of North America was less optimistic. The Mexican peso had crashed, the U.S. dollar had sagged, and the Canadian dollar had slipped badly in comparison with the currencies of North America's competing economies in Japan and Europe. The architects of the FTA and NAFTA (Mulroney, Reagan/Bush, Salinas) and their trade negotiators had been replaced by new national leaders faced by new domestic challenges. The Republican, Gingrich-led nationalism (Contract with America) in the United States, and the Quebec separatism and Western provincial opposition in Canada, has forced a more inward-looking emphasis by the northern NAFTA partners, while Mexico's economic and political turmoil provides even less scope for grand continental or hemisphere plans. The national governments, having given birth to a treaty framework for free trade, accompanied by increased privatization of state enterprises, appear ready to rely upon the private sector to bring forth the promised results. All three countries officially promote NAFTA and its eventual extension to include all the countries of the hemisphere despite the emergence of contradictory initiatives by special interest groups.

Whether the rest of the 1990s has as many unpredicted economic and political surprises as the first 15 months of the post-NAFTA era, when this Introduction was first written, remains to be seen. Whether the private sector is able to take advantage of the now-established framework for continental economic integration, to bring forth projected results, also remains to be seen. What the contents of *NAFTA in Transition* seek to provide, by the retention of chapters from *North America Without Borders*, is an overview of the background and context of issues that have played, and will play, a role in shaping the future of Canada, the United States and Mexico. As a whole it reflects the views of scholars from a broad range of disciplines and with differing professional insights in the three countries. Readers will note that the authors—indeed the editors—sometimes disagree in emphasis and interpretation. No attempt has been made to impose a consensus and the most recent events, noted above, will need to be analyzed in greater depth in the future.

The academic probing of trends and analysis of political events related to continentalization have run parallel to actual events. A consortium of social scientists from Mexico's National Autonomous University (UNAM) and the University of Quebec in Montreal (UQAM) began to examine continentalization trends and implications in 1987, resulting in a series of conferences and publications. When there were hints, in 1989, of the possibility of expanding the Canada–United States FTA to include Mexico, a regional studies group at Baylor University in Waco, Texas sponsored a series of lectures and conferences on regional trade and economic development in 1988 and 1989. It was appropriate, and not surprising, that Texas should have been among those in the forefront of this initiative. Until independence in 1836, the state was part of Mexico. It has had a long Mexican heritage and a close relationship with Mexico since the mid-nineteenth century. It was prescient as well in considering the implications for Canada of a higher degree of integration among the three nations of North America.

Parallel efforts came from the Center for International Studies at Duke University in the fall of 1989, with a conference on Canada–United States–Mexico relations. It was out of the Duke University activity and an independent effort at Western Michigan University on Canada–United States relations that the University of Calgary conference Facing North/Facing South: Contemporary Canada–United States–Mexico Relations took form in the course of 1989–91. *North America Without Borders* derived from a selection of papers presented at that conference. In the same period, other Canadian and Mexican institutions began to host conferences on the emerging free trade debate. These included a colloquium sponsored by the Canada–Latin American Forum in Ottawa, in September 1990, and another at the National Autonomous University in Mexico City, in the summer of 1990. In October 1990, the Partido de Acción Nacional (PAN) sponsored a conference on the Canada–United States FTA in Mexico City. That conference led to a major Mexican publication on the experience of Canada with the Canada–United States FTA negotiations and the results of the agreement.[1] In March 1991, there was a further conference on the North American Free Trade Agreement at the University of Ciudad Juárez, which was especially appropriate because of the high concentration there of the *maquiladora* industries.

In the past several years such national and international gatherings along with publications on aspects of trilateralism and bilateralism have proliferated, drawing together academics, university administrators,

---

1 Maria Teresa Gutiérrez Háces, ed., *Experiencias de la negociación del TLC Canadá–Estados Unidos* (Mexico, 1991).

government officials, labour leaders, women's and other groups, either to assess ongoing processes or to work on strategies for implementing diverse aspects of the NAFTA. In the higher education area the Wingspread Conference (September 1992, Racine, Wisconsin) focused upon an agenda for North American higher education cooperation. This was followed, in September 1993, by the International Symposium on Higher Education and Strategic Partnerships: Mexico, Canada and the United States (Vancouver, British Columbia). Such meetings have included key academic, political and funding agency representatives, such as Ernesto Zedillo, then Minister of Education for Mexico, at the Vancouver meetings. The NAFTA side-agreements on labour and environmental issues, as well as most aspects touched by the agreement, have increased the number of meetings and collaboration across the borders of North America.

The fiftieth anniversary of the establishment in 1944 of formal diplomatic relations between Canada and Mexico resulted in a concerted effort in both countries to sponsor activities that led to conferences focusing upon the Canada–Mexico relationship. Significant conferences took place in Mexico, at UNAM and El Colegio de Mexico, and in Canada, at the Université Laval and the University of Calgary. At these events, plus at annual professional meetings in both countries, and at the IX Conference of Mexican, United States and Canadian Historians (Mexico City, October, 1994) the past, present, and future of continentalization and NAFTA was a dominant theme. The November 10–13, 1994 conference at the University of Calgary, with the theme of "Canada–Mexico Relations: Past, Present and Future," was the inaugural meeting of the Canadian Association for Mexican Studies, at which Dr. Jorge Carpizo, Mexico's Minister of the Interior, gave the opening address. The NAFTA factor has been instrumental in this growth of academic activity, whose focus has quickly become an integral part of university curriculums in all three countries.

If NAFTA has been a catalyst for increased academic activity, the use of its acronym has also identified a cross-cultural recognition dilemma. For Mexicans the Spanish word *nafta* means kerosene, a cheap fuel used for lamps in unelectrified areas. To avoid confusion the Spanish term used has been TLC (*Tratado de Libre Comercio*), the equivalent for the English FTA. For monolingual English speakers, which represent the majority in Mexico's new economic partnership, TLC will most likely be identified, at first glance, with something like "Tender Loving Care." For Spanish publications, both TLC and NAFTA have been recently substituted by TLCAN (*Tratado de Libre Comercio de America del Norte*). At the same time, Mexico has traditionally not considered itself to be part of North America, using the term *norteamericano* exclusively for citizens of the United States. Becoming part of the NAFTA equation, as seen in cultural and academic events, has necessitated a re-evaluation of identity for Mexicans. For all three countries, it will force a re-examination of national identity as the continental economic restructuring process evolves.

While we have employed the structural organization used for *North America Without Borders*, this volume's contents reflect much of what has been taking place since the NAFTA negotiations. All of the chapter authors have been involved, some more intensively than others, in the ongoing debate and analysis of past and future implications. All of the book's five sections include historical background as well as contemporary analysis.

The four chapters in Section I, "Historical Context and the Politics of Emerging Trilateralism," provide the background and historical reasons for the emergence of NAFTA/TLCAN. Taking the last 100 years as a frame of analysis Herman W. Konrad (Chapter 2) argues that the current trade treaty can be seen as a third step in an evolutionary process, the first interrupted by the Mexican Revolution, the second caused by World War II, and the third as a consequence of global competitive factors. The stability of such regional economic comings-together, he suggests, cannot be held as givens. Randall (Chapter 3) focuses upon the shifts in domestic political strategies resulting from NAFTA in the three countries. He suggests that the dominant player, the United States, seeks to strengthen both its domestic and international economic and political positions by entering into this formal relationship. Taking past hemisphere history into consideration, at the same time, he questions whether and how NAFTA may improve and strengthen the formal mechanisms for managing the trilateral relationship. Marquez Perez (Chapter 4) concentrates upon Mexico's recent shift in domestic and regional policies by examining the social neoliberal policies of the Salinas administration that led up to becoming a NAFTA participant and the potential fallout therefrom. Finally, the Gutiérrez Háces contribution (Chapter 5) focuses upon past and present dynamics involved in the Canada–Mexico relationship. Gutiérrez Háces suggests that the United States has been the central shaping force in the trilateral and bilateral dynamics.

Section II, "Economic Perspectives on Free Trade," focuses on the economic rationale for each country's entry into the continental trade arrangement or the potential consequences of that involvement. McRae treats the implications of NAFTA for energy trade, including the possible further liberalization of the Mexican investment environment. Gerber and Kerr examine the important agricultural sector in Chapter 7, linking policies in that area to the broader issue of social policy objectives. The United States, they indicate, had little to lose in this sector, Canada much to protect, and Mexico's interest in using NAFTA plays a central role in social policy reform. In both Mexico and Canada, as recent activities have demonstrated, the agricultural issues will continue to be contentious. In Chapter 8, Castillo Vera broadens the analysis of Mexican, Canadian and United States contexts that affect both traditional binational and future trinational interactions. He argues that both the Canada–United States and the Mexico–United States relationships are loaded with historical content, which will restrict change, while the Canada–Mexico relationship, being largely free from past traditions, is more open to innovation. Alarcón González, in the final chapter (9) of this section, examines the contradictory links between trade liberalization and poverty in Mexico. On the one hand, she sees progress in achieving budgetary stability, but at the expense of increased unemployment, poverty, and extreme poverty.

Section III, "Borderlands, Industry, Labour, and Immigration," moves to questions related to the nature of borders, border regions, and their implications. The southern (Mexico/United States) and northern (Canada/United States) cases are treated by Ganster (Chapter 10) and Victor Konrad (Chapter 11). As Ganster notes, the southern case can be seen as a region (pre-1846 Mexico) with an international border imposed upon it by force, but having retained a regional albeit, now, a growing transborder inter-dependence. In the northern case the political geography has also the same cultural roots—British North America and the 13 independent British colonies—with the bulk of the Canadians located adjacent to the border while the majority of United States residents are more distant from it. Geological factors have shaped a largely north–south land form geography with significant east–west waterways (St. Lawrence River, Rio Bravo). The Adamache, Culos, and Otero contribution (Chapter 12) examines the *maquiladora* industry in terms of its labour and gender implications, beginning as a "labour-intensive, unsophisticated, feminized sector" but expected to become male-oriented and "increasingly flexible, capital-intensive, high-tech operations." Marquez Perez (Chapter 13), on the other hand, examines the Mexican automobile industry as a factor in national industrialization policy, in contrast to the major manufacturers' concerns with global competition. Finally, the Weinfeld (Chapter 14) contribution examines NAFTA as a first stage to less restrictive continental migration flows. This would result in a northward flow of Hispanic influences in view of much higher annual population increases; Mexico, by the year 2020, expected to increase by 60 percent compared to 19 percent and 21 percent increases in Canada and the United States.

Chapters 15–18, in Section IV, "Energy and the Environment," treat important topical issues. Sweedler (Chapter 15) returns to the southern border region of the Californias, where the Tijuana–San Diego cities represent the largest annual two-city international border crossings in the world. This underscores the regional implications of energy and environmental issues. Condon (Chapter 16) looks in the opposite direction, at the differing constitutional national structures in Canada and Mexico that will impact upon implementation of the NAFTA side-agreement on energy (the North American Agreement on Environment Cooperation, or NAAEC). Duquette (Chapter 17) views the broader energy trade in terms of international versus national and regional influences, suggesting that the international factors will continue to overshadow domestic ones of the type that have caused great concerns in Canada and Mexico. And Thompson (Chapter 18) looks at NAFTA and NAAEC implications as they relate to a hierarchy of global, regional, and domestic energy issues.

Throughout the FTA and NAFTA negotiations Canada insisted on keeping its 'cultural industries' out of the negotiations. Cultural questions related to NAFTA and issues which can also be viewed apart from it are dealt with in Section V, "Public Policy and Culture." Chapter 19, by Nevitte, Basañez and Inglehart, takes the broad view in looking at shifts in values based on the 'post-materialist thesis.' It suggests that traditional subsistence security needs are being replaced by quality-of-life objectives in western societies. They argue that this hypothesis can be sustained in the trilateral situation and that there is a convergence of value change in the three NAFTA participants. Castillo Vera (Chapter 20) and Thompson (Chapter 23), respectively, illuminate the differing positions by Mexico and Canada regarding cultural industries. Canada's defensive stance, versus its powerful neighbour, and Mexico's opportunities for penetration into the markets of its neighbour with expanding Hispanic populations, explain why Canada and Mexico will find it difficult to develop a common political strategy on cultural questions. In specific cases, however, as illustrated by the Hoskins, McFayden and Zolf chapter (24), collaborative Canada–Mexico ventures are being planned and implemented. Finally, the Victor Konrad (Chapter 21) and Herman W. Konrad (Chapter 22) contributions show how NAFTA has resulted in increased trinational higher-education objectives and plans, on the one hand, while playing a role in intensified teaching and research about Mexico in Canada and rapidly increasing Canada–Mexico academic linkages independent from NAFTA.

The papers in this volume are designed to address a wide range of these issues, as well as to provide both specialist and general readers with more information on which they will be able to form their understanding about what is actually involved within the international and regional contexts of NAFTA and the trilateral trade debate. They have been selected both for their obvious quality and for their relevance to the current and historical issues. The objective has been to be as comprehensive in coverage as possible, to attempt to understand the full spectrum of economic, political, and cultural implications of the North American developments. We have been especially concerned to broaden the range of discussion from what has often been a narrowly economic one. It has been argued by many proponents of a NAFTA that environmental, social, and cultural issues have no place in what is essentially an economic agreement. The conclusion of the side-agreements as part of the negotiations which made it palatable in the United States Congress underlines that such a view is not accepted in many political circles. A thesis that runs through this volume is that the relationships among nations and societies cannot be understood, let alone legitimately defined, solely in economic terms. One must be concerned with environmental impact, the implications for organized and unorganized labour, for native peoples and other minorities, for women, and with questions of popular and high culture. If the free movement of products across international borders was all there was to international relations, what a simple world this would be! It is our hope that *NAFTA in Transition* will help us to understand the complexity and potential of the issues at stake in North America and the historical route which we have traveled to reach this point in our common histories.

I

Historical Context and the Politics of Emerging Trilateralism

Herman W. Konrad
Departments of History and Anthropology
University of Calgary

2

North American Continental Relationships: Historical Trends and Antecedents

The recent Washington consensus to invoke the fast-track option regarding the United States–Mexico–Canada trade negotiations has accelerated a continentalist process within North America with both antecedents and identifiable trends. The antecedents go back to the late nineteenth century when, in the context of intensified industrialization and foreign capital investments, both governmental and private sector interests in all three countries began actively to pursue policies of greater and freer trade. Though subject to alternating periods of active support and resistance on the part of governments holding power in Ottawa, Mexico City, and Washington, and affected by national and international developments (e.g., the Mexican Revolution, World War I, the Great Depression, World War II, the Cold War, and the emergence of Asian and European trading blocs), the idea of a continental trading bloc has undergone a gradual, but uneven, evolutionary trend. The shape and direction of that trend may be subject to a variety of interpretations depending, in large part, upon its origins, since each country has its own national views, interests, and perspectives. What has not varied is the asymmetrical nature of relationships between Canada and the United States, and between Mexico and the United States.

Fears of dominance and dependence, on the part of Canadians and Mexicans, were and are important issues in the face of disproportionate economic and political influence of a seemingly all-powerful neighbour. Whether the formalization of trade agreements, based on trinational negotiations, can successfully resolve such apprehensions and provide the officially proclaimed mutual and reciprocal benefits for the three countries remains to be seen and will continue to be discussed and debated regardless of the agreements signed. Greater knowledge and awareness of historical antecedents, to complement the current trend of future-focusing, thus becomes a necessary ingredient for a fuller understanding of continental north/south and south/north relationships.

This overview of the past will be both selective and incomplete.[1] It is selective in that it focuses, to a large extent, upon the nature of Canadian–Mexican relationships and the place of the United States, which both links and separates the two countries. It is incomplete in that it assesses primarily the pre-1945 years.

The following historical review begins with the *Porfiriato* period (1876–1910), when Mexico's policy planners sought to limit the role of the federal state in economic development and to open Mexico to greater foreign investment.[2] Their objective was not dissimilar to current strategies designed to produce increased national productivity, a fuller integration into the international economy, and a closing of the gap between Mexico and its more rapidly developing (industrial and technological) northern neighbours. The result was a radical transformation of the Mexican economy, a very substantial United States and European economic role within Mexico, and a notable and visible Canadian presence in specific sectors.

This period represents the first phase of an ongoing continentalist process, though dramatically interrupted by the Mexican Revolution and reshaped by international conflict (World War I) and the Great Depres-

---

1   This overview derives, in large part, from a series of recent papers prepared for a variety of conferences: "Canadian-Mexican Relations: Historical Context and Current Directions" (Calgary, March 1990); "The Reciprocity Dilemma: Canada, Mexico and Current Continentalization Processes" (Mexico City, August 1990); "Tropical Forest Policy and Practice During the Mexican *Porfiriato*, 1876–1910" (San José, C.R., February 1991); "Past as Prologue: The Context of Canada-Mexico Trade Relations" (Ciudad Juárez, March 1991); and "The Context of Canadian and Foreign Investment in Mexico during the *Porfiriato*" (Calgary, May 1991).

2   For Mexican treatments of this period, see Daniel Cosio Villegas, ed., *Historia moderna de Mexico* (Mexico: Editorial Hermes, 1965) and Jesus Reyes Heroles, *El liberalismo mexicano*, 3 vols. (Mexico: Fondo de Cultura Economico, 1974). For non-Mexican treatments, see François-Xavier Guerra, *Mexico: del Antiguo Regimen a la Revolucion*, 2 vols. (Mexico: Fondo de Cultura Economico, 1988); Alan Knight, *The Mexican Revolution*, 2 vols. (Cambridge: Cambridge University Press, 1986); and John Mason Hart, *Revolutionary Mexico: The Coming and Process of the Mexican Revolution* (Los Angeles: University of California Press, 1987). Two examples of the great number of regional studies covering the *Porfiriato* are: Mark Wasserman, *Capitalists, Caciques, and Revolution: The Native Elite and Foreign Enterprise in Chihuahua, Mexico, 1854–1911* (Chapel Hill: University of North Carolina Press, 1984), and Alan Wells, *Yucatan's Gilded Age: Haciendas, Henequen, and International Harvester, 1860–1915* (Albuquerque: University of New Mexico Press, 1985).

sion. A second stage followed in response to the interruption of trans-Atlantic and trans-Pacific commercial linkages caused by World War II, resulting in increased economic integration of Canadian and Mexican economies with that of the United States.

This *de facto* continentalist process, or the regional economic response to international hostilities, was not a byproduct of national policy design, but of a lack of alternatives. In the case of both Mexico and Canada, in the postwar period, alternative economic and commercial strategies have been attempted with mixed results. The current phase of trinational negotiations represents what might be seen as a third major evolutionary step in a more than century-old continentalist process. In the present phase, there appears to be a consensus of governments that greater economic integration is a pragmatic necessity.

The rationale and reasons for this phase vary, as have the historical contexts within which they have developed; yet, there is a common trend. This trend has its basis in the economic interests of private-sector capital, which has consistently viewed national boundaries as barriers to economic development based on productivity, trade, and economic competition. Although national governments take leading roles in formalizing agreements and relationships, their presumed roles may be far less important than the economic systems they represent. This is not to say that they do not influence specific developments; rather, that in the long run, they are role players on a larger stage. For the script is largely determined by other factors, such as demographic trends, technological developments, communication systems, strategic resources (natural and other), ideological persuasions, and what else is happening on the larger international stage—the global village. Such factors were as equally important in the past as they are today, despite the differences in their form and expression.

THE *PORFIRIATO*

The structural adjustments implemented during the 1876–1910 period in Mexico grew out of earlier liberal reforms legislated by the successive governments of Benito Juárez. These reforms sought to broaden the national economic base by encouraging privatization of landholding, increasing productivity, encouraging foreign investment, and furthering modernization. In this pre-industrial era, the Mexican economy was still largely agrarian with exports largely restricted to mineral (gold and silver) extractions. Political turmoil and the impact of the 1860s French intervention prevented implementation of these reforms. With the entrenchment of the Porfirio Díaz regime, a new era of domestic political stability was imposed, considered a precondition for economic development.

This development, seen from the present, and Díaz's *científico* policy strategists, required taking lessons from the richer, more industrialized, European and North American countries. Domestically, the policy of 'peace and process' was articulated, in order to transform Mexico's roughly ten million people into "active citizens, consumers and producers" who through "enterprise and productive vigor" would participate in a "great industrial, agricultural, and manufacturing future" for Mexico.[3]

These views were expressed by Matias Romero, the national treasury secretary, who further argued that:

> what Mexico needs is capital to develop her resources and give employment to labor . . . [but] this will never be developed until those with capital to invest are acquainted with the unparalleled opportunities for safe and profitable investment in Mexico.[4]

In view of having both temperate and tropical climates, foreign as well as domestic observers believed that Mexico could produce a broad range of agrarian products and pay special attention to the increased North American and European demands for tropical products.[5] As Romero put it:

> Mexico has the shape of a cornucopia . . . I look forward to the time, which I do not think far distant, considering our continuity of territory to the United States and our immense elements of wealth, when we shall be able to provide the United States with most of the tropical products . . . which they now import from several other countries.[6]

---

3 Matias Romero, *Coffee and India-Rubber Culture in Mexico Preceded by Geographical and Statistical Notes on Mexico* (New York: G.P. Putnam's Sons, 1898), pp. 76, 80.

4 Ibid., p. 126.

5 Ibid., p. 44. This was a widely shared view, which I have described in greater detail in Konrad, "Tropical Forest Policy" (unpublished paper, 1991). Foreign reporters propagating this idea includes: T.U. Brocklehurst, *Mexico Today: A Country with a Great Future* (London: John Murray, 1883); A.S. Evans, *Our Sister Republic: A Gala Trip through Tropical Mexico in 1869–70* (Hartford, Conn.: Columbian Book Co., 1880); G. Haven, *Our Next-Door Neighbor: A Winter in Mexico* (New York: Harper, 1895); K. Kaerger, *Agricultura y colonizacion en Mexico en 1990*, trans. by P. Lewin and G. Dohrmann (Mexico: Universidad Autonoma Chapingo, 1986); F.A. Ober, *Travels in Mexico and Life Among the Mexicans*, rev. ed. (Boston: Estes and Lauriat, 1887); and W.H. Timmons, ed., *John F. Fenerty Reports Porfirian Mexico, 1879* (El Paso: Texas Western Press, 1974).

6 Romero, *Coffee and India-Rubber Culture*, p. 9. The tropical products frequently mentioned included plantation crops such as coffee, sugar-cane, tobacco, rubber, cotton, bananas, cacao, vanilla, henequen, and rice; a wide range of tropi-

Washington's representative in Mexico, J.W. Foster, shared such views while noting in his dispatches that Mexico, at the beginning of the *Porfiriato*, had the lowest per-capita exportation of "almost all other Spanish American countries." He vigorously endorsed policies of modernization and industrialization, lobbied for the abolition of export taxes and increased mechanized agricultural output. This, he pointed out, would increase Mexico's capacity "for sustaining a large foreign trade," while providing U.S. agricultural equipment manufacturers with new export markets.[7] Mexico's over-dependence upon export of gold and silver, representing 77 percent of all exports in the late 1870s, represented too narrow an economic base. Diversification and industrialization were thus seen as the key to development and progress.

Even before Díaz assumed power, reporters covering U.S. diplomatic missions to Mexico stressed the need for railways, liberal revenue laws, and a period of uninterrupted peace, which would allow Mexico to "supply the United States, Canada and much of Europe" with tropical products. And before the end of Díaz's first term of office, a U.S. industrial deputation was praising his government's policies of prosperity and progress.[8] Both at the official and unofficial level, foreign interests provided encouragement to the Mexican government to open the country to foreign trade and investment.

The *científicos* agreed completely with these foreign views and steps were soon taken to provide domestic conditions favourable for increased foreign involvement in Mexico's economic development. The model of development would be one that had been successfully applied by temperate-zone countries.[9] Little concern or discussion was directed to the fact that Mexico's agrarian sector, a primary focus of development interest, was largely located in tropical zones. Since the federal policy makers were also from temperate, highland, central Mexico, they and their foreign supporters had little understanding of climatic and vegetation growth factors inherent in tropical environments. The grand strategy to

---

cal fruits; tropical forest hardwoods for cabinet-making, lumber, and railroad ties; *palo de tinte* for commercial dyes; chicle for chewing-gum manufacture; grasslands for beef production; and a wide range of indigenous plants sold for medicinal value or as spices.

7 United States National Archives and Records Administration (US/NARA) Record Group (RG) 59, vol. 57, Despatches from Mexico (DM), Reports of U.S. Legation (RUSL), Mexico City, to Secretary of State, Washington, J.W. Foster, July 1877 to July 1879.

8 Evans, *Our Sister Republic*, p. 466, and Timmons, *John F. Fenerty Reports*, p. 326.

9 The U.S. Legation dispatches identify this in a variety of ways, cf. US/NARA, RG 59, vol. 67, DM, while Romero, *Coffee and India-Rubber Culture*, reflects the Mexican views.

convert a traditionally subsistence-oriented rural population into export-oriented wage-labour in forest extraction activities and commercial agriculture, as later developments showed, would run into serious problems.[10]

Most of Mexico was still deficient in systems of transport and communication since Mexico had few navigable rivers, only a rudimentary system of roads, and the country as a whole was a series of unevenly connected regions. To overcome such logistic deficiencies, attention was focused on the construction of a modern system of railroads, telegraph and telephone lines, and improving port facilities to handle international shipping. Lacking domestic capital and experience in such construction projects, generous concessions with favourable subsidies and liberal tax laws allowing for repatriation of profits were offered to foreign investors. Díaz personally insisted on this strategy despite resistance from within his cabinet, by individuals who objected to direct foreign control over strategic national infrastructures.[11]

When Díaz came to power, Mexico had a mere 578 kilometres of railroad and was far behind other Latin American countries in railway construction. By 1895, fifty-five railroad concessions had been granted to foreign and national companies. By late 1898, Mexico had 12,550 kilometres of track in service and had surpassed Argentina and Brazil in completed rail kilometres. The system that emerged now linked Mexico with the United States, its major cities with ports, mining centres, and most provincial capitals. At the same time, urban transit systems were built, and many private companies built narrow-gauge lines, to transport goods and services within large-scale plantations and forest concessions or to seacoast export points. Federal telegraph lines were built parallel to the railway network, increasing from 8,000 to 38,000 kilometres between 1876 and 1898. Including private company lines the total reached 63,000 kilometres. The laying of cables, begun in 1880, provided international links with Central and South America, the United States, and Europe. Domestic and international communications were further facilitated by a ten-fold increase of post offices and postal agencies, resulting in reduced rates (an 80 percent reduction between 1878 and 1896) and greatly increased volumes (from five to 24 million pieces of mail between 1878 and 1896).[12] These transport and communication infrastructures greatly enhanced domestic and international linkages.

The involvement of foreign capital in transforming Mexico's transport and communication systems facilitated the opening of the country to investment in agrarian, mineral, and industrial production. Furthermore,

---

10 Konrad, "Tropical Forest Policy."

11 Romero, *Coffee and India-Rubber Culture*, p. 118, discusses this issue.

12 Ibid., pp. 119–24, 193–220.

gaining access to Mexico's land-based natural resources involved the restructuring of traditional human-land relationships. Previously designated national, public, and communal lands had been opened to private and large-scale access as early as the 1856 Expropriation Law, or Ley Lerdo, and the Díaz administrations then took legislative steps in 1881 and 1884 to allow for claims against formally designated unoccupied land and to introduce a nation-wide survey system.[13]

Within a decade of the land survey regulations, 50 million hectares had been surveyed—Díaz's son being a large player in this activity—of which 16.8 million hectares passed into private hands. By 1896, this total had increased to 30.8 million, and additional lands were made available for purchase at very attractive prices. Depending upon location, the price varied from one peso to 4.5 pesos per hectare. Leading newspapers in Europe and the United States, through full-pages ads and favourable articles, vigorously promoted the land-acquisition and economic participation activities.

By the end of the *Porfiriato*, U.S. capitalists had made enormous investments controlling 40 million hectares, or roughly 20 percent of Mexico's territory.[14] Additional steps taken to encourage foreign economic involvement and produce conditions of apparent stability included international negotiation to resolve long-standing border disputes with Guatemala and the English colony of British Honduras.[15]

In areas where unassimilated indigenous groups resisted the federal and foreign penetrations, as in the case of the Yaqui and Mayo of Sonora and the Maya of eastern Yucatan, the federal army launched scorched-earth campaigns to eliminate resistance.[16] In other rural areas, a special

---

13 For a more detailed analysis of the nature and impact of these laws, see Jan de Vos, *Oro Verde: la conquista de la Selva Lacandona por los madereros Tabasquenos, 1822–1847* (Mexico: Fondo de Cultura Economico, 1988), and Cuauhtemoc Gonzalez Pacheco, *Capital extrajero en la selva de Chiapas 1863–1983* (Mexico: Instituto de Investigaciones Economicas, UNAM, 1983).

14 Romero, *Coffee and India-Rubber Culture*, pp. 124–25; Henry H. Harper, *A Journey in Southeastern Mexico: Narrative of Experiences, Observations on Agricultural and Industrial Conditions* (Boston: De Vinne Press, 1910); John M. Hart, *El Mexico Revolucionario*, trans. by Manuel Arboli (Mexico: Alianza Editorial Mexicana, 1990), pp. 228–30.

15 Diplomatic records and correspondence on negotiations, as maintained by the British Foreign Office, are in Public Records Office (PRO), Foreign Office Record Group (F), 204, Kew Gardens, England.

16 On the Maya question, see Marie Lapointe, *Los mayas rebeldes de Yucatan* (Zamora, Mexico: Colegio de Michoacan, 1983). For the Yaqui and Mayo campaigns, see Francisco P. Troncoso, *Las guerras con las tribus Yaqui y Mayo* (Mexico: Instituto Nacional Indigenista, 1977).

police force, known as the *rurales*, was created to protect the railroads, suppress opposition and, when they took place, to eliminate any signs of social, political, or economic unrest among the rural populations affected by the dramatic economic restructuring of the Mexican countryside.[17] In order to be achieved, progress required peace, for which the Díaz government implemented a domestic big-stick strategy.

The new Mexico of 'peace and progress' offered to the international community by the Mexico City government was met with enthusiasm and increased investments. Equally important were international developments resulting in increased demands for Mexican exports. The opening of the North American Great Plains to commercial agriculture, once settlers and railroads had been firmly entrenched, transformed these regions of Canada and the United States into new areas of economic development. This stimulated major advances in the industrial manufacture of farm equipment. For example, the use of binder-twine for harvesting produced a great demand for the henequen fibre produced in the Yucatan. This state was transformed from one of the most impoverished to one of Mexico's most prosperous.[18]

The growth of U.S. overseas economic activities reinforced foreign investment strategies. Having conquered the temperate zones of continental North America and achieving profitable successes in other parts of Latin America, the financial rewards offered by conditions in Mexico could not be overlooked. Thus, the oligarchy of North American capitalism invested heavily in Mexico's economic development. This was most evident in the railway sector, which allowed for export of Mexico's products to the United States and elsewhere. By 1908, U.S. investment in Mexican railroads was $350 million, compared to the British total of $122 million by 1910. The National City Bank, at this time said to be the largest bank in the world, proved to be a key source of capital. Major investors, including Stillman, Harrison, Rockefeller, and Gould, were all directors of the bank. The National City Bank, plus J.P. Morgan (the Morgan Guarantee Bank) and George Baker (the First National City Bank of New York), represented a consortium of financial interests that dominated the U.S. railway enterprises and provided much of the capital to develop the Mexican railways. Other tycoons, such as Cyrus McCormack (International Harvester), the Grace family, the Hearst family, and Jacob Schiff, extended their commercial interests into a wide range of Mexican ventures.

---

17 Paul J. Vanderwood, *Disorder and Progress: Bandits, Police and Mexican Development* (London: University of Nebraska Press, 1981).

18 See, for instance, Wells, *Yucatan's Gilded Age.*

Such entrepreneurs associated themselves with national and regional interests that shared their financial goals, especially key players in the Díaz cabinets and the elite families in Mexico's state capitals. With capital and strategic Mexican ties, the United States and other foreign investors expanded their already existing activities in ranching, mining, lumber, railroads, banking, and shipping activities into Mexico.[19] And by acting as pro-Mexico lobbyists in domestic financial circles and international capitals, they provided internationally favourable propaganda for the Díaz government.

The international role of foreign investment in Mexico by the end of the first decade of the twentieth century was both substantial and far-reaching. French capital represented 45.7 percent of the capital in Mexico's principal banks and provided capital for the most important textile factories and largest stores. By 1910, according to Hart's figures, 80 percent of the capital in Mexico's financial system was controlled by foreigners, with the principal sources of investment coming from the United States, France, and England. As early as 1902, some 1,112 U.S. companies and 40,000 individuals had invested in a wide range of Mexican economic ventures and properties. And, while the French restricted their investments to banking, commerce, and national industries, the U.S. investors were involved in virtually all sectors of the Mexican economy. By 1902, the latter source had brought $511.4 million of foreign capital into the country.

In the eyes of many, particularly urban and small-town middle-class individuals in the United States, Mexico had become the land of promise and quick fortunes. These individuals invested in land development and tropical commodity ventures, frequently lured on by unscrupulous promoters.[20] Of course, such activities were not restricted to Mexico, keeping in mind that, in the early 1900s, London residents were being promised similar fortunes through investment in land development in recently established Canadian prairie towns such as Winnipeg, Regina and Calgary, and that in the same period one in four actively employed adult males in Calgary was involved in real estate ventures. A decade earlier, the regional economy of southern Alberta was controlled by large

---

19 Hart, *El Mexico Revolucionario*, pp. 186–233, includes an exhaustive analysis of the U.S. investments and sources.

20 Lists of stockholders, identifying origin and structure of companies, were assembled to support postrevolution property-damage claims against Mexico and were handled by the U.S. and Mexico Mixed Claims Commission; cf. Washington National Records Center, Suitland, Maryland (WNRC), Record Group (RG), 76. Harper, *A Journey*, details the 'scam' ventures, information substantiated in the dispatches from U.S. consuls, e.g., from Tuxpan (1879–1906), US/NARA, M. 306.

corporate ranching interests, financed by eastern Canadian and British investors.

The extent of the investment in Mexico, by what Harper called "bogus Mexican development companies," and the results, still await the future historian.[21] What is clear is that many ventures, both small-scale and of great magnitude, had already failed before the beginning of the Mexican Revolution. And while the small-scale foreign stockholder, who had invested in dubious or simply over-ambitious projects in unfamiliar geographical and cultural contexts, lost their investments, the big-time financial entrepreneurs fared much better. For them, the financial rewards were two-fold: in the first instance, from the building of economic infrastructures within Mexico and, in the second instance, from the production, export, and sale of commodities produced in Mexico.

Such successes in the export-oriented economic development strategy of the *Porfiriato* were linked to very favourable concessionary terms offered by the host country and strategic associations with Mexicans. In the Yucatan, International Harvester's monopoly over the henequen market was possible due to the Molinas-Montes family's control over the regional politics and ties with the Díaz government. In Chihuahua, the Terrazas-Creel families controlled regional politics and successful partnerships were established with Hearst (livestock) and Guggenheim (mining and smelting) endeavours.[22] In Tabasco, it was the Venezuela family, with financial linkages with foreign investors (French, Belgian, British, and U.S.) and the lumber ventures.[23] Such relationships proved profitable for both the regional elite families, who controlled state legislatures, and the foreign interests, who produced and exported products in demand in the international markets. Good relations with Mexico City were important as many of the *científicos* were important economic participants as well as architects of economic development.

The Porfirian strategy was a success insofar as it resulted in the expansion and diversification of the Mexican economy and the building of infrastructures for an export-oriented industrial nation. In so doing, it allowed regional elites to become actors in transforming provincial areas from stagnant rural enterprises to commercial export economies. It enabled the elite of politically powerful Mexico City to become directly associated with foreign capital interests. Above all, it allowed foreign capital to expand its international scope, creating in Mexico the basic infrastructures of a turn-of-the-century industrial society. This did not mean that Mexico, as the *científicos* had hoped, became a modern indus-

---

21 Harper, *A Journey*, pp. 55, 76–77.

22 Wells, *Yucatan's Gilded Age*, and Wasserman, *Capitalists*.

23 De Vos, *Oro Verde*, and Gonzalez Pacheco, *Capital extranjero*.

trial nation like those it was attempting to imitate. The bulk of its society remained rural, and its peasant and native populations saw few benefits from the profits accumulated by the elites and foreign participants. Real income, between 1876 and 1910, for the majority of the rural labour force, declined, as did their freedom of movement and civil rights.[24] Other losers were the small-scale foreign investors in questionable land development projects or over-ambitious large-scale ventures. The Mexican Revolution and its long drawn-out struggles for power provided a *coup de grâce* for dreams of quick fortune from foreign investment.

Canadian involvement in this era of Mexican development was rather restricted, both in terms of the focus of investment and the types of investors. For most Canadians, Mexico had been, and remained, a distant, largely exotic and unknown part of the North American continent. British colonial tutelage and the nature of British overseas commerce had provided contacts with the Caribbean rather than the Latin American mainland. Mexican products that reached Canada did so via the United States or through British linkages. The Canadian orientation, in this period when its own industrial infrastructures were being established, was still dominated by commercial relations with England and the United States. Canadian interest in Mexico developed late in the *Porfiriato*, in contrast to much earlier and more intensive U.S. and European involvements, and came about almost by accident by financial actors with recent successes in Brazil and the Caribbean, in utility and transport ventures.[25] The Canadian pattern of involvement, not unexpectedly, in view of its international economic experience at the time, followed directions largely determined by U.S. and British influences. What the Canadians lacked then, as they still do to a large extent, were direct ties with the elite political and economic players within the Mexican commercial establishment.

Despite the virtual absence of serious research about this chapter in Canadian–Mexican relations (with very few exceptions on the part of either Canadian or Mexican scholars), the main outlines of involvement can be identified.[26] The linkages that did develop, and they were impor-

---

24 For a detailed analysis, see Friedrich Katz, *La servidumbre agraria en Mexico en la epoca porfiriana* (Mexico: Ediciones Era, 1980).

25 Christopher Armstrong and H.V. Nelles, *Southern Exposure: Canadian Promoters in Latin America and the Caribbean 1896–1930* (Toronto: University of Toronto Press, 1988), pp. 85–104.

26 Armstrong and Nelles' *Southern Exposure* book is the most serious work to date, covering a much broader context. A pioneering study in the area is J.C.M. Ogelsby, *Gringos from the Far North: Essays in the History of Canadian–Latin American Relations, 1866–1968* (Toronto: Maclean-Hunter Press, 1976). Two unpublished studies focusing directly upon investment in Mexico include Russell E. Chace, "The Mexican Northwestern Railway Company, Ltd.,

tant ones, were the result of opportunistic enterprise by Canadian banking and railway interests. Knowledge about the Díaz promotion campaigns, or the development and investment schemes being promoted in the United States, were not important topics in the Canadian context. Having had a very different relationship with Mexico during the nineteenth century, Canada, and Canadians, held no sense of manifest destiny or civilizing-through-commerce mission toward Mexico. The linkage was to be almost strictly financial, by capitalists who had already been active in such areas as banking, railroads, urban tramways, and power and light in Brazil and Cuba. The foray into Mexico was led by F.S. Pearson, already well-known for his impact on Canadian and Latin American utility development activities. He became the spark plug for getting Canadian investment in Mexican development started. And, between 1902 and 1909, Canada became the location for a list of chartered companies operating in Mexico.[27]

It has been suggested that the reason for incorporation in Canada was the fact "that Canadian Company law offered relatively lax restrictions concerning the issuing of annual reports and the disclosure of financial information."[28] Included were: Mexico City Tramways Company, Mexico City Light and Power Company, Mexican Northwestern Railway Company, Veracruz Electric Light, Power and Traction Company, Anglo-Mexican Electric Company, Monterrey Waterworks and Sewer Company, and Yucatan Power Company.

Canadian banks involved in financing the purchase of these existing facilities (all companies purchased from European or U.S. interests, who had originally established them), which were subsequently chartered as Canadian enterprises, subsequently established branches in Mexico City (Bank of Montreal, 1906, and Canadian Bank of Commerce, 1910). Official Canadian governmental presence was indicated by the establishment of a permanent commercial mission (in 1905) resulting, in quick succession, in the signing of two binational agreements for the establishment of direct Canada–Mexico steamship service along Pacific and Atlantic routes.

The Canadian economic presence in Mexico was welcomed by the Díaz government, already concerned about the dominant position that U.S. capital was exercising and eager to offset such influences by diversifying its source of foreign capital. By now, Canada was also interested in more direct ties with Mexico and in bypassing the U.S. broker or inter-

---

1908–1914," CERLAC Mexico Project Working Paper No. 4, Toronto, 1982 and William E. French, "The Nature of Canadian Investment in Mexico, 1902–1915," M.A. thesis, University of Calgary, 1981.

27 The Canadian activities described are based on sources cited in note 26.

28 See French, "The Nature of Canadian Investment," pp. 63–64.

mediary role in the movement of products between the two countries. The steamship services, subsidized by both the Mexican and Canadian governments, did not result in any significant increase in direct binational trade. Neither survived the Mexican Revolution, which also effectively terminated most of the Canadian investment and ownership role in Mexican utility and railroad infrastructures.

The most important of these Canadian ventures were the Mexican Power and Light Company (an amalgamation of the Mexico City Light and Power Company and the Mexico City Tramways Company) and the Mexican Northwestern Railways Company. The former later became the state-owned Comision Federal de Electricidad, while the latter went bankrupt during the Mexican Revolution. And while these companies involved the "who's who of Canadian finance and entrepreneurship during the first decade of the century," they also had a distinct U.S./European flavour.[29] With intimate links with important U.S. entrepreneurs (e.g., Pearson, Keith, and Farquhar) and capital markets in Europe, Canadian participation was largely dependent upon these non-Canadian interests. The Canadian notion, reflected in the *Monetary Times*, that "Canadians would find more favor in the eyes of the Mejicanos than do their more immediate neighbors to the north, whose strong proclivities towards the game of grab are never quite forgotten by this strong memorized race," held true only to a point.[30] As speculative ventures, their mode of operation did not differ from that of their neighbour, despite the Canadian registry of the companies.

These ventures also had virtually no impact in increasing Mexico–Canada binational trade. With the dominant economic role of the United States in both Canada and Mexico, U.S. interests continued to maximize the benefits derived from continental trade. The Yucatan-produced henequen fibre which reached Canada as binder-twine or other fibre products was exported as raw material from Mexico, bought at monopoly-set low prices, and reached Canada through U.S. channels as manufactured products. Another variation of the triangular trade practised was the way Mexico-produced chicle (the raw material for chewing gums) was transshipped, in-bond, via New York and other U.S. ports, to U.S. subsidiary companies in Montreal and Toronto, from where it was imported to the U.S.-based manufacturing plants at reduced costs, after which the manufactured products were shipped back to Canada. Officially, over half of the U.S. chicle imports came from Canada which, in this case, functioned rather like a *maquilador* role in allowing U.S.

---

29 Chace, "The Mexican," p. 1.

30 *Monetary Times* 38, No. 12 (1909): p. 355, cited in French, "The Nature of Canadian Investment," pp. 63–64.

companies to reduce costs for their raw materials, which added to the profit of the manufactured product.[31] The Mexican tradition of exporting cheap raw materials, with U.S. manufacturers or brokers gaining the rewards from the high prices Canadians paid for raw materials or finished products, became firmly established during the *Porfiriato*.

As an early stage of the continentalization of the North American economy, this era provides a historical context that has not received adequate research attention. This is doubly true for both Canada and Mexico, whose south and north focus has been largely restricted to the most proximate neighbour. Such a limited focus has resulted in a vacuum of historical background for understanding formative processes of the larger economic trends affecting North America as a whole. The idea of a North American common market, involving freer trade between the three countries, was already emphatically articulated in 1908 in terms of "the oneness of the North American Continent in development and destiny."[32]

This was the theme of the annual banquet of the Chamber of Commerce of the State of New York (19 November 1908), attended by high-level diplomatic and business representatives from the United States, Canada, Mexico, and England. The speeches at this event praised Porfirio Díaz as one of the world's greatest statesmen, for having opened the Mexican economy to foreign investment. The banquet theme was expressed in the following terms:

> Here are three great countries occupying practically the whole of this Continent, each of them of great natural resources—and especially as regard Canada and Mexico—of far greater resources than have yet been fully developed. Each was made to supply the needs of the other and to be a market for the other, and thus prosperity of these three countries is naturally connected. The more trade there is between them the better for all. [*great applause*][33]

The contemporary assessment of the *Porfiriato*, by Canadian, U.S., and British statesmen, was that great strides were made in expanding trade within North America and internationally. This (argued James Bryce, the British ambassador to the United States) had greatly strengthened "guarantees for general peace and good will."[34] That the Mexican Revolution and World War I were just around the corner were inconceivable notions

---

31 Wells, *Yucatan's Gilded Age*, and Joseph W. Vander Laan, *Production of Gutta-Percha, Balata, Chicle and Allied Gums* (Washington, D.C.: GPO, 1927), pp. 49–60.

32 Detailed in José F. Godoy, *Porfirio Díaz, President of Mexico: The Master Builder of a Great Commonwealth* (New York: Knickerbocker Press, 1910), pp. 209ff.

33 Ibid., p. 212.

34 Ibid.

for men calling Mexico's President Díaz "one of the greatest men to be held up for the hero worship of mankind."[35] The official Washington view, based on consular reports from within Mexico, evaluated conditions in Mexico in 1907 as "revealing a continuous growth and extension of the country's industrial and vital interests, contemporaneous with the progress of the United States and Canada."[36]

The official Canadian views were hardly less enthusiastic, with Minister of Agriculture Sydney Fisher placing Díaz "among the great statesmen of the day and of the time. We in Canada feel the utmost interest in him and his country, it being a portion of our own continent, conditions there being somewhat similar to the conditions here in Canada."[37] Charles Marcil, the Speaker of the House of Commons, referred to Díaz as "one of the great men of the American Continent" being directly responsible that "the relations between Canada and Mexico are becoming more important every day."[38] Clifford Sifton, then former minister of the interior, evaluated the period of Díaz and Mexico's development in the following terms:

> He has given Mexico a strong, orderly, and efficient administration. He has made life and property safe, he has promoted laws under which the Mexican people have been enabled to peacefully develop the great natural resources of the country and achieve a high degree of domestic comfort and prosperity. Under his administration Mexico has become a modern and progressive country commanding the respect and confidence of the world.[39]

Apart from such diplomatic rhetoric, there were indeed signs that the three North American countries were viewing the destiny of the continent as a common enterprise. This was not restricted to trade and investment but also to other areas of concern, such as the environment. A trinational North American Conference of Conservation of Natural Resources, held in Washington in 1909, agreed to a set of conservation principles which would not only ensure the needs of future generations but also involve active trinational collaboration.[40]

---

35 Part of a tribute made by U.S. Secretary Root, ibid., pp. 213.

36 Ibid., p. 217.

37 Ibid., p. 148.

38 Ibid., p. 168.

39 Ibid., p. 182.

40 Archivo General de la Nación (Mexico City), Gobernacion, S/S, Caja 830, Exp. 1.

When it came to issues involving territorial or border disputes, there was also an expressed willingness to resort to binding arbitration, as in the case of the United States–Mexico Chamizal dispute.[41] This border issue, resulting from the shifting of the Rio Bravo river bed, saw Canada being invited to participate as a neutral member (and president) of the arbitration commission. However, when this commission finally ruled in favour of Mexico's claim, the residents and commercial interests of El Paso's occupants of the disputed area lobbied so successfully to Washington that the Canadian participant was accused of bias and of being in collusion with the Mexicans. This episode of attempted arbitration took place immediately after the *Porfiriato*, in 1911, and it was to take another half century before the issue was finally settled. For then, as has been the case in later periods, if Mexico and Canada appeared—in the eyes of U.S. special interest groups—to collaborate against their interests, opposition that Washington would listen to would be forthcoming.

CONFLICT, DEPRESSION, AND THE IMPACT OF WORLD WAR II

Both the optimism for and activities supporting North American unity in economic development and collaboration were abruptly interrupted by the Mexican Revolution, which dramatically reversed earlier trends. The United States, on the one hand, reverted to earlier so-called big-stick tactics in handling its relations with Mexico (e.g., the occupation of Veracruz), while Canada, on the other hand, seemed to lose interest in Mexican economic involvements.[42] With its involvement in World War I, Canada fulfilled its British imperial obligations, but its regional economic perspective with the U.S. relationship was strengthened. The Canada–Mexico relationship after World War I was not a high priority for either country, despite periodic efforts to re-establish direct steamship services and occasional diplomatic initiatives. Ogelsby concluded that perhaps the main reason for "limited expansion" was that "neither nation has had the ability to talk frankly with the other. Both Canadians and Mexicans have been concerned with self-interest rather than being willing to give way in order to realize developments on a wider scale."[43] The continental perspective gave way to more immediate concerns located closer to home.

Mexicans in search of labour opportunities in the United States moved north, with or without legal papers; many immigrants first land-

---

41 The documentation of this case is extensive; see US/NARA, Decimal File 711.1215, "Relations with the U.S. (1910–29)," M314 (Microfilm rolls 9–13).

42 Ogelsby, *Gringos*, pp. 66–84, traces trade relations.

43 Ogelsby, *Gringos*, p. 82.

ing in Canada soon moved south of the border in search of opportunities there. Whatever expertise had been acquired by Canadian companies in Mexico during the *Porfiriato*, in terms of successful business endeavours, did not translate into new or continuing ventures.

There were less-noticed interactions, as in the case of some 6,000 Canadian Mennonites who migrated to Mexico to enjoy the linguistic, cultural, and religious freedoms they believed they were being denied in Canada. Their migration and subsequent demographic increases, plus maintenance of Canadian citizenship, resulted in this ethnic group becoming, and remaining, the largest Canadian physical presence in Mexico, a population which had increased to over 30,000 by the early 1960s.[44] A 1932 report on foreign residents in Mexico City showed the presence of 104 Canadians compared to 3,575 U.S. citizens. Of the 22,881 foreigners resident in Mexico City at the time, mostly involved in economic activities, the Canadian component was in a distant seventh place, behind Spain, the United States, Germany, France, Britain, and China.[45] The number of Mexicans in Canada was correspondingly insignificant.

The Canada–Mexico relationship was to remain largely dictated by U.S. and British influences. Canadian import of Mexican products (such as coffee, tomatoes, bananas, oranges, mahogany, and henequen products) was via U.S. brokers and its exports to Mexico of manufactured goods were less competitive, price-wise, than U.S. products. The possibility of even negotiating Mexico–Canada trade agreements was further complicated by London's, rather than Ottawa's, control over Canadian external affairs. That Mexican imports, in 1931, were largely from the United States (70 percent) and minimally from Canada (3 percent) reflected the increasing dominance of the North American economy by its strongest country.

In a way, the British factor was almost as much a problem as the intermediary role of the United States. Formal contacts with Mexican foreign affairs officers led to the conclusion that Canada needed its own diplomatic presence in Mexico since, in reference to the role of London and the establishment of trade treaties with Mexico, "it seems clear as day that the present circuitous route is too long for quick direct dealings with people who live right on the same continent."[46] There was even Mexican interest, at least expressed in a letter written in 1931 to the

---

44 Harry Leonard Sawatsky, *They Sought a Country: Mennonite Colonization in Mexico* (Berkeley: University of California Press, 1971).

45 United States, Department of Commerce, Bureau of Foreign and Domestic Commerce, "Foreign Residents in Mexico City, January 28, 1932," US/NARA.

46 Ogelsby, *Gringos*, pp. 72–73.

Mexican president by his minister of communications and public works, that Canada and Mexico should be:

> forming a new economic entity, similar to the American one, as a unique means of freeing ourselves from the poverty-stricken state in which we have always lived in spite of the potential riches of our soil. Probably there are no other two countries in the world susceptible to so admirably perfecting themselves as Canada and Mexico . . . [which are] on the same continent with easy communication by the two oceans.[47]

Talk of forming economic trade entities, during periods of economic depression, had other voices as well. In 1932, the signing of the new Commercial Treaty Regulations between Canada and the British Empire allowed for preferential terms for Canadian import of raw materials from other parts of the empire. In this case, Mexico and the United States had common cause in that Mexican export of raw products to the United States—cotton and henequen were specially identified—resulted in an export market for manufactured goods in Canada by the United States. Canadian preferences for hemp and cotton from other parts of the British Empire would thus "diminish the [U.S.] capacity for consumption in terms of Mexican raw materials" and both Mexico and the United States would lose export markets. To offset the impact of Canada–British Empire trade preferences, the U.S. commercial attaché in Mexico suggested to Washington:

> the possibilities of perhaps getting together with Latin-American countries and other countries outside of the British Empire in some sort of agreement for mutual trade benefit. This commercial restriction on the part of the British Empire will react unfavorably on a large part of the countries not in the agreement . . . we might all get together to form a sort of customs union of our own or in some way, by means based on mutual convenience, offset the effects of the British Act.[48]

Apart from clearly identifying the Mexican and U.S. perception of Canada as already being part of a larger trading bloc within the British sphere of influence, such reactions indicated active interest in forming competitive trading blocs to offset noncontinental commercial trends. Thus, treaty discussions between Canada and Mexico involved more than binational relations, given the existing patterns of economic domination of their trade by the United States and the role of Britain in the external affairs of Canada. The ability of the politically and economically weaker

---

47 Ibid.

48 Charles Cunningham, commercial attaché report, 14 October 1932, Box 351, BFDC, RG 151 US/NARA.

two countries to establish independent binational trade patterns for their mutual benefit—despite the best of intentions—remained minimal. By 1937, Canada was exporting $2.85 million of goods to Mexico, while officially importing $812,000. The Mexican role in Canadian imports was far larger but was in the form of raw materials having been converted into manufactured goods in the United States, and thus listed as imports from that source.[49]

The impact of World War II proved to be significant in that it eliminated much of the British influence in North American economic relations, while greatly increasing the role of the United States. With the interruption of Atlantic and Pacific trading networks, and once the United States entered the conflict, the bulk of its imports were restricted to continental sources. The U.S. economy became the hub, with Mexico and Canada the main spokes of a *de facto* continentalist process under duress. As Messersmith, the U.S. ambassador to Mexico, indicated to his country's consular officers in Mexico City in 1946, Mexico–United States trade represented 55 to 65 percent of total Mexican trade prior to the war, and by 1944–45 it had increased to 83 to 85 percent.[50]

A parallel trend also existed between Canada and the United States. And, as the now totally dominant economic actor on the continent, Washington adopted a strategy of maintaining the *status quo*. The emergence of a Canadian foreign policy independent from London was also a major consideration. In 1944, the two countries exchanged ambassadors and, in February 1946, signed a trade agreement. The diplomatic basis for direct negotiations had finally been established.

The management of continental trade by the United States became a high priority for Washington policy makers immediately after the war. The transcripts of the 2–5 April 1946 consular conference held in Mexico City and attended by all the U.S. diplomatic and commercial officers (as well as the State Department officials sent to brief them) provides an inside view of the postwar Washington strategy. Ambassador Messersmith outlined the economic preoccupations of his country as a prelude to specific targets:

> [W]e recognize today there is no distinction between the political and economic fields; and while we have to be to a certain degree specialists, the preponderance of the economic factors as a determinant of policy is so great that practically all policy, including the most fundamental decisions that states make, depends upon economic considerations.[51]

---

49 Ogelsby, *Gringos*, p. 77.

50 "Transcripts: Proceedings of Consular Conference Held in Mexico City, April 2–5, 1946," WNRC, RG 84.

51 Ibid.

Messersmith's description, in another passage, of Mexicans as "a people who react more to their emotions than to their reason" and in need of guidance, was clearly reflected in the various briefing statements. That Canada fitted into the larger picture as well was indicated in general rather than detailed terms: "Canada, like Mexico, supplied far more than it bought . . . is carefully cultivating its trade relations with Mexico, having recently signed a commercial treaty with the latter nation."[52] Specific instructions regarding the implementation of future continental economic dominance were outlined, largely in terms of getting access to vital information from Mexican private sources, and were considered "more reliable than the official data." The Mexican sources of information included the Benjamin Franklin Institute, the English Language Institute, the Instituto Mexicana-Norteamericana de Relaciones Culturales, the FBI (which had been operating in Mexico since 1942 under the cover of so-called legal attachés) and all consular officers, who were advised to establish personal contacts with publishers, editors, writers, radio station owners, commentators and announcers, and reporters, who, it was cautioned, "may not be particularly pleasant characters."

The seriousness of the communist threat and the need to have as much information on the activities of "communists and the more dangerous fellow travellers" in Mexico was highlighted, as well as an indication that a new intelligence agency (the CIA) would soon be operating to assist in political and commercial espionage. Within the context of the merging Cold War fervour that was to grip Washington, the emphasis upon clandestine information-gathering in a neighbouring country may have had a political rationale.[53] However, more important were the overt admissions that economic factors were the determinants of policy and that it was necessary to use all information available to maintain continental economic dominance in the postwar years.

The degree to which World War II had resulted in a form of economic continentalism, independent of trade negotiations and agreements, was significant. The determination of the major player to maintain its position by influencing the economic policies of its neighbours would invariably also have a reaction.

Most significantly, the pre-1945 years had effectively established an important pattern in the North American political economy, a pattern that has shaped, if not determined, the relationship of the present, and a context which we need to understand in light of the current debate over tri-

---

52 Ibid.

53 For an analogous Canadian situation, see Jean-François Lisée, *In the Eye of the Eagle* (Toronto: Harper-Collins, 1990). The files and documents cited would indicate that Washington used all means at its disposal to affect Canadian economic directions. See, for example, pp. 244–55.

lateral relations. The negotiations, designed to culminate in a trilateral agreement in 1992, derive from a perception of a lack of alternatives. In the case of Canada and Mexico, both countries have attempted to implement strategies to lessen the dominance of the economic role of their most significant trading partner. By the mid-1980s, in the case of Canada, and somewhat later for Mexico, national policy makers had come to the conclusion that neither inward-directed nationalist strategies or so-called third-option policies would provide a counterbalance to rapidly changing global developments. Despite a series of efforts to disengage from the continentalist trends which have evolved during the past half century, they found that the patterns in North America had not changed. For instance, U.S. policies established in the immediate post-1945 period have been refined rather than altered. However, now the threat from prosperous Asian and European trading blocs, rather than Cold War considerations, has become the driving force behind continentalism.

Whether or not Canada and Mexico will be able to achieve the promised levels of increased productivity and prosperity as the result of a trilateral agreement remains a subject of debate. Less debatable is the likelihood that the United States, at least in the short run, will remain the primary economic player on the continent.

Stephen J. Randall, Chair in American Studies and Dean
Faculty of Social Sciences
University of Calgary

Managing Trilateralism: The United States, Mexico, and Canada in the Post-NAFTA Era

INTRODUCTION

It is frankly too early for serious conjecture over whether the conclusion of NAFTA in 1993, precipitated in large part by the "Salinas Opening" to the North, may represent a fundamental reorientation of North American relations. For Canada the FTA represented a consolidation of what had become an economic and trade reality between Canada and the United States, although the debate over its conclusion was no less politically and psychologically divisive and troubling.

For Mexico, however, the 1980s witnessed a dramatic turnaround in Mexican foreign trade, development, and foreign investment policies, embodied in membership in the GATT, wholesale privatization of much public-sector enterprise, and the conclusion of a free-trade agreement with the United States and Canada. In the Mexican case, the shift in trade and economic policies involved substantial institutional change, including the creation in 1983 of SECOFI (the Secretariat of Trade and Industrial Development), which brought together policymakers committed to trade liberalization and economic reforms. A parallel restructuring of PRI took place under Salinas in an effort to locate more power in the hands of technical bureaucracies and away from traditional power groups tied to the old policies of special interests and protectionism. In the United States, the need for new approaches in the 1990s drew the Clinton administration into a conflictual situation with its own party in Congress and with such traditional Democratic Party power bases as American labour. Thus for all three countries the past decade and the implementation of a more trilateral agenda has wrought a political, psychological and economic reorientation that is still very much in transition.

The internal reorientation of politics and policies is not the main issue for this paper; nonetheless, one cannot understand the modification in the trilateral dynamic without understanding that a shift in domestic politics and strategies in each country was a necessary prerequisite for the conclusion of a NAFTA. That broader North American reorientation is only at the early stages of what will be a lengthy process of adjustment. That process will be shaped not only by current political, cultural and economic realities but also by the historical relationship among the countries, their very different approaches to foreign policy, and differing traditions in their respective relations with the rest of Latin America and the Caribbean.[1]

Although we may now speak in terms of a North America without borders[2] and of cultural convergences among the North American countries,[3] such references would have seemed not only premature but also seriously flawed less than a decade ago. For some, such notions are still not only premature but inappropriate. Yet, there is little doubt that the way in which we are increasingly writing, speaking and thinking about North America has undergone a significant change. Historically, at least since the seventeenth century, North America has not been considered a political or even an economic entity. Relations among the three dominant nations of the region—the U.S., Canada and Mexico—have been bilateral in nature: Canada–U.S. on the one hand, U.S.–Mexico on the other, and only marginally Canada–Mexico. Little thought was devoted to the notion of a three-nation collective; indeed I would suggest that such an eventuality was certainly not the objective of either Mexican or Canadian negotiators when they entered the NAFTA discussions. At the outset, even the inclusion of Canada in what was intended to be a U.S.–Mexico bilateral discussion was problematic for Mexico.

Whether NAFTA in itself will contribute to a more integrated North America and in particular to trilateral thinking remains open to debate. The institutional mechanisms in the NAFTA itself are feeble instruments of continentalization; the realities of trade and investment flows, demographic patterns, and cultural affinities, among other variables, tend to favour a continuation of the historical pattern of bilateralism, although the signs of a quickened interest in a broader North American agenda are everywhere: various conferences; the funding initiatives that have come from United States Information Service and Fulbright Program, the Mexican and Canadian governments, Natural Sciences and Engineering Research Council

1   Louis Perez, "Dependency," in Michael Hogan and Thomas Paterson, eds., *Explaining the History of American Foreign Relations* (Cambridge: Cambridge University Press, 1991).

2   Stephen J. Randall, editor (with H. Konrad and S. Silverman), *North America Without Borders? Integrating Canada, the United States and Mexico* (Calgary: University of Calgary Press, 1992).

3   Neil Nevitte, Miguel Basañez, Ronald Inglehart, "Directions of Value Change in North America," in Randall, ed., *North America Without Borders*, pp. 245–60.

and Social Sciences and Humanities Research Council of Canada, among others. Thus, even if the institutions of NAFTA do not compel continental treatment of economic, political, or strategic issues, there has been a gradual shift toward continental or trilateral thinking and a heightened awareness of the issues and problems shared by the three countries.

Both Canadian and Mexican foreign policies have consistently been defined in terms of their relationship to the United States. Both have sought stable and productive relations with their dominant neighbour; yet both have also sought to distance themselves from the U.S., to define their foreign policies in terms that seem distinct from those of the United States. This orientation has been more pronounced in the case of Mexico, whose policies since the first decade of this century have been more decidedly nationalistic toward the U.S. Not only has Mexico historically tended to seek a more defensive posture *vis-à-vis* the United States but it has also at times taken initiatives to assume more of a leadership role in the Caribbean and Latin America as a counterweight to the traditional hegemony of the United States in the region. This is not a posture that Canada has ever assumed, although it may have adopted policies from time to time in the Caribbean and Latin America (as in Cuba and Central America) that were distinct from those of the United States.[4] For Canada as well, the effort to seek autonomy of vision and policies from those of the United States has been a constant refrain, including in the recent Canadian foreign policy review.[5]

Yet integration and NAFTA must be viewed within a broader historical trajectory. The critical dimensions of that larger historical context are several: the evolution of United States strategic and trade policy in general but specifically toward Canada and Mexico; the development of the Canadian and Mexican political economies in relation to the United States; and changes in the international system within which North American trilateralism has evolved.

A combination of national security and commercial interest has served since the late nineteenth century to push Mexico, Canada and the U.S. toward a higher degree of economic integration. It is simply an historical reality that the agenda for that integration has been set largely by the U.S., because of its overwhelming economic preponderance and

---

4   For an overview of Canadian policies in the area see: Stephen J. Randall, "Canada and Latin America: The Dvelopment of Institutional Ties," in Jerry Haar and Edgar J. Dosman, eds., *Dynamic Partnership: Canada's Changing Role in the Americas* (New Brunswick: Transaction Press, 1993).

5   For an overview of Canada–U.S. relations as well as a discussion of the trilateral dimension, see John Herd Thompson and Stephen J. Randall, *Canada and the United States, Ambivalent Allies* (Athens, Ga.: University of Georgia Press, 1994).

because of the national security interests that have driven American foreign policy, especially but not exclusively during the Cold War years. Robert Zoellick, former U.S. under-secretary of state for economic affairs, underlined the importance of North American integration within the larger context of U.S. foreign policy objectives in a 1992 address:

> One feature of United States foreign policy strategy in this post-Cold War world is that our economic policy must become an increasingly critical component of our planning and action. The United States must be economically strong at home and abroad . . . NAFTA is a rare strategic opportunity to secure, strengthen, and develop our continental base, economically and politically, in a way that will promote America's foreign policy agenda, our economic strength and leadership, and global influence . . . The NAFTA would be a key component of a network of global, regional, and bilateral arrangements that promote American interests.[6]

For both Canada and Mexico the Second World War and early Cold War years were important ones in their closer integration with the United States. The economic and strategic demands of war and then the bipolar world of the Cold War created an environment conducive to cooperation. In the Canadian case then U.S. Assistant Secretary of State Adolf Berle effectively captured the nature of the transition that was occurring in Canada during World War II when he commented on an afternoon chat he had in Ottawa with Hugh Keenleyside, then First Secretary in External Affairs. Keenleyside, Berle recalled, had told him that "this is now one continent and one economy."[7]

Prime Minister Mackenzie King recognized the nature of that transition when his government engaged in secret and high-level discussions in 1948 with the Truman administration officials with a view to the elimination of trade barriers between the two countries. Then U.S. assistant secretary of state for economic affairs, Willard Thorpe, suggested that this initiative, which proved abortive, provided a ". . . unique opportunity of promoting the most efficient utilization of the resources of the North American continent and knitting the two countries together—an objective of United States foreign policy since the founding of the Republic." Though the 1948 talks were aborted, in the mid-1950s in the context of bilateral discussions concerning the impact on Canada of the national security clause of the U.S. Trade Agreements Act, senior U.S. officials

---

6 "The North American FTA: The New World Order Takes Shape in the Western Hemisphere," *U.S. Department of State Dispatch*, 3 (13 April 1992), 290.

7 Beatrice Bishop Berle and Travis Beale Jacobs, eds., *Navigating the Rapids, 1918–1971* (New York, 1973), diary entry for 18 March 1941, p. 365.

stressed in a meeting with, among others, C.D. Howe and Lester Pearson, that the U.S. government considered North America a "strategic unit."[8] What was true for Canada seems to have been applicable to Mexico as well. As early as the 1940s, United States policymakers spoke in terms of a "special relationship" between the two nations.

Tensions between the U.S. and its neighbours in the post-1945 years were not strong enough to negate the emergence of a more inter-dependent industrial, investment, and trading environment in North America. The need to look at the three countries in terms of common interests was especially strong during the oil shocks of the 1970s. Even before the second oil shock in 1979, a report prepared in 1977 for Senator Henry M. Jackson's Committee on Interior and Insular Affairs, entitled *The Geopolitics of Energy*, urged that the United States reduce its involvement in the Persian Gulf and seek resources closer to home, including "special relationships" with Canada, Mexico and Venezuela. In a statement that anticipated developments in the 1980s, the report concluded that "should the Mexicans reject assistance in oil development, there are a whole host of additional Mexican interests which could be addressed in a special relationship—trade, investment, labor issues. . . . A special relationship of this sort must necessarily cover areas other than energy raw materials, and the cost to the United States may therefore be higher than a straight oil arrangement. Making such a relationship poli-tically acceptable to Mexico may prove even more difficult . . ."[9]

Crisis followed crisis in the 1970s for American policymakers. Canadian economic nationalism paled by comparison with the fallout from the 1979 Iranian revolution, which not only destroyed the structure of American involvement in Iran but led to another oil embargo against the U.S. Again, America's neighbours proved strategically convenient. In a national television address in mid-1979, President Carter indicated that the U.S. was working closely with Mexico and Canada in the develop-ment of energy policies; although it was anticipated that Canadian oil production would decline, the administration was counting on sharing Canada's hydroelectric power and natural gas. Carter expressed the hope

---

8   Willard Thorpe to Undersecretary of State, Robert Lovett, 8 March 1948, U.S. Department of State, *Foreign Relations of the United States*, IX (1948), pp. 406–410; memorandum on meeting of 26 September 1955 of U.S.–Canada Committee on Trade and Economic Affairs, *Foreign Relations*, IX (1955), pp. 152–53.

9   Melvin A. Conant and Fern R. Gold, *The Geopolitics of Energy*, U.S. Senate, Committee on Interior and Insular Affairs (Washington, D.C., 1977), pp. 138, 146.

that the Alaska natural gas pipeline would by 1985 enable Alaskan and Canadian natural gas to displace almost 700,000 bb/d of imported oil.[10]

U.S. officials also perceived Mexico as a part of the solution to American dependency on foreign sources of oil. By 1978, with the expansion of Mexican oil production, the Pentagon was purchasing Mexican oil for the U.S. Strategic Petroleum Reserve. At that time, the National Security Council viewed Mexico as the most promising source of oil and a means to reduce American reliance on Middle East supplies. The NSC also believed there could be linkage between U.S–Mexican energy trade and other divisive issues in cross-border relations, in particular legal and illegal migration and drug trafficking.[11]

President Carter's efforts to stress the commonality of United States, Canadian and Mexican interests ironically came at the same time that the Liberal government of Pierre Trudeau initiated the National Energy Policy, the Canadianization provisions of which ran directly counter to the traditional American thrust toward continentalism in the use of natural resources. Several of the major objectives of Canadian policy were to make Canadian oil and gas production 50 percent Canadian owned by 1990, discourage foreign investment, encourage exploration and development on federal rather than provincial lands, establish a tax system that would facilitate Canadian investor entry into the industry, and use Petro-Canada as a vehicle for Canadian participation and direction. It was not surprising, therefore, that the Reagan administration would formally object to the direction of Canadian policies, although the dismantling of the NEP owed as much to domestic political reaction as to foreign objections.[12]

Two additional factors which contributed to creating the context and perceived need for a new relationship among the nations of North America, and which led to both the FTA and NAFTA, was the general orientation of the Reagan administration and the economic crisis that overcame Mexico in the 1980s. Both during the 1980 campaign and following inauguration, the Reagan administration consistently articulated the fear that the U.S. was in decline economically relative to Japan and the European community; the old world order was threatened, even after the demise of the Soviet Union in late 1991, with the result that relations with America's major trading partner assumed greater importance. When Reagan took office, the U.S. had a negative trade balance with Canada of

---

10 For Carter's statements see: U.S. Department of State, *American Foreign Policy: Basic Documents, 1977–80* (Washington, 1983), pp. 287–88, 290–91.

11 *Washington Post*, 15 December 1978, cited in Grayson, "Oil in U.S.-Mexico Relations," p. 452.

12 Canada, Department of Energy, Mines and Resources, *The National Energy Program, 1980* (Ottawa, 1980), pp. 17–18, 19, 39, 47, 49, 51.

$7.3 billion; by 1986, when bilateral talks got under way, that imbalance had risen to $23.3 billion. In 1987 the volume of two-way Canada–U.S.trade was worth $125 billion, which was 25 percent of all American trade and 1.5 times the level of U.S. exports to Japan. Canada also remained the main host for U.S. foreign investment. In 1987 U.S. DFI in Canada was $57 billion, representing 20 percent of all U.S. offshore investments, and Canadian DFI in the U.S. was $20 billion.[13] It was therefore not surprising that as early as the 1980 campaign Reagan spoke of creating a North American economic area, perhaps including the Caribbean. In the mid-1980s his administration introduced the Caribbean Basin Initiative, designed to stimulate private investment and economic growth in the area; after his election in 1988, George Bush widened the horizons of the concept to include Latin America in the Enterprise for the Americas Initiative, developed in conjunction with the Inter-American Development Bank.

The main issues here, however, are what interests the three countries share and to what extent NAFTA will contribute to a trilateral agenda and mechanisms to address those issues. For the past decade the countries of North America have been confronted with a strengthened European community, emerging trade blocs in Asia and a strong Asian economic order. At the same time crises in Central America and the Caribbean in the 1980s and early 1990s have underscored the extent to which the countries of North America are vulnerable to socio-economic, political and military dislocation and conflict within the region. The Cuban, Central American and Haitian situations in particular underlined the intensity of pressures generated by peoples displaced by civil strife and poverty. To the commonality of interests inherent in that shared eternal challenge must be added problems of environmental degradation, labour standards, and democratization in the Mexican case.

Clearly it is in the interest of all three countries to adopt a common front in dealing with global issues; yet, the historical institutions do not not readily lend themselves to a trilateral or common front approach. Boundary and water commissions, environmental issues, etc., have traditionally been treated within a bilateral framework. Moreover, there are many institutions and agencies outside the three federal governments which provide input into the cross-border relations. Indeed, it is one of the fundamental features of the two bilateral relationships that there is a remarkable breadth of interests and sometimes interference that cannot be contained within normal diplomatic bounds, whether it is the involve-

---

13 U.S. Department of State, *State Department Bulletin* (April 1987), pp. 22, 24; *Bulletin* (September 1987), p. 16; *Bulletin* (July 1988), p. 23; On trade data see also Department of Commerce, *Statistical Abstract of the United States, 1990* (Washington, 1991), pp. 797, 806.

ment of the legislatures, of citizens' groups, of business interests, or of a multiplicity of city, state or provincial and federal agencies concerned with everything from air and water pollution along the border to job security in the context of debate over NAFTA. This proliferation of legislative, executive, state, city and private entities and agencies in the three countries that have some responsibility for cross-border relations is both curse and blessing. On the negative side of the ledger it is impossible to coordinate all of their activities to ensure consistency of overall policy. On the other hand, as Joseph Nye has suggested for the United States,

> These miniature foreign offices that domestic agencies have developed for dealing with the international aspects of issues with which they are concerned are not merely bureaucratic nuisances. They are needed in the management of interdependence issues that are both domestic and foreign. As the entire government becomes involved in 'international' affairs, it becomes more difficult to reserve a separate section of the agenda for the State Department.[14]

Whether or not Nye's optimism that bureaucratic proliferation provides as much opportunity as dilemma is well-placed, NAFTA does advance the agenda of institutionalization of the trilateral relationship.

NAFTA identifies as one of the six objectives of the treaty to "establish a framework for further trilateral, regional and multilateral cooperation to expand and enhance the benefits of the agreement."[15] Such vague phrasing may translate into considerable institutional cooperation or may mean little in practical application. To date, the three countries have agreed to establish a commission that is mandated to meet at least once a year. Its members, the number of which are not specified, are to be cabinet-level representatives; its decisions, if any, will be reached by consensus. Under the commission comes a secretariat composed of national sections composed of at least twenty-five panelists for each country to serve as arbitrators under the disputes settlements procedures established under Chapter 19 and Chapter 20 of the treaty, as well as members of committees and scientific review bodies.

Neither the secretariat nor the commission appear to have much scope. The secretariat's function is primarily record-keeping; the commission's main activity is to publish the reports of the arbitration committees. Neither body has enforcement or investigative powers or responsibilities and neither has jurisdiction in the critical area of anti-

---

14 Joseph S. Nye, Jr., "Independence and Interdependence," *Foreign Policy* (Spring, 1976), p. 138.

15 *Mexico and NAFTA Report*, 21 April 1994, p. 2.

dumping and countervailing duty determination. More important in this regard is the role of the five-member dispute settlement panels, the decisions of which are to be binding, i.e., their decisions are not to be challenged in the domestic courts of the members. The only recourse is through the "extraordinary challenge procedure," under which a panel decision can be appealed to a court of three judges, drawn from the U.S. federal courts, a court of superior jurisdiction in Canada, or a Mexican federal judicial court. These arrangements pose no challenge to the traditional sovereignty of the three countries; on the other hand, they represent a decided divergence from the European community approach. The failure under NAFTA to establish an umbrella organization which might take decisions buffered somewhat from the vagaries of domestic politics in any of the countries reflects the very traditional nature of the NAFTA agreement and the mutual jealousy of national sovereignty that exists among its members. As well, there are two working groups established under Chapter 20 which retain their strictly bilateral character: U.S.–Mexico and Canada–Mexico.[16]

The two specific areas in which there has been further institutional development during 1994 are labour and environmental standards; those developments are embryonic but suggestive of potential cooperation. In the former area, that is, labour, the three responsible ministers in March 1994 agreed to the creation of the Consejo de la Comisión de Cooperación Laboral to be based in Dallas, to be headed by a Canadian, and to work through the labour ministries in each country. Its function is to monitor the labour accords and to foster trilateral labour sector cooperation, with emphasis on health and safety, employment, productivity and quality. This trilateral body will be supplemented by national offices in each country to respond to complaints about labour practices and working conditions in the other countries.[17] Significantly, the private sector is also taking initiatives in this area. U.S. unions, for instance, have established a solidarity fund to assist Mexican labour in organizing in the industrial sector, generally in competition with the PRI-dominated CTM (Confederación de Trabajadores Mexicanos). Such initiatives from U.S. unions are important, since NAFTA provides only for the suspension of the Treaty's benefits in instances involving child labour or unsafe working conditions.

The three countries have also made progress since implementing the treaty in institutionalizing arrangements in the environmental area. In

---

16 *North American Free Trade Agreement*, Annex 2001.2.

17 *Mexico and NAFTA Report*, 21 April 1994, p. 3. U.S. labour has already filed two complaints about Mexican labour practices at two U.S.-owned plants in Mexico, one owned by Honeywell, the other by General Electric.

March 1994 representatives of the three countries meeting in Vancouver agreed to establish a North American Development Bank, the primary function of which will be to finance environmental clean-up along the always troubled U.S.–Mexico border. The U.S. has committed 10 percent of its share of the bank's loans to projects which are intended to offset the anticipated impact of NAFTA on specific economic activities and groups. The bank, with a capitalization of $3 billion U.S., will be based in San Antonio, Texas, with a branch in Los Angeles. To supplment the work of the bank the countries are establishing an environmental commission for the border area in Ciudad Juarez. As an umbrella organization the three countries have created the North American Commission for Environmental Co-operation. Based in Montreal, the commission includes the heads of the environmental agencies in each country, and is under the initial direction of Victor Lichtinger, a Mexican environmental consultant.[18] Clearly, many of these initiatives are primarily driven by the bilateral relationship between the U.S. and Mexico, the lengthy history of environmental degradation along their border, and the realities of domestic politics; these measures would have been necessary even without a NAFTA, but NAFTA and its side agreements on labour and the environment have clearly facilitated the process by crystallizing support for positive action. In the case of the Development Bank, Clinton administration support for the institution was essential in the fall of 1993 to gain the support of California Democratic Congressman Esteban Torres.[19]

In the final analysis the international relations dynamic in the western hemisphere is in transition. That transition has been fueled by the lost decade and debt crisis of the 1980s in Latin America as well as by the twin realities of historical trends toward closer integration and the contemporary thrust toward regional free trade, investment liberalization, and privatization. It is within that context that relations among the three countries have evolved in the past decade. The challenge that remains is to find the most effective institutional mechanisms available to depoliticize such issues as trade, investment, migration, narcotics, labour and environmental disputes. If history is an accurate guide, the future holds considerable promise, balanced with acute challenges, as different cultures attempt to come to terms with the realities of living with one another in an ever smaller global environment. NAFTA may improve and strengthen the formal mechanisms for managing the trilateral relationship, but ambiguity is likely to remain one of the dominant characteristics of relations among the three societies.

---

18 *Mexico and NAFTA Report*, 21 July 1994, p. 3.

19 Ibid.

Pedro G. Marquez Perez
Department of Political Science
University of Calgary

4

The Social Neo-Liberal Policies of Carlos Salinas de Gortari

The reforms achieved during the administrations of Miguel de la Madrid (1982–1988) and Carlos Salinas de Gortari (1988–1994) ignited a debate concerning the political and economic processes of the reform and the nature of Mexican development policy. Taking into account the world systems shift with the end of the Cold War, the debate questioned the relevance and viability of a statist regime in the context of a trend toward economic globalization and the development of regional trade blocs. Mexican reforms in these years focused on several concerns: the necessity of creating new political spaces for those groups previously excluded from political participation; the necessity to design a new development policy that could solve the crisis produced by the old model based on "import substitution" under "captive markets," which had characterized the development orientation of the country for several decades and which had left the nation with insufficient investment, high public debts and deepening poverty in the country;[1] and the need to reconsider Mexico's relationship to outside markets through the establishment of more efficent production and more consistent and higher standards. The de la Madrid and Salinas governments presented such reforms in terms of continued adherence to the ideals and goals of the Revolution, including individualism, while the role of the state and the bureaucracy especially were transformed.[2]

---

1 Juan Rebolledo, *La Reforma del Estado En México* (México: Fondo de Cultura Económica, 1993), p. 17.

2 Carlos Salinas de Gortari, "Reformando del Estado," *Nexus Magazine*, 148 (April 1990), p. 32.

One of the main controversies of the debate centred on the characteristics and magnitude of the reforms that were being undertaken as the nation shifted from a state-directed economy to one based on "Social Liberalism."[3] The economic reform initiated by President de la Madrid reorientated Mexico into a freer economic regime, first by implementing a mixed economy with an export orientation, later reinforced by the introduction of an open market structure, based on deregulation, privatization, the promotion of foreign investment and the diversification of exports. The social reforms re-evaluated the populist policies that had been followed under the earlier economic model and introduced the Programa Nacional de Solidaridad (PRONASOL—National Solidarity Program). The objective of PRONASOL was to attempt to reconcile the social equity problems of the Neo-liberal model with the reforms—which were seen to be the Achilles heel of Neo-liberalism—and provide the reforms with a mantle of continuity with the values of the Mexican Revolution. Finally, the administration inaugurated a political reform to accommodate the new development model and to respond to the growing demands for a higher degree of political participation in the society.[4]

On the occasion of the 63rd anniversary of the PRI, President Salinas reflected on the direction and nature of his administration's policies:

> Today reform of the Revolution makes Social Liberalism especially relevant; Social Liberalism is consistent with our historic conceptions of the country if we are to reach the goals of sovereignty, justice, liberty and democracy. In that way, we build a new conception of the Revolution, in accordance with our times, proud of the past, but not limited by the previous means used to achieve those ends. Social Liberalism is neither a Neo-liberal reform nor the dominant statism practised in the past. Between those two extremes there must be no confusion.[5]

It is critical to observe that Salinas himself rejected the depiction of his reforms as Neo-liberal. It was audacious novelty for Salinas to proclaim that he was attempting to reform the Revolution, at least the way the Revolution's goals (e.g., land tenure, education and labour) would be

---

3   Salinas de Gortari, *El Liberalism Social*, speech delivered during the 63rd anniversary of the PRI (Mexico: Dirección de Communicación Social de la Presidencia, 1990).

4   For a more general discussion of Neo-liberalism see: Randall Rothenberg, *The Neo-Liberals: Creating the New American Politics* (New York: Simon and Schuster, 1984).

5   For absorbent statism, Salinas referred to the old practice of a large state, responsible for regulating and participating in every economic activity (see Salinas de Gortari, *Liberalism Social*, p. 5).

achieved. "In 1945 the PRI institutionalised the Revolution and in 1992 it intended to reform it."[6] This transition, as Salinas explained it, consisted of adapting the principles of solidarity, liberty, democracy and nationalism that fed the Revolution of 1910 to the new national reality. The main modification associated with Social Liberalism was the rejection of the historical adherence to the notion of the large state as the engine of development.

It has been suggested that Salinas's notion of Social Liberalism was in itself internally contradictory, because of the tensions between the meaning of "social" and "liberal." The individualist principles of Liberalism appeared to be antagonistic to the realization of the more collectivist social goals of the Revolution and of his administration.[7] It should be clear that what Salinas intended was to pursue a liberal policy, with a particular effort to promote social reform in order to realize a balance between the political right and left, thus situating his policies at the critical ideological centre.

Using the same notion of the *sociedad fluctuante*[8] employed by Reyes Heroles to describe the dialectical confrontation between colonialist and revolutionary criollos in the early nineteenth century, and between conservatives and liberals in mid-century, Salinas contended: "these two theories are at odds with each other: the first notion continues with the appearance of the second, and the second cannot flourish freely because of the restraint imposed by the survival of the first. It is the clash between statism and possessive neo-Liberalism; and neither responded to the reforms undertaken as part of the Revolution."[9] Salinas thus presented "Social Liberalism" as a means of achieving a general

---

6   Margarita Bahena-Perez, "Del Liberalismo Revolucionario al Liberalismo Social" ["From Revolutionary Liberalism to Social Liberalism"], *Banca y Comercio*, 17 (Nov–Dec 1993), p. 23.

7   President Salinas advances the notion of Social Liberalism, a doctrine that does not represent the mercantilist and free trade thesis. This is the moment when Salinas faces what I assume will be the biggest discussion of the administration: Social Liberalism. See Arnoldo Cordova, "Liberalismo Social, Invento de Reyes Heroles: una Contradiccion en si Mismo" ["Social Liberalism, Creation of Reyes Heroles: a Contradiction in Itself"], *PROCESO* (9 de Marzo 1992), p. 13.

8   Jesus Reyes Heroles, *El Liberalismo Mexicano, tomo I: Los Origines; Tomo II: La Sociedad Fluctuante; Tomo III: La Integracion de las ideas* (Mexico: Fondo de Cultura Economica, 1957).

9   Salinas de Gortari, *Liberalism Social*, p. 6.

consensus on the economic, social and political development of modern Mexico."[10]

In the presidential speech alluded to earlier, Salinas identified ten features of Social Liberalism: the sovereignty of the state, social justice, freedom, democracy, education, land, native peoples, nutrition, housing, health and the quality of life. In pursuing these values, Salinas contended that he was rejecting the premises of Neo-liberalism. The following discussion examines the veracity of Salinas's contention that he was rejecting the values of that political philosophy.

The strategy used by Salinas to accomplish his objectives consisted of two main elements. First, he defined the ten basic criteria of Social Liberalism in relationship to the Revolution, and delineated the differences between his notion of Social Liberalism and what he contended were the main premises of Neo-liberalism on similar issues. Logically, he discovered several differences as intended; but this comparison was not properly structured because he compared "Social Liberalism and Neo-liberalism." Consequently, he emphasized the social character of the former and its absence in the latter. However, if we attribute some degree of social character to neo-liberalism as well—turning the comparison into "Social Liberalism vs. Social Neo-liberalism"—or exclude it from the first— "Liberalism vs. Neo-liberalism"—then the conclusion is totally different from that reached by Salinas in his speech. Salinas further presented a distorted image of the Neo-liberal doctrine, associating ideas normally attributed to Classical Liberalism rather than to Neo-liberal values.

Initially, as Emeterio Gomez suggests, "Neo-liberalism is not a closed or finished system of ideas; it is not a definitive conjunct of principles that should be accepted or rejected religiously as a block. Neo-liberalism holds a group of postulates inherited from the eighteenth century but in continuing evolution after the Keynesian revolution, permanently exposed to criticism and contrasts with reality, considering the changes of our times."[11] In other words, Neo-liberalism arose from the crisis that Classical Liberalism experienced when confronted with Socialism and Communism, with the result that many of its original postulates were modified, even if basic assumptions were retained. This crisis in Classical Liberalism thus gave place to a new, ideologically more centrist doctrine,

---

10 Manuel Munoz-Patraca, "El Liberalismo Social: Propuesta ideologica del Salinismo," *Revista Mexicana de las Ciencias Sociales*, No. 149 (September 1992), p. 30.

11 Emeterio Gomez, "Reflexiones sobre el Neo-liberalismo" [Reflections on Neo-liberalism], *Revista Mexicana de Ciencias Politicas*, 15 (II trimestre 1989), p. 11. [Referred to hereafter as *Reflexiones*.]

closer to the concept of the "social market economy," and similar to what Salinas called possessive Neo-liberalism, or Social Liberalism.

A brief analysis of some of the ten basic pillars of Salinas's Social Liberalism and their possible linkage to Neo-liberalism is helpful to observe the apparent confusion which Salinas made between Classical Liberalism and Neo-liberalism.

Regarding the issues of social justice, liberty and democracy, Salinas contended that Neo-liberalism was only concerned with the individual rather than the larger concept of the social character of the individual:

> For Neo-liberalism society is only formed by isolated individual participation ruled by "possessive individualism," without taking into consideration other people's interest in its decisions . . . For Neo-liberals, formal liberties are the only guarantees that the state should protect, considering the individual isolated with no ties or duties towards the community . . . The Neo-liberal is committed to a democratic model which considers an isolated individual, without considering its form of organization."[12]

Obviously, the core of Liberalism is liberty and, more concretely, individual liberty; but Neo-liberalism provides for a complex relationship between the individual and society that should be cleared in order to avoid the type of conclusion Salinas reached. Neo-liberalism does not prefer individual well-being or individual selfishness when these work to the detriment of society as a whole, as in the notion of the invisible hand sustained by Classical Liberalism. The criticism of this notion has concentrated on Adam Smith's apparent celebration of individualism, but it is critical to note that the essence of the metaphor is that the community benefits from free individual action. Historically, Liberalism has supported individual liberty to the degree that that individualism also contributed to a broader social welfare.[13] Furthermore, after the crisis in Classical Liberalism, Neo-liberals learned to recognize the profound social problems that could be created from individual liberty egoism. "Neo-liberal opposition against protectionism, corporatism, monopolies and other discriminatory policies finds its basis in the preservation of society through the promotion of individual liberty."[14]

With respect to the issue of sovereignty, Salinas contended that "for Neo-liberalism, the processes of globalization and establishment of

---

12 Gomez, *Reflexiones*, pp. 8–9.

13 Ludwig von Mises, *Socialism* (Indianapolis: Liberty Classics, 1981), p. 53.

14 Octavio Arizmendi Posada, "Convergencia entre Neoliberalismo Economico y Doctrina Social-Cristiana?" *Revista de Ciencia Politica*, No. 21 (November 1993), p. 78.

trading blocks are reasons to sustain that political borders are absurd, nationalism should expire and sovereignty become part of the past. It demands the creation of a world without borders with supranational organisations responsible for regulating national and international issues . . . and it proposes the outside organisation of our elections."[15] Salinas's contention was ill-founded because Neo-liberalism proposes respect for social agreements established on mutual individual interests. In other words, "if anything defines individual liberty, it is political liberty . . . Democracy is in consequence the prerequisite and *sine qua non* condition for the construction of a Neo-liberal society, in other words, free . . . Only democracy can guarantee the real practice of liberty, the law and equal opportunities for all members of society."[16] Respect for law applies in both national and international arenas. Then, if Neo-liberalism promotes free trade among countries, it also respects the legal accord among those countries as sovereign entities.

Even more striking is Salinas's argument that "Neo-liberalism assigns minimum functions and responsibilities to the state and reduces its capacity to regulate excessive abuses resulting from an entirely free market. Its only role is to protect the population from crime regardless of justice."[17] However, Neo-liberalism recognizes the importance of law to guarantee market competition. For Neo-liberalism the law must be paramount. Consequently, democracy and the market are established on the two main pillars of moral and juridical legitimacy. The state's power must reside upon the constitution and equality of the individual before the law, rather than on the government's capacity to control society. Therefore for Neo-liberalism, the executive and legislative powers need to be in balance. If Neo-liberalism demands the reduction of the state power, it means a reduction of the discretional executive power. "Neither during the XVIIIth nor the XXth centuries did liberal thought oppose the state or its power, if it arose directly from constitutional accords among free individuals."[18]

Another example of Salinas's inaccurate critique of Neo-liberalism was his contention that "for Neo-liberals, native people are hindrances from the past that should disappear . . . nutrition, housing, health and quality of life are individual not state responsibilities."[19] But the Neo-liberal conception of democracy "sustains the political freedom of the

---

15 Salinas de Gortari, *Liberalism Social*, p. 6.

16 Gomez, *Reflexiones*, p. 24.

17 Gomez, *Reflexiones*, p. 11.

18 Gomez, *Reflexiones*, p. 14.

19 Salinas de Gortari, *Liberalism Social*, p. 12.

rights of all members of society, including labour and native people."[20] Furthermore, Neo-liberalism does not propose strict laissez-faire, premised on the belief that the free market will guarantee a fair distribution of income. After the Keynesian revolution, Neo-liberalism accepted that the market could create a social gap, that must be solved by direct action in the social sphere. Consequently, as advanced by Milton Friedman, Neo-liberalism suggests the practice of direct subsidies to the poorer segments of society.[21] Neo-liberalism defends democratic capitalism with equal chances and opportunities for all members of the population. "The social problems cannot be left aside; the only possible solution is to promote social expenditure with a flexible strategy, respectful of economic profitability,"[22] and PRONASOL follows the Neo-liberal directive.

From the above, one may conclude that the argument used against Neo-liberalism in reality applied to Classical Liberalism instead. Since the term "Social Liberalism" was in the first instance adopted from nineteenth-century Mexican history and in the second instance from Classical Liberalism then criticism would be more accurately directed at Salinas's own policies than at Neo-liberalism itself.

Furthermore, two important premises of Neo-liberalism are found in Salinas's reform: first, the nature of money for Neo-liberalism is different than for Classical Liberalism. After the Keynesian revolution, Neo-liberalism recognized the inflationary problems which derived from the production of money by a central bank, since there is constant pressure from society on government to solve problems of economic liquidity. Neo-liberals proposed two possible solutions: first, the abolition of central banks through the total privatization of the monetary system; or second, the existence of a central bank under complete constitutional control to prevent expansion of the monetary supply. Salinas's economic reform promulgated the independence of the central bank from the state, and promoted a law to forbid any sector—including especially the president— from requesting the expansion of the money supply, policies closer to Neo-liberalism. In accordance with Neo-liberalism, the state's capacity to respond to those pressures must reside with the constitution and not with

---

20 Gomez, *Reflexiones*, p. 27.

21 Rosario Green, *Los Mitos de Milton Friedman* [The Myths of Milton Friedman] (Mexico: Centro de Estudios Economicos y Sociales del Tercer Mundo, 1983), p. 21.

22 Gomez, "Reflexiones sobre el Neo-liberalismo" [Reflexions on Neo-liberalism], *Revista Mexicana de las Ciencias Politicas*, 89 (1989), p. 27. [referred to hereafter as "Neo-liberalismo."]

executive discretion.[23] At the same time, Classical Liberalism is largely silent on monetary policy.

Second, for Neo-liberalism, macroeconomic equilibrium plans—such as Salinas's macroeconomic stabilization program—may only be accomplished by a strong state. However, at the time Classical Liberalism emerged, economic theory had not developed a macroeconomic stabilization strategy. Therefore it made no sense to establish a firm economic policy to guarantee basic macroeconomic equilibrium on the balance of payments, public finances and monetary policies. From the Neo-liberal perspective, macroeconomic projects require strong states—not large states—capable of resisting pressures from the different economic elements challenged by the macroeconomic policy. "The market can only be reconstructed from the state; in other words, it can only be conceived as the product of a conscious—ethical, juridical, constitutional and political—decision of society."[24] In the Mexican case, the macroeconomic reform was built upon a strong presidential system responsible for attaining accords in the political, economic and social realms.

It would appear, as a result, that Salinas's "Social Liberalism" policy may more meaningfully be called "Social Neo-liberalism." Employing Salinas's logic, "Social Neo-liberalism" and not "Social Liberalism" is the centre point between—pure Neo-liberalism on the one hand and statism on the other.

But why the rejection of this term? The answer lies in two complementary, key issues: on the one hand, the success of Salinas's reform heavily depended on his success in gathering enough support to defeat the strong *status quo* forces of the previous economic and political system. The Neo-liberal adjective of Social Neo-liberalism implied a right-wing policy and consequently the potential lack of support from the left—or conservative—forces, and could be easily misinterpreted as an intended ideological separation from the Revolution's goals and the PRI's ideology. On the other hand, the term "Social Liberalism"—copied from Reyes Heroles—provided the reform with "historical legitimacy." That is, it linked Salinas's project not only with important elements of Mexico's history, but also established a closer relationship between Salinas's leadership and other successful initiatives in the country's history. In other words, the term connected Salinas's reform with the triumphant Liberal reform of 1857 and the Revolution of 1911, as well as linking Salinas with such national heroes as Benito Juarez and Francisco I. Madero.

---

23 Charles Peters, *A New Road for America: The Neo-liberal Movement* (Madison: Madison Books, 1985), p. 161.

24 Peters, *A New Road*, p. 170.

In summary, Social Liberalism—and not Social Neo-liberalism—allowed Salinas to built an apparently ideologically centrist policy which, because of its historical legitimacy, could garner support from the left wing, while also collecting support from the right wing. "With the term, the president found a rich spring to abandon the old social democracy schemes, and aim for a centre policy to avoid the characterisation as fully Neo-liberal."[25]

---

25 Federico Reyes Heroles, "Salinas habla ahora de Justicia Social; Vamos a ver Hasta Donde Llega" ["Salinas Talks about Social Justice; Let's See How Far He Gets"], *PROCESO* (9 de Marzo 1992), p. 11.

Maria Teresa Gutiérrez Háces
Centre for United States Studies
National Autonomous University of Mexico

5

Canada–Mexico: The Neighbour's Neighbour

I

Towards the end of 1990, when Mexico and Canada decided to negotiate a trilateral free trade agreement with the United States, they suddenly had to confront an undeniable fact: during the past fifty years, neither one had advanced in its knowledge of the other. By late 1993, with a final document and the signing of the parallel agreements, the negotiations for the North American Free Trade Agreement (NAFTA) had concluded. Throughout the negotiating process, those who were in one way or another connected to NAFTA tried to gain expertise, in the shortest time possible, regarding the most relevant issues about the Canadian economy, history and policy in order to define a strategy for the Mexican negotiating team. Overall, I would call that strategy defensive rather than complementary. Although much data was collected and many documents were drafted, the information that was gathered about Canada was mostly related to issues considered important in relation to the negotiation itself and did not focus on those aspects that would lead to a greater knowledge of, and understanding between, the two societies.

Apart from the negotiations, another process developed, one which, in my opinion, was of equal importance. Towards the end of 1990, a growing number of individuals and organizations in Canada began to study Mexico from their own professional and political perspectives. This phenomenon, a spontaneous encounter of two societies, was and is a process which in most cases was independent of Mexican or Canadian official agencies.

Thus, there were two parallel movements towards this mutual discovery. One began and grew as a need by groups directly involved, basically bureaucrats at all levels of government from those departments which considered themselves most affected by the negotiations, including

Commerce and Industrial Development, Foreign Affairs, Agriculture, Labour, and Mines and Natural Resources. At this level, in my opinion, the Mexican negotiating team hesitated, and decided to concentrate its energy on its strategy regarding the United States. Not much time was spent on creating a "Canada file" which could later serve as the basis for future negotiations, since the main worry was the agreement with the United States.

This attitude clearly reflects what was and will continue to be the Achilles heel of Mexico–Canada relations: the overwhelming presence of the United States in its neighbours' political and economic affairs. During the Canada–U.S. negotiations, Canada also committed a great deal of its human and monetary resources to the bilateral agreement. When the time came for the trilateral negotiations, it felt that it wasn't necessary to repeat that effort. Regarding Mexico, the Canadians focused on protecting acquired interests and trying to obtain new advantages from the trilateral relationship. Later, the official Mexican group, which included representatives from both the government and the private sector, felt that it should rectify its strategy and pay more attention to Canada. This change came about when groups opposing NAFTA, and trade unions, began a debate which addressed the need to answer two important questions:

Why was the first free trade agreement unpopular in Canada?

What lessons might Mexico learn from the Canadian experience and thus avoid making the same mistakes during the negotiations?

Towards the end of 1990, two important conferences in Mexico became the watershed between the old and a new attitude towards Canada. The first was organized by the National Action Party (PAN), traditionally a middle-class party, politically right-wing and historically the PRI's main opposition, whose members for the most part come from the private sector and have an enormous influence in industry and commerce. Eighteen renowned Canadians were invited to discuss the U.S.–Canada bilateral agreement and the Canadian negotiating experience. The diversity of speakers reflected the diversity of contemporary Canadian society. Various political opinions and parties were represented from government and private sector representatives, as well as dissidents, academics, and representatives from the different provinces.

Since it was an event organized by a centre-right political party, the public was much larger than that which would have attended a conference sponsored by a left-wing organization. The conference had important consequences; entrepreneurial groups learned much from their Canadian interlocutors, the COECE (Entrepreneurial Export Council), which represented the Mexican private sector during the negotiations, was directly influenced by the Canadian Business Council on National Issues' experience. The Mexican negotiating team prepared a good deal of its strategy starting from the Canadian experience, and agencies such as PEMEX listened attentively to the discussion on negotiations related to energy.[1]

During the second conference, which was held only a few days after the first, more than forty Canadians from various social organizations and trade unions spoke out against the bilateral free trade agreement. Their statements came as a surprise to the Mexican public, who suddenly became aware of important aspects of the Canadian situation and some of its contradictions. This conference also had important consequences. It spawned the Mexican Action Network which, to date, has encouraged the only serious debate regarding Mexico's role in the NAFTA negotiations. It also had an impact on the Mexican labour movement because it revealed the huge disparities that exist between the two countries regarding salaries, social security, labour rights and union practices. Another important result was its impact on public opinions which, in turn, led to the creation of the parallel agreements.[2]

It is worth noting that both conferences featured Canadians who were willing to go to Mexico and speak on issues which were until then unknown to most Mexicans. Mexico's participation in the process of mutual discovery came later. Generally speaking, those Mexicans who travelled to Canada were part of *ad hoc* missions, usually official, that tried to solve a particularly complex aspect of the negotiations *in situ*. Their knowledge of Canada was limited to issues on their agenda. However, during 1992 and at the beginning of 1993, the pressure exerted by the U.S. government and certain civil organizations in Canada, who were concerned about elections and human rights in Mexico, forced Mexicans into seeking a closer relationship with Canadian political organizations. Mexico's Federal Electoral Institute became interested in Canada's 1992 Constitutional Referendum and 1993 federal election, and Mexican delegates attended the Conservative Party convention and also the Quebec and Liberal Party conventions.

All of this leads me to conclude that, over and above the trilateral agreement, the civil society in both Mexico and Canada has cleared away the smoke screen that separated the two countries. In the future, the human flow of information between these nations will not easily be stopped, nor will it be dependent on commercial exchanges or investment ventures. The parallel agreements, together with the trilateral agreement, have given rise to a new relationship which will compel both Mexicans

1   T. Gutiérrez-Háces, ed., *Experiencias de la Negociación del T.L.C. Canadá–Estados Unidos* (Mexico: Epessa, 1991).

2   *Red Mexicana de Acción Frente al Libre Comercio, La Opinión Publica y las Negociaciones del Tratado de Libre Comercio: Alternativas Ciudadanas* (Mexico, 1991).

and Canadians to exchange knowledge and opinions, and, above all, as citizens of the North American bloc, to coordinate their policies.

Although the most intense part of the negotiation has been the debate concerning U.S. interests, we cannot deny that the Canadian presence and initiative regarding Mexico has been greater than that of the United States. The number of Canadian businesspersons reaching Mexico increased from 1,036 in 1988 to 7,762 in 1991; in 1988 there were 952 business visitors registered by the Canadian Embassy, in 1991 that number rose to 2,931. To this we must add all the Canadians who have travelled to Mexico seeking their professional counterparts. Recently, more than seven hundred university students met in Vancouver and proposed the creation of an educational project for North America. Worthy of note is Canada's ability to initiate and encourage processes in favor of, or against, NAFTA in Mexico. The same cannot be said of the United States.

II

The relationship between Mexico and Canada did not begin in 1990, nor in 1970 when Trudeau's foreign policy looked to Latin America as an answer to the Third Option. The relationship dates back to the end of the nineteenth century. In 1865, representatives from four British colonies (Canada, Nova Scotia, New Brunswick and Prince Edward Island) met in Quebec to discuss the possibilities the Mexican market offered as a commercial alternative to the U.S. market. In 1847 Mexico lost half of its territory to the United States and, as a result, like Canada, feared American expansionism and was unsure of its future as an independent state. With respect to Canada, as its Reciprocity Treaty (1854–1866) with the United States was reaching an end, the Confederate Trade Council sent its first mission to Latin America to explore potential markets.

This points to the fact that both Mexico and Canada have lived through similar, though not always concurrent, processes. Their relationship to the United States shares a common past which yields an instructive lesson. Since their beginning as independent nations, both were interested in establishing alternate markets to reduce the excessive weight of the U.S. economy. Both Mexico, which had won its independence from Spain in 1821, and Canada, still part of the British Empire, were worried about their relationship with the United States.

What were the Canadians who travelled to Mexico in the nineteenth century like? The early commercial missions were deeply distrustful of the Mexican government. Armed uprisings were not uncommon and they created a negative image for foreign investment, which the Canadians didn't wish to ignore. The first trade mission never arrived in Mexico, although it drafted a "Report of Commissioners for British-North America

TABLE 1. BILATERAL COMMERCE MEXICO–CANADA
1979–1992 (MILLIONS $ CAN)

YEAR	MEXICAN EXPORTS TO CANADA	CANADIAN EXPORTS TO MEXICO	BALANCE
1979	208	236	28
1980	345	483	138
1981	974	715	-259
1982	998	440	-558
1983	1000	375	-625
1984	1437	350	-1,087
1985	1331	391	-940
1986	1175	397	-778
1987	1169	522	-647
1988	1319	486	-833
1989	1698	603	-1,095
1990	1730	594	-1,136
1991	2574	441	-2,133
1992	628.1	154.5	-473.6

Source: Statistics Canada.

Appointed to Inquire into the Trade of the West Indies, Brazil and Mexico." Mexico was crumbling, together with Maximilian's empire, and it wasn't in the least attractive to those Canadians who were travelling to Latin America with limited resources.[3]

We can speak of a significant Canadian presence at the beginning of this century, when a group of venturesome entrepreneurs invested in the modernization of Mexico's infrastructure. In 1900 these business pioneers, who came to the fore during a period of great economic prosperity in Canada, considered Latin America the ideal place to increase their capital and make fantastic deals. Everything seemed to come together. In Mexico,

---

3   J. Ogelsby, *Gringos from the Far North* (Toronto: Macmillan, 1989).

Porfirio Díaz's regime was characterized by his energetic rule; foreign investment was considered necessary to modernize the country, and a certain amount of ill-will towards the United States favoured the presence of other countries in Mexico. Canada, with its ties to the British Empire, and its moderately independent stance *vis-à-vis* the United States, was an attractive alternative.

Porfirio Díaz knew that without railroads, telegraphs, electricity and urban transport the modernization process would be impossible. Those who had built the Canadian Pacific Railroad were looking for new markets. This convergence of interests couldn't have been more favourable. The Canadians were convinced that the profits they could make in Mexico would be greater than any they could make if they remained in their own country. Those Canadians were not much different from their twentieth-century counterparts. They thought that Canada's economy set limits which would sooner or later affect their gains. Furthermore, the business pioneers of the early 1900s were confident that the market niche they were going to establish outside of Canada could not be contested; their specialty was technology applied to utilities in the service sector and to transportation and communications.

Canadians in Mexico were the first to apply management principles combined with state-of-the-art technology and an efficient administration of earnings. They profited from the commercial routes the British had opened in Latin America. Conscious of their advantage over Mexican, Brazilian or Argentinean entrepreneurs, they decided to exploit the benefits offered them by the international conjuncture: a British Empire that was retreating from Latin America, an economic sector that was not controlled by the United States, and an urgent need to modernize the infrastructure of many Mexican cities that were anxious to be linked with other cities, both in Mexico and abroad.

The turn-of-the-century Canadians constantly repeated that market imperfections only made local economies more interesting. Thus, Canadian investment in Mexico focused on the transfer of mature technology to marginal regions, where the foreign investors and engineers who built the country's first hydroelectric plants were acclaimed as gods. Technological expertise, managerial skills, and the repatriation of capital from Canada to Mexico came together in the building of an empire of urban services that gradually connected Mexico's economic arteries.[4] Besides, the Canadians were able to obtain a higher rate of return in Mexico than in their own country, and they also benefited from their

---

4   Gutiérrez-Háces, "Experiencias y Coincidencias de Una Vecinidad Bajo el Libre Cambio: Canadá, México y Estados Unidos," in V. Bernal et al., *La Integración de México a Estados Unidos y Canadá: Alternativa o Destina* (México: Editorial siglo XXI, 1993).

superiority over local resources, miserable wages, tax exemptions, the availability of free land—and, if that were not enough, the consent of a dictatorship that allowed them a freedom and impunity unheard of in Canada.

In 1902 Fred Stark Pearson went to Mexico and visited the waterfall formed by the Necaxa river. He outlined a project, of the construction of a hydroelectric plant, to the Mexican government and his financial backers in Canada. Shortly thereafter, with capital from Montreal, he founded the Mexican Light and Power Company, which competed with the German-owned Mexican Electric Works until the latter was bought—in cash—by the Canadians. Pearson then signed a contract whereby his firm would supply electricity to Mexico City until the year 2012.[5] Pearson's company serviced not only city streets but industry, mines, trains and trolley cars. In 1906 Pearson was president of Mexico City's Streetcar Company; Canadians held 75 percent of the shares.

In 1911, Canada and Great Britain accounted for 89 percent of foreign investments in telegraphs, telephones, water, electricity and hydroelectric plants. The United States controlled six percent, France four percent, and Holland one percent. That same year, 38 percent of total foreign investments in Mexico corresponded to the United States, 29.1 percent to Canada and Great Britain, 26.7 percent to France, 1.9 percent to Germany and 1.6 percent to the Netherlands. These figures reflect Canada's relative weight in the Mexican economy at the beginning of this century. Canadians, such as Pearson and others, had discovered that integrated utility monopolies could be created in Mexico, and they didn't lose the opportunity to do so.

Foreign banks arrived in Mexico together with the above-mentioned investments, among them the Bank of Montreal and the Canadian Bank of Commerce, both of which were established to guarantee and regulate the use of Canadian capital for the business pioneers. The first Trade Commissioner from the Canadian government—A.W. Donly—was sent to Mexico in 1905. Donly's designation introduced a new stage in Canada's foreign policy. The new-found economic space in Latin America was of interest not only to a few Canadian businessmen; now it was a matter of concern for the government as well.

In 1910 the Mexican revolution abruptly cut short the budding relationship. Electric companies, railroads and streetcars were soon affected since the first social revolution of this century needed all means of

---

5 C. Armstrong and H.V. Nelles, *Southern Exposure* (Toronto: University of Toronto Press, 1988); D. McDowall, *The Light* (Toronto: University of Toronto Press, 1988); Ogelsby, *Gringos*; James Rochlin, *Discovering the Americas* (Vancouver: UBC Press, 1994); William French, *The Nature of Canadian Investment in Mexico* (MA thesis, University of Calgary, 1981).

TABLE 2. THE 25 MAIN CANADIAN ENTERPRISES IN MEXICO

NAME	YEAR OF CREATION	SOCIAL CAPITAL[a]	% FOREIGN INVESTMENT[b]
Oro de Sotula	1989	120.6	100.00
Sandoz	1994	88.0	100.00
Bombardier-Concarril	1992	72.5	100.00
Magna International de México	1991	52.1	100.00
Corporación E. G.	1990	48.4	50.10
Operadora Azucareradel Pacífico	1990	47.0	66.66
Cambior de México	1993	26.2	100.00
Amerpack	1993	18.9	16.53
Cambior Metates	1993	16.8	80.99
Minerales Libertad	1994	12.5	45.95
Purity	1994	7.1	51.00
Minera Teck	1992	6.4	100.00
Inmobiliaria Seal	1993	5.7	33.33
Cambior Exploración	1993	5.0	67.77
Ventramex	1994	4.7	100.00
Ventramex holding	1994	4.7	100.00
Soter	1992	4.0	33.00
Matol Botánica de México	1992	3.9	40.00
Advanced Profiles	1991	3.5	100.00
Sandoz Químicos	1994	3.0	99.94
Stuart Entertainment	1991	2.2	100.00
SRT de México	1992	2.1	100.00
Cambior Suaquiverde	1993	2.0	58.99
Ilco Iusa	1990	1.2	40.00
MC Extursion	1991	1.2	100.00
Subtotal 25 enterprises		559.7	85.53
Total Canadian enterprises 1989–1994		578.0	85.20

[a] Millions of Mexican new pesos. [b] Percentage of capital in direct investment.
Source: *Expansión*, March 1995.

communication for its cause. Six years later, the Canadian banks closed their Mexican offices. The revolutionary decrees were not in keeping with their interests; the days of endless privileges had given way to a new national policy.

Thus, between 1905 and 1916, events in Mexico led to important changes in Canada's attitude. The newly erected business empire crumbled, and most Canadians were forced to leave behind what they had built without filing a legal claim or receiving indemnity, because all their affairs were handled by Great Britain. Years later, in 1938, when the British government broke diplomatic relations with Mexico after it expropriated foreign oil companies, Canada's presence in this country was further debilitated since it did not have an official, independent diplomatic representative.[6]

Here we can close the first stage in Mexico–Canada relations, but not without mentioning the following six points which will help us understand subsequent stages:

1. There are two different types of actors in Mexico–Canada relations. The first is made up by investors and entrepreneurs who decide to venture into Mexico on their own; the second type consists of those few government representatives who, since 1905, have been sent to Mexico. Both are a reflection of the Canadian society at the beginning of the twentieth century, when private economic groups were not as identified with the government strategy as was later the case.
2. Great Britain's economic and political presence was a key factor in evaluating Mexico–Canada relations (as U.S. presence is today). The fact that Canada settled its diplomatic affairs through Great Britain conditioned that relationship to such an extent that on more than one occasion Canada, because of its dominion status, came into conflict with Mexico.[7]
3. Canada's official presence in Mexico reflects not only the development of the Canadian ministry of Foreign Affairs, created in 1909, but the debate on foreign policy, diplomatic relations and international trade policies in Canada.
   In 1920, Canada's Trade Commissioner in Mexico was reprimanded because he had interviewed several Mexican government representatives regarding investment opportunities in Mexico. This attitude

---

6 Lorenzo Meyer, *Su majestad Britanica contra la Revolución Méxicana, 1900–1950* (México: El Colegio de México, 1991).

7 Herman Konrad, "Le Dilemme de la Reciprocité de Canadá, le Méxique et la continentalisation aujourd'hui," in Dorval Brunelle and C. Deblock, *L'Amérique du Nord et L'Europe communautaire* (Montreal: Les presses de L'Université du Québec, 1994).

Table 3. Canadian Exports to Mexico by Provinces ($ millions)

	1988	1989	1990	1991	1992
Atlantic provinces	17,522	23,184	15,568	26,308	66,974
Ontario-Quebec	277,953	439,045	510,835	403,649	456,664
Western provinces	194,981	157,956	116,960	94,581	246,930
Total	490,456	620,185	643,363	524,538	770,573

Source: Statistics Canada.

changed radically after 1946, when Mexico and Canada signed a Reciprocal Trade Agreement.[8]

4. During the first stage of the relationship, the Canadian government learned that in order to do business in Mexico it had to follow the state of relations between business and government, and between investment, trade and finance, and Mexican nationalism.

5. Canadian entrepreneurs—past and present—are interested in an investment strategy focused on transportation, telecommunications and services related to natural resources, such as water, oil and mines.

6. Canadians in Mexico are aware of the fact that they must establish ties with the local market and create an interlocking chain of services. The difficulties of applying this strategy are closely related to their negotiating power *vis-à-vis* economic sectors that, to this day, are governed by state monopolies: oil and mines, telecommunications, electricity and highways.

III

Possibly the greatest difference between the first Canadians in Mexico and those who began to arrive during the 1940s was that the latter lived according to the parameters set by the Cold War. The Cold War affected the entire sphere of international relations, and the world was governed under a bipolar system. For Mexico and Canada this situation was especially important because their proximity to the United States overrode any political or commercial decision they might try to mutually establish. A few examples illustrate the climate that prevailed between 1940 and 1990.

Canada first established diplomatic relations in Latin America with Argentina, Brazil and Chile; surprisingly, *not* with Mexico, with whom

---

8 David Winfield, Canadian Ambassador to Mexico, "What are Canadians Doing in Mexico?" (mimeo of address in Toronto, 1990).

TABLE 4. CANADIAN EXPORTS TO MEXICO BY
MAIN PRODUCTS 1990–1992 ($ MILLIONS)

PRODUCT	1990	1991	1992
Motor vehicle parts	109.4	127.1	157.6
Iron & steel products	67.7	46.3	87.8
Aircraft & parts	39.1	17.3	20.8
Bituminous coal	0.0	2.2	32.1
Telecom equipment	40.0	21.8	61.0
Newsprint	15.9	34.9	28.3
Asbestos	13.4	16.0	12.7
Milk powder	72.5	13.4	24.9
Sulphur	28.8	19.8	7.5
Rape or colza seeds	0.0	0.0	13.0
Meat & livestock	23.6	31.6	49.9
Wood pulp	27.7	21.2	20.2
Cooper	0.0	0.0	12.2
Furniture & furnishings	0.9	24.0	7.0
Electrical boards	0.6	0.1	7.2
Barley, oats, canary seed	0.7	5.1	9.4
Petroleum oils	5.1	16.1	6.9
Wheat	8.4	25.0	108.7
Others	189.3	160.5	103.5
Total	643.4	560.7	770.6

Source: Statistics Canada.

it had commercial ties since the early 1900s. The answer to this must be found in U.S. hemispheric policy: the United States felt that Canada should support them to prevent South America from forming alliances with totalitarian governments. This can be documented in the correspondence between Cordell Hull, Sumner Welles, Franklin D. Roosevelt and Mackenzie King.

The United States always compelled Mexico and Canada to support its political and commercial positions. As regards the former, Canada has long been pressured into sharing U.S. geopolitical projects; respecting the latter, U.S. free trade and entrepreneurial positions were an important influence on Canada, which was co-founder, with the United States, of the GATT. Mexico did not accept free trade as part of its economic policy until 1986—and lived until then through a period filled with conflicts— while Canada adopted this policy at the end of the 1940s. Both Mexico and Canada built their industrialization with protectionist tariff policies; Mexico maintained those policies from 1944 to 1982, Canada until 1979.[9] Possibly one of the greatest differences between the two countries lies in their decisions regarding foreign investment and state control of natural resources. Until close to 1970 Canada officially considered that foreign investment was a great asset for economic development, while Mexico held a stricter position and put obstacles in the way of its entry to the country. Mexico began to nationalize its natural resources in 1938, when it expropriated foreign oil companies; Canada did not attempt to implement a nationalistic oil policy until the 1970s and 1980s.[10]

When Canada expressed its desire to participate in the Pan American Union in 1942, U.S. influence on Canadian foreign policy was flagrant. The United States censored Canada's initiative, indicating that it didn't want Canada to join because it might give Great Britain the opportunity to interfere in hemispheric affairs. Only recently, in 1990, did Canada become a member of the Organization of American States.[11]

These are some of the elements that conditioned the relationship between Mexico and Canada. Notwithstanding, in 1946 a Canadian Trade Mission to Latin America led to the signing of a trade agreement with

9 D. Wolfe, "Canadian Economic Policy, 1945–1957," *Journal of Canadian Studies,* vol. 13 (1978).

10 Gutiérrez-Háces, "Canadá: del Nacionalismo y la diversidad Política a las realidades de la continentalización," in Gutiérrez-Háces and Monica Verea, eds., *Canadá en Transición* (México: El Colegio de México, 1994); Mel Watkins, *Foreign Ownership and the Structure of Canadian Industry* (Ottawa, 1968); A. Rotstein, "Is There an English Canadian Nationalism?" *Journal of Canadian Studies,* vol. 13 (1978).

11 Rochlin, 1994; Brian Stevenson, "Foreign Policy and the Canadian Setting" (El Colegio de México, mimeo, 1994).

TABLE 5. MEXICAN EXPORTS TO CANADA
BY MAIN PRODUCT ($ MILLIONS)

PRODUCT	1990	1991	1992	% 92/91
Automotive vehicles	127.7	716.2	602.1	-16
Automotive parts	436.3	538.2	688.4	28
Radio, telephone, audio	146.6	143.5	199.4	39
Ignition wiring sets	89.2	105.0	118.8	13
Engines & engine parts	300.2	224.9	139.4	-38
Vegetables	79.3	48.6	43.1	-11
Petroleum oils	56.8	97.6	188.4	93
Air conditioners	32.0	57.0	73.1	28
Fruit, coffee & nuts	68.5	56.8	55.5	-2
Air filtering systems	33.6	26.7	66.4	149
Kitchen appliances	13.7	23.3	0.0	0
Carpets, fabrics & yarns	27.8	30.2	31.7	5
Springs (iron or steel)	10.4	15.4	14.3	-7
Furniture	33.6	21.2	14.9	-30
Toys	12.6	12.2	0.0	0
Clothing	9.1	11.5	13.5	17
Glass articles	12.8	15.7	0.0	0
Data processing machines & parts	0.0	127.8	105.7	-17
Electrical lighting & signalling equipment	0.0	27.5	34.1	24
Beer, wine and spirits	0.0	15.5	17.7	14
Others	239.6	265.1	344.8	30
Total	1,729.8	2,579.8	2,751.1	7

Source: Statistics Canada.

Mexico. A code of conduct was established, based on the principle of Most Favored Nation, a position based on its status as developing country that Mexico also wielded in its commercial relations with the United States. Starting with this agreement, the relationship began to flow through diplomatic channels; the arrival of businessmen or trade missions was handled by the Canadian Embassy, which opened its doors in 1944. In 1953, the possibility of creating a Mexico–Canada Chamber of Commerce was discussed; by then, economic conditions in Mexico were stable and the country was interested in doing business with Canada. But it was not until 1969 that entrepreneurs founded the Canadian Association for Latin America (CALA). Canadian diplomatic documents from this period reflect uncertainty regarding Mexico's political outcome, expressing many of the concerns that had been set forth by the nineteenth-century business pioneers. The constant fear of a devaluation of the peso, inflation, and labour troubles did not help to encourage Canadian initiatives.

In 1959, Adolfo López Mateos became the first Mexican president to make an official visit to Ottawa. A few months later, Prime Minister John Diefenbaker returned the visit. Let's not forget that this period was when C.D. Howe's policy of U.S. investment in Canada came under fire.[12] This was the first time that the proximity between the two countries was mentioned. It was also Mexico's first attempt to appear on the international scene, specifically in North America. These two heads of state ended a stage of discreet diplomacy and began a period of moderate international activism, which included looking for economic spaces that would be supplementary and alternate to those offered by the United States. These two visits were the immediate precedents of the Third Option Policy maintained by both countries under Prime Minister Trudeau and President Echeverría.

The high point in Mexico–Canada relations, before 1990, came in 1968 with the arrival of the Canadian Ministerial Mission. Their report led to the famous white book, *Foreign Policy for Canadians*, which contains Mitchell Sharp's broad outline of Canadian foreign policy. The Canadian International Development Agency (CIDA) and the Export Development Corporation were founded that same year, the former to coordinate Canadian participation in developing countries and the latter to finance Canadian exports. Shortly after, still in 1968, a Joint Ministerial Committee was established in Mexico to study issues of common interest to the economy and politics of both countries.

The 1970s began with a commercial diplomatic infrastructure geared to facilitating and consolidating a new phase in Mexico–Canada relations, one in which investments and business became a priority. From 1970 on, most of the diplomatic correspondence I was able to examine in the National Archives of Canada reflects a governmental and entrepreneurial disposition to enter into the Mexican market. The problem, however, was that this decision to open alternate markets in Mexico and Canada confronted serious obstacles. U.S. foreign policy towards both its neighbours

---

12 Knowlton Nash, *Kennedy & Diefenbaker* (Toronto: McClelland and Stewart, 1990).

flared up—for example, Nixon levied tariffs on imports entering the United States in 1971; the nationalistic atmosphere in the two countries had a negative social counterpart—guerrillas in both Mexico and Canada led to the flight of domestic and foreign capital; the United States applied political pressure in trying to modify Canada's and Mexico's active diplomacy.[13]

In sum, it was a complex period. Both governments wanted to improve the bilateral relationship, but the method they chose was censured by the United States. Thus, economic problems arose because Mexico and Canada depended on a bilateral trade balance, which at the time was impeded by U.S. protectionism.

The years between 1980 and 1995 have seen a rise in cooperation by committees in various economic sectors: energy, agriculture, environment, finance, tourism, forest resources, and migration, among others. In 1980, the two countries created a committee for co-operation on energy, because of the particular relevance of the energy sector to each country and to the balance of trade between them. In effect, during that period, and until 1984, the balance of trade favoured Mexico. With the fall of oil prices on world markets, Mexico increased its exports of manufactured goods to Canada, counting Canada as one of its ten main trading partners.[14] In 1981, the two nations signed a commercial agreement on agricultural commodities, under which Canada sold wheat, powdered milk, barley, breeding cattle, and other products to Mexico. Other agreements pertaining to tourism, forest products, and migration were also concluded in 1988. Together these developments helped to prepare the way for the conclusion of NAFTA as well as closer bilateral ties.

Since 1985, the Canadian Export Development Corporation has maintained approximately ten lines of credit in Mexico, amounting to almost $720 million. Moreover, the Canadian International Development Agency (CIDA) is supporting more than twenty-five projects involving investment development and Canadian technology transfer to Mexico. During Brian Mulroney's visit in 1990, ten new agreements related to customs, duties, trade and investment were signed. Worthy of note is the agreement regarding the identification of new markets and dispute settlements.

This avalanche of agreements, resolutions, memoranda and presidential visits leads us to believe that the official intention was to place the bilateral relation within a framework that was closer to the new international economic reality. In 1987 Canada initiated a new commercial

---

13 Gutiérrez-Háces, "The Place of Canada in United States–Mexico Economic Relations," in S.J. Randall and Herman Konrad, eds., *North America Without Borders* (Calgary: University of Calgary Press, 1992).

14 Gutiérrez-Háces, ed., *Experiencias de la negociación del T.L.C.* (1991).

TABLE 6. CANADA-MEXICO MERCHANDISE TRADE
1985–1992 ($ MILLIONS)

YEAR	EXPORTS TO MEXICO	IMPORTS FROM MEXICO	TOTAL TWO-WAY TRADE
1985	398.740	1325.999	1724.739
1986	403.583	1163.433	1567.016
1987	530.168	1165.406	1695.574
1988	500.800	1327.729	1828.529
1989	603.100	1698.400	2301.500
1990	643.400	1729.800	2373.200
1991	560.700	2579.800	3140.500
1992	770.600	2751.100	3521.700

Source: Statistics Canada.

strategy towards Mexico, thus preparing itself for the eventuality of an extended free trade agreement. Independent of this co-operative relationship between the two governments, one can observe in Mexico an increasing number of Canadian firms, which have strengthened direct lines of co-operation with their Mexican counterparts. Recently *Expansión*, a Mexican economic journal, published a list of the 25 main Canadian enterprises in Mexico between 1989 and 1994.

For instance, Northern Telecom Canada Inc. and Novatel were involved in establishing the first cellular telephone system in Mexico City. They also won the tender for the provision of equipment in five of the nine regions designated by the Mexican government. As a result, Canada exported telecommunications equipment worth $26 million to Mexico, in contrast with only $5 million the previous year (1989). SPAR Aerospace is participating in the development of a satellite which is intended to replace the present Morelos Satellite System. Another leading firm has signed a contract with the Mexican Secretary of Communications and Transport to develop a spectrum management system. As well, Canadian technology is being used in Mexican agriculture and in the vaccination of Mexican cattle.

Clearly, the commerce between Canada and the United States is far more significant than that with Mexico. In effect, the bilateral trade between Canada and Mexico was in the order of $2.3 billion in 1989, of which Mexican imports from Canada represented only one per cent of total Canadian imports. Nonetheless, compared to other Latin American countries, Mexico is Canada's main trading partner. By way of comparison, in the same period the United States–Canada trade represented a value of $185.8 billion, or more than eighty times the value of Canada–Mexico trade.[15] In the past fifteen years, the trade between Canada and Mexico has shown considerable dynamism. For instance, Mexican exports increased more than eight times. Canadian exports to Mexico, on the other hand, peaked in 1981 at a value of $715 million, and have not again reached that level, falling to $603 million in 1989. Mexican exports to Canada in 1989 were three times higher than in 1980.

But in the current period, after the NAFTA negotiations, we can affirm that Canada and Mexico have only just begun to develop their trading partnership to its full potential. In 1992, Mexico ranked fifth as a source of imports to Canada and fourteenth as a destination for Canadian exports. Less than two percent of Canada's 1992 imports came from Mexico while less than one percent of Canada's exports went there. Even so, Canada's trade relations with Mexico are broader and more substantial than with any country in Latin America. Two-way trade totalled more than $3.5 billion in 1992, and recent trends suggest that it could easily double in the next few years.

The asymmetrical nature of their respective trade regulations has made it easier for Mexicans to export to Canada than for Canadians to export to Mexico. Mexico's trade surplus with Canada declined slightly in 1992, but still remained at a high of about $2 billion. Canadian exports to Mexico increased 37 percent in 1992, recovering from a 13 percent drop one year earlier. This export performance, as mentioned in Rayman's Report, can be attributed to stronger Mexican demand for Canadian wheat, iron and steel products, coal products, copper, telecommunications equipment and motor vehicle parts, milk products, and meat and livestock. Since 1985, Canada's exports to Mexico have almost doubled, rising by approximately 93 percent. Meanwhile, as Ruth Rayman documents, imports from Mexico grew by nearly 7 percent in 1992. Most of this increase can be attributed to imports of radio, telephone and audio equipment, automotive parts, petroleum oils, and air filtering systems. Since 1985, imports from Mexico have more than doubled, rising by 107 percent.

The composition of exports between the two countries has also evolved significantly in recent years. While in 1986 Canada exported manufactured goods such as automobile parts and accessories, railroad rails, and gas turbines, since 1989 the emphasis has shifted more to raw materials and agricultural products such as turnips, powdered milk and wheat, and less on manufactured products, such as auto parts and telecommunications products.[16] In turn, Mexico has increased its exports of

---

15 Royal Bank of Canada, *Perspectivas para un Acuerdo de Libre Comercio entre México y los Estados Unidos* (Mexico: mimeo, 1990).

16 Canadian Embassy, Internal Reports, 1990.

TABLE 7. SOME EXAMPLES OF CANADIAN
MAQUILADORAS OPERATING IN MEXICO

COMPANY	CDN BASE	MEXICAN SITE	TYPE	PRODUCTS	START
Custom Trim	Waterloo	Matamoros	Subsidiary	Leather-wrapped steering wheels	1984 /85
Dicom System	Toronto	Cd. Juarez	Sub-contract	Smoke detectors	1988
Dominion Gro.	Toronto	Cd. Juarez	Subsidiary	Wiring hamesees and assemblies	1987
Fleck Manuf.	Toronto	Nogales, Cd. Juarez, Imuris	Subsidiaries	Wiring hamesees and assemblies	1985
Ideal Equip.	Montreal	Matamoros	Subsidiary	Sewing machine parts	1978
Noma Indust.	Toronto	Cd. Juarez	Subsidiary	Artificial Christmas trees and lights	1990

Source: Conference Board of Canada.

manufactured goods and agricultural products (notably green coffee, fresh tomatoes, chile, and orange juice), mining products (mainly copper and silver), and petroleum and its derivatives, which continue to constitute a significant part of Mexican exports to Canada.

The Canadian firms that have recently been established in Mexico specialize in exporting technological skills related to telecommunications, mining, environment, and water treatment. By the end of 1992, accumulated Canadian direct investment in Mexico totalled U.S. $580 million. During 1992 alone, Canadians invested $88 million (U.S.) in Mexico, a substantial 18 percent increase over 1991, but Canadian investment still comprises only 1.5 percent of total foreign direct investment in Mexico, ranking ninth in 1992. However, it is growing more quickly than investment from all other countries except Switzerland and the United Kingdom.

Today, Canada's economic presence in Mexico is apparent at various levels:

1. As an indication of Canadian state strategy;
2. As part of the specific interests of a certain province. Some, like Quebec and Ontario, have a greater presence in Mexico than others;
3. As private individuals. The number of small and medium-sized businesses involved in joint ventures in remote parts of Mexico, far from the oversight of the Canadian Embassy, is astounding;
4. As part of transnational firms with main offices in the United States that have been relocated from Canada to Mexico;

5.   As large Canadian firms, such as Bombardier, Northern Telecom, Novatel, SPAR Aerospace, that operate with provincial and/or federal support.

In most cases, Canadian investors prefer joint ventures and in general they avoid Taylorist forms of production. On several occasions they have expressed that they do not wish to participate in projects which would oblige them to deal directly with large numbers of workers or trade unions. Regarding Concarril, the large state-owned enterprise, Bombardier demanded the reduction of the labour-management contract and didn't invest in the company until the union had accepted the new terms. Bilateral trade between Mexico and Canada has undergone an interesting transformation. During the past ten years, the level of Mexican exports increased eight times more than Canadian exports to Mexico. Canada reached its best level in 1981 ($715 million) and has never regained it.

The export structure has changed significantly over the past few years. In 1986 Canada's exports to Mexico were mainly manufactured goods, such as auto parts, railroad tracks, and gas turbines. In 1989 it started to export agricultural products, such as turnip seed, powdered milk, and wheat; its manufactured exports increased only in tele-communications equipment. Mexico, on the other hand, has stressed a tendency towards exporting manufactured goods; oil and its derivatives are an important part of its sales to Canada.

Mexico offers Canada a promising opportunity for investment. If it were to cater to Mexico's new needs, Canada could reproduce the old business pioneer strategy and take advantage of a demand for services related to the environment, petrochemical, telephone and computer industries, geology, topography and biotechnology. Canadian expertise implies an economic presence that is less aggressive than pillaging investments which do not offer Mexico new knowledge or training, and in many cases lead to serious social problems in the short run. According to recent data, towards the end of 1991 Canadian investment in Mexico was located in 201 firms: 40 in mining and extraction, 77 in manufacturing, 22 in commerce, 4 in construction, 1 in transportation and communications, 18 in financial services, and 39 in community services.

Finally, I believe that today the real challenge Canada faces in Mexico is that of building a specific trade strategy, less spontaneous than those built in the past, based on the supposition that the reshaping of tasks of production on the international level will give it an opportunity in the Mexican service sector. The very dynamics of the commercial opening in Mexico is forming a new economic structure whose needs, to date, cannot be fully met by Mexicans alone. There is an enormous technological gap, part of which Canada can surely fill. And we mustn't forget that in applying NAFTA, new necessities and legal requirements will arise. It would be utopian to think that Mexico can confront the impact produced by NAFTA on its own, without any kind of support from abroad. There are great vacuums in Mexico in the areas of technological knowledge and professional training, which put it at a disadvantage as it faces the great changes imposed by the globalization process. In this context, Canada can play an important role as an innovative partner.

II

Economic Perspectives on Free Trade

Robert N. McRae
Department of Economics
University of Calgary

6

The Emergence of North American Energy Trade Without Barriers

INTRODUCTION

This chapter concentrates on the forces which underlie energy trade within North America. Although the scope is North American, more emphasis is placed on Canada–United States trade. Only oil and natural gas trade are considered, despite the fact that coal and electricity are also traded.

The United States produces both oil and natural gas; however, there has been excess demand for both commodities since the 1950s. Hence, Canada exports oil and natural gas to the United States, and Mexico exports oil. Data for both the volume and value of Canada's oil and natural gas exports and imports are displayed in Tables 1 and 2; the volume of U.S. imports of oil from Canada, Mexico and the world is shown in Table 3.[1]

Canada, Mexico and the United States have all, at one time, used government intervention to restrict exports (or imports). Since the mid-1980s, Canada–United States trade has been relatively free of government intervention; however, the Mexican government still controls the flow of oil to the United States. In the 1970s and 1980s many governments restricted the development of and trade in energy products. Generally,

---

1   More recent data and a forecast are contained in United States and Canadian reports, Department of Energy (1995) and Natural Resources Canada (1995), respectively. Net oil imports into the U.S. are expected to rise to over 48 percent of demand in 1996, due to an increase in petroleum demand of between 1.4 and 2.5 percent per annum, and a decline in oil production of between 2 and 3 percent per year. Natural gas imports into the U.S. (from Canada) are expected to increase to about 13 percent of U.S. demand by 1996 because of relatively strong domestic demand growth of about 2.5 percent per annum and a decline in domestic production of about 1 percent.

TABLE 1. Exports of Oil and Natural Gas from Canada

Year	Crude Petroleum		Natural Gas	
	Volume million m^3	Value million $	Volume billion m^3	Value million $
1970	38.3	649	21.8	206
1971	43.1	787	25.6	251
1972	54.2	1008	28.5	307
1973	66.8	1482	29.2	351
1974	53.0	3420	27.2	494
1975	41.7	3052	26.9	1092
1976	29.0	2287	27.0	1617
1977	19.2	1751	28.2	2028
1978	15.6	1573	25.0	2190
1979	16.7	2405	27.9	2889
1980	12.4	2899	22.8	3984
1981	9.5	2505	21.6	4370
1982	12.2	2728	22.1	4755
1983	16.8	3457	20.0	3848
1984	20.9	4404	21.1	3923
1985	27.5	5917	25.3	3912
1986	33.6	3774	20.9	2483
1987	35.8	4855	27.7	2527
1988	41.0	4010	36.3	2929
1989	37.5	4462	37.9	3023
1990	35.0	5529	40.7	3279
1991	43.1	6041	44.8	3339
1992	46.6	6683	56.6	4361

Source: Canadian Association of Petroleum Producers (1993).

governments have abandoned their attempt to control the oil and gas industry, except in OPEC and centrally planned economies; yet in Latin America, even with the extensive liberalization and privatization that has occurred in the 1980s and 1990s, a strong legacy of statism remains in critical sectors such as energy. Mexico, which also underwent substantial liberalization following the economic crisis of the early 1980s and entry into GATT in 1986, retains major control over the oil industry and its activities. One day, Mexico may go through some of the same transformations as Canada in relaxing government control. This paper focuses, however, more on the Canada–United States bilateral relationship, with the result that it is instructive to note the transition in policy orientation which took place in Canada in the course of the late 1970s and 1980s, as those policy changes influenced Canada's energy industry and its trading capacity.

The next section contains a description of the economic consequences to the Canadian oil and gas industry during a period of regulation. In contrast, the third section describes the economic consequences of deregulation. The fourth section contains a brief description of Mexico's role in energy trade with the United States, and a comparison of its energy industry with that of Canada. The impact of NAFTA on energy trade is explained in the fifth section. The last section has some summary remarks.

REGULATION OF ENERGY IN CANADA[2]

Nearly all Canadian oil and natural gas production is from the western provinces of Alberta, Saskatchewan and British Columbia. In 1992, Alberta produced about 75 percent of crude oil, all synthetic oil and 85 percent of natural gas; British Columbia produced about 11 percent of natural gas; and Saskatchewan produced about 20 percent of crude oil.[3]

The three energy-producing provinces account for only about 25 percent of the population of Canada. The energy policy disputes of the 1970s and 1980s were partially caused by the uneven distribution of population and energy reserves within Canada. Consumers' interests were to keep

---

2 Much has been written describing the regulatory policies in Canada and the United States, and analyzing their economic consequences. For example, see J.F. Helliwell, M.E. MacGregor, R.N. McRae, and A. Plourde, *Oil and Gas in Canada: The Effects of Domestic Policies and World Events* (Canadian Tax Foundation, 1989); G.C. Watkins, "Eccentric Orbits: Canadian Oil and Gas Pricing, 1947–1987" in G.C. Watkins, ed., *Petro Markets: Probing the Economics of Continental Energy* (Vancouver: The Fraser Institute, 1989), pp. 105–40; and A.W. Wright, "History as Prologue: Lessons from Canadian and United States Energy Policy, 1970–1988" in G.C. Watkins, *Petro Markets*, pp. 17 –39.

3 Canadian Association of Petroleum Producers, *Statistical Handbook*, Calgary (September, 1993).

TABLE 2. IMPORTS OF OIL AND NATURAL GAS INTO CANADA

Year	Crude Petroleum		Natural Gas	
	Volume million m³	Value million $	Volume million m³	Value million $
1970	33.0	415	336	5.1
1971	38.9	541	454	7.0
1972	44.7	681	446	7.6
1973	52.1	943	416	7.8
1974	46.3	2646	261	5.8
1975	47.4	3302	296	7.8
1976	44.0	3280	254	8.8
1977	38.0	3215	0.1	-
1978	36.8	3457	1.7	0.1
1979	35.3	4497	3.2	0.2
1980	32.7	6919	2.9	0.3
1981	30.7	8004	4.1	0.6
1982	19.7	4979	2.5	0.5
1983	14.6	3319	1.1	0.2
1984	14.8	3376	0.9	0.2
1985	15.9	3700	1.0	0.2
1986	20.2	2885	1.8	0.3
1987	21.8	3179	-	-
1988	23.5	2824	-	0.3
1989	28.3	3608	-	0.2
1990	31.8	5300	-	0.5
1991	30.8	4489	-	32.2
1992	29.4	4142	0.1	50.0

Source: Canadian Association of Petroleum Producers (1993).

energy prices low and to restrict exports in order to secure supply for domestic use. Producers wanted energy prices to reflect their opportunity cost (international prices) and to have no restrictions on exports. In an oversimplified sense, the consumers were represented by the federal government, and the producers by the governments of the producing provinces, especially Alberta.

The struggle amongst the competing stake-holders really began in the 1960s with the expansion of energy supplies from western Canada into populous central Canada, and ended in 1986 with the deregulation of oil and natural gas industries. A brief history of the regulatory period will show how far the governments had to move when the industry was deregulated. Government policy involved a combination of regulating prices and sales opportunities, and discriminatory taxation. Government regulations were unable to respond very effectively to external shocks to the energy market. Regulations had an impact on the demand for and supply of natural gas and oil, and on the industrial structure.

Natural gas and oil are fundamentally different from other commodities, in that they are owned by the provinces.[4] As resource owner, the provinces have an obligation to extract the rent (surplus value) from its exploitation. Overlapping jurisdiction and disagreements over how to share the rent between the federal and provincial governments and between the producers and consumers led to the policy actions (i.e., regulations) of the 1970s and early 1980s, described below.

In the early development of the petroleum industry, natural gas was often found as a by-product of oil exploration. Until long-distance pipelines were built in the mid-1950s, natural gas was only used in local markets. In order to secure the financing for building long-distance natural gas pipelines, long-term sales contracts were negotiated, which included a basically fixed price, with only the possibility of a modest price escalation.

As both the oil and natural gas pipeline network expanded into central Canada and the United States, sales increased dramatically. This was the market response to relatively low and stable prices, ample supplies which were available at prevailing prices, and growing economic activity.

The international oil crisis of late 1973 had repercussions in the Canadian energy market, affecting both price and sales. The international price of oil increased by about 400 percent. The response of the Canadian government was to regulate the domestic oil price so that it would be lower than the international price, and to regulate the price of natural gas so that it would be lower than the heating-equivalent value of the domestic price of oil. Nevertheless, the domestic price of natural gas rose

---

4   Energy resources are owned by the federal state in Mexico, and owned by a combination of private landowners, state and federal governments in the United States. In Canada, the federal government owns the mineral rights for the offshore region and in the Yukon and Northwest Territories.

Table 3. United States Imports of Crude Oil

Year	From Mexico		From Canada		Total U.S. Imports	
	millions of bbls	% of U.S. imports	millions of bbls	% of U.S. imports	millions of bbls	% of U.S. oil demand
1970	-	-	245.3	19.7	1248.1	23.3
1971	-	-	263.3	18.4	1432.9	25.8
1972	-	-	312.4	18.0	1735.3	29.0
1973	0.5	0.0	365.4	16.0	2283.5	36.1
1974	0.6	0.0	288.8	12.9	2230.9	36.7
1975	25.7	1.0	219.2	9.9	2210.3	37.1
1976	31.7	1.2	135.7	5.1	2676.4	41.9
1977	64.7	2.0	101.8	3.2	3207.1	47.7
1978	115.4	3.9	90.5	3.0	2993.8	43.5
1979	158.9	5.2	99.1	3.2	3062.1	45.3
1980	185.5	7.4	73.0	2.9	2512.6	40.3
1981	171.4	8.2	59.9	2.9	2095.1	35.7
1982	235.3	13.0	78.0	4.3	1806.2	32.4
1983	279.7	15.9	100.1	5.7	1758.5	31.6
1984	241.1	12.6	124.7	6.5	1917.9	33.3
1985	261.0	14.5	170.8	9.5	1806.3	31.5
1986	226.5	10.1	208.2	9.2	2254.0	37.9
1987	219.6	9.1	222.0	9.2	2410.8	39.6
1988	246.5	9.2	249.1	9.3	2690.4	42.5
1989	261.2	8.9	230.0	7.9	2921.8	46.2
1990	251.3	8.6	234.5	8.0	2916.6	47.0
1991	276.9	9.9	271.4	9.7	2783.8	45.6
1992	288.2	10.0	291.6	10.1	2883.3	46.0

Source: American Petroleum Institute (1994)

sharply, although probably not as much as it would have under an un-regulated market. The price of natural gas exports was set at a higher level than domestic natural gas. Canada took advantage of the willing-ness of U.S. customers to pay prices that were higher than their own because they had a shortage.

The Canadian government was concerned about a possible shortage of natural gas[5] and oil in Canada. The U.S. shortage would have spilled over into Canada if our exports had been allowed to increase and domes-tic prices had not been allowed to increase. Oil and especially natural gas sales had grown rapidly, reserve additions were getting smaller, and consequently the life index (a measure of inventory) began to fall. The Canadian government adopted a nationalistic policy of "Canadian re-serves for Canadians," which prohibited additional exports of natural gas to the United States, reduced exports of light crude oil to zero over a five year period (see Table 1),[6] and forced Canadian oil further east into the Montreal market through a government-subsidized extension to the Inter-provincial Pipe Line (IPL) oil pipeline. The Canadian government had always been concerned about the future supply of gas for Canadians, and prior to approving any exports, the National Energy Board (NEB) used the "exportable surplus test" which required about 25 times the annual consumption of gas to be available in reserve.

Despite higher royalties and taxes, producer netback prices for oil and natural gas rose, and the industry responded by making more dis-coveries, especially in Alberta. Nevertheless, exploration effort was targeted at finding natural gas. On the demand side, sales continued to grow, but at a lower rate, since the prices were higher.

In 1979 and 1980 international oil prices again rose by over 100 percent, and most experts predicted they would continue to rise. The response of the Canadian government was to introduce the National Energy Program (NEP) on October 28, 1980. The NEP affected the oil and gas industry. It was hurt by the continuation of "made in Canada" price regulation for oil and gas whereby the price of natural gas was tied to the low domestic price of oil, and by new taxes, such as the Petroleum and Gas Revenue Tax (PGRT) which was a non-deductible gross royalty on production, the Natural Gas and Gas Liquids Tax (NGGLT) which was a consumer tax applied to domestic and export gas sales, and the COSC (Canadian Ownership Special Charge) which all consumers had to pay

---

5 It should be noted that there was a huge swing in perception in Canada from the notion of substantial surplus of natural gas in the late 1960s to the notion of shortage of gas in the mid-1970s. This was partially due to the pessimistic forecasts provided by companies which were attempting to get permission to build a natural gas pipeline from the Arctic.

6 Exports of heavy oil were not affected.

in order to "Canadianize" the industry. On the positive side, the Petroleum Incentive Payment (PIP) grants were a small benefit to Canadian-owned firms, including Petro-Canada, which was owned by the federal government.

Numerous changes to the pricing and taxation elements of the NEP were made over the 1980–85 period in response to representations from Canadian oil and gas firms, flat then falling international oil prices, the deregulation of oil markets in the United States in 1981, and the gas bubble (surplus) in the United States.

The market actions with respect to demand for and supply of natural gas were quite dramatic and instructive. The higher price for domestic natural gas and the slowdown in economic activity meant that the demand for natural gas levelled off. The export price got too far above the U.S. price and the shortage in the United States had given way to a surplus, so natural gas export sales fell substantially below the authorized export levels. In general, natural gas producers did not enjoy higher netback prices even though the domestic price had risen because taxes and royalties had risen by an equivalent amount. The exceptions were small Canadian-owned gas firms.

ENERGY MARKET DEREGULATION IN CANADA

The federal government deregulated Canadian oil markets in 1985, and natural gas markets a year later. For natural gas, that meant no more "exportable surplus" policy; for oil it meant no more restrictions on export levels; for both oil and gas it meant no more price controls and no more special taxes, such as the PGRT, NGGLT and COSC. For oil producers it meant freedom to sell to any market; consequently, oil shipments to Montreal fell and shipments to the U.S. midwest rose. Such a dramatic change was difficult for governments, especially the federal government. The Energy Options report strongly endorsed the use of markets for efficient allocation of energy resources and urged the use of a non-discriminatory and neutral tax system for the energy industry.[7] This report, produced by a 23-member panel of non-government experts under the direction of the respected Thomas Kierans, made the changes more palatable to those who opposed the abandonment of government intervention.

In 1986, the international oil price fell by about 50 percent, and because of deregulation, the Canadian oil price automatically fell. The decline in the domestic oil price also dragged down the price of natural gas since it is a competitive fuel in many markets. But natural gas had

---

7 Energy, Mines and Resources Canada, *Energy and Canadians into the 21st Century: A Report of the Energy Options Process* (Ottawa, 1988).

additional problems because the U.S. gas bubble had driven down, and would continue to force down, natural gas prices in the United States, and the previously-mandated 25-year surplus requirement meant that there was also a surplus in Canada.

Deregulation of natural gas markets was complicated because of the role played by gas pipelines as owner of the natural gas they transported. Consequently, regulators forced the gas pipelines to become common carriers, whereby they would transport gas for any customer for a tariff.

The oil and natural gas markets have responded to the drastic changes in a myriad of ways.[8] Natural gas sales in the domestic market and especially in the export market expanded, but not enough to offset the price decline. It was not until 1993 that natural gas prices began to significantly increase. As mentioned above, oil markets began to expand along an economically more profitable north-south axis rather than the government induced east-west axis. Oil which had previously been shipped to Montreal through the IPL expansion line (subsidized by the federal government as a supply security measure) was being diverted to U.S. destinations, primarily in the mid-west (PADD II) district.

Once natural gas pipelines were forced to act as common carriers, deregulation allowed direct negotiations between producers and consumers, long-term contracts with a take-or-pay clause were no longer the norm, and instead a variety of contracts with different conditions and maturity dates developed, as did a flourishing spot market.[9] In oil markets the notion of pro-rationing by the Alberta government was abandoned. The NEB (on behalf of the federal government) abandoned the practice of requiring a surplus test prior to issuing long-term export permits for natural gas. In fact, many export permits were issued sans formal hearing.

Canada–United States energy markets became more highly integrated. Petroleum firms responded to deregulation by unleashing their entrepreneurial spirit. For example, firms specializing in natural gas attempted to increase sales through convincing users of oil and/or coal to switch to natural gas, and convincing gas users to switch suppliers. Producers have been very successful in expanding sales of natural gas to U.S. customers. In fact, export sales in 1993 were almost triple those in 1986. In order to satisfy the demand, new pipelines have been constructed to send gas to the eastern U.S. states and to California.

---

8   The impact of deregulation on the export (and import) volumes of oil and natural gas, described below, can be seen in Tables 1 and 2.

9   Several reports by the National Energy Board contain an excellent explanation of the market adjustments made in the natural gas industry. See National Energy Board, *Natural Gas Market Assessment: Natural Gas Supply, Western Canada* (Calgary, 1993).

Against all odds, Canadian production of light crude oil remained fairly constant rather than falling as predicted. In the last few years, production has even increased.[10] Technological improvements have been the key factor. Oil pipeline capacity constraints have meant forgone export sales. However, IPL expanded its pipeline capacity in 1994 to accommodate the higher export volumes of oil.[11]

The price collapse in the mid-1980s and deregulation have meant that firms have had to react to having less revenue, so they paid less for land sales, laid off workers, especially in the exploration and development departments, and lobbied the provincial government for royalty relief. The latter request has been granted through various temporary and permanent royalty relief schemes. Generally, decisions by the oil and gas industry are dictated by the market rather than government regulation.

The future for the natural gas industry looks promising.[12] The excess supply situation for natural gas appears to have dissipated. Prices have risen, and demand for natural gas should continue to increase, especially as consumers become more sensitive to its relatively low level of environmentally damaging emissions and therefore switch fuels. Also, natural gas sales for co-generation plants are expected to continue to increase dramatically. Western Canada appears to have a plentiful supply of gas, recoverable at today's prices, and technological advances are helping to keep exploration and development costs down. The industry will always be subject to volatility in prices. For instance, after finally reaching a post-1986 high in 1993, prices fell significantly in 1994. High storage capacity in both the United States and Canada, mild winter weather, and a high number of successful new wells led to the price collapse.[13]

The future for the oil industry is more clouded. The average discovery size has been declining for some time; however, the supply price has been held in check by technological advances, such as horizontal drilling and three-dimensional seismic. The National Energy Board expects oil production to continue to increase for several more years

---

10 National Energy Board, *Canadian Energy: Supply and Demand 1993–2010* (Calgary, 1994).

11 M. Heath et al., *Expanding U.S. Markets for Canadian Crude Oil* (Calgary: Canadian Energy Research Institute, 1993).

12 The National Energy Board (*Natural Gas Market Assessment*) and Natural Resources Canada (*Canada's Energy Outlook*) have published their forecasts for oil and natural gas in Canada for at least the next twenty years.

13 United States, Department of Energy, *Short-Term Energy Outlook: Quarterly Projections–1995 Q1* (Washington, DC, 1995); Natural Resources Canada, *Canadian Natural Gas Exports: Evaluation and Outlook* (Ottawa, 1995).

before the inevitable decline begins.[14] Exports of oil to the U.S. are expected to remain at their current high levels for several more years.

THE ROLE OF MEXICO IN NORTH AMERICAN ENERGY TRADE

Mexico has large reserves of oil and natural gas, and has a long history of producing oil for export.[15] It is interesting to note that oil exports to the United States have been relatively constant since the early 1980s despite the increase in aggregate U.S. oil imports. Except for a brief period in the early 1980s, Mexico has not exported natural gas. In 1994, Mexico once again began exporting a small quantity of natural gas to the United States. Mexico has not sought to enter the U.S. gas market largely because its producers do not see a significant opportunity at present, given current price and production costs. Eighty-five percent of all gas produced is associated gas (produced along with oil) and Mexico has no storage capacity. Although Mexico has unrealized potential, PEMEX does not have the capital for large-scale gas development; therefore, exports will remain negligible.[16] In addition, Mexico now imports some natural gas from the United States into the northern border region. Imports from the United States were virtually zero until 1988, and then they increased rapidly to a peak of 94 Bcf in 1992 before dropping precipitously to only 28 Bcf in 1994. The devaluation of the peso in December 1994 and the slowdown or cancellation of electric power fuel switching (oil to gas) investments lead to the sharp decline.[17]

The market structure[18] for the petroleum industry is completely different in Mexico than in Canada or the United States. The constitution enshrines ownership of petroleum with the Mexican government. The

---

14 National Energy Board, *Canadian Energy*.

15 Mexico actually became a net importer of oil in the late 1960s and early 1970s. Mexico exported virtually no oil to the United States from 1970 to 1974.

16 Natural Resources Canada, *Canadian Natural Gas Exports*.

17 Natural Resources Canada, *Canadian Natural Gas Exports*.

18 The domestic natural gas market in Mexico is underdeveloped. For instance, in 1994 PEMEX consumed 42 percent of natural gas in petrochemical plants (with two of those plants accounting for 40 percent), the state electricity company CFE consumed 19 percent, the industrial sector consumed 34 percent, and the residential sector consumed just 4 percent. There are only 12 local distribution companies (LDC) and they only account for 10 percent of total sales. Amazingly, about 68 percent of the LDC sales volume comes from two industrial customers, and only 25 percent from 541 residential customers. See E. Estrada, "Opportunities for Natural Gas in Mexico," *Proceedings of CERI North American Natural Gas Conference* (Calgary, 1995).

federal state not only owns the petroleum resource but it also reserves the exclusive right to explore, develop, produce and market that resource. These activities are the mandate of the petroleum monopoly, PEMEX. Although President Carlos Salinas de Gortari was instrumental in opening up the Mexican economy to international competition and in arranging the North American Free Trade Agreement (NAFTA) with Canada and the United States, the exploration and development dimensions of the oil and gas industry remain protected from domestic and foreign competition.

A state-owned monopolistic firm is not very nimble in price setting, often not able to raise enough investment capital from its shareholder (Mexican government), not efficient in its activities (over-staffed[19]) and probably not using the latest technology. Such problems lead to unrealized profit potential. In other words, some of the rent associated with petroleum exploitation is being dissipated.

In contrast with the Canadian petroleum industry, the Mexican industry is not subject to competitive market forces. The Canadian industry has always been characterized by some degree of competition, even though it was once dominated by large foreign-owned multinational firms. As described in the section on deregulation in Canada, once governments switched from regulatory intervention in the petroleum industry to allowing markets to function, the petroleum industry flourished. The Canadian governments were unable to keep their regulatory environment functioning effectively during the 1973–84 period of changes in the international energy marketplace. It is inconceivable that the governments would have been capable of managing the industry in the turbulence of the post-1985 markets. Nevertheless, the Mexican government is still active in regulating the petroleum industry through its ownership of PEMEX.

I conjecture that if Mexico were to break the monopoly power of PEMEX and allow competition, the petroleum industry would produce more oil and gas at a lower cost, and hence increase its exports. Consequently, the industry would be capable of returning more revenue to the state. I believe the Canadian experience after deregulation could be used as evidence for this claim. If Mexico were to deregulate and restructure its petroleum industry, energy products from Mexico would probably replace some of Canada's sales to the United States.

---

19 For instance, when competition was recently permitted in the petroleum sector in Argentina, the state petroleum enterprise, Yacimientos Petroliferos Fiscales (YPF), laid off 46,000 workers from a total workforce of 52,000 (*acumen* [January/February 1995], p. 36). Of course, many of these workers would remain in the oil sector.

NAFTA AND ENERGY TRADE[20]

It should be noted that the North American Free Trade Agreement (NAFTA), just like its predecessor, the Canada–United States Free Trade Agreement (FTA), makes it difficult for the federal government to regulate the Canadian energy industry under nationalistic principles, such as forcing Canadian energy prices to be lower than those in the United States, and/or to withhold supplies from the U.S. market.[21]

However, according to Watkins, the Mexican government negotiated the NAFTA so that the energy industry is basically exempt.[22] The energy provisions of the Mexican constitution remain paramount. They agreed not to use price discrimination in energy trade with the United States, but would not agree to restrictions on their ability to control the volume of energy trade. For instance, in case of an energy shortage, the proportionality provision of the Canada–United States FTA does not apply to Mexico. However, Watkins believes that NAFTA could be "seen as providing a lever to prise open the Mexican energy sector over time in a way that would lead to greater and more efficient integration of North American energy flows."[23]

Hence, NAFTA allows asymmetric regulations to exist in energy trade, and this is advantageous for Canada. Since NAFTA only came into effect on 1 January 1994 and there have been few changes affecting the energy industry, there is no point in examining the energy trade flows to get a rough impact of NAFTA.

CONCLUSIONS

In contrast to the heavily regulated energy markets, especially in the period prior to 1985, Canadian energy markets are working efficiently, and should not be re-regulated—no matter what sort of external shocks

---

20 Plourde and Waverman describe energy trade in the pre–North American Free Trade era. See A. Plourde and L. Waverman, "Canadian Energy Trade: The Past and the Future," in G.C. Watkins, ed., *Petro Markets*, pp. 141–80.

21 See J.N. McDougall, "The Canada-U.S. Free Trade Agreement and Canada's Energy Trade," *Canadian Public Policy*, 17, No. 1 (1991), pp. 1–13; R.N. McRae, "Canadian Energy Development Under the Free Trade Agreement," *Energy Policy*, 19, No. 5 (1991), pp. 473–79; and G.C. Watkins, "NAFTA and Energy: A Bridge Not Far Enough?" in S. Globerman and M. Walker, ed., *Assessing NAFTA: A Trinational Analysis* (Vancouver: The Fraser Institute, 1993), pp. 193–225.

22 Watkins, "NAFTA and Energy."

23 Watkins, "NAFTA and Energy," p. 222.

occur. Firms in a competitive market must be able to respond to the unexpected. Competition does not exist in Mexican energy markets. PEMEX is in control. One should remember that the government (federal state in Mexico and province in Canada) is the resource owner, and as such has an obligation to capture any rent associated with exploitation.

One of the reasons for studying the period of energy regulation in Canada is to explain the economic consequences of government regulations. Government intervention distorted market responses and led to economic waste. The economic waste due to price controls alone has been estimated to have cost the Canadian economy billions of dollars. Mexico could learn from Canada's experiences.

James Gerber and William A. Kerr
Department of Economics
San Diego State University

7

Trade as an Agency of Social Policy: NAFTA's Schizophrenic Role in Agriculture

INTRODUCTION

Agriculture is consistently one of the most contentious sectors when changes to trade policy are considered. From initial discussions of the repeal of British "Corn Laws" at the end of the eighteenth century to the Uruguay Round of the General Agreement on Tariffs and Trade, changes to agricultural trade policy have produced heated debates.[1] The Uruguay Round almost foundered a number of times over agricultural issues. Changes to trade policy are always going to be subject to debate because the process creates losers as well as winners. Those with a vested interest in the status quo can be expected to object. In agriculture, however, the debate often seems to transcend trade policy to become a major social policy issue. This broader social policy debate has been at the centre of the North American Free Trade Agreement (NAFTA) provisions on agricultural trade and has produced an entirely different result when one compares the Canada–United States interface in agricultural trade with the United States–Mexico interface. Hence, the NAFTA, rather than presenting a single regime for agricultural trade in North America, has produced instead two trade policy regimes with contradictory aims. This paper will explore the reasons for this apparently schizophrenic result.

---

1 For a discussion of the long history of the agricultural trade debate, see for example, W.A. Kerr and R.J. Foregrove, *An Assessment of the Protectionists' Position in the Canada–U.S. Reciprocity Debate of 1846–1854*, Discussion Paper No. 119, Department of Economics, The University of Calgary, 1989. For a discussion of more current aspects of the agricultural trade debate, see W.A. Kerr and J.E. Hobbs, "A New Era of Corn Laws: Agricultural Trade with the European Community—1992 and Beyond," in G.M. MacMillan, ed., *The European Community, Canada and 1992* (The University of Calgary Press, 1994).

While the result of the NAFTA for most goods and services and over the three possible interfaces—Canada–United States, United States–Mexico and Canada–Mexico—is an unambiguous reduction in trade restrictions, in agriculture the Canada–United States interface is protectionist while the United States–Mexico interface is trade liberalizing.[2] In part, this reflects the stylized fact that Canadian and U.S. agricultural products are substitutes while Mexican and U.S. agricultural products are substitutes. These divergent results, however, also arise from the existence of different social policy objectives for the agricultural sectors in Canada and Mexico. If one examines the NAFTA provisions relating to agricultural trade, it seems clear that the major provisions were driven by Canadian or Mexican imperatives, rather than those of the United States. There are three reasons for this. First, any change in the agricultural trade regime in North America was likely to provide only small gains for the American economy.[3] Hence, agriculture was not a priority area in the trade negotiations for the United States.[4] Second, for the most part, U.S. agricultural trade was already quite open to both Canadian and Mexican products so there was little to lose from further liberalization. Finally, the shift to significantly greater use of contingency protection measures (antidumping and countervail actions) as the focus of U.S. protectionist policies since the late 1970s had reduced the need for other forms of protection. The allowing of U.S. agricultural producer groups and agribusiness firms to easily initiate dumping and countervail actions (along with the provision of liberal criteria for granting protection based on a preliminary finding of the United States International Trade Commission)

---

2   The Canada–Mexico interface is itself schizophrenic, with Canada's agricultural sector protected and Mexico's opened to trade. As Canadian–Mexican agricultural trade is, however, very small and is likely to remain so, this interface schizophrenia simply reflects the differences exhibited by the more important geographically contiguous interfaces. As a result, the Canada–Mexico interface will be largely ignored in the subsequent discussion.

3   For example, Texas, California, and Florida were expected to be the states most affected by changes to the United States–Mexico interface, but even for these states the available research suggests that the effects would be small. In the case of Texas, see Texas Department of Commerce, *Texas Consortium Report on Free Trade* (Austin: Business Development Division, 1991), and for California the various articles in *California Agriculture*, 45, No. 5, 1991. For all three states see R. Cook et al., *NAFTA: North American Free Trade Agreement, Effects in Agriculture* (Park Ridge, IL: American Farm Bureau Federation, 1991).

4   This does not mean, however, that in the case of particular industries, such as the heavily protected sugar industry, the Florida citrus industry or the avocado industry in California, that the United States failed to act to provide for certain vested interests through the retention of protectionist measures.

reduced the need to lobby for other forms of protection. While there were considerable concerns in Canada regarding the capricious use of contingency protection measures by the United States, these were not confined to the agricultural sector. They became a major focus of the more general Canada–United States Trade Agreement (CUSTA) negotiations and, hence, transcended purely agricultural issues.

As with most developed countries, agriculture in Canada is a labour-shedding sector. Rapid and sustained technological change in almost all sectors of agriculture has meant that fewer and fewer farmers are needed to produce larger quantities of agricultural output.

Declining real prices have led to financial difficulties for a considerable proportion of farmers. As independent businessmen who stand to lose most of their assets as well as their family home, they have had a strong interest in finding effective ways of influencing the political process. Further, as the exit of farmers and farmland consolidation tends to affect the viability of the wider rural community, farmers have been able to find ready allies in their political battles. As a result, the major focus of social policy toward the agricultural community has been to slow the rate at which farmers are forced to exit the industry. Trade policy in agriculture has simply been an adjunct to this social policy. As trade liberalization is likely to increase the rate of exit of farmers from the least efficient agricultural activities, it was resisted in the name of the more general social policy toward agriculture. The rate of technological change had been greatest in the dairy and poultry (eggs, chicken and turkey) industries in Canada. The domestic social policy which developed to slow the process of exit in these industries was, first on a provincial basis and later federally, supply management marketing boards. By restricting supply, prices could be kept high. The restricted supply then had to be allocated among producers—a process which could be structured so as to keep additional farmers in the industry.

The higher prices arising from controls on supply, however, could face a competitive threat from imports—particularly from the U.S. poultry industry, which has received almost no government assistance. To make the supply management marketing board system viable, import restrictions in the form of quotas were imposed at almost exclusionary levels. These non-tariff restrictions were allowed under the GATT's weak provisions on agriculture. On the other hand, the beef and pork industries, where technological change had been much slower (and, hence, the pressure on farmers to exit much less), prior to the CUSTA trade were virtually unfettered and subsidy levels low.

In cereals, particularly prairie grain crops, where exports predominate, prices were determined in the international market. As both the United States and Canada were exporters, under competitive conditions significant cross-border trade was not likely. However, as subsidies and marketing arrangements for grain crops existed, cross-border trade would have made both countries' grain systems more difficult to manage. In particular, the Canadian Wheat Board's monopolization of prairie grain marketing would have been complicated by cross-border movements. As a result, a tacit agreement existed between Canada and the United States to limit cross-border movements. The actual mechanism was import licences effectively controlled by the Canadian Wheat Board. Licences to import U.S. grains were seldom issued. In return, the Canadian Wheat Board voluntarily did not market grain in the United States. Canada also levied seasonal tariffs on some fruits and vegetables and various forms of protection were given to the grape-growing/wine industry.

The major thrust of the Canadian negotiating strategy regarding agriculture was to ensure that its major social policy initiative, the supply management system, remained in place. Trade liberalization would have been particularly detrimental in the supply management industries because the quota system had, to some extent, prevented economies of scale from being achieved. As a result, few of the existing farmers in these industries would have been able to survive import competition even if the industry as a whole might have survived the dismantling of supply management.

The only other Canadian priority at the CUSTA negotiations with a direct impact on agriculture was the desire to improve Canadian security of access to the U.S. market by reducing the perceived capriciousness of U.S. contingency protection actions.[5] As some Canadian agricultural products had been the subject of both dumping and countervail actions in recent years, they were expected to benefit from any progress made on this high-priority item in the Canadian government's negotiation strategy.

Basically, the aim of the Canadian government was to prevent international trade forces from acting in their natural role as a signal for resources to move from inefficient to efficient uses. As the numbers of farmers in supply managed industries were relatively small and the costs which the supply management system imposed on Canadian society considered acceptable—at least by the government—the social policy objective took precedence over the general trade liberalization objective.

In Mexico, on the other hand, the NAFTA is seen as a valuable aid to a major social policy reform in agriculture. The government of President Salinas initiated a major structural reform of the Mexican economy. The Mexican government has, along with many other countries, determined that its long-standing economic development strategy based on import substitution and heavy state involvement in the means of production was not likely to produce sustained levels of economic

---

5   See D.L. McLachlan, W.A. Kerr and A. Apuzzo, "The Canada–U.S. Free Trade Agreement: A Canadian Perspective," *Journal of World Trade*, 22, No. 4, 1988.

growth. As a result, with the encouragement of the World Bank and the International Monetary Fund (IMF) and prompted by its 1986 accession to the GATT, an extensive program of deregulation and privatization was initiated.[6] In agriculture, the aim had been self-sufficiency in food production.[7] Mexican food self-sufficiency was promoted by high levels of protection, particularly through the use of import licences for staple cereals such as corn.

Agriculture, which contributes only a small amount of Mexican GDP, provides employment for approximately one-quarter of the population. Population growth, however, was outstripping gains in output. A major constraint to increased agricultural productivity was perceived to be the rural land tenure system. One of the fundamental changes initiated was the reform of the rural land tenure system.

Trade liberalization, under the auspices of the NAFTA, was seen as a major adjunct to the domestic reform process. While deregulation, privatization, and, in the case of agriculture, land reform could be initiated domestically, the pace of structural reform may be slow because those with vested interests in the existing system may have sufficient power to restrain the pace to change. Privatized government corporations may have sufficient market power to prevent competitors from entering. Deregulation may be proposed from the centre, but bureaucrats may be able to prevent it from being put in effect by controlling information and stifling challenges to its authority. Basically, by limiting competition, the pace of reform can be slowed by those who will lose from the process of reform.

Trade liberalization can provide the missing aspect of competition. Competition from imports can provide the price signals for resources to move from inefficient to efficient activities. It will likely be much more difficult for privatized ex-government monopolies to exclude imports than to raise barriers to entry for potential domestic competitors. Foreign firms are more likely to be able to access information on the removal of regulations and be better able to insist that bureaucrats implement changes than local citizens who are dependent on bureaucrats' goodwill. Hence, trade liberalization becomes an important mechanism whereby the centre can impose its reforms on the wider society. As the centre effectively controls trade negotiations, trade policy becomes an important

---

6 Sylvia Ostry, "The NAFTA: Its International Background," in S.J. Randall, ed., *North America Without Borders"* (Calgary: University of Calgary Press, 1992), pp. 21–29.

7 L.A. Marks, K.K. Klein and W.A. Kerr, "Efectos Economicos de la Biotecnologia— Estudio de Case: La Industria Mexicana de la Papa," in W.R. Jaffe, ed., *Analisis de Impacto de Las Biotecnologias in la Agricultura: Aspecto Conceptuales y Metodologicos* (San Jose: Instituto Interamericano de Cooperacion Para la Agricultura, 1991).

instrument of social policy. The Mexican government's negotiating strategy with regards to agriculture was a direct opposite to that of Canada because it was looking to NAFTA to be a major instrument of social change.

The United States perceived that considerable new export potential would arise from the opening of the Mexican agricultural market. As Mexico was anxious to grant concessions for agricultural imports, there seemed little to argue about. The major concern of the United States revolved around the issue of migratory pressure in the Mexican labour market. While there were concerns expressed about the effect of land reform on the agricultural labour market, no consensus was formed on whether migratory pressure would be increased or decreased. As migratory pressure was high with the land tenure system which was in place, the experiment with agricultural reform was at least consistent with other reforms which were expected to reduce migratory pressure. There was no conflict between the Mexican government's interest in using competition from imports as a spur to social change and the U.S. goal of increased exports.

THE CANADA–UNITED STATES AGRICULTURAL TRADE INTERFACE

Canada's major objective relating to the agricultural sector was achieved in the CUSTA negotiations. The major pillar of its social policy[8] in the agricultural sector, the supply-management system was exempted from trade liberalization. Small increases in the size of import quotas were conceded but the system remained intact. In grains, future trade liberalization was provided for, but only when the subsidy levels in the two countries were equal. Elaborate formulas were set out for the annual calculation of grain subsidy levels. As U.S. subsidies were considerably higher than those in Canada, no immediate change in the existing system was contemplated. Tariff removal, with some safeguard provisions in case of import surges, was agreed to in the case of fruits and vegetables. A number of joint committees on regulatory harmonization in agriculture were established.[9]

---

8 There are, of course, a large number of policy measures applied in the agricultural sector. Most of those, however, are primarily economic in intent and focus on risk-reduction, access to technology and alleviation of the adverse effects of short-term income fluctuations.

9 W.A. Kerr, "The Canada–United States Free Trade Agreement and the Livestock Sector: The Second Stage Negotiations," *Canadian Journal of Agricultural Economics*, 36, No. 4, 1988.

On the broader issue of U.S. contingency protection measures—which was important for a number of products, including cattle and hogs—considerable headway was made. Instead of appeals to the U.S. International Trade Commission/Department of Commerce[10] having to be argued in U.S. courts, they would be conducted by bilateral panels with the power to "remand" them (i.e., send them back for revision). Further, and very importantly, there was a commitment to devise mutually acceptable definitions of what constituted dumping and an "unfair subsidy" and under what conditions anti-dumping and countervailing duties could be applied. For example, in existing U.S. procedures no account is taken of the level of domestic subsidies received by U.S. producers when the levels of countervailing duties to be applied are calculated. As a result, even if U.S. subsidies were larger than those paid to Canadian producers, countervailing duties are calculated only on the basis of Canadian subsidies.

Seven years were allowed for the new, mutually acceptable definitions to be devised. Part of the reason for the delay may have been to ensure that the provisions arrived at by Canada and the United States would be consistent with those reached at the Uruguay Round of the GATT. When the CUSTA was being negotiated, a GATT agreement appeared to be a lot closer than it actually was.

While the immediate Canadian objectives regarding supply management were met, the process of trade liberalization in other areas meant new pressures threatened the viability of the supply-management system. In the CUSTA, it was agreed that all tariffs, including those on processed food, would be removed either immediately or over a phase-in with a maximum of ten years. As tariffs were removed on processed foods, Canadian processors who used Canadian supply-managed products as inputs faced increased competition from U.S. processed food imports. As Canadian food processors only had access to higher-priced Canadian poultry and dairy products, U.S. firms exporting processed products gained a cost advantage. The market share of Canadian processors declined and marketing-board quotas exceeded domestic requirements. This problem has yet to be satisfactorily resolved and it remains a threat to the supply-management system. In addition, the international price differentials in milk and poultry products may have been one of the major contributors to large-scale cross-border shopping. The government was forced to tighten up border-crossing procedures and to leave personal exemptions on imports extremely low—$300 per year. The failure

---

10 In Canada, the responsibility for contingency protection is divided between the Department of National Revenue and the Canadian International Trade Tribunal. Their determinations are also subject to bilateral review.

to liberalize personal exemptions in conjunction with commercial trade liberalization led to considerable public annoyance.

A far greater threat to supply management as a social policy instrument, however, came from the Uruguay Round GATT settlement. While the Canadian government tried to have the GATT exemptions, which allowed import quotas to be used to protect the supply-management system, retained in the new agreement, it did not succeed and the quotas have been changed into tariffs of equivalent value. The degree of protection provided by quotas increases as prices in external markets fall. The amount of protection provided by tariffs, however, is fixed. As a result, tariffs provide the supply-management system with much less protection than import quotas.[11] The Canadian government, in an attempt to sustain supply management, has set the new tariffs at the highest possible level it could justify on a historical basis. This unilateral announcement of tariff rates came to the attention of the U.S. government and the issue has been brought up at subsequent trade discussions. The priority given to maintaining the supply-management system by the Canadian government is well understood by the U.S. trade negotiators. One suspects that they have been very adroit at obtaining concessions in other areas by threatening actions against the trade measures that are used to protect supply management.

In terms of contingency protection, the bi-national panels set up under the CUSTA had, at the time of the NAFTA signing, remanded U.S. decisions on pork, live hogs, and red raspberries. The duties applied by the U.S. contingency protection agencies were either reduced or eliminated in each case. Hence, the CUSTA achieved part of Canada's objectives for agriculture.

Buried in the fine print of the NAFTA, however, is a lifting of the seven-year deadline for arriving at new countervail and dumping definitions and procedures. It did not appear that the United States was willing to accept new restraints on this effective method for diffusing domestic protectionist pressures. Further, little real progress was made at the Uruguay Round regarding dumping or countervail. In the case of actionable subsidies—those which are not prohibited outright but merit investigation—to prevent countervailing duties from being applied, it is now up to the exporting country to prove that its subsidies do not cause "serious prejudice" to the importer's industry. This means that the Canadian government must satisfy the U.S. authorities that its subsidies do not cause the undefinable "serious prejudice" to U.S. industry. This may be a step

---

11 For a detailed discussion see W.A. Kerr, "Can Canadian Dairy Farmers Survive in an Open North American Marketplace?" *Advances in Dairy Technology*, 4, 1992.

backward in terms of Canadian objectives regarding more secure access to the U.S. market.

Agricultural trade relations between the two countries took a new, and undesirable, turn in the summer of 1994. Within a few years of the signing of the CUSTA, changing market conditions led to the convergence of Canadian and U.S. grain subsidies—and the subsequent opening up of cross-border grain trade. Due to a combination of circumstances, this led to significant increases in exports of durum wheat (used primarily as an ingredient of pasta) from Canada to the United States in 1993 and 1994. The U.S. administration chose to use direct pressure rather than the mechanisms of the CUSTA to satisfy its concerns regarding the rapid increase in durum imports. It pressured the Canadian government to "voluntarily restrict" its exports. One of the threats it used was that of opening the question of the tariff levels put in place to protect supply management. The Canadian government agreed to restrict its exports. This suggests that shoring up its agricultural social policy by continuing to support supply management may be more important than attempting to maintain the NAFTA system. As a result, agriculture is likely to remain a contentious trade issue in the Canada–United States trade interface of the NAFTA.

THE MEXICO–UNITED STATES AGRICULTURAL TRADE INTERFACE

In the NAFTA, Mexico agreed to eliminate its most trade-restricting import policy in agriculture: the import licensing system for grains. The most important crops affected are corn, wheat, barley and potatoes. In some cases, the licensing system was replaced by tariffs which would be subsequently removed over a maximum of ten years. Other tariffs were either removed immediately or phased out on five- or ten-year schedules. Provisions were made for cooperation in health and sanitary regulations and a committee was set up to monitor implementation, to reduce trade-distorting subsidies and to advise on private commercial disputes. Basically, with some phase-in provisions, the Mexican government followed its strategy of opening agricultural markets to foreign competition.

The most important crop, in terms of Mexico's social policy objectives for the agricultural sector, was corn. Most non-export crops received on average only 15 percent protection prior to NAFTA. Corn prices, on the other hand, were 70 percent above the world price. Corn is grown by subsistence farms as well as commercially. Corn is also the key ingredient in tortillas, the main staple food in Mexico.[12] Hence, corn is the key crop in agricultural reform.

Mexican agriculture is far less productive than its share of the labour force would predict. Agriculture produces about 9 percent of GDP with a labour-force share of nearly 26 percent. Rural incomes are about one-third the national average and 70 percent of the population below the official poverty line live in rural areas in spite of the fact that these areas contain only about 30 percent of the population.

The Mexican agricultural economy is a dual economy which is dominated by approximately 400,000 commercial farms (about 10 percent of the total number of productive units) that control nearly one-half the land and produce the vast bulk of exports. The agricultural economy also contains about one million small family farms, many of which are semi-collectivized on *ejidos*, which control about 40 percent of the farmland. A third type of production unit consists of perhaps 1.5 million rural subsistence farms which survive on just 10 percent of the farmland. In addition to these three groups, there are also a roughly estimated 600,000 to 700,000 landless agricultural workers.[13]

Another way to divide the agricultural economy is between private farms and the semi-collectivized agricultural units known as *ejidos*. *Ejidos* are groups of 20 or more farmers who have organized to petition the federal government for land under Article 27 of the Constitution of 1917. This clause provided the landless with the right to request "excess" land, which was defined as any land in a private holding that exceeded specified maximums—100 hectares of irrigated cropland, 300 acres of irrigated orchards or more land than was necessary to maintain 500 head of cattle. Enforcement of these limits, however, has been arbitrary and their precise definition appears to have been much less clear than it might appear. The ambiguity involved in determining precisely when a farm exceeded the limits, whether it should be classified as a ranch or a crop-producing farm, and how to deal with diversified farms, all added a significant degree of uncertainty to the tenure of both private and *ejido* farmers. This system is assumed to have created barriers to long-term capital improvement. Private farmers could never be sure whether the rights to their land were secure and, hence, would not make investments.

Successful petitioners to the federal government were given land which they were usually required to cultivate individually. Pasture and forest lands are held in common and few *ejidos* work land communally.

---

12 S. Levy and S. von Wizenbergen, "Labor Markets, Migration and Welfare: Agriculture in the North-American Free Trade Agreement," *Journal of Development Economics*, 43, 1994.

13 P. Martin, *Trade and Migration: NAFTA and Agriculture* (Washington, Institute for International Economics, 1993).

In addition, Mexico recognizes the rights of its indigenous communities to farm and own land communally where such rights antedated the European invasion.

Of the over 100 million hectares controlled by *ejidatario*[14] and agrarian communities, only 21 percent is in agricultural production (not counting pasture). The average size of each individual's plot is estimated at 9.44 hectares. Clearly, a significant portion of *ejido* land is nonarable and 72 percent of the total area is held communally.[15]

The constraints placed on ownership of farm land within an *ejido* pertained primarily to its disposal. In essence, the constitution of Mexico provided a "use right" to an *ejidatario*, but not a "disposal right." Farmers were allowed to make their own cropping decisions, but were prohibited from renting, selling, or sharecropping their plots. In general, the plots were inheritable, but they were not allowed to be divided among heirs. *Ejidatario* who abandoned their land or who broke the rules of tenure were subject to having their land confiscated by the *ejido* leadership. There is a general consensus, however, that this form of punishment was very irregularly inflicted, that renting and sharecropping were common and that an active land market flourished.[16]

Agricultural policy under the administration of Carlos Salinas de Gortari has been characterized as a move to "privatize the incentives driving primary sector production, to modernize rural life . . . and to allow the untrammeled integration of Mexican agriculture . . . into the international system."[17] The liberalization of agricultural policy has two parts. The first part is to convert the extensive system of producer subsidies into direct income payments. This change will allow Mexico to meet its GATT commitments regarding trade-distorting subsidies. It is also essential if international price competition is to provide the stimulus for the movement of resources within the Mexican economy. The second part is a modification of Article 27 of the Constitution. It is the second

---

14 The word *ejidatario* refers to the person(s) in charge of the individual plots within an *ejido*.

15 B. DeWalt, M. Rees and A. Murphy, *The End of Agrarian Reform in Mexico: Past Lessons, Future Prospects*, Transformation in Rural Mexico Series, Number 3, Ejido Reform Research Project, Centre for U.S. Mexican Studies, University of California, San Diego, California, 1994 and from the institute of statistics in Mexico, INEGI, Censo Agropecurio: Resultados Preliminares, Aguascaluntes, 1992.

16 DeWalt et al., *The End of Agrarian Reform in Mexico* and J. Heath, "Evaluating the Impact of Mexico's Land Reform on Agricultural Productivity," *World Development*, 20, No. 5, 1992.

17 S. Sandersen, "Mexican Public Sector Food Policy Under Agricultural Trade Liberalization," *Policy Studies Journal*, 20, No. 3, 1992, p. 434.

part of the liberalization movements that has created the most controversy and that raises the most basic questions about agricultural policy.

President Salinas proposed constitutional modifications in 1991, and in early 1992 they were passed by the legislature. In February of 1992 the Agrarian Law implementing the constitutional amendment was passed. The amendments accomplish the following: they end the obligation of the federal government to redistribute land; create a legal right for an *ejidatario* to obtain personal title to their land with the corresponding rights to sell, rent, or sharecrop; permit joint ventures with outsiders; and permit foreign direct investment in agricultural production on *ejido* lands. Previous restrictions on the size of landholdings by a single landowner are kept and corporations are limited to 2,500 hectares of irrigated land.[18]

Three new institutions were created to carry out these reforms: the Agrarian Ombudsman (Procuraduria Agraria), the National Agrarian Registry (Registro Agrario Nacional) and the Superior Agrarian Tribunal (Tribunal Superior Agrario). One of the roles of the Agrarian Ombudsman is to regularize the property within *ejido*s as well as to settle the backlog of land claims and petitions. An offshoot of the role of the Ombudsman is the Program for the Certification of Ejido Rights and Titling of Urban Lots (PROCEDE) which will provide legal property titles. The Registry institution records transactions involving *ejido* and communal lands, and registers boundaries. The Superior Agrarian Tribunal is a national-level court responsible for administering justice along with Agrarian Tribunals (Tribunales Agrarios) in each state.

The *ejido* reforms have been viewed as either the abolition of *ejido*s or their resurrection in a more dynamic and market-oriented form. Reform proponents within the Salinas administration argue that it will allow the continuation of subsistence farming, which is an important safety net, and income supplement, while avoiding the social disruption of complete abolition. Others see it as a way to prepare agriculture for stiffer competition and to reduce the costs of government subsidies.[19] Both of these views are consistent with the trade-liberalization-as-an-agent-of-social-change thesis.

One of the underlying assumptions of the reforms is that the constant threat of redistribution has been the source of significant inefficiencies in agriculture. Large-scale private farms operated under conditions of uncertainty deriving from the possibilities for eventual redistribution. As any holding in excess of the constitutionally established minimums was

---

18 The restrictions on individuals' landholding are easily circumvented, however, by registering land in the names of family members.

19 W. Cornelius, "The Politics and Economics of Reforming the Ejido Sector in Mexico: An Overview and Research Agenda," *LASA Forum*, 23, No. 3, 1992.

always open to an *ejido* petition, landholders could never be sure of their continued use of land. Of course, investments in fixed farm infrastructure made the land more productive and, hence, more valuable to potential members of an *ejido*. The lack of transparency in the rules governing confiscation and the scope for political intervention fed into a system of political patronage which only heightened the degree of uncertainty over future outcomes. As a consequence, greater security in property rights could potentially increase the willingness of private farmers to invest for the long term in capital improvements.

From the standpoint of the *ejidatario*, constraints on land use in the form of prohibitions against land markets reduces the scope of permissible activities and probably contributes to inefficiencies. Although rental, sharecropping, and outright selling of land to fellow *ejido* members (and even to outsiders) is not uncommon, the technical illegality of these activities means that selective enforcement remains a possibility and, in turn, increases uncertainty. These restrictions have probably made it harder to work off the farm and to gain outside income sources. As a consequence, capital improvements are probably fewer than they would have been in a different institutional setting. Furthermore, the absence of a provision allowing for land to be rented out reduces the ability of *ejidatario* to receive compensation for capital improvements.[20]

The lack of capital and capital improvements is one of the major reasons why yields in Mexico are often less than in the U.S. or Canada.[21] For example, only 45.3 percent of *ejidatario* and 37.3 percent of private farmers have access to tractors.[22] The American Farm Bureau Federation's 1991 survey of NAFTA's impact on agriculture cites, among other factors, a technology gap between Mexico and the United States and the poorer quality of Mexican post-harvest marketing and handling infrastructure as two of the primary obstacles for Mexican horticultural crops competing against U.S. products.[23]

The scarcity of capital in Mexican agriculture could be partially overcome through foreign investment—which is now permitted on *ejido*s. This would parallel the strategy in other parts of the economy which is relying on significant inflows of foreign capital to initiate the process of

---

20 Heath, "Evaluating the Impact of Mexico's Land Reform on Agricultural Productivity."

21 R. Cook et al., *NAFTA: North American Free Trade Agreement, Effects in Agriculture.*

22 INEGI, *VII Censo Agropicurario.*

23 Cook et al., *NAFTA: North American Free Trade Agreement, Effects in Agriculture.*

economic growth and was one of the Salinas administration's motivations for the modification of Article 27 of the Mexican constitution.[24]

There are two potential problems which may arise from this strategy for raising agricultural productivity. First, there is an enormously difficult and contentious task ahead to regularize the property rights of all landowners. Nearly three-quarters of all *ejido* lands are not parcelled and lack official boundaries. Even within the parcelled landholdings, there are few surveys of boundaries. Furthermore, the encroachment of urban areas onto *ejido*s and the passing of use rights to outsiders under the pre-reform legislation has produced a jumble of conflicting and poorly defined land claims. Before significant amounts of foreign capital will enter directly into agricultural production, these issues must be settled.

Second, even if the issue of property rights were to be resolved, it is unlikely that U.S. investors will be willing to put their money into primary agriculture, although Japan or other third parties may act differently. Total U.S. foreign direct investment in agriculture, forestry and fishing in all countries has averaged only $33.4 million over the five-year period 1989–1993, a small fraction of one percent of total U.S. foreign direct investment.[25]

A much more likely scenario is investment in food processing. This type of activity is consistent with current patterns of U.S. foreign direct investment and has already occurred in significant amounts in Mexico (see Table 1). Multinational food-processing companies often supply local producers with preferred seed varieties and technical know-how, as well as contracting for the entire crop. In this indirect sense, capital and technical information may become increasingly available to Mexican farmers.

The ability of the farm sector to raise capital in the domestic market may also be limited. One the one hand, the reduction in direct subsidies has meant a decline in credit availability through official government lending agencies such as Banrural, the government rural development bank. Between 1988 and 1992, Banrural decreased the percentage of *ejidatario* it lent to from 88 percent to 33 percent.[26] Furthermore, 40 percent of Mexico's agricultural advisors have been laid off or shifted to other work and the budget of the agency for forestry and agricultural research (Instituto Nacional Investigaciones Forestales y Agropecuario) has been

---

24 Cornelius, *The Politics and Economics of Reforming the Ejido Sector in Mexico.*

25 Bureau of Economic Analysis, "Capital Expenditures by Majority Owned Foreign Affiliates of US Companies." *Survey of Current Business*, 74, No. 9, 1994.

26 R. Salinas de Gortari and J.L.S. González, *Rural Reform in Mexico: The View from the Comarca Lagunera in 1993*, Transformation in Rural Mexico Series, Number 4, Ejido Reform Research Project, Center for US–Mexican Studies, University of California San Diego, San Diego, 1994.

TABLE 1. UNITED STATES FOREIGN DIRECT INVESTMENT IN MEXICO,
TOTAL AND FOOD PROCESSING

Year	Total Direct Investment (TDI)	Direct Investment in Food Processing (DIFP)*	DIFP ÷ (TDI)
1990	10,313	1,119	10.8%
1991	12,501	1,382	11.1%
1992	13,723	1,371	10.0%
1993	15,413	2,334	15.1%

* Food and Kindred: Standard Industrial Classification, Major Industry Group 20.
All figures are in millions of current dollars.
Source: Bureau of Economic Analysis, "U.S. Direct Investment Abroad: Detail for Historia Cost Position and Related Capital and Income Flows 1993," *Survey of Current Business*, 74, No. 8, 1994.

cut by 50 percent.[27] The bright spot in this picture is the aforementioned reduction in uncertainty with respect to property rights and the incentives this offers to private farmers. In addition, the validation of the status quo with respect to the rights of *ejidatario* to work off the farm and sharecrop or sublet their land provides a mechanism for bringing more capital into the *ejido*s. The major question remains as to what institutions will arise to supply capital to the agricultural sector.

Even with the price signals provided by international competition, it seems very unlikely that productivity levels will rise significantly without additional investments. Hence, the social policy objectives associated with trade liberalization in agriculture and the modification of the constitution greatly depends on an altered incentive system which will induce foreigners, private farmers, and *ejidatario* to take a longer view of Mexican agriculture. For many producers, the longer view probably entails leaving the agricultural sector altogether. With the disappearance of price floors and subsidies for credit and inputs, many farmers will undoubtedly not be able to farm profitably. The conversion of subsidies to direct income payments under the PROCAMPO program (Programma Nacional de Apoyos Directos al Campo) will permit some marginal farmers to survive, but these payments are scheduled for complete phase-out by 2008.

Modernization of the farm sector in Mexico will undoubtedly create a significant displacement of the rural labour force. It is also likely to generate increased international migration. Martin has observed that "policies that accelerate economic growth—including privatization, land reform, and freer trade—produce a migration 'hump'; that is, temporarily

27 T. Bardacke, "Nuevo Giro en Política Agrícola," *Este Pais*, Septiembre 1992.

more migration. . . . A migration hump accompanies industrialization in countries with an emigration tradition or in which workers are recruited to go abroad."[28] Migration humps are a worldwide and relatively common phenomenon.

Luis Tellez, undersecretary of agriculture under President Salinas, is quoted as having predicted that by early in the next century, the share of the labour force in agriculture will have dropped from its current 26 percent to around 16 percent.[29] This shift of 10 percent of the labour force is equivalent to around nine million persons if one includes dependants. The Mexican government believes that this displacement is the price required for agricultural modernization. The Mexican government has few resources to mitigate the costs of the hump; the costs will largely be borne by those displaced. One potential means of lowering those costs is migration to the United States. This aspect of the change in rural social policy is of the greatest interest to the United States.

Three forces will determine the share of dislocated rural dwellers that choose to seek employment in the United States. These are (1) the supply-push factors in Mexico, (2) the demand-pull factors in the United States, and (3) the extent of existing network linkages to the United States. The first factor originates with the reform of agriculture, including the validation of the right of *ejidatario* to sell their land. It will be intensified if the economic reforms do not provide sufficient growth in the urban economy to create enough jobs to absorb the natural increase in the labour force plus the hump expected from agricultural reform.[30]

Demand-pull factors inside the United States are most apparent in California, particularly within the horticultural sector (fruits, nuts, vegetables, and specialty crops such as flowers). Although perfectly capable of mechanization, California horticulture remains relatively labour-intensive as a result of the downwards trend in farm labour wages relative to machinery costs throughout most of the 1980s.[31] Additionally, growers have traditionally depended on Mexican labour, either through guest-worker programs such as the Bracero Program, or simply through the hiring of undocumented workers.

---

28 P. Martin, *Trade and Migration: NAFTA and Agriculture*, p. 2.

29 Cornelius, "The Politics and Economics of Reforming the Ejido Sector in Mexico."

30 Mexico's labour force grows at a rate of about 900,000 persons per year; the economy has been creating approximately 300,000 to 400,000 jobs. One consequence is the rapid growth of the informal sector in recent years. Another is the more or less permanent sending abroad of 200,000 to 300,000 people. Martin, *Trade and Migration: NAFTA and Agriculture*.

31 Martin, *Trade and Migration: NAFTA and Agriculture*.

One outcome of this traditional dependence on Mexican labour is the presence of family and village networks linking Mexicans to jobs in California. In some areas of Mexico, the extent of these linkages is extraordinary. For example, one study of land reform in the state of Michoacan reported that 80 percent of *ejidatario* interviewed had worked in the United States at some point.[32] In another study, the authors report that more than half the *ejidatario* in one community in San Luis Potosí had work experience in the United States.[33] These are probably extreme cases but they attest to the existence of well developed network linkages between Mexico and the United States.

Opinions from inside the *ejidos* contrast with this gloomy view of social dislocation. The results of a survey of 1,000 *ejidatario* conducted in 1992 suggest that the vast majority of *ejidatario* and private farmers agreed with the constitutional reforms and the Agrarian Law of 1992 (77 percent and 79 percent, respectively).[34] Given that the undersecretary of agriculture predicted a shift of agricultural labour which is equivalent to nearly 40 percent of the agricultural labour force, it is interesting to note that 82 percent of the *ejidatario* claimed that they will continue to farm in the new institutional environment

The fact that *ejidatario* see themselves in a very different light than economic forces seem to be placing them in leads to what is one of the most important issues facing newly elected President Zedillo. The question is whether the entire set of agricultural reforms can continue without inducing extreme levels of social and political conflict.

The armed rebellion in the state of Chiapas, which began with the formal initiation of the NAFTA agreement and which threatens to break out again, is one possibility. The EZLN rebels' demands include the repeal of the modification of Article 27 of the Constitution and the redistribution of the large landholdings in the state.[35] Chiapas represents one of several regions where land redistribution has never been carried out and where inequality has created severe social and political problems. There are large backlogs of petitions for land, and the regularization of land titles will be an extremely bitter process.

---

32 J. Gledhill, *Casi Nada: A Study of Agrarian Reform in the Homeland of Cardenismo* (Austin: University of Texas Press, 1991).

33 D. Barkin and B. DeWalt, "Sorghum in the Mexican Food Crisis," *Latin American Research Review*, 23, No. 3, 1988.

34 Salinas de Gortari and J.L.S. González, *Rural Reform in Mexico*.

35 N. Harvey, "Rebellion in Chiapas: Rural Reforms, Campesino Radicalism and the Limits to Salinismo," *Rebellion in Chiapas*, Transformation of Rural Mexico Series, Number 5, Ejido Reform Research Project, Center for U.S.–Mexican Studies, University of California, San Diego, San Diego, 1994.

In one sense, the protest in Chiapas is reminiscent of the farm protest movement in the United States during the latter part of the nineteenth century. The introduction of railroads and commodity markets, together with falling prices (input and output), tied farmers into the world market and created a growing sense of frustration in farmers over the loss of control over their lives. In the 1880s and 1890s, midwestern U.S. farmers were convinced that they were the victims of a system that was controlled by the wealthy and powerful. Small-scale farmers and landless agricultural workers in Chiapas perceive themselves as similarly abused by a system outside their control.

The analogy with the United States ends, however, with the fact that the poverty and inequality faced by the rebels in Chiapas is extraordinary. Even though Chiapas is perhaps the poorest state in Mexico, several other regions are not far ahead. If one or two other regions experience similar conflict, the result could be catastrophic; yet, the agricultural reform movement, while necessary, runs precisely this risk.

It seems clear that the United States took a risk when it agreed to extend the process of continental trade liberalization to Mexico. An unreformed Mexico presented a picture of slow economic growth and rapidly rising population. This had two implications for the United States. The first was already being experienced: the consistent flood of illegal immigrants. Without reform, this could only grow and create increased social tensions in the United States. The second was the potential for political instability in Mexico itself and the problems this would create for U.S. security. Without reform of the Mexican economy, there was no means to alter these potentially disruptive forces.

The election of the reform-minded President Salinas presented an opportunity to alter these forces. The risk associated with supporting the reform process, in part through the NAFTA, was that the forces set in motion by domestic institutional reform and trade liberalization would create an untenable degree of social disruption before the benefits from the expected economic growth could be reaped. Agriculture, with its large labour force and low productivity, was the key. It is not yet clear whether the "hump" of displaced agricultural workers will increase the number of illegal immigrants in the United States to politically unacceptable levels, or lead to political instability in Mexico itself. One thing is clear: the liberalization of agricultural trade embodied in the NAFTA has been important in putting the social policy changes in rural Mexico in motion.

CONCLUSION

The central postulate of this chapter is that as the United States saw little advantage to be directly gained for itself in changes to the agricultural trade relations in North America, Canada and Mexico were allowed to set the agricultural agenda in the CUSTA/NAFTA negotiations. This has led to a schizophrenic trade regime for agriculture within the NAFTA. These divergent agricultural trade policies have arisen from the different social policy priorities for the agricultural sectors of Canada and Mexico. In Canada, the social policy objective has been to retain as many human resources in the agricultural sector as possible. Trade liberalization, with its resource-shifting implications, threatened the supply-management system put in place to achieve Canadian social policy objectives. As a result, in the CUSTA and subsequently NAFTA deliberations, Canada negotiated exemptions from trade liberalization for the dairy and poultry industries from a largely indifferent United States and Mexico.

In Mexico, liberalization of agricultural trade was expected to play a central role in social policy reform in agriculture. Competition with imports was expected to provide a stimulus for the movement of resources, particularly labour, in the agricultural sector. While liberalization of agricultural trade could have been undertaken unilaterally in Mexico, having it part of a larger NAFTA trade agreement made it easier to justify politically for the reform-minded regime of President Salinas. The United States, while realizing the risks involved, agreed with the Mexican government's assessment of the need for reform.

Hence, agriculture is likely to remain a contentious issue, either directly or indirectly, in the process of economic integration in North America. In Mexico, the forces put in motion in the rural sector as a result of domestic reforms and trade liberalization will have far-reaching effects in agricultural productivity, Mexican immigration, and possibly political stability in Mexico itself. The latter are far more important to the United States than any of the direct agricultural trade issues involved.

In Canada, the failure to liberalize trade in supply-management marketing-board commodities creates an "Achilles heel" for Canada in future trade negotiations. While the United States may see no significant benefit to liberalizing trade in dairy and poultry products, it can use Canada's social policy commitment to advantage by applying it as a lever to force concessions in other areas. In the future, agriculture and related issues may still cause problems within the NAFTA. The U.S. government decision to step outside the formal NAFTA mechanism in the 1994 dispute over Canadian exports of durum wheat—and the Canadian government's acquiescence to "voluntary" export restrictions—is particularly disturbing. One can only speculate as to the degree of commitment to the NAFTA the United States will show if it is faced with increased illegal immigration in the wake of agricultural reform in Mexico.

Gustavo del Castillo Vera
Director, Department of United States Studies
El Colegio de la Frontera Norte

8

Institutional Concerns and Mechanisms Developing from Tripartite Free Trade Negotiations in North America

The purpose of this paper is to develop an understanding of the tripartite relationships existing in North America and the ways these relationships will define the nature of the negotiating process of a free-trade agreement between Canada, the United States, and Mexico. In this paper, a typology will be presented which attempts to outline the possible relationship existing between public and private actors in these three countries and their expected preferences, either for an intensification of the bilateral relationships existing between them, or their preferences for more of a continentalist perspective. It is these preferences that will set the parameters for a North American Free Trade Agreement (NAFTA) negotiating process. The preferences involved are those of collective actors organized around professional or functional organizations of the private sector, and the bureaucracies and decision-making centres of the public sector. Over time, when these preferences are expressed in a collective fashion, they create the structural conditions for present and future negotiations.

This analysis develops a typology of private and public behaviour in North America along a so-called integration continuum, where the poles are characterized by bilateralism, on the one hand, and continentalism, on the other. Continentalism is not represented by the signing of a free trade agreement (FTA) in North America but is only a stage along this continuum, where true continentalism would imply the full integration of the countries in a common market.

As a starting point for this analysis, I propose that, all things being equal, the starting point for negotiations of a North American FTA will tend to favour bilateral negotiations between Mexico and the United States, as was the case between Canada and the United States (under the already signed FTA), given the fact that the significant and most meaningful trade relationship between these countries is of a bilateral nature.

TABLE 1. PROPOSED PREFERENCES BY ACTORS ALONG A
BILATERALIST–CONTINENTALIST CONTINUUM

Country	Sector	Bilateralism	Continentalism
Mexico	Private	Favoured for historical reasons in dealing with United States[a]	
	Public	Favoured for historical reasons in dealing with United States[a]	Undefined (data not available)[b]
Canada	Private		Undefined (data not available)[b]
	Public		Objects to hub-spoke model FTA umbrella[a]
U.S.A.	Private	Favoured by smaller industries[a]	Favoured by nationalists[a]
	Public	Favoured by country-desk negotiators[a]	Favoured by multi-lateralists[a]

[a] = preference indicated; [b] = no preference indicated.

In other words, the proposition as stated in the works of Lipsey and Schott, that an umbrella FTA might emerge which will favour a continentalist perspective, would be false.[1] In empirical terms, the research posed by these two propositions involves the comparison between bilateralist tendencies and the more general multilateralist thinking within the policy-making centres in North America.

Within this context, the typology being presented consists of a three-by-two matrix which outlines the preferences between public and private actors for intensified bilateralism or a general continentalist perspective as shown in Table 1.

The object of this analysis is to explain the matrix. A second approach would involve the conceptualization of the relationship between decision-

1 Richard G. Lipsey, *Canada at the Mexico–U.S. Trade Dance: Wallflower or Partner?*, Commentary No. 20 (Montreal: C.D. Howe Institute, 1990); and Jeffrey J. Schott, *Free Trade Areas and U.S. Trade Policy* (Washington, D.C.: Institute for International Economics, 1989).

making processes in three asymmetrically placed countries, and between the state and the civil societies in these nations.

THE MEXICAN CONTEXT: THE RUT OF HISTORY

Mexican dealings with the United States differ significantly from those of Mexico with Canada. Specifically, the trade relationship between Mexico and the United States has both empirical and policy components. In the recent past, these two components have differed and have been the cause of objections in the United States and within Mexico, where the private sector has opposed many of the country's foreign economic policy initiatives. These experiences are similar to the Canadian experience and will be treated later.

Over the years the unidirectional nature of Mexican trade with the United States has been reinforced, creating a *de facto* integration of the U.S. and Mexican economies. In spite of the nature of trade, Mexican foreign economic policy has not been unidirectional. This shifting policy has had serious costs for Mexico in its relationship with the United States, although, in the last ten years, public policy seems to have taken a more cogent direction.

The most significant policy deviation from the actual pattern of trade was the so-called third option undertaken under President Luis Echeverría. The policy shift was congruent with other policy initiatives of that administration, but the shift in trade policy was intended to overcome a perceived dependency on the United States. In the context of resurgent Mexican nationalism, policy-making shifted to an effort to diversify Mexico's export markets. Mexico became an active participant in the United Nations Conference for Trade and Development (UNCTAD), while also having the United Nations adopt a measure on the Rights and Obligations of Nations which was an attempt to legally define the manner of relations between North and South. The intent to change Mexico's relationship with the United States through UNCTAD and the Rights and Obligations resolution irritated the United States and led to a period of tense economic relations until 1981.[2] These policies also alienated the Mexican business community, which opposed the ideological statist rhetoric, while favouring protection from competitive pressures from abroad.

The dichotomy between bilateralism and continentalism takes on an added dimension in the Mexican case, involving the reliance on a trading

---

2   Gustavo del Castillo Vera, "Politica de comercio exterior y seguridad nacional en Mexico: Hacia la definicion de metas para fines de siglo," *Frontera Norte,* 1, No. 1 (1989).

system set up as an alternative to the General Agreement on Tariffs and Trade (GATT) by the developing countries and relying on the United Nations. Mexican participation reinforced this system and alienated the United States, which preferred Mexico to be a member of the GATT.[3] The real question is whether the Mexican public and private sectors conceived this alternate system as an adequate mechanism to articulate its trading needs with the United States.

Mexico has participated actively in multilateral institutions, including such world lending institutions as the World Bank, the International Monetary Fund (IMF) and the Inter-American Development Bank. Rosario Green has documented the shift which occurred in the structure of lending toward Mexico in terms of the institutions involved.[4] This shift basically substituted world institutions for American ones during the decade of the 1970s. Mexico's latest choice of bilateralism over multilateralism is not out of lack of experience but the result of other factors.

It is possible that what appears as a shift toward bilateralism in Mexico's foreign economic policy may be confined to the commercial dimension; yet, severe constraints on Mexico's policy options remain, strengthening continued bilateralism through the intervention of the United States as Mexico deals in multilateral forums like the IMF or the World Bank. Further, as a North American free trade agreement gathers strength over time, pressure will mount to harmonize standards and fiscal and monetary policies, thus intensifying the bilateral relationship. Under these conditions, it is possible to envisage a time when, because of a North American FTA, Mexico will necessarily be integrated into that multilateral process of decision-making centred around the Group of Seven or some other regional mechanism.

One area where much closer co-ordination will have to take place is in defining monetary policy so that some sort of stable exchange parity can be achieved at a continental level so that distortions in relative prices are not introduced in the trading relationship. In this sense, clear bilateral, or even tripartite, actions such as an FTA will also involve consideration of the possible roles which Mexico will have to play in multilateral groupings. This certainly will be the case if an FTA is signed between Mexico, Canada, and the United States, coupled with the proposal by the Bush administration that hemispheric free trade be allowed to go forward under such programs as the Enterprise for the Americas initiative. Mexico can play a significant role *vis-à-vis* the rest of Latin America, providing it with the experience of bilateral negotiations with the United States.

---

3   Personal interviews in Washington, D.C., 1978, 1979, and 1980.

4   Rosario Green, *Estado y banca transnacional en Mexico* (Mexico City: Centro de Estudios del Tercer Mundo (CEESTEM)/Nueva Imagen, 1981).

Mexico could also provide a possible FTA model which Latin American countries might follow in their relations with the United States, or it could encourage trade with Mexico through trade agreements to offset the effects of trade diversion from Latin America.

During the mid-1980s, the distance between the empirical realities of United States–Mexico commercial relations and Mexican foreign economic policy began to come closer together, finding a congruence that had been lost during the Echeverría and López Portillo governments. This congruence expressed itself in an intensification of the formal bilateral relations between the two countries in the form of an Agreement on Subsidies and Antidumping, in 1985, and a later more comprehensive one, known as the Framework Agreement of 1987.[5]

These two agreements were the logical results of the significance of the intense trading relationship between the two countries and of the inherent problems which develop out of such a relationship.[6] It is worth noting that the subsidies agreement came after Mexico had effectively failed the so-called injury test for its export products to the United States and was facing an increasing number of countervailing and antidumping actions which threatened its exports.[7] This element of uncertainty, of not knowing what the rules will be, is central in explaining both Mexico's and Canada's foreign economic policy toward the United States. Their actions, to the present, are directed toward diminishing that level of uncertainty.[8] It must be clear that the loss of the injury test was directly related to Mexico's refusal to join the GATT in 1979.

Mexico joined the GATT in 1986, apparently strengthening the country's multilateralist option.[9] Yet there are at least two important

---

5 Gustavo del Castillo Vera, "Mexico-Estados Unidos: del SGP a un acuerdo bilateral de comercio," *Comercio Exterior,* 36, No. 3 (March 1986).

6 Gustavo del Castillo Vera, "El proteccionismo estadounidense en la era de Reagan," *Comercio Exterior,* 37, No. 11 (November 1987).

7 Gustavo Vega, "Las relaciones comerciales entre Mexico y Estados Unidos: Evolucion reciente y perspectivas para el futuro," in Gustavo Vega, ed., *Mexico ante el libre comercio con Norte America* (Mexico City: El Colegio de Mexico and the Universidad Tecnologica de Mexico, 1991).

8 Jeffrey J. Schott and Murray G. Smith, eds., *The Canada–United States Free Trade Agreement: The Global Impact* (Washington: Institute for International Economics, 1988). See also Richard G. Lipsey and Murray G. Smith, *Taking the Initiative: Canada's Trade Options in a Turbulent World,* Observation No. 27 (Montreal: C.D. Howe Institute, 1988); and Richard G. Dearden, Michael M. Hart and Debra P. Stager, *Living with Free Trade: Canada, the Free Trade Agreement and the GATT* (Halifax: Institute for Research on Public Policy, 1989).

9 Gustavo del Castillo Vera, ed., *Mexico en el GATT: Ventajas y desventajas* (Tijuana: El Colegio de la Frontera Norte, 1988).

dimensions that have to be looked at in this context. The first is the ideological-political spin which Mexican decision-makers gave to Mexican participation in the GATT, and the second has to do with the process and mechanics of the negotiations themselves which made Mexico's participation possible.

Mexico's participation in the GATT was portrayed by decision-makers in Mexico City as the best means to resolve trade conflicts with the United States and as the mechanism which would guarantee that Mexican exports received fair treatment in the world economy. It was felt that the GATT rules and conflict-resolution structures would protect Mexican goods worldwide, especially in the United States. Since the United States would now be obligated to grant Mexico Most Favoured Nation (MFN) status, spurious U.S. dumping and injury accusations would be inhibited, thereby stabilizing the conditions of United States–Mexico trade.

Through this action, Mexico felt that the instrument to engender better trade relations with the United States had been set in place, particularly since the mechanics of joining the GATT had involved intense bilateral negotiations between the two countries. Since the United States was Mexico's largest trading partner, negotiation on tariff bindings and duty reduction took place in Washington. In fact, because of the intense negotiations between the two countries, Mexico's GATT membership can be interpreted as one additional bilateral agreement with the United States which carried other multilateral benefits.

The Framework Agreement with the United States, in 1987, reinforced the trend toward bilateralism. The principal feature of this agreement is that for the first time, a mechanism for conflict resolution between the two countries was created which put in place deadlines for conflict resolution. The agreement also stipulated that the countries would first seek resolution within its framework before resorting to the GATT. Finally, the agreement set up a number of working groups which would lead to further trade negotiations along sectoral lines, some sectors being of crucial importance to the United States, such as intellectual property rights and patent protection, investment features, telecommunications, and agriculture. Included in this list were sectors which represented the U.S. interests at the Uruguay Round, and it was felt that if a bilateral agreement could be reached with Mexico, it would set an important precedent within the GATT. It now appears that the Canada–United States Free Trade Agreement is the precedent which the United States sought.

Under the Framework Agreement, Mexico saw its voluntary restraints on steel exportation lessened, thereby increasing its exports, as well as an increase in its textile quota. One American negotiator informed this author that the working groups did not really become operational for a variety of reasons, mostly political ones; by the time they could have been operational again in 1990, Mexico had opted to seek a free-trade agreement with the United States.[10]

Toward the end of the decade, the private sector came to the conclusion that exporting to the United States was the means to survive. The contraction of the internal market still continued as the result of a lack of credit and an enormous decrease in the purchasing power of Mexicans due to a drop in salaries since 1982. The private sector thus began to move away from its reliance on traditional protectionism. By the late 1980s, Mexico experienced a boom in exports and some restructuring, with oil ceasing to be the principal source for foreign exchange, replaced by manufactured exports.[11] A recent International Trade Commission report has Mexican exports to the United States being represented by manufactures by 76.5 per cent and by fuel and other raw materials with only 9.1 per cent.[12] One other shift was even more significant; industry began to feel that a free-trade agreement between Mexico and the United States was the best mechanism to promote Mexico–United States economic ties. A survey of Mexican firms, carried out by this author in late 1989, indicated that 64.1 per cent of firms favoured a free-trade agreement with the United States.[13] This radical shift in Mexican thinking took place at the same time that top-level Mexican policy makers were in Japan and Europe seeking investment for Mexico; these trips resulted in apparent failure, convincing them that a stronger union with the United States was a wise, if not the only, policy alternative.

Thus, by the end of the decade, Mexico had found congruence along three dimensions, a phenomenon which had not occurred in modern times. This congruence related the empirical content of the trading relationship between Mexico and the United States to a shift in the protectionist tendencies of the private sector. Finally, public policy reflected the interests of the Mexican state to incorporate these shifts into measures which protected both of these new realities by seeking formal mechanisms which guaranteed the possibilities and presence of Mexican goods in the North American market.

---

10 Confidential interview in Washington, D.C., 25 March 1991.

11 Mario Dehesa, "The Export Specialization Pattern of Mexican Manufactures," in Claudia Schatan, Cassio Luiselli, and Darryl Mcleod, ed., *Mexico-Estados Unidos; la integracion macroeconomica* (Mexico City: Centro de Investigacion y Docencia Economicas [CIDE], 1989).

12 United States International Trade Commission, *Review of Trade and Investment Liberalization Measures by Mexico and Prospects for Future United States–Mexican Relations*, USITC Publication 2326 (Washington, D.C.: USITC, October 1990).

13 Gustavo del Castillo Vera, "Politica publica y privada: El acuerdo de libre comercio y firmas manufactureras mexicanas," *Comercio Exterior*, in press.

One further dimension which will not be treated in this paper has to do with the other aims of the Mexican state in seeking a free-trade area encompassing all of North America. Besides protecting the private sector in these markets, the political machinery of the contemporary Mexican state would certainly find its survival chances enhanced (though not guaranteed) by a successful agreement, which would alleviate the dire economic situation which Mexico has endured since the decade began. This is an important dimension which cannot be ignored because of the significance which failure to obtain an FTA will represent for future Mexican political stability.[14]

Changes in Mexican export performance and private-sector adoption of economic liberalization policies, together with public-sector efforts at developing better articulating mechanisms with the United States, make it possible to explore the future preferences and actions of private- and public-sector actors in Mexico in the drive toward further economic and social integration on a continental level. It is in this context that recent actions in Mexico to incorporate public actors into the decision-making process of foreign economic policy has to be evaluated. The question is whether the mechanisms which have been set up to integrate public and private thinking are the most appropriate ones leading private and public actors to adopt a continentalist perspective, or whether these mechanisms will actually reinforce the bilateralist tendencies described above.

Early in the 1980s, Mexican private-sector participation was activated after the failure of the Joint Trade Commission, under the auspices of the Bilateral Commission. The Joint Trade Commission made little progress because there was a lack of political will. As a result, in 1983, a committee of Mexican–United States businessmen petitioned the United States Trade Representative for bilateral negotiations on a trade agreement.[15] This bilateral problem-solving approach made sense at the time because of the increased concern in the business sector that Mexico's loss of Most Favoured Nation status would lead to conflict between the two countries. As a result of their actions, the 1985 agreement on subsidies and counter-

---

14 Although this has been an obvious point in most academic discussions on the subject of contemporary United States–Mexican relations, few policy makers in the United States and Mexico were willing to acknowledge the issue. This attitude has been changing, with one informant in Washington referring to it as a "national security concern for the U.S." and which will be brought up if it appears that Congress will not give the fast-track approval for negotiations with Mexico. Confidential interview in Washington, D.C., 8 April 1991.

15 Gustavo Vega, "Las relaciones comerciales entre Mexico y Estados Unidos: Evolución reciente y perspectivas para el futuro," in Gustavo Vega, ed., *Mexico ante el libre comercio con Norte America* (Mexico City: El Colegio de Mexico and the Universidad Tecnologica de Mexico, 1991), p. 181.

vailing duties was signed between the two countries. Still, these isolated private-sector actions do not compare with private-sector participation in the United States.

In the United States, there are approximately 1,000 so-called advisory groups which are consulted when major foreign economic policy decisions have to be taken.[16] These groups participate at all stages of policy development and congressional consideration.[17] This arrangement was institutionalized in the 1974 Trade Act.[18] In Mexico, the process is much newer and substitutes groups for the corporately organized chambers. The process is too new to evaluate.

There is one important element which has to be considered here: because the liberalization initiatives and the search for appropriate mechanisms have fallen upon the state, it is likely that, in the short term, the mechanisms to incorporate private-sector thinking in the decision-making process will also be defined by the public sector. Thus, it will be very difficult to evaluate the degree of private-sector influence on foreign economic policy.

Foreign economic policy-making in Mexico will likely reflect an unusually high degree of consensus; there will be little dissent over the content of such policies. The state will select the actors and determine the forums in which they will be heard, creating a controlled consensus.

In this context, what has Mexico's response been to Canada's participation in the negotiations between Mexico and the United States? Mexico initially indicated it was only interested in a bilateral agreement with the United States, and it was not until later that Mexico favoured tripartite negotiations. Yet the trade data indicate that certain economic sectors such as textiles, steel, petrochemicals, and the auto sectors, instead of being complementary, are sectors where a good deal of competition will occur in the U.S. market between Canadian and Mexican products.[19]

---

16 Thomas M. Franck and Edward Weisband, *Foreign Policy by Congress* (New York: Oxford University Press, 1979).

17 For a general review of interest group participation in foreign economic policy making, see Raymond A. Bauer, Ethiel de Sola Pool, and Lewis Anthony Dexter, *American Business and Public Policy: The Politics of Foreign Trade* (Chicago: Aldine-Atherton, 1972). For two more recent and excellent studies on the making of foreign economic policy making, see I.M. Destler, *Making Foreign Economic Policy* (Washington, D.C.: Brookings Institution, 1980) and I.M. Destler, *American Trade Politics: System Under Stress* (Washington, D.C.: Institute for International Economics, 1986).

18 Trade Act of 1974, 19 U.S.C., S2211(*a*), Supp. V, 1975.

19 Michael Hart, *A North American Free Trade Agreement: The Strategic Implications for Canada* (Ottawa: Centre for Trade Policy and Law, Carleton University, 1990).

One could have expected the private sectors of the two countries either to favour an FTA in order to acquire conflict-resolution mechanisms or to oppose an FTA in order to maintain present, preferential access for their export products in U.S. markets.

In spite of this, the procedures for tripartite negotiations are still undefined, manifesting a certain hesitancy between the three partners as to how to approach each other. Early in the discussions, the status of the Canada–United States FTA in tripartite negotiations was unclear. It now appears that all three countries have accepted the FTA as the umbrella, the guiding light, for the tripartite negotiations. In spite of this, early in 1991, letters of understanding were signed guaranteeing the removal of Canada whenever the Canadian presence threatened to slow down progress between Mexico and the United States.

A possible outcome would be a tripartite agreement within the existing FTA, and complementary, joint bilateral agreements between Mexico and the United States and between Mexico and Canada dealing with additional issues and exceptions to the trilateral agreement. In fact, the structure envisaged here would be similar to the existing GATT agreement where not all member countries have signed the different code attached to the GATT. How extensive such exceptions will be may determine the degree of real economic integration in North America.

Mexico and the Continentalist Perspective: Canada, the Far Northern Neighbour

This discussion leaves unresolved the question of how Mexico has managed its relationship with Canada, and whether this past relationship can set the basis for a continentalist perspective. Even though Mexico–Canada trade is minor compared to United States–Mexico trade, it is still larger than Mexico's trade with all of Latin America. In spite of this, until 1990 there were no formal trade mechanisms between the two countries, thus limiting exchanges between their respective private sectors, while at the same time, public-sector transactions between the two countries have been kept to a minimum. Michael Hart has noted that the absence of such institutional arrangements and of a strong trade history has significantly undermined the development of closer linkages.[20] This situation contrasts severely with the intensity of bilateral agreements existing between

---

20 Ibid., pp. 67, 69.

Canada and the United States where the number of agreements is much greater.[21]

As the possibilities of a North American FTA took on more realistic proportions, the number of Mexico–Canada agreements rapidly increased, especially during 1990 when Mexico sought new Canadian investments and trade, formalizing these arrangements in a framework agreement. In spite of the rapidly increasing trade between Mexico and Canada which saw Canadian exports to Mexico grow by 160 per cent between 1988 and 1989 and Mexican exports to Canada gained 28 per cent in the same time period, Canadian analysts of this relationship indicate that there has been a Canadian perception that the relationship is marginal.[22]

The perception of marginality in the relationship extends to those sectors where Mexican and Canadian products are likely to compete in the U.S. market. The principal conclusion is that although there are exports of similar products, they reach different markets within the United States, with Canadian exporters concerned primarily with the Northeast and Midwest United States and Mexico focused on the Southwest.[23]

This lack of Canadian preoccupation with Mexico could be a source for a continuation of its past emphasis of the bilateral relationship with the United States. Nevertheless, on the basis of past experience, it is possible to hypothesize that:

1. as the bilateral relationship between Canada and Mexico increases in intensity, the greater the hindrance to develop a meaningful tripartite relationship or a continentalist perspective; and

2. because the trading relationship continues at a low level of intensity, little effort will be given to improve the relationship or to design the mechanisms which will permit the intensification of the bilateral relations.

This would be the case, in part, because existing bilateral mechanisms act as institutional barriers to a more continentalist perspective. These barriers to that perspective are not the only ones. One of the most

---

21 Gustavo del Castillo Vera, "Relaciones continentales en Norte America: Un analisis de las relaciones tripartitas Mexico-Estados Unidos-Canada," *Foro Internacional*, 28, No. 3 (January–March, 1988).

22 Investment Canada, *Canada–U.S.–Mexico Free Trade Negotiations: The Rationale and the Investment Dimension* (Ottawa: Investment Canada, 1990), p. 6; and Department of Finance, Canada, *Canada and a Mexico–United States Trade Agreement* (Ottawa: International Trade and Finance Branch, 1990), p. 17.

23 Canada, *North American Trade Liberalization: Sector Impact Analysis* (Ottawa: Industry, Science and Technology Canada, September, 1990), p. 2.

important barriers is the existing national trade legislation and the political medium in which that legislation is implemented. At the present time, there is an ongoing debate in Washington as to whether the North American FTA falls under a multilateral or bilateral negotiation. The question is not purely academic, since it might well determine the future of such an agreement, in the sense that, if it should fall under the definition of a multilateral agreement, then Senate approval is necessary, while the Executive could negotiate a bilateral agreement without Congressional approval. Although the status of the North American FTA could well be a moot point, other national legislation certainly affects international negotiations.

From this perspective, the costs sustained by any change in the bilateral direction of economic relations in North America would appear to be greater than the benefits derived from a tripartite relationship between the three countries in the continent. This situation can be documented with two recent cases involving the relationships between Canada, the United States, and Mexico.

In 1979, at the time of the Mexican oil boom, the United States nominated a special ambassador to Mexico, in addition to its normal ambassadorial representation in Mexico City. His function was to handle the intensification of the United States–Mexico bilateral relationship, because of the new importance given to Mexico as a first-class resource country deriving from its newly found oil deposits and because Mexico was fast becoming a new recipient of major international loans.

This special ambassador found the Mexican State Department bureaucracy poised against him, since he was the only such ambassador outside of the formal bureaucratic structure; Canada also felt aggrieved because the appointment appeared to challenge the idea of a Canada–United States special relationship. Consequently, Canada lobbied Washington to make a comparable appointment for Canada. Fortunately for Washington and the Canadians, the office of this special ambassador was dismantled at the beginning of the Reagan administration when the Mexican crisis developed and Mexico went back to being a Third World country. The second instance of Canadian impatience came recently after its signing of the FTA, when Mexico announced its intention to negotiate an FTA with the United States. Previous to Mexico's announcement, Canada had made it very clear that its agreement with the United States was not one which would allow Mexico "to enter through the back door."[24] When, in June 1990, Mexico expressed its desire to sign an FTA with the United States, Canada's immediate response was chagrin and a

---

24 Gustavo del Castillo Vera, "Politica de comercio exterior y seguridad nacional en Mexico: Hacia la definicion de metas para fines de siglo," *Frontera Norte*, 1 (January–June 1989).

sense of betrayal.[25] In this sense, one institutional arrangement had the potential for slowing down new commercial arrangements. Almost one year went by before Canada and Mexico agreed, in February 1991, that a tripartite trade negotiation in the form of a North American FTA was possible and desirable.

CONCLUSIONS

It is not sufficient to say that the North American FTA will bring about the conditions for close economic ties and co-operation between the three countries of North America. What is important is that the North American FTA may provide some institutional provisions which can ameliorate the existing bilateralism. Yet this optimistic scenario has been questioned by Canada after the signing of its FTA with the United States. There are two dimensions which have been brought up by Canada's External Affairs evaluation of the first year of operations of the Canadian–United States FTA. The first is the continuing *ad hoc* nature of the relationship, in spite of the formal mechanisms which were instituted under the FTA. Second is the so-called administrative discretion which still exists, especially in the United States, to interpret provisions of the FTA. The External Affairs report evaluating the FTA states that "an examination of the current cases between Canada and the United States indicates that the delay, consultation, and negotiation that have been a feature of the past treatment of disputes will likely remain."[26] With respect to the second dimension, it concludes that "in some respects, rather than gaining Canada exemption from harassment, the FTA seems to have licensed even more 'aggressive' harassment of Canadian trade practices by the United States.[27]

It seems clear that, while it is necessary to have the infrastructure in place to enforce foreign economic policy agreements, national interests and legislation will still determine how nations approach one another. A good example of how national legislation can be manipulated to reduce the effectiveness of international agreements such as the FTA is indicated by the report cited so far. One particularly telling reference states that the

25 Gustavo del Castillo Vera, *Proceedings from the North American Congress for Latin America* (NACLA, forthcoming).

26 Senate Committee on Foreign Affairs, Senate of Canada, *Monitoring the Implementation of the Canada–United States Free Trade Agreement*, Issue 22 (Ottawa: Senate of Canada, 27 March 1990), p. 106.

27 Ibid., Introduction, n.p.

old Tariff System of the United States (TSUS) tariff classification system remains in place.[28]

What seems clear is that national institutions, and the instruments which are designed to provide the basis of relations among the three countries of North America, are distinct, with Mexico differing most sharply from the others. For Mexico, the public sector has historically set the guidelines for its relations with other countries, especially the United States. On the other hand, in Canada and the United States, private-sector pressure groups have encountered a fertile medium to develop, and they have also been given the forums for public expression which relate them to the mechanisms where public policy is made.

In relation to the ongoing discussions on a North American FTA, the benign neglect which characterized Canada–Mexico relations seems difficult to overcome since few instruments are in place to define the nature of this relationship. Yet this might well be a blessing, in that these two countries are in a situation where they are free of past historical experiences and can design the instruments which will serve them to become better trading partners, with or without a North American Free Trade Agreement.

---

28 Ibid., p. 3.

Diana Alarcón González
Departamento de Estudios Económicos
El Colegio de la Frontera Norte

Trade Liberalization, Income Distribution, and Poverty in Mexico: An Empirical Review of Recent Trends

Amidst a sharp contraction of the economy triggered by the 1982 debt crisis, the Mexican government initiated one of the most ambitious programs of trade liberalization ever intended in order to reorient the structure of the Mexican economy. By 1990, Mexico had made the transition from a protected economy to a relatively open economy. Traditional mechanisms of trade protection had been eliminated or cut down substantially.[1] In the initial years of trade reform, the exchange-rate policy maintained a certain margin of undervaluation in order to promote exports.

Similar to the experience of other developing countries, however, policies to restructure the economy were implemented in a framework of sharp macroeconomic instability. Fiscal and balance-of-payments deficits were dealt with through policies of stabilization which were intended to reduce the level of national expenditures and bring it into line with national income.

Contradictory forces were set in motion which would have mixed effects on welfare. Structural adjustments—as a systematic attempt to increase the level of income through the reallocation of resources towards their most efficient use—would provide the basis to increase the level of

---

This paper was written in November 1994 before the currency devaluation in December of that year. The sharp contraction of the economy, the difficulties in reorganizing production, and the deep social and political tensions arising throughout the country confirm the ideas expressed in this paper.

1   For a full description of these processes see Chapter 4 of Diana Alarcón, *Changes in the Distribution of Income in Mexico and Trade Liberalization* (El Colegio de la Frontera Norte, 1994).

production, increase exports and, in the context of a labour-abundant economy, increase the level of employment creation. In that sense, economic restructuring would have a beneficial impact over the standards of living of the working population. To the extent that the economy became more open to the international economy, distortions in the domestic market, characteristic of import substitution industrialization, would be reduced, which would set the conditions for improving the distribution of income. By contrast, policies of stabilization are concerned with the short-term macroeconomic stability of the country. They are intended to restore short-term balance of payments and budget stability. By design, policies of stabilization generate sharp contractionary tendencies in the economy that lead to employment losses and the reduction of public expenditures. Very frequently, the contraction of government expenditures affects the provision of key social services that serve large segments of the population.

Trying to assess the welfare implications of structural adjustments as distinct from the contractionary effects of stabilization policies in the context of specific country studies is a very difficult question. Economic restructuring implies the reallocation of resources to their most efficient use. In the process, however, less efficient operations are displaced. Job losses in the sectors of the economy that cannot resist the pressure from intensified competition are part of the process of resource reallocation under economic restructuring. The extent to which employment and wage losses can be identified within economic restructuring, or if a recession in the economy is generated by policies of stabilization, or the operation of longer term tendencies, is empirically difficult to separate out. Most of the time, observed trends will be the result of the complex interaction of all these factors. Rather than trying to establish artificial causal links between macroeconomic adjustment in Mexico and its welfare implications, I intend to provide some evidence of the evolution of key indicators of welfare during the period of stabilization and structural adjustment. In particular, I concentrate on the evolution of income distribution and the incidence of poverty.

REVIEW OF MACROECONOMIC PERFORMANCE

The performance of the Mexican economy through the 1980s and 1990s has been rather poor. The heterodox approach adopted by the Mexican government reduced the level of inflation from the three-digit inflation rates that prevailed in the early part of the 1980s, to one digit. Frequently, the continuous inflow of foreign capital through 1994 was also quoted as one of the successful signs of macroeconomic stability.

On all other counts, however, the performance of the economy is far less impressive. Efforts to stabilize the economy have not been able to produce any meaningful sustained growth (see Tables 1 and 2). The average yearly growth of the gross national product (GNP) has been 2.5 percent in the 1987–93 period. When population growth is taken into account, the average GNP per capita has been negative throughout the period of adjustment.

One of the explicit objectives of structural adjustment is to alter the composition of economic output. By liberalizing the economy, resources are freed to flow towards their most efficient use. One result of this should be to increase the share of tradable goods in the economy. The time frame for adjustment may yet be too short to evaluate the reallocation of resources that may be taking place in Mexico. So far, however, there is not much evidence of major resource reallocation. The share of tradables (defined as the production of agricultural, mining, and manufacturing goods) in relation to total production has remained fairly stable throughout the period of adjustment, approximately one-third of total production.[2] The proportion of manufacturing production, however, has increased from 21.3 percent in 1987 to 22.3 percent of the total value of production in 1993.

The economic performance of sectors producing tradable goods has been heterogeneous. Agricultural production and mining have both remained fairly stagnant. The average rate of growth of the former was 0.5 percent per year between 1987 and 1993. The manufacturing sector has produced a more dynamic growth of 3.5 percent per year on average. Within manufacturing, exports of machinery and equipment are actually leading the way and their importance in total manufacturing production has increased (from 17.3 percent in 1987 to 23.1 percent in 1993). Exports of manufactured goods have shown very fast rates of growth. Nowadays they constitute Mexico's main exports. From three-fourths of total exports in 1991, the share of manufacturing exports increased to 81.9 percent in 1993. They represented as much as 93.7 percent of total non-oil exports in that same year. Within manufacturing, the fastest growing sectors are precisely those associated with exports. Machinery and equipment are the largest component of total manufacturing exports and its share in the value of exports is increasing. In 1991, machinery and equipment accounted for 63.3 percent of total exports of manufactures. By 1993, it was 66.7 percent of the total, and by March 1994 it was already 70 percent of total manufacturing exports.

Unfortunately, the rapid growth of manufacturing exports has not led to any substantial increase in employment. In fact, employment in

---

2 Nontradables, by exclusion, are defined here as the value of production in construction, electricity, commerce, and transportation, as well as financial, community, and banking services.

TABLE 1. MACROECONOMIC INDICATORS

	1980	1987	1988	1989	1990	1991	1992	1993	1994ª
GNP at 1980 prices (growth rates)	9.2	1.9	1.3	3.3	4.5	3.6	2.8	0.4	2.4
GNP per capita (growth rates)	5.4	-0.1	-0.6	1.5	2.7	1.9	1.2	-1.0	1.0
(%) Manufacturing exports to total exports	19.5	47.6	56.0	55.2	52.0	58.7	60.8	80.3	81.8
(%) Manufacturing exports to non-oil exports	59.8	82.1	83.2	84.2	83.4	84.4	87.2	93.7	93.2
(%) Manufacturing imports to total imports	87.2	89.1	89.6	89.8	91.0	94.0	93.7	94.2	94.1
Trade balance ($ millions)ᵇ	-3,058	8,433	1,667	-645	-4,433	-11,063	-15,934	-13,480	-18,990
Trade balance to GNP	-2	5.5	0.2	-1.3	-1.8	-3.9	-6.3	-5.4	N/A
Share of tradables in total outputᶜ	N/A	33.6	33.6	33.8	34.2	34.0	33.6	33.1	31.7
Share of manufacturing in total output	N/A	21.3	21.7	22.5	22.8	22.9	22.8	22.3	22.7

Tradables include the value of agriculture, mining and manufacturing production. ª To July 1994. ᵇ A negative sign indicates a trade deficit. ᶜ Since 1991 manufacturing exports include exports from maquiladoras.
Source: Own construction based on INEGI, NAFINSA, Quinto Informe de Gobierno.

manufacturing has been contracting in relation to the preadjustment period. By March 1994, employment in manufacturing was only two-thirds of the level of employment prevailing in 1980. Moreover, the most dynamic exporting sectors within manufacturing are showing the largest loss of employment. By March 1994, employment in machinery and equipment was only 67.8 percent of its 1980 level.

Maquiladora activities are one of the few areas where employment is rapidly growing. With over two thousand establishments by March 1994, maquiladoras employ 557,658 workers, equivalent to over 17 percent of the labour force in manufacturing. Most of the maquiladoras are concentrated in the northern border states. Although maquiladoras have made an important contribution to the creation of employment in Mexico, the nature of this type of activity has very few multiplier effects in the economy. Less than two percent of inputs used in *maquiladora* production originate in Mexico. The rest are temporary imports from abroad. Their net contribution to the creation of demand for domestic inputs, employment generation in other sectors, and thus their overall contribution to the development of the country, is very limited.

Unemployment figures in Mexico do not capture the extent of the problem. The lack of an unemployment compensation system makes it difficult for people to remain unemployed for long periods of time. Open unemployment throughout the period of adjustment has fluctuated around 3.5 percent. However, one indication of the overall loss of unemployment in this period is the rapid growth of the informal employment sector.

In relation to balance-of-payments stability, the rapid growth of manufacturing exports has not helped to relieve external trade deficits. The trade surplus associated with undervaluation in the exchange rate in the period 1983–87 is rapidly turning into a large trade deficit. In 1993, the trade deficit was 3.5 times larger than the deficit observed in the preadjustment period and the difference between the value of imports and exports has widened since 1988. By March 1994, the trade deficit was clearly associated with the imports of intermediate and capital goods, which is presumably supporting the expansion of manufacturing exports.

On all counts, therefore, the pattern of specialization that is arising from the economic restructuring of the Mexican economy is generating deep structural problems. The process of integration with the rest of North America is leading to a pattern of specialization that runs counter to Mexico's resource endowments. Even though in relation to its trading partners, Mexico's abundance of cheap labour provides an opportunity to expand employment and thus disseminate the beneficial impact of trade reform, contractionary macroeconomic policies have failed to provide the framework for a more efficient allocation of resources, a framework that would promote Mexico's comparative advantage in international markets through the production and exports of labour-intensive goods.

On the contrary, the manufacturing sectors identified as the most dynamic exporting sectors are precisely the ones that are rationalizing production in a capital-intensive direction, and are also dependent on imported inputs and capital goods. The result is a major displacement of workers away from manufacturing activities and the worsening of Mexico's trade account.

Trade liberalization in the context of a generalized contraction of the economy has led not only to a very distorted process of economic restructuring with a pattern of specialization that does not correspond to

Table 2. Employment and Wage Indicators

	1980	1987	1988	1989	1990	1991	1992	1993	1994[a]
Manufacturing employment	100	87.0	86.8	88.8	88.8	87.3	84.0	77.9	74.5
Employment in mach. & equip.	100	77.1	78.4	81.8	83.1	82.7	79.1	71.8	68.1
Mean income, manufacturing Total	100	69.0	68.7	74.8	77.5	82.2	89.4	93.3	93.2
Blue-collar workers	100	62.7	60.5	62.0	62.7	64.6	68.7	70.4	68.6
Share of *maquiladora* employment in manufacturing employment	4.9	12.6	16.0	17.5	N/A	N/A	N/A	16.8	N/A
Share wages in disposable personal income	40.6	32.1	30.6	29.5	28.1	29.0	N/A	N/A	N/A

[a] To July 1994.
Source: Base de Datos de INEGI, 1994.

Mexico's resource endowment, but also to large welfare costs. In the next two sections, I review two key aspects of these costs: income distribution trends and the incidence of poverty during the period of adjustment.

INCOME DISTRIBUTION TRENDS

Inequality in the distribution of income has been a characteristic feature of Mexico's economy. Differences in the methodologies for data collection and in the design of household surveys make it difficult to establish long-term trends in the distribution of income prior to the implementation of trade reform in the 1980s. Among the many studies that have looked into the question, however, there is wide consensus in the conclusion that income distribution in Mexico is large when compared to other developing countries.[3]

---

3   See Alarcón, *Changes in the Distribution of Income*, Ch. 3.

In 1984, the institute of statistics in Mexico (INEGI) initiated a series of Income Expenditure Surveys that are fully comparable.[4] The availability of reliable statistics on the income and expenditure patterns of households for 1984, 1989, and 1992 is extremely valuable in understanding the evolution of income distribution during the period of economic restructuring. Nineteen eighty-four can be roughly identified as the year prior to the initiation of policies of trade liberalization. Although exchange rate policies to promote exports have been in place since 1982, trade reform was not initiated until mid-1985. Observations collected in 1989 and 1992 provide valuable post-trade liberalization data. Income and expenditure patterns for 1992 are particularly interesting. One would think that 1992 provides a clearer picture of longer-term trends since more time has passed since the initiation of trade reform.

The distribution of income in Mexico became noticeably more unequal during the period 1984 to 1992. Gini coefficients of the distribution of total income rose sharply from 0.429 in 1984 to 0.469 in 1989 and then rose again to 0.475 in 1992 (a 10.7 percent increase overall).[5] There are several forces pushing towards greater income inequality during this period. First is the increasing share of profit and personal service income in relation to total household income, at the same time as these two income sources became more concentrated in the top deciles. Second, as a result of the sharp contraction of agricultural production during the period of adjustment, the share of income generated by agriculture and livestock activities decreased as a proportion of total household income. Since these income sources (especially agriculture) are the traditional income sources of the poorest segments of the population, any decline in its share with respect to total household income tends to accentuate overall inequality.

Third, the wage share of total household income has actually decreased from almost 47 percent in 1984 to 46.4 percent in 1989, and 45.4 percent in 1992. During the period of economic restructuring, wages

---

4   For a discussion of the level of comparability of the 1984, 1989, and 1992 Income Expenditure Surveys, see INEGI, *Encuesta Nacional de Ingreso-Gasto de los Hogares* (Documento Metodólogica, 1992).

5   Coefficients should be regarded as a rough approximation since they are based on ranking households by total household income and on grouping data by deciles. When Gini coefficients are calculated from micro data and households are ranked by per capita income, inequality measures increase. Using the appropriate methology, Gini coefficients were as high as 0.488 in 1984 and 0.519 in 1989. See Nora Lustig, *The Remaking of an Economy* (Washington, D.C.: The Brookings Institute, 1992), and Alarcón, *Changes in the Distribution of Income*. Equivalent values for 1992 are yet to be established since tapes for the 1992 income expenditures survey have just been released.

moved in a U-shaped pattern. In 1984 the distribution of wage income was very similar to the distribution of total household income. In 1989, as wages were compressed in a downward direction, their distribution became more concentrated among the lower-income deciles. But in 1992, as white-collar workers started to recuperate the value of their pre-adjustment real wages, total wage income became more unequally distributed.[6]

Income distribution trends are consistent with the overall performance of the Mexican economy. The contraction of agricultural production, together with the loss of jobs identified in manufacturing activities, have generated a sharp contraction in the income sources of the poorest sectors of the population. The rapid increase in capital-intensive manufacturing exports, on the other hand, may be well behind the increasing importance of industrial profits and income from personal services (where professionals' service income is reported). Thus income inequality during the period of adjustment reflects not only the lack of growth of the Mexican economy, but may also be reflecting the emergence of a pattern of specialization that is not conducive to job creation.

POVERTY

Consistent with patterns identified in the distribution of income, studies on poverty in Mexico lead to the conclusion that poverty, especially extreme poverty, has been increasing during the period of adjustment.[7] Using a poverty line equivalent to 1.25 times the value of a food

---

6   Diana Alarcón and Terry McKinley, "Wage Differentials in Mexico from 1984 to 1992: a Profile of Human Capital and Earnings," paper presented at the Conference on the Impact of Structural Adjustment on Labour Markets and Income Distribution in Latin America (San José, Costa Rica, 7–10 September, 1994).

7   There are several studies about the evolution of poverty in Mexico. While there are slight differences in the definition of poverty lines and some studies adjust income to render it comparable with National Income Accounts, they all point at an intensification of extreme poverty, especially in rural areas. See Alarcón, *Changes in the Distribution of Income*; Enrique Hernández-Laos, "Alternativas de Largo Plazo para Erradicar la Pobreza en México," in *Frontera Norte* Special Issue (El Colegio de la Frontera Norte, 1994), pp. 155–69; Nora Lustig and Ann Mitchell, "Poverty in Times of Austerity: Mexico in the 1980s," revised version of a paper presented at the XIII Latin American Meetings of the Econometric Society (Caracas, Venezuela, January 1995); and Miguel Székely Pardo, "Estabilización y Ajuste con Desigualdad y Pobreza: El Caso de México," *El Trimestre Económico*, 61 (1), No. 241 (January–March 1994).

consumption basket that provides 2,082 calories and 35.1 grams of protein, Levy estimated that 19.5 percent of the population in Mexico were afflicted by extreme poverty.[8] Using the same methodology to assure comparability of results, Alarcón concluded that 23.6 percent of the Mexican people in 1989 were below the extreme poverty line.[9]

Studies on poverty suggest that the policies of stabilization and structural adjustment implemented in the late 1980s imposed a heavy cost on low-income households and a disproportionately high cost on rural households in particular. The sharp decline of the agricultural sector in the 1980s translated into an increasing proportion of extreme poverty being concentrated in rural areas.[10] When the incidence of poverty, the income gap, and the distribution of income among the poor are taken into account, it turns out that by 1989, rural areas constituted as much as 80 percent of the population living in extreme poverty in Mexico.[11]

Although no independent calculations have been made about the incidence of poverty in 1992,[12] a joint study by INEGI and CEPAL suggests that the extent of poverty decreased slightly in 1992 in relation to 1989, although it is still higher than the extent of poverty registered in 1984. Although the incidence of poverty, according to this study, decreased slightly in 1992, the absolute numbers of poor people in rural areas actually increased throughout this whole period.[13]

Again, as difficult as it is to establish the links between specific policy decisions and their social outcome, the evolution of poverty in Mexico reinforces the idea that the performance of the economy in the postliberalization period has not done much to alleviate the living conditions of vast segments of the population. Whether the prevalence of

---

8 Santiago Levy, *Poverty Alleviation in Mexico*, Working Paper Series No. 679 (Washington, D.C.: World Bank, 1991).

9 For a discussion of the methodology used in these two studies, see Alarcón, *Distribution of Income*, Ch. 7.

10 For a reference on poverty measures and the contribution of rural areas, see T. McKinley and D. Alarcón, "The Prevalence of Rural Poverty in Mexico," in *World Development* (forthcoming).

11 Alarcón, *Changes in the Distribution of Income*, Ch 7.

12 Partly because the tapes that contain the most recent income expenditure survey have just been released.

13 The methodology used by INEGI and CEPAL is different to other studies of poverty in Mexico. Through a series of methodological adjustments, poverty measurements tend to decrease. According to their estimates 15.4 percent of the population were below the extreme porverty line in 1984, 16.2 percent in 1989, and 16.1 percent in 1992. See CEPAL-INEGI, *Magnitud y Evolución de la Pobreza en México, 1984–1992* (Mexico City: ONU-CEPAL and INEGI, 1993).

poverty, especially rural poverty, can be attributed to the conditions of recession of the Mexican economy, to the inertial effect of longer-term tendencies, or if, rather, they are attributed to the emergence of a new pattern of specialization that is not allocating resources efficiently, the point is that, so far, large segments of the population have not been incorporated into the dynamics of economic restructuring. And unless those trends are reversed, the prevalence of poverty in the country questions the social sustainability of economic restructuring.

Conclusion

So far, the process of economic integration with the rest of North America has been very costly in terms of its welfare effects. The experience of almost a decade of adjustment seems to indicate that the benefits that can be derived from economic integration are contingent upon a larger set of issues. On the one hand, it is true that the liberalization of trade in Mexico provides a great opportunity to restructure the economy more efficiently, but the "magics" of the market in the context of a more open economy depend upon the ability of the economy to respond to greater openness. It depends on the rate of investment that the country is able to achieve, particularly on those production sectors and activities that create employment. After all, the reallocation of resources is not static. One cannot think of resource reallocation as the process of disinvestment in some sectors in order to promote investment in sectors where a country like Mexico would have a comparative advantage—the most labour-intensive sectors that could create employment and would therefore have the most beneficial effects in terms of income distribution and poverty reduction.

Resource reallocation occurs at the margins. It occurs in the framework of a dynamic, fast-growing economy in which investment flows to the sectors where Mexico has a comparative advantage, and in the context of the North American Free Trade Agreement (NAFTA), resources should flow to the most labour-intensive operations that create employment.

Economic policy so far has, however, to a large extent suppressed the benefits of trade liberalization. Mexico's obsession to reduce inflation, to promote foreign investment flows, and to create an image of exchange-rate stability has, in effect, suppressed the long-term beneficial effects of trade liberalization. It has depressed the extent of resource reallocation to those labour-intensive activities where Mexico would have a comparative advantage in the context of an integrated North American market.

Thus, domestic economic policy does play a role in shaping the outcome of a more open, integrated economy, whether it be active policies or a more indirect form of intervention such as the exchange rate policy.

Domestic policy, however, is only one side of the coin. The other side of the coin is the rules and regulations of trade in the larger North American region. Formal trade agreements (the NAFTA in particular) do not necessarily mean free trade. There is a whole range of nontariff restrictions that create "uncertainty and prejudice the smooth functioning of flexible production."[14]

In closing the gap between the rich and the poor in Mexico, we need to be concerned with *two* gaps: an external gap with respect to our two North American trading partners, and a domestic gap associated with the large social and regional disparities characteristic of Mexico. There are thus two parallel agendas, one that is concerned with the deepening of a NAFTA in the sense of promoting the actual conditions of free trade where Mexico can develop a pattern of specialization consistent with its comparative advantage in labour-intensive products, and a second, domestic agenda which is concerned with the generation of a process of integration conducive to sustainable development, that is, to the promotion of economic growth with employment creation.

The recent experience of adjustment indicates that we need to go back to the basics, to the ABCs of economics, to commonsense intuition, and to building our own Mexican competitive advantage in accordance with our own resource endowments and greater investment in human capital which is, after all, our most important insurance for the future.

---

14 Sidney Weintraub, "Making the Most of North American Integration: The Challenges," commissioned paper presented at the Trinational Institute on Innovation, Competitiveness and Sustainability (Whistler, B.C., 14–21 August, 1994).

III

Borderlands, Industry, Labour,
and Immigration

Paul Ganster
Director
Institute for Regional Studies of the Californias
San Diego State University

The United States–Mexico Border Region and Growing Transborder Interdependence

INTRODUCTION

The territorial interface between the United States and Mexico constitutes one of the most dynamic and complex border regions of the world. It is an area characterized by rapid population growth, accelerated urbanization, political change, and economic change. Two very different systems meet at the boundary between Mexico and the United States. It is where the developed, industrialized world meets the developing world; it is where the North meets the South. One of the most distinguishing features of this border region is its economic asymmetry. It has the strongest contrasts in the entire world in terms of economic differences from one side of the boundary to the other. A border born in war and characterized by conflict over many decades, it is nonetheless a binational region that clearly evidences growing integration and increasing levels of transborder cooperation. This paper will highlight these important trends within the historical context of the region. First, an historical overview of the region's development will be provided. Then, the major features of the contemporary border, including the major conflictual issues, will be detailed. Finally, growing transborder interdependence and integration will be discussed.

HISTORICAL OVERVIEW OF THE BORDER REGION

The United States–Mexican border region initially was the northern fringe of the Spanish colony of New Spain and then, after 1821, of the newly independent republic of Mexico.[1] Characterized by sparse settlements based on mining and ranching, the northern region was never effectively settled nor occupied by Mexico, a new nation that experienced nearly a half-century of internal disorder after independence. Mexico lost much of its northern territories, first through a revolt of Anglo settlers in Texas in 1835, and then through a war between Mexico and the United States in 1846. The Treaty of Guadalupe Hidalgo that was signed in 1848 to end the war ceded much of the north to the United States. This, along with the sale of parts of New Mexico and Arizona by the Gadsden Purchase in 1854, established the international boundary between Mexico and the United States that endures today.[2]

Early Border Development. The war with Mexico opened a vast area to the dual forces of Manifest Destiny and the dynamic U.S. economy. Economic cycles of mining, ranching, and agriculture—in combination with the building of extensive railroad networks—led to rapid economic development of the Southwest of the United States in the late nineteenth century. Linking of transportation networks of the United States and Mexico encouraged the development of border cities. At every major transportation route crossing the international boundary, customhouses and service industries for trade developed on both sides of the boundary, giving rise to population centres that eventually emerged as the twin-city settlement pattern that characterizes the region today.

The interdependence of the U.S. border region with Mexico was evident relatively early. Increasingly, trade was a factor, but also important was the fact that much of the labour for the development of railroads, mines, ranches, agriculture, and urban areas in the South-western border region came from Mexico. The flow of labour was conditioned, of course, by the dual push-pull factors of lack of jobs in Mexico and labour needs in the United States. Since Mexico's north was isolated from the national economy, the United States was the historical trading partner for Mexican northerners. Mexican-border urban centres developed in response to economic stimuli from across the border, and Mexican

---

1 For treatments of the historical development of the borderlands, see David J. Weber, ed., *New Spain's Far Northern Frontier: Essays on the American West, 1540–1821* (Albuquerque: University of New Mexico Press, 1979) and his edited work, *Myth and the History of the Hispanic Southwest* (Albuquerque: University of New Mexico Press, 1988), and Paul Ganster, Bernardo García Martínez, and James Lockhart, "Northern New Spain," in Norris Hundley, ed., *Historical Atlas of the U.S.–Mexican Border* (Tucson: University of Arizona Press, forthcoming).

2 Richard Griswold del Castillo, *The Treaty of Guadalupe Hidalgo: A Legacy of Conflict* (Norman: University of Oklahoma Press, 1990).

border-city growth became dependent upon the U.S. settlements and regions to the north. These elements have been present in the border region for more than a century and continue in significant ways today.

For much of the second half of the nineteenth century, the border region was a frontier characterized by lawlessness, violence, and lack of strong governmental controls.[3] Indian groups, whose traditional paths of migration were cut by the international boundary, sporadically raided across the border. When pursued by troops back into the other country, diplomatic protests resulted. Transborder banditry and cattle rustling were also common occurrences, as were filibustering expeditions, most usually launched from U.S. territory, with the intent of capturing undefended areas of Mexico's north to establish independent states.

Relative peace and order finally came to the region by the 1880s with extension of railroads throughout the U.S. border region, economic development, and defeat and confinement to reservations of most of the marauding Indian groups.[4] In Mexico, a half-century of internal disorder was brought to a close with the rise to power of Porfirio Díaz, who was to dominate Mexican politics until 1910. Díaz ruthlessly suppressed rural violence and restored order to the nation's border. His regime instituted policies that enabled individuals and companies to amass huge land holdings, evicting traditional small holders, communities, and villages from the lands that had been worked by families and communities for centuries. This new landless class often joined the migratory stream north from Mexico to search for work in the expanding U.S. economy.

In the north, in Chihuahua, Sonora, and Baja California, foreign and Mexican companies acquired title and/or concessions to huge tracts of land for development purposes from the Díaz government. Typical was the case of Ensenada, Baja California, where first an American company, and then an English company, were involved in an ambitious plan to establish colonies of foreign immigrants and bring economic development to the region. Although the effort collapsed, it did lay the foundation for the development of Ensenada and is testimony to the importance of such efforts in the rise of urban areas in the Mexican border region.[5]

The violent upheavals in Mexico during the 1910 Revolution, some of which spilled over into the United States, are an example of how

---

3   Oscar Martínez, *Troublesome Border* (Tucson: University of Arizona Press, 1988).

4   Edward H. Spicer, *Cycles of Conquest: The Impact of Spain, Mexico, and the United States on the Indians of the Southwest, 1533–1960* (Tucson: University of Arizona Press, 1981).

5   David Piñera, *American and English Influence on the Early Development of Ensenada, Baja California, Mexico* (San Diego: Institute for Regional Studies of the Californias, San Diego State University, 1995).

conditions in Mexico directly affected lives and property in the U.S. border region. Mexican revolutionaries often operated from safe bases in U.S. border-towns. Mexicans of all classes fled the violence and many settled on the U.S. side of the border and remained even after restoration of relative peace in Mexico by the 1920s.

Prohibition in the United States provided stimulus for economic growth in Mexico's northern border cities as they became the sites of tourism development centred on gambling, entertainment, and alcohol.[6] Although during the 1920s Mexican border towns grew and their economic bases broadened with the creation of agricultural industries and other jobs, development was very much dependent upon the twin city across the border. With the ending of prohibition in 1933 and the deepening Great Depression, the Mexican border-towns were hard hit, revealing extreme dependence on the adjacent U.S. border towns. Tijuana, with a narrow economic base linked to tourism and isolated from the Mexican economy, was particularly affected. Mexican border-cities did not recover until the World War II era brought prosperity that continued with the Sunbelt expansion of the U.S. Southwest in the post-war period. Mexican border-cities expanded rapidly, so that by 1960 their populations had grown enormously: Mexicali (281,333); Ciudad Juárez (276,995); Tijuana (165,690); Matamoros (143,043); and Reynosa (134,869).[7]

Labour Flows. Shortly after the end of World War I, the United States entered a sharp recession that had important implications for the border. With the economic downturn, many Mexican workers, along with some U.S. citizens of Mexican descent, were expelled from the United States as immigration restrictions were imposed and enforced. During the mid and late 1920s, with the expansion of the American economy, Mexican labour flows were welcomed back to provide excellent, low-cost labour to grow-ing cities, ranches, mines, and transportation infrastructure. With the Great Depression, national attention focused on Mexican workers and there were large-scale forced repatriations that returned Mexican workers

---

6 Manuel A. Machado, Jr., "Booze, Broads, and the Border: Vice and U.S.–Mexican Relations, 1910-1930," in C. Richard Bath, ed., *Proceedings of the 1982 Meeting of the Rocky Mountain Council on Latin American Studies* (El Paso: Center for Inter-American and Border Studies, University of Texas, El Paso, 1982), pp. 349–61. Ovid Demaris, *Poso del Mundo* (New York: Pocket Books, 1971), pro-vides a journalistic view of this period on the border. Also, T.D. Proffitt III, *Tijuana: The History of a Mexican Metropolis* (San Diego: San Diego State Univer-sity Press, 1994); Oscar J. Martínez, *Border Boom Town: Ciudad Juárez since 1848* (Austin: University of Texas Press, 1975).

7 Martínez, *Border Boom Town*, p. 161.

across the border.[8] This was a pattern that was repeated every time there was an expansion/recession cycle in the United States. These episodes have been the source of bitter feelings on the part of Mexicans and have disturbed the lives of border residents. Immigration continues to be a source of conflict between Mexico and the United States. To a large extent, immigration is a border issue, for the flows are across the border, the U.S. border states receive most of the undocumented workers, and the migratory flows have great impacts on the Mexican border-cities.

The economic development of the Southwest accelerated in the post-World War II period with the Sunbelt growth phenomenon of the United States that was mirrored on Mexico's northern frontier by extremely rapid urban development. The demographic explosion, rapid urbanization, and increasing transboundary economic, cultural, and social linkages increased interdependence with Mexico all along the border. Increasingly, what occurs on one side of the boundary has negative or positive impacts on the other side. A key factor in the economic development of the U.S. Southwest and border was Mexican labour. In 1942, in response to the wartime labour shortage in the United States, Mexico and the U.S. agreed to a guest-worker program to allow temporary contracting of Mexican labourers to work in the United States, initially in agriculture, but later in other occupations. The program, known as the Bracero Program, was extended beyond the wartime emergency and was terminated in 1964. Nonetheless, driven by poverty and lack of jobs in Mexico and attracted by employment in the United States, the flow of Mexican labour northward has continued to the present time in the form of illegal migration. The movement of Mexican migrants into the United States has profoundly affected border communities and today constitutes a key issue for the border region.[9]

Over the years, as many Mexicans acquired visas for work in the United States and as many border Mexicans acquired U.S. citizenship, a significant group of commuter workers developed along the entire border region. Living in the Mexican twin-city and commuting to work at jobs in the United States, these workers are an important regional economic force. For example, in the San Diego–Tijuana region there are between 20,000 and 30,000 men and women who cross daily to work in the United

---

8   See Abraham Hoffman, *Unwanted Mexican Americans in the Great Depression: Repatriation Pressures, 1929–1939* (Tucson: University of Arizona Press, 1974) for a discussion of these repatriations.

9   For a brief overview of the Bracero Program, see Karl M. Schmitt, *Mexico and the United States, 1821–1973: Conflict and Coexistence* (New York: John Wiley & Sons, Inc., 1974), pp. 214-220; also, Richard B. Craig, *The Bracero Program: Interest Groups and Foreign Policy* (Austin: University of Texas Press, 1971).

States.[10] Paid in dollars, these individuals benefit from devaluations of the peso and account for important retail purchases in the United States. Often earners of low wages in the United States, these commuters are middle class by Mexican standards. They often live in Mexico not only for cultural preferences, but also for lower housing and living costs. In addition to providing high-quality and low-cost labour, these workers benefit the U.S. border cities in another way. San Diego has a serious shortage of affordable housing and in the case of the commuter workers, Mexico meets that basic infrastructure need.[11]

Border Industrialization Program. Mexico, fearing significant unemployment as the Bracero Program ended and guest workers returned from the United States, established in 1965 the Border Industrialization Program. Designed to generate jobs in Mexican border-cities through establishment of assembly plants, or *maquiladoras*, the program initially enjoyed modest success. Beginning in 1984, stimulated by simplified regulations and lower wages brought by the devalued peso, the industry saw yearly increases in employment that averaged more than 20 percent on an annual basis, as shown in Table 1.

The importance of the *maquiladora* industry to the border region should not be underestimated. On the Mexican side of the international boundary, the industry stimulated significant job creation and produced a group of managers and technical personnel in an industry that was competitive on a world level. Other areas of Mexican industry were not globally competitive since Mexican economic development policy from the 1940s favoured import substitution industrialization, heavy protection for national producers, and great state participation in the economy with parastate industries and companies of all sorts. The *maquiladora* industry, through job creation and investment, helped the northern border became one of the most economically dynamic regions of Mexico, even during the severe economic downturn of the early and mid-1980s.

For decades the most visible element of border economic integration from the perspective of the U.S. border communities was through retail purchases made by Mexican shoppers on the U.S. side of the border. Mexico's northern border was a free zone that recognized the northern economy's isolation from the Mexican national economy and close linkages to the U.S. economy. This policy, which continues currently, acknowledges that enforcement of customs regulations by Mexico at the

---

10 Lawrence A. Herzog, "Border Commuter Workers and Transfrontier Metropolitan Structures along the United States–Mexico Border," *Journal of Borderlands Studies*, 5, No. 2 (Fall 1990), pp. 1–20.

11 Paul Ganster, "Affordable Housing in San Diego and Tijuana and Transborder Linkages," unpublished manuscript, 1993.

TABLE 1. NUMBER OF PLANTS AND WORKERS
IN THE *MAQUILADORA* INDUSTRY, 1974–1994

Year	Number of Plants	Annual Growth Rate: Plants	Number of Jobs	Annual Growth Rate: Jobs
1974	455	—	75,974	—
1975	454	–0.2	67,214	–11.3
1976	448	–1.3	74,496	10.8
1977	443	–1.1	78,433	5.3
1978	457	3.2	90,704	15.6
1979	540	18.2	111,365	22.8
1980	620	14.8	119,546	7.3
1981	605	–2.4	130,973	9.6
1982	585	–3.3	127,048	–3.0
1983	600	2.6	150,857	18.7
1984	672	12.0	199,684	32.4
1985	750	13.1	211,968	6.2
1986	890	17.1	249,833	17.9
1987	1,125	26.4	305,253	22.2
1988	1,396	24.1	369,489	21.0
1989	1,665	18.6	429,725	16.3
1990	1,938	17.1	460,258	7.1
1991	1,914	–1.2	467,352	1.5
1992	2,075	8.4	505,698	8.2
1993	2,166	4.4	540,927	7.0
Average Annual Growth Rate of Plants and Jobs				
1974–78		0.1		4.5
1978–84		6.6		14.1
1984–93		13.9		11.7

Source: Comisión Económica para América Latina y el Caribe, *México: La industria maquiladora* (N.P.: 28 October 1994, LC/MEX/R.495), Table 30, based on data from Instituto Nacional de Estadística, Geografía e Informática.

international boundary was futile. Many U.S. border communities reported significant negative impacts with the peso devaluations of 1976, 1982, and 1994–1995 that decreased the value of the peso versus the dollar and made it difficult for many Mexicans to continue to cross into the United States to shop.[12]

The expansion of the *maquiladora* industry in the early 1980s coincided with a decline in Mexican retail purchases. Many local officials in U.S. border communities noted the positive economic impact of establishment of *maquiladoras* in adjacent Mexican twin cities and began to actively recruit U.S. and other companies to relocate to the Mexican side of the border. For the first time, many business and political leaders as well as members of the general public in U.S. border communities became aware of the symbiotic relationship with their Mexican neighbours. Beginning in the mid-1980s, then, U.S. border communities began to see significant opportunities in expanded economic relations with Mexico. This was particularly true in the smaller U.S. border communities, especially along the lower Rio Grande in Texas, where regional economies were narrowly based on agriculture and Mexican retail purchases.[13] These communities viewed *maquiladoras* as an opportunity to broaden the regional economic base and actively recruited companies to locate across the border in nearby Mexican cities. This change in mentality led to strong support in border communities for the North American Free Trade Agreement that took effect January 1, 1994. It also culminated in enhanced border interactions in areas of life other that those strictly related to trade and commerce, pushing U.S. and Mexican border-communities to cooperation on many fronts.

---

12 See, for example, "Impact of the Peso Devaluation on Retail Sales in San Diego County," *San Diego Economic Bulletin*, 33 (March 1985), and the *Impact of Increased United States–Mexico Trade on Southern Border Development* (Washington, D.C.: United States International Trade Commission, 1986). The effects of the December 1994–January 1995 devaluation of the peso are still not clear.

13 Jerry R. Ladman, "The U.S. Border Regional Economy: Interdependence, Growth and Prospects for Change," in Stanley R. Ross and Jerry R. Ladman, eds., *Views Across the Border*, 2nd ed. (Tempe: Latin American Center, Arizona State University, forthcoming). Of course, the *maquila*-generated employment benefitted Mexican border cities economies as well. Salvador Mendoza Higuera et al., "Tijuana: Short-Term Growth and Long-Term Development," in Norris C. Clement and Eduardo Zepeda Miramontes, eds., *San Diego–Tijuana in Transition: A Regional Analysis* (San Diego: Institute for Regional Studies of the Californias, San Diego State University, 1993), pp. 57–64.

Restructuring the Mexican Economy. Over the course of the last decade, Mexico has undergone a profound revolution in its economic development policy, changing from a highly protected domestic economy with strict controls on imports and foreign investment and heavy state participation in many sectors of the economy to an open economy with liberalized import and investment laws.[14] These changes have been important for the border region.

The changes in Mexico's economic policy initiated under the presidency of Miguel de la Madrid (1982–1988) and continued under Carlos Salinas de Gortari (1988–1994) have significantly altered the economic relations between the United States and Mexico. Mexico's decision to enter GATT (General Agreement on Tariffs and Trade) in 1986 quickly produced the elimination of import licences and reduction of tariffs, providing much greater access for U.S. exporters to Mexican markets. Additional changes in Mexico's trade, investment, real estate, and *maquiladora* laws and regulations followed, and these measures liberalizing the Mexican economy produced a significant increase in United States–Mexican trade. Since most bilateral trade moved goods by land transportation, trade-related activities boomed in the border cities. At the same time, infrastructure in the border cities, including customs facilities, ports of entry, and roads became saturated.

North American Free Trade Agreement. In the spring of 1990, President Salinas requested that Mexico and the United States discuss implementation of a free-trade agreement between the two countries. Canada, which already had a free-trade agreement with the United States, joined in and the three countries negotiated the North American Free Trade Agreement that took effect on 1 January 1994. Debate over approval of NAFTA was particularly intense in the United States Congress and focused national attention on environmental conditions in the border region and potential impacts of the treaty on border communities. In response to strong criticism of existing governmental efforts on the border environment, U.S. and Mexican authorities developed the Integrated Border Environmental Plan of the United States–Mexico Border Region (IBEP).[15] Other important actions included negotiation by Mexico and the United States of side agreements to NAFTA that led to the establishment of the North American Development ment Bank (NADBANK) and the Border Environmental Cooperation

---

14 "Mexico. Foreign Investment Report. Winter 1994/1995" (México, D.F.: U.S. Embassy, 1994).

15 U.S. Environmental Protection Agency and Secretaría de Desarrollo Social, *Integrated Environmental Plan for the Mexican–U.S. Border Area (First Stage, 1992–1994)* (Washington, D.C.: USEPA, 1994).

Commission (BECC). The BECC will analyze border environmental issues and certify priority infrastructure projects for funding by NADBANK.

The recent history of the border region, culminating with the NAFTA process, has seen a fundamental change in the role that the border region plays domestically in Mexico and the United States and also internationally in the bilateral relationship. Historically, the border has been politically marginalized in the polity of Mexico and the United States. The NAFTA process helped transform the border from a region that merely received policy from Washington, D.C. and Mexico City to a region that began to initiate actions that became national and bilateral policy. The border was a key to the passage of NAFTA and will likely retain a strategic role in the unfolding economic integration of the two partners.

After one year of NAFTA, many of the hopes of the supporters of NAFTA have been realized with respect to Mexico–United States trade. During the first nine months of NAFTA, American exports to Mexico grew 22 percent and imports from Mexico expanded 23 percent. The United States' surplus on this trade was up to $1.8 billion and the U.S. Department of Commerce estimated that this expansion of exports to Mexico accounted for 130,000 U.S. jobs.[16] At the end of 1994 a note of uncertainty was interjected into NAFTA as Mexico fell into a severe economic crisis that was compounded by the transition from the Salinas presidency to that of Ernesto Zedillo on 1 December 1994, and a continuing series of political crises, including the Chiapas rebellion, disputed gubernatorial elections, and the assassination of several prominent political leaders. A devaluation of the peso, by as much as 40 percent relative to the dollar at the end of the year and early in 1995, had predictable impacts on the border region in terms of decreases in Mexican shoppers in U.S. border cities. The devaluation severely affected the middle class in Mexico's border cities, where many expenses such as rents are pegged to the value of the dollar. However, it is too soon to determine what the long-term effects of this period of economic adjustment will be.

MAJOR CHARACTERISTICS OF THE BORDER REGION

Historical forces have produced a border region of some diversity from east to west. For example, on the U.S. side, the eastern half of the border is poorer, more Hispanic, and with a narrower economic base than on the western end, which is wealthier, has a broader economic base, and is

---

16 For discussions of the first year of NAFTA, see "Happy Ever NAFTA?" *The Economist*, 333, No. 7893 (December 10, 1994); Jim Weddell, "NAFTA, One Year After," *Hispanic*, 7, No. 10 (November 1994), pp. 52–56.

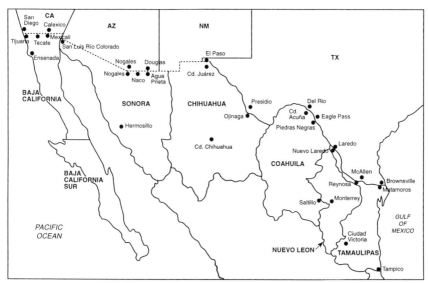

Figure 1. United States–Mexico Border Region.

more Anglo in population and culture. On the Mexican side, there is also some east-west differentiation, principally with respect to economic development. The western end of the Mexican border is more dynamic economically than elsewhere along the border. There are also strong contrasts from north to south across the border. The human settlement of the borderlands is one of twin cities separated by expanses of lightly populated deserts, mountains, or in the lower Rio Grande, agricultural land or undeveloped rolling plains with scrub vegetation. Figure 1 illustrates clearly the twin-city settlement patterns of the border region.

While the natural systems extend seamlessly across the border, the international boundary marks a very clear dividing line between two very different human systems. Some features of these systems do not extend across the border; others demonstrate a surprising degree of transboundary interaction with counterpart features from the other country. A review of the different components of the Mexican and U.S. systems that meet at the border will serve to highlight the extent of integration present in this transboundary zone.

Political and Legal Systems. The juxtaposition at the border of the highly centralized Mexican political system with the decentralized federal U.S. political system has broad implications for the daily lives of border residents. The differences in the two political systems historically have hindered bilateral cooperation on transborder issues of importance to border residents. While the foreign-relations departments (the U.S.

Department of State and the Secretaría de Relaciones Exteriores [SRE]) are technically in charge of developing and implementing foreign policy, the Mexican SRE is much more successful than its U.S. counterpart in controlling and supervising transborder contacts and relations between Mexican government agencies at the state, local, and federal levels and their counterparts in the United States. Due to the federal system of the United States, many different government agencies make decisions with foreign implications; in effect, they are making foreign policy. Thus, at the federal level, the U.S. Department of Agriculture, U.S. Customs Service, Immigration and Naturalization Service, Environmental Protection Agency, Department of Commerce, and many others regularly implement decisions that have concrete impacts on the transborder region. Agencies from the U.S. border states and from the city and county local governments likewise initiate policies that have importance for Mexico and its border region. While the U.S. State Department tries to monitor these actions, it does not attempt to enforce absolute control. However, in Mexico, policy tends to emanate mainly from, and is more tightly controlled by, SRE.

This same centralized/decentralized dichotomy is visible in differences of the two legal systems that stand in sharp relief at the border. Water law is a good illustration of this point. In the United States, jurisdiction over underground water supplies, even those that cross state and international boundaries, is with the different states. In Mexico, however, water law is federal law. The government of Mexico could negotiate an arrangement with the United States to resolve the problem of unregulated exploitation of critical transborder aquifers that supply most of the water for the twin cities of El Paso, Texas, and Ciudad Juárez, Chihuahua. However, the U.S. government cannot negotiate a groundwater treaty without changing water law in four states—California, Texas, Arizona, and New Mexico—a nearly impossible task.[17]

Historically, the border region was neglected by both federal governments. Far removed geographically from the national capitals, the border region did not have large and important political constituencies. In the Mexican case, the traditional forces of regionalism meant that Mexico City viewed the northern border with suspicion. The border region typically has been a pawn in the relations between the two countries. Often federal decisions that affected the border region were made for reasons unrelated to the border. For example, at various times, the U.S. government has ordered increased inspections of incoming pedestrians and vehicles at the ports of entry on the United States–Mexico border to discourage the southward movement of tourists, causing great

---

17 Robert D. Hayton and Albert O. Utton, *Transboundary Groundwaters: The Bellagio Draft Treaty* (Albuquerque: CIRT, University of New Mexico, 1990).

economic hardship in the tourist-dependent Mexican border-communities. The real purpose of these actions was to pressure the Mexican government to improve its cooperation on drug-trafficking matters. Typically, policies and decisions made in the national capitals had a big impact on the border, yet border residents had little input in these decisions.

Differences in the political and administrative structures often make local transborder cooperation difficult. Direct administrative counterparts often do not exist in each of the twin cities. Usually, local government agencies in the United States are able to initiate projects independently and develop financing. Mexican local agencies usually are not only constrained by restricted mandates for independent action, but have extremely limited financial and technical resources and trained human capital.[18]

Another difference in the political and public administration systems of the two countries that has important implications for local border relations is the nature of public service and office holding. In the United States, the majority of local, state, and federal government employees fall under various sorts of civil-service systems. This assures that the professional staffs most responsible for the day-to-day running of agencies will remain in place even when there is a change in the elected officials. In Mexico, the situation is quite different. There, with the change of administrations, whether federal, state, or local, government employees at all levels are replaced by new political appointments. Hence, continuity and institutional memory are much more fragmented in public administration on the Mexican side of the border. An additional element is that in Mexico upward career movement often means jumping from agency to agency through a series of political appointments. While this produces individuals with significant experience in many areas of government, it tends to work against the most capable people staying in one agency to provide leadership and continuing expertise. Bureaucrats in the United States tend to advance careers through promotion within the same agency, continually upgrading their knowledge and skills in that one particular area. Thus, all of these factors constitute bottlenecks for effective binational governmental cooperation.[19]

---

18 Administrative complexities regarding transborder environmental projects are discussed in Clifton G. Metzner, Jr., ed., *Water Quality Issues of the California–Baja California Border Region* (San Diego: Institute for Regional Studies of the Californias, San Diego State University, 1988).

19 Many problems of transborder government communication are discussed by Joseph Nalven, "An 'Airy Tale along the Border," *New Scholar*, 9 (1984), pp. 171–199.

Economic Asymmetries. A key characteristic of the economic relationship between the two neighbours, and one that is especially apparent in the border region, is economic asymmetry. The 1994 Gross Domestic Product (GDP) of the United States was $6,600 billion, approximately 18 times that of Mexico's GDP of $373 billion. The Gross Regional Product (GRP) of the greater Los Angeles area exceeds the GDP of Mexico, but with one-tenth the population. At the border regional level, the County of San Diego has a GRP of over $60 billion and that of the Municipality of Tijuana is probably around $3 billion. The combined annual governmental budgets of the County of San Diego and the City of San Diego are equivalent to the GRP of the Municipality of Tijuana. Although such marked asymmetry is less marked elsewhere along the border, the disparities are still significant.

These enormous economic asymmetries make transborder cooperation by government entities difficult due to the great differences in physical and human resources available to each side. Attempts to collaborate on regional transborder air-monitoring have been repeatedly frustrated because Mexican agencies have not had trained personnel, laboratories, and monitoring equipment, and thus felt they could not participate equitably in a binational effort.[20] Joint environmental infrastructure projects, for instance, repeatedly have been stillborn because of financial and technical constraints on Mexican administrative units, not because Mexicans lacked interest in cooperation.

Demographic Features. The United States–Mexico border region, for purposes of population studies, is best defined by administrative units adjacent to the border: 25 counties in the states of California, Arizona, New Mexico, and Texas; and 35 municipalities in the Mexican states of Tamaulipas, Nuevo León, Coahuila, Chihuahua, Sonora, and Baja California. The demographic picture for this region is complex, for not only are two countries involved, but the border zone is one of the most dynamic regions demographically and economically in each country. Reliable data that are comparable across the border are generally difficult to obtain for the border region, so precise analysis of demographic characteristics is not always possible.[21]

Both U.S. and Mexican border populations are highly urbanized, as seen in Table 2. The more arid western end of the border tends to be more highly urbanized than the eastern end in the lower Rio Grande Valley, where more small, agricultural-based settlements exist in the areas

---

20 Nalven, in "An 'Airy Tale," makes this point.

21 John R. Weeks and Roberto Ham Chande, *Demographic Dynamics of the U.S.–Mexico Border* (El Paso: Texas Western Press, 1992).

TABLE 2. URBANIZATION OF BORDER MUNICIPALITIES AND COUNTIES

Municipality or County	Percent of Population in Urban Core
Tijuana, Baja California	81.0
San Diego, California	93.2
Ciudad Juárez, Chihuahua	96.0
El Paso, Texas	96.1
Webb County, Texas (City of Laredo)	95.7
Nuevo Laredo, Tamaulipas	98.0
Santa Cruz, Arizona (City of Nogales)	76.7
Nogales, Sonora	97.0
Cameron County, Texas (City of Brownsville)	74.0
Matamoros, Tamaulipas	78.9

Source: Data for the Mexican border municipalities are for 1970 and are from Mario Margulis and Rodolfo Turián, *Nuevos patrones de crecimiento social en la frontera norte: La emigración, documentos de trabajo* (México D.F.: El Colegio de México, Centro de Estudios Demográficos y de Desarrollo Urbano, 1983), Table C2; U.S. data are for 1980 and are from the *County and City Data Book*.

outside the urban cores. The Municipality of Tijuana's lower level of urbanization is due to development of luxury housing along the coastal strip and emergence of outlying urbanized areas such as Rosarito.

In addition to urban concentration, border populations have been, and continue to be, distinguished by rapid growth rates. Swift demographic expansion has brought a continuing infrastructure- and urban-services crisis in border cities, particularly in the Mexican cities that had fewer resources and ability to cope with the burgeoning demand. Table 3 clearly demonstrates this urban dynamism. The populations of both the Mexican and the U.S. border zones have, over the long run, exceeded natural growth rates. Migration is the most important factor shaping the demographic picture of the binational border region. For example, Tijuana's population grew 6.9 percent between 1987 and 1988; 1.9 percent of the growth was natural increase and 5 percent was the result of immigration. During the same period, Ciudad Juárez saw a 1.8 percent

TABLE 3. ANNUAL GROWTH RATES OF TWIN CITIES BY DECADE

City	1940–1950	1950–1960	1960–1970	1970–1980	1980–1990
San Diego	6.4	7.1	2.1	2.6	2.4
Tijuana	13.4	9.8	6.4	4	5.0
Calexico	1.9	2.4	3.3	4.3	2.6
Mexicali	12.8	10.4	4.4	2.5	2.5
Nogales, AZ	2.0	1.8	2.3	7.5	2.2
Nogales, Sonora	7.7	6.3	3.4	2.7	4.9
El Paso	3.5	11.2	1.6	3.2	1.9
Ciudad Juárez	9.4	7.5	5.1	3.3	3.8
Eagle Pass	1.3	6.6	2.7	3.9	−.4
Piedras Negras	7.6	7.6	−.04	7.2	3.6
Laredo, TX	3.1	1.8	1.4	3.3	3.0
Nuevo Laredo	7.0	4.9	5.0	3.0	0.8
McAllen, TX	6.9	6.3	1.5	7.6	2.4
Reynosa	3.4	8.1	6.6	3.4	3.2
Brownsville	6.1	7.5	9.1	6.2	1.5
Matamoros, Tamaulipas	11.0	7.3	4.2	3.1	3.5

Source: For the United States, Peter L. Reich, ed., *Statistical Abstract of the United States–Mexico Borderlands* (Los Angeles: UCLA Latin American Center Publications, 1984), and *County and City Data Book*, 1983. For Mexico, Margulis and Turián, Cuadro C2. The 1980–1990 annual growth rates are calculated from David Lorey, ed., *United States–Mexico Border Statistics since 1900. 1990 Update* (Los Angeles: UCLA Latin American Center Publications, 1993).

natural increase and a 7.5 percent increase from migration.[22] In 1980, 48.9 percent of the population of the border counties and municipalities consisted of migrants. Of the 48.9 percent, 8.4 percent were from a foreign country. The 1980 population of the Mexican border municipalities had 31.8 percent migrants while the figure for the U.S. border counties was 58.2 percent. Eleven percent of the migrants in the Mexican border municipalities were foreign born while the figure was a much larger 20 percent for the U.S. border counties.[23]

U.S. border communities are further distinguished by considerable numbers of undocumented immigrants who are primarily from Mexico. For example, estimates for San Diego County indicate that there were about 96,000 undocumented aliens in San Diego County by the end of 1986. For 1993, estimates of undocumented immigrants in San Diego County are as high as 220,000.[24] Most of these individuals are Mexicans. The data in Table 5 show that most illegal aliens arrested in the San Diego region and elsewhere along the border are from Mexico, and it is reasonable to conclude that the preponderance of undocumented aliens in the border region are Mexicans.

The growing number of Spanish-speaking individuals in the United States, largely in the Southwest, and the close personal ties they have with Mexico is another factor that adds to the commonality of interests and interdependence between the two countries at the border. The Hispanic, or Latino, percentage in border cities has been significant and is increasing, as illustrated by Table 4. The growth rate of this segment of the population is considerably higher than the majority Anglo sector. While the total U.S. population increased 11.5 percent from 1970 to 1980, the Hispanic population increased 61 percent during that same period. Approximately 60 percent of the growth of the Hispanic population is due to natural increase; the remainder is due to immigration. Thus, the

22 David E. Lorey, ed., *United States–Mexico Border Statistics since 1900* (Los Angeles: UCLA Latin American Center Publications, 1990), Table S129, pp. 53 ff.

23 U.S. Department of Commerce, Bureau of Census, *County and City Data Book*, 10th edition (Washington, D.C.: U.S. Government Printing Office, 1983), and Peter L. Reich, *Statistical Abstract of the United States–Mexico Borderlands* (Los Angeles: UCLA Latin American Center Publications, 1984).

24 Joseph Nalven, *Impacts and Undocumented Persons: The Quest for Usable Data in San Diego County, 1974–1986* (San Diego: Institute for Regional Studies of the Californias, San Diego State University, 1986); R.A. Parker and L.M. Rea, *Illegal Immigration in San Diego County: An Analysis of Costs and Revenues* (Sacramento: California Legislation, Senate Special Committee on Border Issues, 1993).

TABLE 4. PERCENT LATINO POPULATION OF U.S. BORDER CITIES

City	1980, percent Latino	1990, percent Latino
Los Angeles	27.5	34.6
San Diego	14.9	20.7
El Paso	62.5	68.9
Laredo	93.0[a]	93.5
Brownsville	87.3[a]	89.8

[a] 1985 data.
Source: *Statistical Abstract of Latin America*, 25 (Los Angeles: UCLA Latin American Center Publications, 1987), Table 667; 1990 data from *1990 Census of Population and Housing* (Washington, D.C.: Bureau of Census, 1991).

combination of declining growth rates for the Anglo population, high natural rates of increase for Hispanics, and Hispanic immigration is dramatically shifting the ethnic composition of border states such as California.[25] In border cities like San Diego, this "Hispanization" process is especially apparent. The decade 1980–1990 saw the local Hispanic population increase from 14.9 percent to 22 percent of the total population. The border region is becoming more Hispanic, which has interesting political implications, both domestically and internationally, particularly in regions such as San Diego, where the shift from Anglo to Latino has been dramatic.[26]

25 *Characteristics of California Population: 1985 Update and Projections to 1990, 1995, 2000* (Palo Alto: Center for Continuing Study of the California Economy, 1986), p. 204; "1990 Census. Race and Hispanic Origin Population Change, 1980–1990," *INFO* (March–April 1991), publication of SANDAG, San Diego Association of Governments.

26 The connection between the Latino population and U.S. and Mexican foreign policy is explored in R.R. Fagen, "The Politics of the United States–Mexico Relationship," in C.W. Reynolds and C. Tello, eds., *U.S.–Mexico Relations: Economic and Social Aspects* (Stanford: Stanford University Press, 1983), p. 344; R.O. de la Garza, "Chicanos and U.S. Foreign Policy: The Future of Chicano-Mexican Relations," J. Gómez-Quiñones, "Notes on an Interpretation of the Relations Between the Mexican Community in the United States and Mexico," and C.H. Zazueta, "Mexican Political Actors in the United States and Mexico: Historical and Political Contexts of a Dialogue Renewed," in C. Vásquez and M. García y Griego, eds., *Mexican–U.S. Relations: Conflict and Convergence* (Los Angeles: Chicano Studies Research Center and Latin American Center, 1983).

TABLE 5. ARRESTS OF UNDOCUMENTED IMMIGRANTS
BY U.S. BORDER PATROL
(ALL FIGURES BY FISCAL YEAR, OCTOBER 1–SEPTEMBER 30)

Year (Fiscal Year)	United States–Mexican Border			San Diego Sector (San Diego County, Parts of Riverside County)		
	Total	Mexicans	OTMs (Other than Mexican)	Total	Mexicans	OTMs (Other than Mexican)
1986	1,615,844	1,573,068	42,776	629,656	614,608	15,048
1987	1,122,067	1,099,577	22,490	500,327	492,276	8,051
1988	942,561	912,753	29,808	431,592	420,580	11,012
1989	852,506	807,932	44,574	366,757	355,136	11,621
1990	1,049,321	1,020,256	29,065	473,323	465,794	7,529
1991	1,077,876	1,058,078	19,702	540,347	535,709	4,638
1992	1,145,574	1,132,148	13,426	565,581	562,487	3,094
1993	1,212,886	1,195,951	16,935	531,689	526,851	4,838
1994	979,101	963,132	15,969	450,152	445,990	4,162

Source: Immigration and Naturalization Service, Statistics Division, Washington, D.C.

Border Culture. The presence of Hispanic populations on both sides of the international boundary, stimulated by important transboundary economic ties, has encouraged strong social and cultural linkages. Although difficult to quantify, these social and cultural aspects of interdependency are nonetheless real and growing. Oscar Martínez, in his recent work titled *Border People*, as well as in earlier works, discusses the emergence of groups of borderlanders who participate in a vibrant border culture that is firmly linked to Mexico and to the United States.[27] These individuals, who are able to function in both cultures and to participate in activities on both sides of the border, in some ways represent the future of the border. At the current level of interdependence, the percentage of these persons in the total border population is not large, but as the region moves towards more advanced integration the number of specialists who are fully functional on either side of the border will increase.

In a number of areas along the border, binational cultural activities are prospering. Transboundary cultural events in fine arts, classical and contemporary music, and literature are ubiquitous. The California–Baja California border region has a growing tradition of border literature. Symphony halls in Mexicali, Tijuana, and San Diego regularly draw patrons from the other side of the border. San Diego's Museum of Contemporary Art and the Centro Cultural in Tijuana have initiated projects on border art and art of the other nation, and a binational group of artists—the Border Art Workshop/Taller de Arte Fronterizo—is active on both sides of the border.[28] The San Diego Repertory Theater offers plays in Spanish, not only for the U.S. Spanish-speaking population, but also for the Mexican audience. The San Diego–Tijuana Sister Cities Society, which first became active in 1993, has concentrated on these sorts of

---

27 Oscar J. Martínez, *Border People: Life and Society in the U.S.–Mexico Borderlands* (Tucson: University of Arizona, 1994), and his "Border People and Transnational Interaction," in Paul Ganster and Eugenio O. Valenciano, eds., *The Mexican–U.S. Border Region and the Free Trade Agreement* (San Diego: Institute for Regional Studies of the Californias, San Diego State University, 1992), pp. 97–104.

28 For examples of border literature, see José Manuel Di-Bella, Sergio Gómez Montero, and Harry Polkinhorn, eds., *Mexican/American Border Writing. Literatura de frontera México/Estados Unidos* (Mexicali and San Diego: Dirección de Asuntos Culturales de la Secretaría de Educación Pública y Bienestar Social and Institute for Regional Studies of the Californias, San Diego State University, 1987) and Harry Polkinhorn, Gabriel Trujillo Muñoz, and Rogelio Reyes, eds., *The Line: Essays on Mexican/American Literature* (Calexico and Mexicali: Binational Press of San Diego State University and the Universidad Autónoma de Baja California, 1988).

cultural activities with considerable success in bringing people together from both sides of the border.

Transboundary linkages are also to be seen all along the border in the area of popular culture. *Corridos* and other traditional Mexican folk songs are encountered everywhere in the binational border region, as are traditions in popular literature and folk tales, humour, folk medicine, and other beliefs. Youth movements, such as that of the *cholos* from East Los Angeles, spread to U.S. and Mexican border cities and ultimately to Mexico City.[29] Sports are also a feature of the transboundary popular cultural life. Professional and intercollegiate athletic teams regularly draw fans from the other side of the boundary.

Higher Education in the Border Region. An aspect of culture that is of great importance in the border region is higher education, for these institutions train the leaders who will manage the region in the future.[30] The border has seen a slow process of transborder cooperation on faculty research, faculty exchange, student exchange, and joint programs. The process is now moving more rapidly, under the impetus of NAFTA, as more students, faculty, and administrators realize that to be competitive, university graduates must be able to operate on both sides of the border, in both languages and cultures.

Relations between universities in Mexico and the United States along the border have to some extent paralleled broader social and economic trends and relations between the two countries. Until relatively recently, the Mexican university system was poorly developed in terms of physical and human capital. Resources were largely concentrated in Mexico City, which exacerbated the position of provincial and border institutions. Over the course of the last decade, a number of Mexican border universities have shown a significant growth and development, and thus have been

---

29 See José Manuel Valenzuela Arce, *A la brava ése* (Tijuana: El Colegio de la Frontera Norte, 1988), for a discussion of *cholos*. Also see Steven Loza, *Barrio Rhythms: Mexican American Music in Los Angeles* (Champaign: University of Illinois Press, 1993) for a discussion of the influence of Los Angeles barrio music on Mexico.

30 Paul Ganster, "Education, the Border Region, and Free Trade," *Proceedings of the Annual Meeting of the Rocky Mountain Council on Latin American Studies, 1991* (Albuquerque: Center for Latin American Studies, University of New Mexico, 1992), and his "La educación superior en la frontera México–Estados Unidos ante el TLC," *Comercio Exterior*, 44, No. 3 (marzo 1994), pp. 242–248; Judith I. Gill and Lilian Alvarez de Testa, *Understanding the Differences: An Essay on Higher Education in Mexico and the United States* (Denver: Western Interstate Commission for Higher Education, 1994).

more able to engage in productive interactions with counterpart entities in the United States.

In part, the emergence of border universities is the result of the oil boom of the 1970s that generated funds to send many Mexicans abroad for Ph.D. or Master's training; the deteriorating quality of life in Mexico City which has led many young scholars to relocate to the border and the provinces; a conscious attempt to decentralize higher education in Mexico; and the relative prosperity of Mexico's northern border during the economic crisis of the 1980s. Baja California particularly saw qualitative changes in higher education in the late 1970s and early 1980s with the establishment of a number of scientific research centres in Ensenada, the establishment of El Colegio de la Frontera Norte (COLEF) in Tijuana and other border cities, and the emergence of research and graduate programs within the different units of the Universidad Autónoma de Baja California (UABC). By the mid-1990s, Mexican universities in Ciudad Juárez, including the Universidad Autónoma de Ciudad Juárez, the Instituto Tecnológico de Ciudad Juárez, the Ciudad Juárez branch of the Instituto Tecnológico y de Estudios Superiores de Monterrey (Monterrey Tec), and the Ciudad Juárez office of COLEF, had developed new research interests and cooperative working arrangements across the border. As well, Monterrey Tec had established a strong presence in all Mexican border states except for Baja California.

As more of a parity relationship has emerged between Mexican and U.S. border universities, collaboration and exchange activities have increased. Over time, many faculty from the Mexican institutions have obtained advanced degrees at U.S. border universities and faculty for the U.S. border universities have taught at Mexican border universities. These contacts have sometimes led to establishment of joint research projects and student and individual faculty exchange programs. The oldest centre of transborder university cooperation is probably the El Paso–Ciudad Juárez area, with the University of Texas, El Paso (UTEP), taking the lead in collaboration with counterparts at the Universidad Autónoma de Chihuahua and the Universidad Autónoma de Ciudad Juárez. These relationships have been facilitated by the presence of a large group of border scholars at UTEP and the practice of permitting students from Ciudad Juárez to study at UTEP, paying the same fees as Texas students. The most active centre of transborder university cooperation is in the California–Baja California region. For many years faculty from San Diego State University (SDSU) have taught courses at a number of Baja California institutions, including UABC, COLEF, and Centro de Enseñanza Técnica y Superior (CETYS), and faculty from Mexican border universities regularly teach courses at SDSU.

Recently, some U.S. and Mexican universities in the border region have begun to explore ways to increase interaction of Mexican and U.S. students. For example, SDSU and UABC in 1994 launched a cooperative program in international business. In this program, students from UABC, and CETYS University will spend significant amounts of time at SDSU and Southwestern College, a community college in San Diego. SDSU students will likewise study on the other side of the border at UABC or CETYS University. Participant students will graduate with degrees from SDSU and from either UABC or CETYS. The international dual degree was devised rather than a joint degree program due to regulatory issues and differences in the structures of undergraduate education in the two countries.

Although there is movement in the direction of better articulation of Mexican and U.S. universities in the border region, much more change is needed to adequately serve the needs of the region, now and in the future. This contrasts strongly with Europe, where joint advanced degree and research programs have been created in the Regio Basiliensis region of France, Switzerland, and Germany, and an area-wide undergraduate program for the European Economic Community has been developed. Nevertheless, U.S. and Mexican border universities have taken a leadership role on bilateral cooperation and programmatic development, reversing the traditional role of the border region. Instead of simply following national trends, the border region is providing innovation in this important area.

BORDER ISSUES

As the United States–Mexican border region has grown and developed, new areas of conflict have emerged as traditional issues have continued. The border location makes the ordinary business of public administration and resolution of routine issues much more difficult and complicated than might otherwise be the case. Concerns that might have a relatively simple domestic solution often become quite complicated in a transborder, international framework. The next section provides an overview of the most important issues that affect border communities.

Environmental Issues. Mexico and the United States have very different traditions regarding environmental protection and policies. Mexico has been more concerned with creation of jobs and providing people with basic services such as potable water rather than with preventing and cleaning up industrial pollution or with providing sewage treatment and collection. Mexican officials often felt that environmental protection and rigorous standards were a luxury that developing countries could afford but were an unfair burden for Mexico. These different approaches to the environment stood out in strong contrast at the border and were, at times, a source of conflict between twin-city communities and between countries.

At the border, not only is there often a lack of agreement as to exactly what constitutes environmental problems, but there are great differences in economic resources available for environmental protection. And when the two sides agree that an environmental problem does exist, often there is a significant difference in opinions as to how remediation should be undertaken. U.S. policymakers tend to favour large and costly engineering solutions that depend on relatively sophisticated and expensive technology. Mexican decision-makers tend to favour less expensive, low-technology solutions. It is interesting to note that in the 1990s, U.S. border communities faced with new budgetary constraints are now beginning to look more at low-technology, low-impact solutions to environmental infrastructure issues instead of the usual high-technology, high-cost approaches.

I. Water Quality and Supply Problems.[31] The United States–Mexican border region is characterized by its aridity, particularly on the central and western parts of the border, and many of the regions of the border find water in short supply for the growing urban populations and agricultural enterprises. San Diego currently imports about 95 percent of its water from the Colorado River and from northern California; Tijuana increasingly depends upon water imported through an aqueduct from the Colorado River. El Paso and Ciudad Juárez rely on underground water supplies that are shared, but not regulated, and are projected to last only another 15 to 20 years. The major population centres of the border do not have a secure supply for this basic resource.

Since all surface waters in the border region are fully allocated by international treaties and since groundwater deposits are very limited, there is simply no more new water available for future growth. The traditional wisdom in border communities has been that water reclamation, combined with conservation, is the only viable solution for providing an adequate long-term water supply for sustainable growth and development in the region. However, water reclamation involves significant capital costs for infrastructure and major energy costs for reclamation and pumping. Recently, attention has turned to an examination of developing water markets that would permit transfer of water from agriculture to urban uses. In the case of California, only five percent of agricultural water would have to be transferred to urban uses to assure an adequate supply for the foreseeable future. Participating in trans-

---

31 Metzner, *Water Quality Issues of the California–Baja California Border Region* , and Clifton G. Metzner, Jr., ed., *Water Quality Issues of the San Diego–Tijuana Border Region* (San Diego: Institute for Regional Studies of the Californias, San Diego State University, 1989) provide a discussion of water quality issues in this region, including low-technology and traditional solutions to the problems.

boundary water markets might be a viable alternative for Mexican border cities in order to avoid huge infrastructure costs.

The two major river systems of the border region are the Colorado River and the Rio Grande. Both of the basins have in the past been subjected to intensive development through irrigation, storage, and flood control projects. Those on the Colorado River include the Hoover Dam that provides management primarily for production of hydroelectricity. Release of runoff downstream occurs according to the needs of electric power generation or when the storage system is at capacity; release of water is not timed for the benefit of downstream users, including Mexico.[32] The water resources of the Rio Grande are also well developed. The part of the watercourse shared by Mexico and the United States has seen the development of a series of international dams, jointly constructed and administered by the two countries.[33]

Surface and groundwater supplies are threatened everywhere along the border due to raw sewage dumping, fertilizer and pesticide contamination of agricultural runoff, and industrial- and hazardous-waste pollution. Pollution of these water sources in effect decreases the availability of water supplies, or at the very least, makes it more expensive to treat the water to the point where it is usable for human consumption. Pollution of groundwater resources also has the potential of permanently affecting the aquifers and eliminating those supplies from possible use by humans.

There are important problems of contamination of surface streams and rivers by sewage in all of the border twin-city pairs from Brownsville-Matamoros to San Diego–Tijuana. In most cases, this contamination has transboundary impacts. For nearly 50 years, authorities in San Diego have been concerned about renegade flows of sewage from Tijuana. For the past decade or so, the flow of sewage into the United States from Mexico has grown to its present level of about 12 million gallons per day (mgd). Although in 1988 Tijuana built a new treatment plant, it was soon over capacity and the amount of untreated wastewater continues to grow.

After years of difficult negotiations between Mexico and the United States, in the fall of 1989, Presidents Bush and Salinas signed an agreement to build a binational treatment plant on the U.S. side to treat sewage

---

32 See Gary D. Weatherford and F. Lee Brown, eds., *New Courses for the Colorado River: Major Issues for the Next Century* (Albuquerque: University of New Mexico Press, 1986) for a discussion of the Colorado River and the use of its waters.

33 See, for example, Stephen P. Mumme, "Engineering Diplomacy: The Evolving Role of the International Boundary and Water Commission in U.S.–Mexico Water Management," *Journal of Borderlands Studies*, 1, No. 1 (Spring 1986).

from Tijuana and from some areas of the southern part of San Diego. The project will be jointly financed, with the United States paying the majority of the cost. The plant will not be ready until 1996 or after, and it still faces a number of legal hurdles before full construction can begin.

Elsewhere along the border, serious sewage problems exist. All Mexican border cities discharge significant amounts of untreated sewage into the environment. Particularly problematic is the case of Mexicali, where the Río Nuevo passes through the Mexicali Valley and then through urban Mexicali where it receives discharges of raw sewage from residences and businesses, industrial waste, and the outflow from the municipal sewage treatment plant. The river then passes into the United States near Calexico in the Imperial Valley, and has been characterized as the most polluted river in the United States. Mexican authorities have initiated a program of enforcement of environmental codes and have obligated many industrial polluters to clean up their discharges into the river and sewage system. Within the last several years, State of California agencies have begun to work with Mexican authorities to evaluate point source pollution control projects in Mexicali, for the first time contemplating spending California and federal funds in Mexico on a binational project. This approach is the most cost-effective, given the lower cost of dealing with pollution before it enters a body of water, and represents an important change in attitude by Mexican and U.S. officials on resolution of border issues.[34]

All Mexican cities along the Rio Grande discharge raw sewage into that body of water.[35] These discharges have noticeably contributed to the deterioration of the quality of water in the river and have increased the costs of filtering and treating the water for human consumption. There is some concern that the contamination will also have negative effects on ecosystems near the mouth of the river. Many of the areas of the flood plain on the U.S. side are inhabited by poor Hispanics who have purchased lots from farmers who illegally subdivided agricultural fields. The subdivision residents, many of whom are illegal immigrants from Mexico, have constructed houses and for water supply have simply dug shallow wells into the high water-table of the flood plain. These wells not only are contaminated with agricultural chemicals but also with human waste, as they are often located relatively close to the pit privies installed by the occupants. These *colonias*, with a population of perhaps some 150,000, have chronic health problems related to the contaminated water supply,

---

34 See the presentation by Phil Gruenberg outlining these studies in Metzner, *Water Quality Issues of the California–Baja California Border Region.*

35 See Richard Alm and Bruce Tomaso, "Dirty Water: U.S. Must Live with Border Pollution or Aid Mexico's Cleanup," *Transborder Resources Report*, 4, No. 2 (Summer 1990).

including high rates of infectious hepatitis and infant diarrhea.[36] In fact, the health statistics are quite similar to those of the Mexican residents on the other side of the river.

II. Hazardous and Industrial Waste. With the growth of manufacturing and the *maquiladora* industry, there has been a great increase in industrial waste in the border region.[37] Largely because of the lack of infrastructure and regulatory and enforcement capacities in the border region, particularly in Mexico, only a small percentage of hazardous waste from border *maquilas* is being disposed of in a fashion that would meet generally acceptable international standards. The rest is being stored (often improperly), dumped in municipal landfills, or discharged into the wastewater collector system. Some individuals and groups have taken advantage of the border to illegally transport and dump hazardous materials on the Mexican side. So the traditional function of border regions as a haven for lawless elements has continued in new forms.

The chemical pollution of surface waters and groundwater has potentially serious consequences for the region's water supply. Reclamation is made impossible or prohibitively expensive when the water to be reused has significant chemical contamination. The treatment necessary to safely remove these contaminants is simply too expensive to justify reclaiming this polluted water. Improper disposal of waste has serious implications for human populations in the region.

III. Air Pollution. As the size of border twin-city pairs increased, air quality became an important transborder problem. The most serious cases are in the El Paso–Ciudad Juárez region and in the San Diego-Tijuana region. In these areas, air pollution is generated from sources in two countries and is transported by winds to affect the entire air basin. Sources of pollutants tend to differ on each side of the border. Uncontrolled burning of trash, industrial air pollution from cement factories in urban areas, dust raised from vehicular traffic on unpaved streets, electrical power generation with fuel oil rather than natural gas, leaded fuel, poor maintenance of vehicles, lack of pollution-control equipment on motor vehicles, and the older vehicle fleet are particular problems on the Mexican side. Enforcement of U.S. federal and state air quality regulations has brought improvement regarding pollution sources on the U.S. side—including significant reduction in industrial pollutants and motor-vehicle pollutants—but the continued growth of populations and numbers of vehicles has made improvement in quality of air difficult. A

---

36 David C. Warner, "Health Issues at the U.S.–Mexican Border," *Journal of the American Medical Association*, 265, No. 2 (January 9, 1991).

37 *Integrated Environmental Plan for the Mexican–U.S. Border Area* provides data on this.

complicating factor for the San Diego–Tijuana regions is the periodic transportation by prevailing wind of pollution from the Los Angeles air basin. At every border town, long lines of idling vehicles at the border crossings, in part due to drug-interdiction policies of the U.S. Customs Service, contribute significantly to air pollution.

Topography and other features have combined to make El Paso almost continually in noncompliance with E.P.A. standards for air quality. In large part this is due to pollutants produced in Ciudad Juárez and to high levels of pollutants associated with the border crossing lines.[38] Consequently, until an international air basin pollution-control authority is established, little can be done to alleviate the situation in this twin-city pair. The El Paso–Ciudad Juárez region is leading the way with an innovative effort to develop an air-basin management authority, where both cities and countries would cooperate to protect a common resource.[39]

IV. Bioresource Issues. The impressive growth and development of the borderlands over the past decades have produced significant negative impacts on the native flora and fauna and ecosystems of the region. Expansion of urban areas, destruction of native habitats through grazing activities or agriculture, lowering the water table through excessive pumping of water deposits, and impacts of recreation on fragile eco-systems have all had important consequences on the border region. While efforts have been made to protect certain endangered species such as the masked bob-white and the white-winged dove, it has been difficult for U.S. and Mexican authorities to adequately cooperate to establish trans-border biosphere reserves to protect habitats of species that live on both sides of the border.[40]

Resolution of Border Environmental Issues. The 1983 Border Environ-mental Agreement, signed by the presidents of Mexico and the United States, established a framework mechanism for dealing with the range of border environmental problems. Because the International Boundary and Water Commission, a Mexican–U.S. agency charged with maintaining the

---

38 Robert Gray, Jesús Reynoso, Conrado Díaz Q., and Howard Applegate, *Vehicular Traffic and Air Pollution* (El Paso: Texas Western Press, 1989).

39 See Peter Emerson, "Solving Air Pollution Problems in Paso del Norte," in Alan Sweedler, Paul Ganster, and Patricia Bennett, eds., *Energy and the Environment in the California–Baja California Border Region* (San Diego: Institute for Regional Studies of the Californias, San Diego State University, 1995); and his "Why Not Trade Pollution, Too?" *The New York Times* (January 1, 1995).

40 Discussion of border bioresource issues is to be found in Paul Ganster and Hartmut Walter, eds., *Environmental and Bioresource Issues of the United States–Mexico Borderlands* (Los Angeles: UCLA Latin American Center Publications, 1989).

boundary and allocating surface waters, restricted its activities to a few water contamination issues, it was felt necessary to establish a more comprehensive way of dealing with the growing number of border environmental issues. The 1983 Agreement created a series of working groups to meet regularly to deal with transboundary pollution issues and also called for participation in the process by researchers, universities, and state and local governments. These efforts produced a series of annexes dealing with specific issues, such as the smelter pollution of the Sonora-Arizona region, the binational sewage treatment plant of the San Diego–Tijuana region, expansion of the binational sewage treatment plant for Nogales, Sonora, and Nogales, Arizona, and the binational treatment plant for the Laredo–Nuevo Laredo region.

Despite some successes, the U.S. federal government has been slow to respond to transboundary pollution problems that technically are a federal responsibility but which have local impacts. However, the great debate in the United States prior to the approval of NAFTA by Congress produced a commitment by the President and Congress that border environmental concerns would be addressed. The first concerted effort to address the many border environmental issues was development by the U.S. Environmental Protection Agency and its Mexican counterpart, the Secretaría de Desarrollo Social (SEDESOL): the Integrated Environmental Plan for the United States–Mexican Border Area (First Stage, 1992–1994). This plan laid out major border environmental problems and identified specific solutions, mainly in the areas of enforcement and infrastructure projects. In addition, an environmental side-agreement to NAFTA was negotiated and signed by Mexico and the United States, creating the Border Environmental Cooperation Commission (BECC) and the North American Development Bank (NADBANK). As mentioned above, the purpose of BECC is to examine and approve border infrastructure projects for funding by NADBANK.

Given the increased level of federal attention to border environmental issues and the promise of significant funding via NADBANK, border communities have responded by developing priorities and plans for projects to address environmental infrastructure concerns. For example, in the case of San Diego–Tijuana, the two mayors have recently established the Binational Environmental Task Force to approach environmental infrastructure needs on a binational, regional basis.

Immigration Issues. A major aspect of the United States–Mexican relationship has been international migration. Migration issues are very much border issues since border communities and states are most heavily impacted. Both push and pull factors, both supply and demand, are evident in this phenomenon. Mexican development and social policies over the last half-century have produced one of the most inequitable societies in the world in terms of income distribution. These policies have produced the concentration of enormous wealth in the hands of the few, and poverty along with lack of adequate social investment for the masses. For decades, even during periods of sustained growth under the Mexican "economic miracle," waves of economic refugees have fled north from Mexico, first from the rural near-north, then from the rural south, and now increasingly from urban Mexico. In the past, the United States clearly benefitted from this flow of migrants, through the incorporation of energetic and motivated workers into entry-level positions in the economy and through the rich culture and traditions these people have brought with them. Over the past several decades, the costs and benefits of this arrangement increasingly have been critically examined in the United States to the point where it has turned into a continuing national debate.

Late in 1986 Congress passed the Immigration Reform and Control Act (IRCA) that was designed to stem the flow of undocumented immigrants into the United States by imposing penalties on employers who hired undocumented workers and, at the same time, to provide legalization for people who had been in the country illegally since 1982. The amnesty aspect of IRCA enabled some 2.7 million people to enter the legalization process. The attempt to control the flood of undocumented people has been less successful, although enforcement efforts at the border have increased over the last several years with increased staffing for the Border Patrol and construction of an eight-foot-high steel fence at key points along the border. Arrests of undocumented immigrants fell after the passage of IRCA but the number of people detained increased until 1993 and 1994, when increased enforcement and fence construction activities once again slowed the flow.[41] Table 5 includes data from 1986 through 1994. It should be noted that these figures include multiple arrests of the same individual and that the total number of arrests varies according to the deployment of patrol agents. Border patrol officers estimate that two or three times the number arrested successfully cross into the United States. Despite these caveats, the data clearly demonstrate the scale of the flows of undocumented workers at the border and indicate that nearly one-half the activity is concentrated in the San Diego region.

Although a number of studies have suggested that undocumented workers in the United States contribute as much or more in taxes as they use in public services, it is clear that the costs and benefits of undocumented immigration are somewhat different according to region. A 1990 study by the County of San Diego suggested that local governments incurred significant burdens in the areas of indigent health care,

---

41 "Border Fence Update," information sheet from the United States Border Patrol, San Diego Border Patrol Sector, February 1995.

administration of the criminal justice system, public education (kindergarten–12th grade), social services, and crime (particularly residential burglaries and auto theft) due to the presence of large numbers of undocumented persons in the county.[42] This analysis was followed in 1992 and 1993 by two reports of the California State Senate Special Committee on Border Issues that pulled together available data and presented estimates of costs incurred by local and state government agencies in providing services to undocumented immigrants in San Diego County.[43] When coupled with similar studies undertaken for Los Angeles, the negative fiscal impacts of undocumented immigrants have become quite clear to policymakers and the general public, although hotly contested by some academic researchers and supporters of the rights of undocumented immigrants. The cost to local governments in San Diego County of all services provided to undocumented immigrants probably exceeds several hundred million dollars each year.

Even the benefits to employers of cheap labour of undocumented people are now beginning to be questioned. Traditionally, undocumented workers were largely an invisible phenomenon in places such as San Diego County, toiling as field workers, in restaurants, and as construction workers, maids, and gardeners. The visibility of undocumented persons has changed considerably as work in agriculture has shifted and as luxury housing developments have spread to canyons and other formerly isolated areas of the county where more than 10,000 migrants reside in rude, makeshift shelters, forced to do so by the high cost of housing or by the desire to save money to remit to Mexico. Now migrants congregate on streets or in front of businesses waiting for employers to pass by. Or they walk door-to-door asking for work.

As the economic recession advanced in the border region in the 1990s, undocumented immigrants increasingly were perceived as presenting job competition to unemployed groups in the United States, particularly minority youth, and as drains on public budgets through expenditures on social services, medical care, education, and criminal justice. One small city in San Diego County where migrants congregate declared a state of emergency. Elsewhere in the region, disaffected residents formed a "Light Up the Border" movement to protest the inability of the federal government to control the flow of people into the

---

42 County of San Diego, Department of Transborder Affairs Advisory Board, "Consultations in Cost and Benefits of Migration in the San Diego Region: A Local Response" (San Diego, CA: 1990).

43 Parker and Rea, *Illegal Immigration in San Diego County*.

United States.[44] The states of Texas and California initiated legal actions against the federal government, requesting reimbursement for state expenditures for undocumented immigrants since the federal government failed to control the entry of persons without proper documentation. Undocumented immigration became a major theme of the November 1994 elections in California with Proposition 187 on the ballot. Basically, Proposition 187 was a grass-roots initiative designed to deny undocumented immigrants in the state access to social, non-emergency medical, and educational services. The proposition passed easily, despite strong opposition from Hispanic groups and surprisingly direct involvement by Mexican government officials and political figures. Although Proposition 187 possibly will never be implemented due to challenges in the court system, it is a strong indicator of the mood of residents in California that may presage similar movements elsewhere along the border.

Border Crossing Issues. Flows of documented people across the border are also a source of irritation for border residents due to long waits at the border in order to cross from Mexico into the United States. Everywhere along the border, the number of people and vehicles crossing has increased significantly, which is a good indicator of growing interdependence between the two countries and of integration of the binational border region. As can be seen in Table 6, northbound legal crossings at San Diego have grown from 33 million in 1985 to more than 56 million in 1994. A crossing total of 40 million per year would mean approximately 800,000 pedestrians and 1.8 million vehicles crossing each month. Table 7 provides annual crossing figures for the entire United States–Mexican border.

As interactions have increased between the Mexican and U.S. parts of the twin-city pairs along the border, more and more border residents have been inconvenienced by excessive delays at crossing due to saturated infrastructure, inadequate staffing of border checkpoints by U.S. Customs and the Border Patrol, and inspection policies that emphasize drug interdiction and determining the migratory status of crossers. The perception of many local people is that this is another case of a federal responsibility not being discharged properly and local border residents are forced to suffer the consequences. As more border residents are involved in activities on the other side of the border, they suffer delays and inconvenience because of inadequate infrastructure for vehicular, pedestrian, and commercial crossing. Although both Mexico and the

---

44 Paul Ganster, "Percepciones sobre los costos y beneficios de la migración mexicana en el condado de San Diego," *Revista Mexicana de Sociología*, 53, No. 3 (julio–septiembre 1991), pp. 259–289.

TABLE 6. BORDER CROSSINGS INTO THE UNITED STATES
AT SAN DIEGO, CALIFORNIA, 1956–1990
(By fiscal year, October 1–September 30)

Year	Aliens	Citizens	Total	Annual % Change
1956	4,174,052	9,758,034	13,932,086	
1960	10,127,001	8,204,772	18,331,773	7.10
1965	10,588,808	11,491,351	22,080,159	3.79
1970	15,018,902	12,343,251	27,362,153	4.38
1975	22,164,979	14,050,212	36,215,191	5.77
1980	21,973,132	13,125,039	35,098,171	–0.62
1985	17,330,535	15,818,417	33,148,952	–1.14
1990	38,860,112	27,166,558	66,026,670	14.78
1991	33,565,633	15,851,838	49,417,471	–5.63
1992	37,733,173	18,219,434	55,952,607	2.52
1993	35,043,013	17,949,937	52,992,950	–5.29
1994	36,847,424	19,737,852	56,585,276	6.78

Source: David E. Lorey, ed., *United States–Mexico Border Statistics since 1900: 1990 Update* (Los Angeles: UCLA Latin American Center Publications, 1993), Table S22. 1991–1992 data are from U.S. Immigration and Naturalization Service, *Statistical Yearbook of the Immigration and Naturalization Service,* 1992 (Washington, D.C.: U.S. Government Printing Office, 1993). The San Diego border crossings include San Ysidro and Otay ports of entry.

United States benefit from the increased trade flows across the border, border residents receive the negative impacts of saturated infrastructure.

Law Enforcement and Criminal Justice Issues. A continuing problem for most U.S. and Mexican communities along the border is in the area of law enforcement and criminal justice issues. The fact is that very different legal codes meet at the border, that very different administrative and law enforcement structures are present, and that the traditional use of the border by criminals for illegal activities makes the administration of

TABLE 7. CROSSINGS INTO THE UNITED STATES ALONG THE
UNITED STATES–MEXICAN BORDER
(BY FISCAL YEAR, OCTOBER 1–SEPTEMBER 30)

Year	Total Crossings	Alien Crossings	Percent Alien Crossings
1985	176,844,524	105,771,089	60
1986	193,019,856	116,978,424	61
1987	195,920,926	118,768,977	61
1988	225,970,850	138,264,511	61
1989	244,395,272	149,249,020	61
1990	253,494,906	158,294,654	62
1991	235,336,948	151,581,043	64
1992	252,529,133	164,028,528	65
1993	269,349,987	175,472,973	65
1994	306,981,268	299,592,936	65

Source: *INS Statistical Yearbook*, various years; Immigration and Naturalization Service, Statistics Division, Washington, D.C.

justice and maintenance of law and order particularly challenging in the border context. The large number of local, state, and federal law enforcement agencies involved make matters more complex and difficult to coordinate. In the Imperial Valley in California, for example, there are at least fourteen U.S. law enforcement agencies operating, and just across the border in Mexicali there is an equivalent number of Mexican agencies.[45]

Concerns in U.S. border communities regarding law enforcement issues focus on a number of areas. In every border city in the United States a significant amount of the local auto theft is directly linked to organized groups operating out of Mexico.[46] Once in Mexico, the vehicles generally are registered with false documentation obtained from cooperating Mexican

45 See Robert L. Wilhelm, "The Transnational Relations of United States Law Enforcement Agencies with Mexico," *PCCLAS Proceedings, Change and Continuity*, 14, No. 2 (Fall 1987), pp. 157–164.

46 Michael V. Miller, "Vehicle Theft Along the Texas-Mexico Border," *Journal of Borderlands Studies*, 2, No. 2 (Fall 1987), pp. 12–32.

officials and then sold to Mexican consumers. Traditionally, Mexican border law-enforcement authorities have provided little cooperation in vehicle recovery efforts. Thefts and burglaries committed by individuals and groups from Mexico are ongoing problems for U.S. border communities. Organized gangs sometimes use juveniles (under 18) so that if caught they will be sent back to Mexico and not prosecuted in the United States. Drug trafficking is another area of significant concern in border communities.

Although in theory a federal problem, every border community feels the impact of such illegal activities, not only through the negative social effects of drug use and related criminal activities, but through enforcement activities that focus on the border region. The long delays often encountered for crossing commercial goods and individuals into the United States are to a large degree attributable to inspections for drugs. The cumulative effect of such delays, in terms of the economic costs of wasted time and in terms of ill-will generated, is appreciable. Drug trafficking is due in large part to consumer demand in the United States and to a lesser extent to production and trafficking operations in Mexico and elsewhere. Drug trafficking and related issues have their origins largely outside the border region, but their impacts affect border residents in disproportionate ways.

Mexican communities cite a number of issues related to transborder criminal activities. Mexican criminals frequently avoid prosecution by fleeing to U.S. border communities. There is considerable smuggling of consumer goods into Mexico at the border, although as NAFTA is phased in, price differentials will disappear and the incentive for smuggling these goods will be eliminated. Finally, Mexico is concerned about the illicit flow of firearms across the border from the north.

The NAFTA era has brought better transborder cooperation on criminal-justice and law-enforcement matters. There is a better spirit of teamwork on both sides. Professionalization of law enforcement agencies is improving in Mexico and there is increased attention to training and continuity of personnel. U.S. agencies have become more sensitive to their counterparts' capabilities and shortcomings and tend to take a more realistic approach in addressing day-to-day matters. However, Mexico and the United States do not have effective extradition treaties. That, along with difficulties in transborder collaboration by law enforcement, means that criminal elements are still able to use the border to escape prosecution. While over the past five years transborder law enforcement cooperation has improved, economic asymmetry realities and concerns about sovereignty, as well as the very complexity of the issues, will continue to produce concerns for border residents in this area.

GROWING TRANSBORDER LINKAGES

All of the above features of border life serve to link the two sides of the border together and provide continuities from south to north and north to south that enable us to speak of the border as a geographical region. The two parts of this region are far from Washington, D.C. and Mexico City, and people on the border often feel neglected by the national capital when dealing with transboundary issues of local, but vital, concern. Thus, over the years, border residents have evolved a whole range of informal arrangements to deal with transborder aspects of their daily lives. Examples that come to mind are seen in the informal, but regular, cooperation of fire departments, health authorities, and police to deal with emergencies without the intervention of either federal government. At some point, this sort of interaction will begin to bear upon the national policies of each country and will begin to redefine the nature of the relationship that exists between the U.S. and Mexico.[47] Transboundary linkages, both informal and formal, reflect the increasing interdependency of the two nations, particularly in the border zone. To some degree, on the microlevel, interdependency offsets aspects of asymmetry, producing a more collaborative, parity relationship at the local level. Growing transborder linkages and interdependency between the United States and Mexico has given U.S. border communities a much larger presence on the Mexican side. This has created a powerful lobby to temper the asymmetrical use of power by Washington, D.C. *vis-à-vis* Mexico.

The border region of 1995 is very different than the border region of 1980 in terms of transborder interdependence and cooperation. The great burst of activity stimulated by economic linkages between the two neighbours and NAFTA built upon slow progress made over many decades. The economic forces in the border region, first the *maquiladora* industry and then the opening of the Mexican economy that culminated with NAFTA, have driven broad changes elsewhere in the bilateral relationship, particularly as manifested at the border. NAFTA made the border a priority for both countries, particularly the United States. Beginning at the time of the discussion about the NAFTA treaty in 1993, many U.S. federal agencies began to pay greater attention to border-related issues within their areas of competency. This has had several effects. First, all this activity has raised the visibility of the border in Washington, D.C. Second, the clients and constituents of these agencies in the border region have participated in greater levels of activity. Finally, these agencies have tended to renew relations and establish new linkages with counterpart Mexican agencies and some part of the activities have border components.

---

47 Ivo B. Duchacek, "International Competence of Subnational Governments: Borderlands and Beyond," and the other essays in Oscar J. Martínez, *Across Boundaries: Transborder Interaction in Comparative Perspective* (El Paso: Texas Western Press, 1986).

At the regional level along the border, particularly within the frame-work of the twin-city pairs, transborder interactions have demonstrated a remarkable florescence due to the processes and circumstances des-cribed in this essay. In the San Diego–Tijuana region, for example, the micro-regional expansion of transborder contacts and linkages has been significant over the past decade or so, particularly from 1993 and the NAFTA discussions.[48] The growth of collaborative relations has been across the board, including local and state government agencies, higher education, non-governmental organizations of all sorts, private busi-nesses, chambers of commerce, and civic and cultural groups. While many of these transborder relationships go through a predictable process of initial contacts and activities, disillusionment, and decline, there is clearly an increase in solidly grounded projects and endeavours by parti-cipant groups. These usually bring measurable benefits to both sides by establishing mutually advantageous interactions. The sum of all these small efforts has been to significantly expand the number of actors in the two communities that are involved in transborder activities and to move the entire binational region farther along the path towards increased interdependence and integration.

Anecdotal information suggests that this process is ubiquitous along the border. Despite short-term setbacks associated with economic cycles and political difficulties, the level of transborder interaction is increasing over the long and medium term. The United States–Mexican border re-gion is so dynamic that it is not easy to predict how far the process of integration will advance. Nevertheless, Mexican and American border communities have made much progress towards conceptualizing and managing their regions in a transborder mode.

NAFTA has been a catalyst, for it made border issues a high priority on the bilateral agenda and brought increased federal involvement and funding to border issues, particularly by the U.S. federal government. At the same time, the longstanding inclination of the U.S. government and the decentralization process in Mexican public administration have com-bined to facilitate greater transborder cooperation at the local level in the border region. Increasing transborder linkages in most areas and increas-ing interdependence economically, socially, and culturally are clear indicators of the direction of change in the United States–Mexican border region. This zone that is the interface between two asymmetrical partners is moving towards regional integration.

---

48 Paul Ganster, "Transborder Linkages in the San Diego–Tijuana Region," in Norris C. Clement and Eduardo Zepeda Miramontes, eds., *San Diego–Tijuana in Transition: A Regional Analysis* (San Diego: Institute for Regional Studies of the Californias, San Diego State University, 1994), provides a discussion of the process and a listing of San Diego organizations with ties in Mexico.

Victor Konrad
Executive Director
Foundation for Educational Exchange
Between Canada and the United States

Borderlines and Borderlands in the Geography of Canada– United States Relations

After over 500 years of cumulative immigration, population mixing, and differential growth, North American societies remain decidedly plural, yet their peoples continue to roam a vast continent to which they can all legitimately lay claim. Together, these societies are shaping a postmodern map of North America, a map comprised of vectors, regions, and locales.[1] More apparent, once again, is the understanding, if not the outright acknowledgement, among an increasing number of North Americans, that they share a continent. These sentiments have prevailed before as the continent was discovered, settled, and shaped.

Today, they find expression in free trade and clean air agreements, in seasonal accommodations, and in strong relationships across boundaries. The landscapes of North America reflect the history of differential growth and development among the neighbour countries, but they also sustain a geography of continuity across borders. "North America runs more naturally north and south than east and west as specified by national boundaries."[2]

This essay encompasses the symbolic geography of vast North American landscapes. It extends beyond the national realm to identify

---

1 Joel Garreau, *The Nine Nations of North America* (Boston: Houghton Mifflin, 1981). See also Glen E. Lich and Joseph A. McKinney, eds., *Region North America: Canada, United States, Mexico* (Waco, Texas: Baylor University Press, 1990).

2 Lauren McKinsey and Victor Konrad, *Borderlands Reflections: The United States and Canada*, Borderlands Monograph Series 1 (Orono: University of Maine Press, 1989), p. iii. See also Pritt J. Vesilind and Sarah Leen, "Common Ground, Different Dreams," *National Geographic*, 117, No. 2 (February 1990), pp. 94–127.

commonalities in the borderlands. The symbolic landscapes of localities and regions are measured across the border between Canada and the United States but relate to the United States–Mexico borderlands as well. The objectives are to explore what national and regional images work across the border and to evaluate what images prevail in the borderlands and where.

The Elusive Borderlands

North America works as a continent because the borderlands are effective regions of exchange. As soon as borders were defined, borderlands emerged as regions of differentiation and mediation between the United States and its neighbours. These borderlands, and particularly the Canada–United States borderlands, have worked so well that they remain overlooked and generally underestimated for their contribution to the continental dynamic. Furthermore, the relatively benign continental relationships are undervalued because the borderlands work well and they remain pervasive but subtle.

This paper proceeds with the idea and characterization of borderlands.[3] The focus is on the United States and Canada, but the context is North America. The relevance of borderlands study to the trilateral relationship of Mexico, the United States, and Canada is implicit throughout this study, and it is based on the mitigating role of borderlands in the bilateral relationships between Mexico and the United States, and the United States and Canada. The conceptual discussion will be brief; the borderlands concept and its application to the Canada–United States border are developed elsewhere.[4]

First, it is necessary to define some of the integrative elements that make the Canada–United States borderlands both elusive and effective, but before doing this it is useful to place the borderlands concept among other formulations of North American development. Then, three expressions of the Canada–United States borderland relationship are offered to illustrate the interplay of image, tradition, and reflection: the continent-wide temperate-woods tradition, settlement continuity, and the borderlines and borderlands of imagination.

---

3   For an early recognition of the borderlands, see S.B. Jones, "The Cordilleran Section of the Canadian–United States Borderlands," *Geographical Journal*, 89 (May 1937), pp. 439–50. For a current wide-ranging recognition, see Glen Allen, "Vanishing Frontiers, Barriers Come Down in the Borderlands," *Macleans*, 103, No. 26 (25 June 1990), pp. 46–49.

4   McKinsey and Konrad, *Borderlands Reflections*.

In the introduction to their book, *Border Landscapes,* Julian Minghi and Dennis Rumley stress their interest in "the reverse of the regional model. We focus on edges, not the cores of regions."[5] They explain that

> the boundary creates its own distinctive region, making an element of division also the vehicle for regional definition. This paradox is at the core of the borderland concept. Boundary dwelling characteristics, unique to either side of the line become dominant moulders of the cultural landscape within the shadow thrown by the boundary, and yet these characteristics disappear as one moves away from the borderland in either direction into the territorial domain of the states divided.[6]

The premise of the borderlands concept is that North America is oriented north and south, and that commonalities tend to blur distinctions between regional neighbours. Neighbours across the border may have more in common than citizens across the country. This relationship does not diminish the allegiance of Mexicans, Americans, and Canadians to their respective sovereign authorities in Mexico City, Washington, D.C., and Ottawa, nor does it reduce their tendency to identify and express nationalist sentiments.[7]

For example, virtually all Canadians live in the borderlands shared with the United States, are acutely aware of the borderlands relationship, and delineate the border with precision. Most U.S. residents live beyond the borderlands. Those who live close to Canada acknowledge the borderlands less than their neighbours across the border. These Americans see a light border shadow that extends only a short distance into the United States, in contrast to Canadians who visualize a darker presence extending across the boundary.

Americans are generally less concerned about cross-border influences from the immediate north. Their attention is captured by the borderlands shared with Mexico. This benign neglect irritates Canadians, who do not wish to be overlooked and who insist on being treated in a special way. Americans, on the other hand, need to be jolted into seeing the elusive borderlands between Canada and the United States.

The jolt has come in the imperative to seek a formula for more effective North American economic integration. In this move toward a new realization of North American relationships, the borderlands assume

---

5 Julian Minghi and Dennis Rumley, *Border Landscapes* (New York: Routledge, 1991), p. 2.

6 Ibid.

7 Victor Konrad, Deryck Holdsworth, and Wilbur Zelinsky, "Focus: Nationalism in the Landscape of Canada and the United States," *Canadian Geographer,* 30, No. 2 (1986), pp. 167–80.

added significance as the joints of continental articulation. North America is being re-conceptualized as a unique continental amalgam where culture remains decidedly plural and political lines are sustained, yet social forces move people across boundaries within a vast and relatively under-populated land mass.

This concept of North America defines a continent that is more complex and vigorous and, consequently, more effectively integrated than the simple layering of Canada beyond the United States and Mexico below it. Key elements of integration were set in place as the three countries, and particularly Canada and the United States, emerged as independent, yet interdependent, entities. Because the countries show distinct national developments, the formation of the integrative elements is veiled, but it is evident in the borderlands landscapes.

Before I proceed to identify and discuss some of these integrative elements, it is necessary to place this discussion in the context of formulations of North American development. Part of the problem in seeing and understanding the borderlands in North America is the limited consideration given to the relationship between the borderlands concept and formulations of North American development, namely the frontier thesis in the United States, and the Laurentian, Metropolitan, and Archipelagian theses in Canada.[8]

It is not so surprising that the borderlands concept has seen limited application to the Canada–United States boundary, for it is apparent that formulations of Canadian development need to distance the Canadian experience from that of the Americans. However, what is surprising is the lack of connection between the frontier thesis and the borderlands concept. Historian David J. Weber concludes that Frederick J. Turner's frontier thesis, although readily applicable to the southwestern borderlands, was not applied by Bolton and the disciples of the so-called borderlands school because they were "far more interested in the impact of Spaniards on the frontier than the influence of the frontier on Spaniards."[9] Furthermore, the Boltonians rejected Turner's idea that the frontier democratized Hispanic institutions.

From this initial differentiation, the two schools of thought moved apart, and so did the concept of the frontier in Mexico and the United States. In the United States, the frontier came to embody democratization, consolidation, individualization, and nationalization. It imparted a character of practicality, inquisitiveness, restlessness, optimism, and inventive-

---

8 R. Cole Harris, "Regionalism and the Canadian Archipelago," in L.D. McCann, ed., *Heartland and Hinterland: A Geography of Canada*, 2d ed. (Scarborough: Prentice-Hall Canada, 1987), pp. 533–59.

9 David J. Weber, "Turner, the Boltonians, and the Borderlands," *American Historical Review*, 91, No. 1 (February 1986), p. 68.

ness to those who confronted it. In essence, the frontier assumed mythic proportions in the United States, whereas in Mexico the frontier never developed the same mythic importance in letters and popular culture.[10] In Canada, the idea of the frontier was applied by Harold Innis, his contemporaries, and followers, in their works, but again, as in Mexico, the frontier thesis did not gain mythic importance.[11]

A balanced application of Turner's frontier thesis, throughout North America, could have provided valuable comparisons of North American development. Instead, the idea of an American frontier has been ratcheted between parallel borders from east to west, not to define the place of the United States in North America, but to promote democracy and to differentiate American and European experiences. In the long run, the frontier thesis has defined the place of the United States in North America, and it has differentiated the United States from Canada and from Mexico.[12] Furthermore, this differentiation has delineated the borderlines and has overlooked the borderlands.

The unfortunate result of all of this is that, today, in a time when borderlines are becoming less important and borderlands are attracting more attention, North America continues to embrace formal borders and border formalities.[13] Now, it is necessary to focus more on "local and regional interests *across* the boundary."[14]

In North America, where boundary confrontations are limited, and immense cross-border flows are an everyday occurrence,[15] acknowledgement of this "crucial reorientation of issues"[16] is slow, probably because North Americans have not yet adjusted their separate national outlooks

---

10 F.J. Turner, "The Significance of the Frontier in American History," in G.R. Taylor, ed., *The Turner Thesis Concerning the Role of the Frontier in American History*, 3d ed. (Lexington, Mass.: D.C. Heath, 1972), p. 3; and Weber, *Turner*, p. 78.

11 A.R.M. Lower and Harold A. Innis, *Settlement and the Forest and Mining Frontiers* (Toronto: Macmillan, 1936).

12 John A. Price, "Mexican and Canadian Border Comparisons," in E.R. Stoddard et al., ed., *Borderlands Sourcebook* (Norman: University of Oklahoma Press, 1983), pp. 20–23.

13 See, for example, the proceedings of the international symposium on "Boundaries and the Cultural Landscape," *Regio Basiliensis*, 22, Nos. 2 and 3 (1981).

14 Minghi and Rumley, *Geography*, p. 16.

15 The *National Geographic* features a colourful article and a superb map to convey the magnitude of the cross-border flows. See *National Geographic*, 177, No. 2 (February 1990), pp. 94–127; map on pp. 106–7.

16 Minghi and Rumley, *Geography*, p. 16.

to a new vision of North America as a workable continent.[17] Without this new way of looking at the continent, they tend to overlook the borderlands landscapes of accommodation and visualize instead the most evident components and symbols of national landscapes emphasized by statist alignment.

NORTH AMERICA: CONTINENT OR CONCEPT?

Although evolved by longitudinal progression, North America is governed by latitudinal layering. It is evident that the United States intervenes between Canada and Mexico and that it concedes only bilateral relationships. Supranational ties within the continent remain unfulfilled; subnational linkages articulate America's relations with its neighbours. North America does not behave like other continents. The cross-wise layering of political lines, cultural areas, and social movements over an indelible north-south geographical template has resulted in a uniquely integrated structure with, perhaps, the most effective infrastructure in the world. North America may well be a concept beyond a continent, but as we prepare to celebrate the discovery of North America, most of us are seeing the workings of the entire continent for the first time.

Our vision of North America may be clouded by nationalist sentiment, but it is really underdeveloped due to the limited multilateral relationships maintained within the continent. Even if we travel extensively throughout North America, as many of us do, we tend not to associate the parts of the whole but rather to differentiate them. We make considerable efforts to distinguish east from west, north from south, cold from warm, rich from poor, and so on. Given these constraints and tendencies, our vision of North America is incomplete and often inaccurate.

As North America moves toward greater economic integration, there is a need among its residents to recognize the social, political and cultural implications of this change in perspective.[18] There are well-established guideposts to these implications as many of North America's social, political, and cultural phenomena have been continental in scope and continent-wide in impact throughout this century. For example, migration extends beyond the latitudinal borders to encompass the entire continent. Borderland landscapes record and display impacts of this kind in the

---

17 Jonathan P. Doh and Peter J. Stephens, "The New York/Quebec Partnership: A Case Study in Accelerating Linkages" (a paper submitted to the University of Maine at Orono project on Canada–United States borderland communities and issues, known as the "Borderlands Project," April 1990).

18 Pierre-Paul Proulx, *Trade Liberalization and Regional Development in North America: A Canadian's Perspective*, Cahier 8814, Département de Science Economique, Université de Montréal (1988).

land arrangements, building styles, and crops that extend across the border. In all likelihood, North American economic integration will extend existing social, political, and cultural patterns.

The question of greatest concern to Americans, Canadians, and Mexicans alike is: in whose favour will these extensions emerge? Overwhelmingly, the sense has been that the interests of the economic superpower will be served first. This impression may be valid, in some instances, but it is not supported with regard to all of the patterns now evident. As expressed earlier, North America simply does not behave like other continents.

In order to appreciate this difference, and in order to understand more thoroughly what North America is, both as a continent and as a concept, it is necessary to evaluate the growing number of views and opinions from abroad, to take note of new views of the continent; to allow that new forms of continental realization beyond boundaries may be positive forces; and to employ our new systematic data-analysis technology to understand North America's complexities. New approaches may be applied to the comprehensive assessment of the North American continent. Among these are the better levels of resolution available through advances in geographic information systems: a continent-wide rationalization of east-west dimensions with north-south alignments, the definition of borderlands patterns on the land,[19] mapping continent-wide sequences and series in environmental change, and displaying cross-border resource definitions for effective international management.[20]

For many of us, temporary migrations throughout North America are an accepted pattern of modern life. Seasonal occupations and homes, and a new post-industrial transhumance draws us to all quarters of North America and homing instincts take us back to ideals and permanent connections. We find ourselves knowing the entire continent but not knowing it at all.

All of this exchange, mobility, and rapid adjustment is possible today because subnational linkages were extended through the borderlands in the past, and because these ties have been maintained throughout the twentieth century. Lauren McKinsey and I have shown elsewhere how

> subnational cultures spread across the border through a vernacular expression rather than a more literate one and, consequently, did not herald the advance of either an American or Canadian (British) national

---

19 See, for example, H.A. Reitsma, "Agricultural Changes in the American-Canadian Border Zone, 1954–1978," *Political Geography Quarterly*, 7, No. 1 (January, 1988), pp. 23–28.

20 Victor Konrad et al., eds. *The Gulf of Maine Conference: Proceedings* (Orono: University of Maine Press, 1990).

culture. In this way, nineteenth-century migrations created an inter-locking of culture that is a unique, North American heritage for people on both sides of the border.[21]

Today, these latent cultural bonds underlie new dimensions of inter-action in the borderlands. For instance, Quebec has sought to revive Franco-American ties in New England, and expand cross-border trade, especially with regard to the sale of electricity. "The potential for multi-billion-dollar electricity sales is an understandable incentive for activating a cultural link that had become largely passive in recent decades."[22]

The work on subnational cultural linkages suggests one form of inte-gration in the borderlands. Other forms are evident in the borderlands landscapes that knit together Canada and the United States. Among these are extensions of transportation routes, consistent land-use patterns, linked energy grids, and co-ordinated resource management. The follow-ing considerations are merely a selection of the integrative elements that convey the depth of tradition and the power of image and reflection in the borderlands landscape.

The Temperate-Woods Tradition. Lumbering the temperate forests of North America engaged woods workers, farmers, river drivers, teamsters, bosses, and bankers, from Canada and the United States, in one of the most extensive resource extractions of the nineteenth century. Whereas the regional operations are well documented, and an extensive literature is generally available for lumbering in each region's forest domains, few studies have acknowledged the continent-wide scope and progression of this grand undertaking.[23] During the nineteenth century and into the twentieth century, the temperate forests of North America, from New England and the Maritimes in the east to British Columbia, Washington, and Oregon in the west, and even north to Alaska and the Yukon, pro-vided what was to become the clearest delineation of the borderlands across the continent. David C. Smith links the components of this exten-

---

21 McKinsey and Konrad, *Borderlands Reflections*, p. 14.

22 Ibid.

23 A.R.M. Lower, *The North American Assault on the Canadian Forest: A History of the Lumber Trade Between Canada and the United States* (Toronto: Ryerson, 1938); David C. Smith, *A History of Lumbering in Maine, 1861–1960* (Orono: University of Maine Press, 1972); Richard W. Judd, "Timber Down the Saint John: A Study of Maine-New Brunswick Relations," *Maine Historical Quarterly*, 24, No. 1 (Summer, 1984), pp. 195–218; and W.E. Greening, "The Lumber Industry in the Ottawa Valley and the American Market in the Nineteenth Century," *Ontario History*, 62 (1970), pp. 134–36.

sive borderlands zone in his article "The Logging Frontier."[24] In this essay, Smith traces the westward movement of loggers, techniques, machines, capital, and traditions. Other scholars, among them Richard Judd, Edward Ives, and W.E. Greening, trace the cross-border weave that defines the temperate-woods tradition.[25]

The woods industries have contributed, and continue to contribute, to Canada–United States economic ties and tensions, to lead to political problems and solutions, and to extend a shared cultural history resulting from the migration of workers back and forth across the border as the timber frontier advanced from east to west. Recent contributions to the literature, some commissioned for the Borderlands Project, show that the United States–Canada borderlands derived in part from an inter-regional and transnational temperate-woods tradition that originated in the international region of the northeast.[26] This notion has simmered for a long time, as, for instance, in the work of A.R.M. Lower on the cross-border lumber industry.[27]

Today, the temperate-woods tradition remains as a legacy recorded but muted in the landscape of the borderlands. Extensive woods operations, spreading across hundreds of miles, including virtually all of the forested lands from the Gulf of Maine to Puget Sound, are visions of the past recorded in stories, documents, and photographs. The forests have grown back to shade most of the legacy on the land, but the landscape analyst will find the evidence under the canopy. Overgrown roads, sluice dams on streams, ubiquitous stumps, and even entire trains rusting in the woods are found throughout the temperate forests.

Still used today are the expertly crafted wooden houses built in the towns associated with the lumberwoods. New England adaptations of classical revival and Victorian styles are evident in Michigan, Ontario, Montana, British Columbia, and Washington, and among other border states and provinces. Tracts of stumps amid an interlacing of curvilinear woods roads created a landscape of arboreal devastation and resource extraction that obliterated evidence of the international boundary.

---

24 David C. Smith, "The Logging Frontier," *Journal of Forest History,* 18, No. 4 (October, 1974), pp. 96–106.

25 Judd, "Maine–New Brunswick Relations"; Greening, "Lumber Industry"; Edward D. Ives, *Larry Gorman: The Man Who Made the Songs* (Bloomington: Indiana University Press, 1977); and *Joe Scott: The Woodsman Songmaker* (Chicago: University of Illinois Press, 1978).

26 Stephen J. Hornsby, Victor A. Konrad, and James J. Herlan, eds., *The Northeastern Borderlands: Four Centuries of Interaction* (Fredericton, N.B.: Acadiensis Press, 1989).

27 A.R.M. Lower, *North American Assault.*

Lumbermen with interests in both Canada and the United States cleared their tracts in the same way with the same men, animals, and machines.

In the upper Saint John valley, Robert Connors lumbered on both sides of the river boundary, with operations at Seven Islands in Maine and in the Madawaska District of New Brunswick.[28] The boundary was of little consequence to Connors and his contemporaries and successors who carried the temperate-woods tradition to other forested regions west and north. Between mid-nineteenth century and World War I, the lumbermen defined a borderlands interaction and fashioned a borderlands landscape that mediated the distinction between Canada and the United States.

Many of the predominant features of this shared landscape have receded into the regrown forests of the twentieth century, or they have been removed by agricultural expansion and settlement growth. Consistent with the often subtle and elusive nature of the borderlands, the landscape evolved by the temperate-woods tradition holds its rewards for the trained eye of the geographer and for the observer of history on the land.

Settlement Continuity and Contrast. Another vivid expression of the borderlands may be found in the continuities and contrasts between settlements paired across the boundary between Canada and the United States. Some of the most fascinating insights about the borderlands, and Canada–United States relations in general, are found in the settlements that face each other across the border. In these places, one can find the values and institutions that pull the countries together and those that push the countries apart.[29]

In his comprehensive unlayering of the nineteenth-century societies of Portland, Maine, and Saint John, New Brunswick, historian Robert Babcock shows how competition and development are co-ordinated in the borderland:

> The new steam and railway technology of the mid-19th century rapidly diffused throughout the region, forging alliances among New England and Maritimes entrepreneurs whose ancestors had been fighting each other only a few decades earlier.[30]

---

28 Kathryn Olmstead, "Palace in the Wilderness," *Echoes*, 6 (1989), pp. 37–44.

29 Seymour Martin Lipset, *Continental Divide: The Values and Institutions of the United States and Canada* (Toronto and Washington: Canadian-American Committee, sponsored by the C.D. Howe Institute and the National Planning Association, 1989; New York: Routledge, 1990); and *North American Cultures: Values and Institutions in Canada and the United States*, Borderlands Monograph Series 3 (Orono: University of Maine Press, 1990).

30 Robert H. Babcock, "Capitalist Development in the New England–Atlantic Provinces Region" (a paper submitted to the Borderlands Project, April 1987), p. 22.

Other studies, of coordinated development between Windsor and Detroit,[31] and of symbiotic relations between the two Saults,[32] support the finding that relationships between communities changed, often rapidly and drastically. Yet, in these studies and others submitted to the Borderlands Project, there is always re-affirmation that, even in their differences, U.S. and Canadian borderland communities shared a common, prevailing, co-operating purpose.

Borderland settlements have often originated and sustained common landscapes to display a shared sense of community. Not only are they spatially proximate, economically integrated, and socially related, but, as border communities, they are "shaped in some direct and immediate way by that border."[33] In the St. John valley of Maine and New Brunswick, the river served as the 'main street' to link settlements on both sides. St. Leonard, New Brunswick, and Van Buren, Maine, may be two towns, but they are essentially one community. That is illustrated by the case of François Violette, considered the founder of Van Buren; two of his sons lived on the Canadian side of the border. "Because the bonds of family and church crossed the river, it united people and did not divide them."[34]

In the St. John valley, the agricultural landscape, and the settlements, on one side of the river reflected the features on the other side of the river. The river joined 'long lots' extending into the forested upland from the alluvial plain. It mirrored sinewy French-Canadian street villages with prominent churches, similar houses and barns and identical crops.[35]

A sense of cross-border community prevails in the St. John valley, but the border imposed along the river now serves to divide the cultural area as well as to unite it. For example, inhabitants of Van Buren and St. Leonard retain the evidence of family connections and cultural continuity inside their houses. In contrast, the exterior of the homes and the outward appearance of properties often signal the inhabitants' allegiance, either to U.S. or Canadian material culture.[36]

---

31 J.F. Barlow, "Windsor, A Suburb or a Satellite of Detroit?" (a paper submitted to the Borderlands Project, 1988).

32 Graeme S. Mount, "Sault Ste. Marie, A Borderland?" (a paper submitted to the Borderlands Project, July 1988).

33 Roger Gibbins, *Canada as a Borderlands Society*, Borderlands Monograph Series 2 (Orono: University of Maine Press, 1998), p. 3.

34 Jacques LaPointe, "A Bond, not a Boundary," *Echoes*, 6 (1989), pp. 45–47.

35 Victor Konrad, "Against the Tide: French Canadian Barn-building Traditions in the St. John Valley of Maine," *American Review of Canadian Studies*, 12 (Summer 1982), pp. 22–36.

36 Victor Konrad and Michael Chaney, "Madawaska Twin Barn," *Journal of Cultural Geography*, 3, No. 1 (1982), pp. 64–75.

A sense of symbolic differentiation, often keyed by the prominent display of national icons, is accomplished in communities united by the interlocking of culture, faith, and family. In the east, where cultural enclaves were divided by subsequent boundaries, the juxtaposition of community across the border with statist allegiance, designated by the boundary, produces complex borderland landscapes of interwoven continuity and differentiation. In the west, where the boundary was determined before settlement, the differences have often been clear from the outset. Roger Gibbins, writing for the Borderlands Project, describes the differential impact of the international border on Osoyoos, British Columbia, and Oroville, Washington. Both communities had populations of approximately 4,000 in 1972, shared the same climate and agricultural foundations, but did not share the same advantages nor display the same landscape features, and the course of their development was markedly different.[37]

Dual or twin communities may be actually quite different from each other because they serve as the physical crossing points between the two societies.

> Like border places of unequal size, twin cities mediate cultural differences where cross-border flows are concentrated in narrow exchange corridors. Here boundaries appear stronger and cultural ties are less apparent. Where cross-border flows are selective or subdued, cultural ties appear stronger and boundary lines are less apparent. Lying astride the boundary, then, twin cities may be isolated from the rest of their region in either country, or they may be the link points in well-established corridors. For example, the Sault Ste. Maries and the Niagaras are sites of cultural conversion. Here, the parallax is most extreme. Patrick McGreevy has designated Niagara Falls as the "end of America and the beginning of Canada, a frontier where Americans still deny the finality of the border, and a place where Canadians celebrate its firm establishment."[38]

McGreevy's designation has generated responses from Canadian geographers who question the symbolic power that he attributes to this "border place,"[39] and from American geographers who support the long-

---

37 Gibbins, *Canada*, p. 7.

38 McKinsey and Konrad, *Borderlands Reflections*, p. 12. See also Patrick McGreevy, "The End of America: The Beginning of Canada," *Canadian Geographer*, 32, No. 4 (1989), pp. 307–18.

39 Ronald Bordessa and James M. Cameron, "The End of America: The Beginning of Canada—A Commentary," *Canadian Geographer*, 34, No. 3 (1990), pp. 264–69.

standing myth that the border is not a meaningful boundary.[40] Rather than reducing the validity and power of McGreevy's assertion, these differentiated objections clearly underscore the differential development and functions of border places. These places are, at once, the link points and the break points in the borderlands, and without them the borderlands landscape would be more difficult to discern.

BORDERLINES AND BORDERLANDS OF THE IMAGINATION: A SUMMARY AND A BEGINNING

Between Canada and the United States, much of the borderlines and borderlands is in the eye of the beholder. Those trained to read the landscape may discover a strong, differentiating line in place, but, in all likelihood, they will find a richly layered transition between two countries. The overlays may be viewed in many different ways. One vivid perspective comes from the accomplished writer Clark Blaise:

> Anything to do with "borders" speaks to me personally. I am animated by the very thought of border; crossing the border is like ripping the continent, tearing its invisible casing. I look upon borders as zones of grace, fifty miles wide on either side, where dualities of spirit are commonplace.[41]

This kind of response may go well beyond the emotions felt by most of us as we go about our daily business of crossing between Canada and the United States. But are our sentiments really that different? For Americans living near the border, for all Canadians, and particularly for Canadians, like Clark Blaise, who have lived on both sides of the border, the border is a personal experience, and the borderlands are recognized landscapes where the experiences accumulate. We recognize not only our border experiences but also those of others who live in the borderlands. The literary critic Russell Brown splits and splices border concepts in an effort to determine the origin of the elusive borderlands:

> We have so far found two quite different ideas of border. The first defines Canada in terms of difference, in terms of what lies on its other side or of what it does not or will not admit: it expresses as both the dividing line and the sanctuary line. The second is the border that draws all things into it, the place identified with the middle-ground, with the

---

40 Janet Baglier, "The End of America: The Beginning of Canada—A Response," *Canadian Geographer*, 34, No. 3 (1990), pp. 270–71.

41 Clark Blaise, *The Border as Fiction*, Borderlands Monograph Series 4 (Orono: University of Maine Press, 1990), p. 1.

union of opposites, and with mediation. The first of these is the border-line; the second the borderland.[42]

Viewing the borderlands as the middle ground allows the observer, or the analyst, to imbue a linear concept with spatial dimension, to recognize the substance of place and the configuration of landscape on and beyond a line. Here, differentiation, as in the case of McGreevy's Niagara Falls or Gibbins' Osoyoos and Oroville, both occurs and is mediated. Frances Kaye, devoted to the interpretation of western literary landscapes, conveys a regional interpretation:

> The very idea of Borderlands, particularly in the Prairie/Plains where the border is most abstractly a geometrical concept, implies a distinction between the two sides of the border, in this case, Canada and the United States. Further, it may imply both a region of blending and a region where contrasts are most precise simply because two cultures, two nations, meet face to face on territory differentiated only by that political abstraction, the border.[43]

Whereas a borderlands region of blending and precise contrasts may be most evident in the prairies and plains of the western interior of North America, regional characterizations of the borderlands are recognizable in each section along the continental boundary. The underlying physical geography of the cross-border region defines a unique template for borderlands interaction in each case.

For both Canada and the United States, borderlands stand as frontiers of national orientation. They appear juxtaposed, and, as we have learned in the discussions of symbolic landscapes and of national frontiers presented in this essay, the axes of Canadian and U.S. geographical orientation are at odds with each other. It is precisely this juxtaposition which contributes depth and meaning to the borderlands shared by the two countries.

---

42 Russell Brown, *Borderlines and Borderlands in English Canada: The Written Line*, Borderlands Monograph Series 4 (Orono: University of Maine Press, 1990), p. 44.

43 Frances Kaye, "Borderlands: Canadian/American Prairie/Plains Literature in English," (a paper submitted to the Borderlands Project, 1989), p. 1.

Robyn Adamache, Simon Fraser University
Claudia Culos, Simon Fraser University
Gerardo Otero, Simon Fraser University

12

Gender, Work and Politics in Mexico's Maquiladora Industry

Mexico's silent but sure integration into the North American economy in the past decade has involved profound changes in gender relations. Increasing numbers and proportions of women have been incorporated into the labour force, either through the formal or the informal sectors of the economy. Although the new economic roles for women have involved obvious changes in their overall work load, their traditional role in the household and society continues to be largely unchanged. Therefore, the oppression of women resulting from traditional patriarchal relations is now aggravated by class exploitation in industrial production, as waged workers. Moreover, the relations of production that women experience, for example in the *maquiladora* industry, borrow and reinforce patriarchal norms that originate in the reproductive sphere of social life.[1] Therefore, the exploitation that women face in production jobs takes on a distinctly gendered form.

The purpose of this paper is to explore the recent changes experienced by Mexican women in their economic and household relations, and extrapolate some political and economic scenarios of what may lie ahead now that the North American Free Trade Agreement (NAFTA) is in place.

---

1 In this paper we refer to reproduction and reproduction activities of women in the same way that Helen Safa and Cornelia B. Flora do: not only bearing and rearing children, but also "the process by which society replaces the material goods it has consumed through production for use in the household, maintains the labour force, and reinforces or recreates the institutional structure—including cultural norms and values." Helen I. Safa and Cornelia Butler Flora, "Production, Reproduction and the Polity: Women's Strategic and Practical Gender Issues," in Alfred Stepan, ed., *Americas: New Interpretive Essays* (New York: Oxford University Press, 1992), p. 132.

In order to accomplish this, we focus on women in the *maquiladora* sector because NAFTA is likely to encourage more *maquila*-type industrialization in Mexico, at least in the initial phases of North American integration. Because implementation of the NAFTA is just beginning, we can only propose probable outcomes and implications. Thus, rather than arriving at conclusive findings, the goal of this paper is to formulate theoretically and empirically informed hypotheses for a future research agenda.

The first section develops some conceptual tools to understand the political participation of Mexican women as a result of economic changes accelerated by North American integration. The following section discusses the structural trends in women's participation in the labour market, with a focus on the *maquiladora* sector. With this background, four possible scenarios are proposed in the third section, as likely outcomes for gender, work and politics.

GENDER, WORK AND POLITICS

Women's insertion into a traditionally male-dominated formal economic system has been a response to the changing demands of international capital as well as to economic crises. This insertion has had both direct and indirect effects on the social dynamics occurring within and outside the home. Within this context of change, it soon becomes apparent that women are active participants rather than passive recipients of change. Therefore, women's political participation has been and continues to be a reflection of alterations occurring in both the private and public realm of women's daily lives. As new crises arise, or as present ones are exacerbated by national and international economic policies, both formal and informal movements develop in order to address specific problems stemming from these crises.

Generally speaking, the issues, strategies, and character of women's movements in Mexico have been categorized by social scientists as being focused around two discrete sets of concerns: (1) feminist or strategic and (2) feminine or practical. According to this dichotomy, the former type of organization focuses on specifically feminist concerns such as violence against women, reproductive rights, and gender oppression and exploitation in the workplace. Usually, middle or upper class women have addressed issues that reflect their relatively privileged status. Education and a higher income have allowed these women a louder voice in the political arena, and, like women involved in feminist movements in advanced capitalist countries, they have been able to focus on specific gender issues as separate from broader political and social problems.

In contrast, lower-income women in Mexico have traditionally been involved in popular movements with the primary intention of addressing reproductive issues of interest to the community of which they are a part.

There has arisen a certain paradox in the way women have come to participate in social movements and develop an identity. The most important participation by women has been in the urban popular movements, rather than in movements centered in the work place. The notable phenomenon is that women have built on the traditional expectations of their roles as mothers to posit demands on the State, so that they can fulfill those expectations.[2] This is a somewhat paradoxical situation since it is precisely the biological constraints of female reproduction which have been used to legitimize women's subordinate position in Mexican society. However, it is women's reinterpretation of the images associated with the power of motherhood which has led to the change in their political role from "visible but silent participants to visible and vocal participants."[3] Living conditions have been so dismal that the very conditions for economic reproduction at the household level have been threatened. In view of this, women have developed what Kaplan has called "active motherhood." In this form of political participation, activist mothers address predominantly class-based needs according to traditional expectations of motherhood while subverting dominant political relations. Thus, "activist motherhood" may be seen as a step toward social change in gender relations and as a condition for broader political change.[4]

Although the image of the self-sacrificing mother has been instrumental in allowing lower-income women a voice in the political sphere, the limitations of that image must also be recognized. Women's conceptualization of the power of motherhood and society's conceptualization of that image can be quite different. The question then must be raised: can an image that simultaneously subordinates women and allows them a certain degree of political autonomy be used to achieve an equal say in political, social, and economic decision-making?

From this kind of reflection, we should realize that the ambiguities associated with gender and its relationship with class are such that an examination of women's past, present, and possible future roles in the political sphere based on the notion of motherhood can become overly simplistic. This is especially so given the profound changes that economic modernization has had and will continue to have in the private sphere.

---

2 Temma Kaplan, "Female Consciousness and Collective Action: The Case of Barcelona, 1910–1928," *Signs*, 3 (1982); Kathleen Logan, "Women's Participation in Urban Protest," in Joe Fowaraker and Ann Craig, eds., *Popular Movements and Political Change in Mexico* (Boulder and London: Lynne Rienner, 1990), pp. 150–159.

3 Joann Martin, "Motherhood and Power: The Production of a Woman's Culture of Politics in a Mexican Community," *American Ethnologist*, 17 (August 1990), pp. 470–490.

4 Kaplan, "Female Consciousness," and Logan, "Women's Participation," p. 158.

One such change that has directly affected the traditional sexual division of labour and women's involvement in political movements has been the incorporation of women into the formal labour market.

It is also important to note that the practical-strategic dichotomy used to categorize women's movements has been called into question on several grounds. For instance, Lynn Stephen illustrates through three case studies of women's movements in Mexico that there is a significant convergence of interests and issues–both strategic and practical–between different grassroots groups. First, the act of women subverting power relations in order to have their demands heard is in itself a challenge to traditional stereotypes, even if these demands relate to the practical concerns of traditional gender roles. Second, women have concerns that are simultaneously strategic and practical, and these interests change over time and from place to place.[5]

Futhermore, Safa and Butler Flora suggest that movements that begin as struggles over practical issues often become politicized and transformed into a more strategic focus as women's gender consciousness is raised through grassroots activism.[6] As Kathleen Logan has argued, a more ambitious option for working class women is to develop a popular (i.e., class-based) feminism that seeks to redress both class and gender issues:

> Popular feminism would allow women to continue to work collectively for improvements in the lives of the entire community as opposed to improvements in the lives of individuals. A feminism so defined would also permit low-income women to address issues that symbolize their subordination as *women*, such as male violence, institutionalized discrimination, and the lack of reproductive freedom.[7]

The involvement of feminist advisors in popular movements has in some cases helped in transforming "active motherhood" into popular feminism. Thus, on one hand, we have a predominance of women participating as the grass roots of urban social movements in Mexico. These women probably remain in the home for the most part, although many also work

---

5   Lynn Stephen, *Women's Grassroots Organizing in Latin America: Bridging the Feminine/Feminist Dichotomy*, forthcoming (Austin: University of Texas Press). Lynn Stephen, "Democracy for Who? Women's Grassroots Political Activism in the 1990s, Mexico City and Chiapas," in Otero, *Neoliberalism Revisited: Economic Restructuring and Mexico's Political Future*, forthcoming (Boulder, CO: Westview Press).

6   Safa and Flora, "Production, Reproduction and the Polity."

7   Logan, "Women's Participation," p. 159.

in the informal sector, including industrial homework.[8] On the other hand, we have an increasing number of women working in *maquiladora*-type industries who experience subordination on two fronts: first, class exploitation resembling that of the traditional industrial proletariat; and second, gender subordination that substantially colours this relation and governs relations inside and outside of the factory. It is a matter of contention whether this type of employment is emancipatory for women. It may be beneficial in that it gives women some earning power and independence outside of the home, and this may provide them with the opportunity to participate in political movements. As well, since 20 to 30 percent of Mexican women are the main income earners of the household[9] and many more are significant contributors, *maquila*-type employment is a necessity in most cases. However, if this independence only means that women are free to be exploited in paid production as well as in the private sphere, then it is not necessarily emancipatory. In this case, the locus of subordination has been shifted or transformed, but not eliminated. A combination of class exploitation and gender oppression on the factory floor is added to gender inequalities in the home.

Just as poorer women's participation in the political sphere was prompted by the increasing difficulty in meeting practical needs in the reproductive sphere, so too were many women workers who had entered the productive arena compelled to address their needs as workers through political organization. Therefore, the changes that occurred through industrialization have resulted in the growth and development of women's movements which brought to the fore problems and issues facing women whose productive and reproductive roles were becoming increasingly interconnected.

Popular organizations such as CONAMUP and CIDHAL (Coordinadora Nacional de Movimientos Urbanos Populares [in Mexico]; and Comunicación, Intercambio y Desarrollo Humano en América Latina, respectively) have started with the premise that community-based organizations can be more effective than those specifically focused on the work place. Because women's incorporation into the paid work force has meant an increase in actual labour (double shift) and an exposure to different forms of gender inequality outside of the community and household context, many popular women's movements have linked com-

---

8   Lourdes Benería and Martha Roldán, *The Crossroads of Class and Gender. Industrial Homework, Subcontracting, and Household Dynamics in Mexico City* (Chicago: University of Chicago Press, 1987).

9   Barbara Ehrenrich and Annette Fuentes, "Life on the Global Assembly Line," in Alison M. Jagger and Paula Rothenberg., eds., *Feminist Frameworks: Alternative Theoretical Accounts of the Relations Between Women and Men* (New York: McGraw Hill, 1992, 1984), p. 32.

munity, work place, and gender issues with the goal of uniting women through common experiences in and out of the home. Therefore, what began as movements struggling for change based on the popular conception of motherhood has slowly evolved into movements which acknowledge the multi-faceted nature of women's roles. Not only are women struggling to be recognized as mothers, but also as paid workers, and essentially as women. Thus, issues of class and gender have steadily been given a space in women's popular organizations.

The intersection of these issues has both strengthened and modified the underlying symbolism of motherhood. With all of its cultural connotations, the image of motherhood has provided women with an important tool for their incorporation as vocal participants in the public sphere. As well, the expansion of women's roles into the paid productive arena has led to a greater degree of political and gender consciousness that could only have developed out of the interaction between work and the home, the public and the private spheres.

One key question that results from these changes is: how will women's new roles in paid production be combined with women's traditional reproductive roles in shaping their political participation and the formation of identities? An empirical question is to what extent do these roles overlap in the same social actors, and how do class and gender concerns intersect to shape women's lives? If it is the case that most women working in *maquiladoras* are single, this would have different implications than if they are also in charge of their households as wives or as single mothers.

Transformations in the *Maquiladora* Industry: Stakes for Female Workers

Mexico's dynamic *maquiladora* industry is a concrete example of economic restructuring in which the forces of international capital interact with local conditions and gender relations to produce a rather perverse form of economic integration. Transnational corporations (TNCs) are drawn to Mexico by its cheap, abundant (often female) labour force and political stability, which allow these firms to increase profitability and remain competitive on the world market. The *maquiladora* industry was initiated in 1966 as a response to the termination of the Bracero Program, which allowed Mexican labour to work legally in the United States. One of the main goals of promoting the *maquiladora* industry was to stem unemployment resulting from the end of this program. Under Mexican law, companies import component parts duty-free into Mexico for assembly. The finished product is then exported back to the United States for sales and distribution. At this stage, duties are paid only on the labour value added through assembly, as stipulated in the United States Tariff Code.

Thus the main lure for businesses is low wages for labour-intensive processes within larger (often world-wide) integrated production arrangements. Indeed, since the early 1980s, Mexican wages have been getting progressively cheaper as a result of ongoing peso devaluations. Since its inception, the *maquiladora* industry has grown substantially and undergone many changes. It is estimated that by 1980, there was a total of 620 *maquiladora* firms operating in Mexico employing approximately 100,000 workers,[10] whereas by 1992, 2064 such firms were in operation with a corresponding work force of 517,629.[11] This employment figure can be approximately doubled due to the effects of indirect employment generated by the *maquiladoras*. Together, direct and indirect employment in *maquiladoras* constitutes about 2 percent of the total economically active population in Mexico—the same amount by which the Mexican labour force expands *each year*.

Since the late 1980s, the *maquiladora* industry has been undergoing fundamental changes in terms of work organization, the level of technology being used in production processes, the types and stages of production that are being transferred to Mexican plants, and the gender composition of the labour force. The *maquiladora* industry is in the process of evolving from (or rather, adding to) its roots as a labour-intensive, unsophisticated, feminized sector.[12] As more levels of the production process (other than just labour-intensive stages) are shifted to Mexico, the industry is becoming increasingly vertically integrated. The result is a "new" or "post-fordist"[13] form of *maquiladoras* which consist of increas-

---

10 Gary Gereffi, "Mexico's Old and New Maquiladora Industries: Contrasting Approaches to North American Integration," forthcoming in Gerardo Otero, *Neoliberalism Revisited.*

11 BID (Inter-American Development Bank), "América del Norte: La Maquiladoras en México en Visperas del TLC," *Comercio Exterior*, 43, No. 2 (Mexico, 1993), 159–161.

12 Gereffi, "Mexico's Old and New *Maquiladora* Industries"; Kathryn Kopinak, "The Maquiladorization of the Mexican Economy," in Maxwell A. Cameron and Ricardo Grinspun, eds., *The Political Economy of North American Free Trade* (Montreal and Kingston: McGill-Queen's University Press, 1993); Ruth Pearson, "Male Bias and Women's Work in Mexico's Border Industries," in Diane Elson, ed., *Male Bias in the Development Process* (Manchester: Manchester University Press, 1991); Leslie Sklair, *Assembling for Development: The Maquiladora Industry in Mexico and the United States* (Boston: Unwin Hyman, 1989); Susan Tiano, "Maquiladora Women: A New Category of Workers?" in Katherine Ward, ed., *Women Workers and Global Restructuring* (New York: ILR Press, 1990); Patricia Wilson, *Exports and Local Development: Mexico's New Maquiladoras* (Austin: University of Texas Press, 1992).

13 Wilson, *Exports and Local Development.*

ingly flexible, capital-intensive, high-tech operations with more skilled and technical employment positions which often go to men rather than women.

However, there is no consensus as to the implications that these transformations in the industry will have for female *maquila* workers. Assessments of the effects of these changes on women workers tend to vary according to how one views the *maquiladora* industry more generally; that is, whether one subscribes to what Susan Tiano categorizes as either the integration thesis or the exploitation thesis regarding women and *maquila* employment.[14] Supporters of the integration view argue that assembly work is a positive, liberating step for women because it takes them out of the reproductive sphere and into the public sphere of formal, paid employment. This explanation is aligned with the liberal feminist-inspired approach of developmentalism and with modernization theory. Developmentalism is the theory of women and development pioneered by Esther Boserup (1970), which argues that women have been marginalized from the development process. According to the advocates of this perspective, providing access to paid employment for women in the *maquiladoras* will solve the problems of gender inequality and give women a voice in development. Much akin to modernization theory, the integration camp argues that as women are integrated into industrial employment and gain skills and Western knowledge and values, they will slowly move up the job hierarchy, thereby realizing the benefits of development. Thus, following this line of thought, *maquiladora* employment is a vehicle for progressive change because it enables women to earn an income (no matter how small it may be), and achieve some independence and presumably a higher status *vis-à-vis* unpaid reproductive duties.[15]

According to proponents of the integration thesis, the new *maquiladoras* should be seen as a positive transformation of the industry, which will also benefit women as long as equal access to employment is established and maintained. The new *maquiladoras* will offer female workers highly skilled, higher-paying jobs, further improving their position in Mexican society. Not only will women be employed, but they will be employed in better, higher-status jobs (as compared to the old-style *maquilas*), more equally sharing the fruits of the development process. Once again, similar to modernization theory, women will have the opportunity to move one more rung up the ladder of modernization and equality by attaining higher skills and better jobs.

---

14 Tiano, "Maquiladora Women."

15 Safa, "The New Women Workers: Does Money Equal Power?" *NACLA Report on the Americas*, 27, No. 1 (1993), pp. 24–29.

In light of the empirical evidence of women's subordination within the *maquiladora* industry, and the inequality of women within more developed countries despite so-called equal access to employment, we do not support this naïve view of the export processing industry in Mexico. As well, the seemingly global phenomenon of the "double shift" of paid employment followed by unpaid reproductive work in the home, calls into question the benefits of work outside the home in terms of the overall workload that women are saddled with. Furthermore, considering that relations on the factory floor often mimic patriarchal relations in the home, the liberation potential of *maquila* work is questionable.

This is not to say, however, that *maquila* employment has no benefits for women workers, especially if one takes into account the scarcity of opportunities and alternatives. Rather, we would argue that a more critical approach following the exploitation thesis and inspired by socialist feminism holds more explanatory power than the integration thesis. Since the exploitation thesis is well documented and thoughtfully explained by many authors writing on women in international factory production and, more specifically, the "old" style *maquiladora* industry in Mexico, only a brief summary of the main points is necessary here.[16]

---

16 Cf. Lourdes Benería and Gita Sen, "Class and Gender: Inequalities and Women's role in Economic Development—Theoretical and Practical Implications," *Feminist Studies*, 8, No. 1 (1982), pp. 157–76; Jorge Bustamante, "Maquiladoras: A New Face of International Capitalism on Mexico's Northern Frontier," in Maria Patricia Fernandez-Kelly and June Nash, eds., *Women, Men and the International Division of Labor* (Albany: State University of New York Press, 1983); Diane Elson and Ruth Pearson, "Nimble Fingers Make Cheaper Workers: An Analysis of Women's Employment in Third World Export Manufacturing," *Feminist Review*, 7 (Spring 1981), pp. 87–107; Elson and Pearson, "The Subordination of Women and the Internationalisation of Factory Production," in Sandra Young et al., eds., *Of Marriage and the Market: Women's Subordination in an International Perspective* (London: CSE Books, 1981); Maria Patricia Fernandez-Kelly, "Broadening the Scope: Gender and International Economic Development," *Sociological Forum*, 4, No. 4 (1989), pp. 611–35; Fernandez-Kelly, *For We Are Sold, I and My People: Women and Industry in Mexico's Frontier* (Albany: State University of New York Press, 1983); Annette Fuentes and Barbara Ehrenreich, "Life on the Global Assembly Line," in Alison M. Jagger and Paula Rothenberg, eds., *Feminist Frameworks: Alternative Theoretical Accounts of the Relations Between Women and Men* (New York: McGraw Hill, 1982); Ehrenreich and Fuentes, *Women in the Global Factory* (Boston: South End Press, 1982); Linda Lim, "Capitalism, Imperialism and Patriarchy: The Dilemma of Third World Women Workers in Multinational Factories," in Fernandez and Nash, *Women, Men*; Devon Pena, "Tortuosidad: Shop Floor Struggles of Female Maquiladora Workers," in Vicki L. Ruiz and Susan Tiano, eds., *Women on the U.S.–Mexico Border* (Boulder, CO: Westview Press, 1991); Safa, "Runaway Shops and Female Employment: The Search for

Proponents of the exploitation thesis regarding the old-style *maquiladoras* hold that employment within this industry is not necessarily emancipatory for women because the preference for female labour is based on their subordinate position within the private sphere which is reinforced and transformed in the public sphere of paid production. Thus, these authors take the position that it is "the relations through which women are integrated into the development process that need to be problematized and investigated."[17] According to this line of thought, women are relegated to "low-skilled," repetitive, monotonous jobs which often provide only low wages and shoddy working conditions including paternalistic, patriarchal relations within the factory. Mexican women form a vast pool of cheap, exploitable labour for the assembly industry, and are hired based on their supposedly innate, 'natural' manual dexterity and docility or ability to withstand the rigours of repetitive, monotonous, highly supervised production processes. However, the degree of exploitation varies between different types of *maquiladora* industries. For example, Tiano points out that working conditions and pay tend to be better in the electronics industry which is dominated by large transnational firms and hires mainly young women, as compared to the garment industry which more often consists of small subcontractors which hire more mature workers.[18] It is clear, then, that this approach is incorporating issues of gender, age and class under capitalist relations in order to more fully explain women's insertion within the *maquiladora* industry. But what of race?

Fernandez-Kelly argues that "in areas such as the Mexican-American border where racial, ethnic, national and religious differences are generally nonexistent, gender takes their place."[19] In the case of the female *maquiladora* workforce, women are preferred over males and selected on the basis of presumptions of gender- (and age-) specific characteristics and behaviours rather than traits associated with a particular racial group. However, as the industry disperses geographically within the country this may change, and certainly if we were discussing a country such as Guatemala where Indians have traditionally been a target of foreign capital, the issue of race or ethnicity could become more central. However, imperialist relations between the United States and

---

Cheap Labor," *Signs: Journal of Women in Culture and Society*, 7, No. 2 (1981), pp. 418–33; Sklair, *Assembling for Development*; Tiano, "Maquiladoras in Mexicali: Integration or Exploitation?" in Vicki L. Ruiz and Susan Tiano, eds., *Women on the U.S.–Mexico Border* (1991); and Tiano, "Maquiladora Women: A New Category of Women?" (1991).

17 Elson and Pearson, p. 87.

18 Tiano, "Maquiladoras in Mexicali."

19 *For We Are Sold*, p. 72.

Mexico are the basis on which the relations between U.S. transnationals and *maquila* workers is structured. In as much as imperialist relations are based on racist and relativistic conceptions such as manifest destiny and 'the white man's burden', so too are the *maquiladoras* promoted based on the assumption that U.S. firms are helping Mexican workers who would otherwise be destitute and unable to develop their country by themselves. Likewise, the 'evolution' of the *maquiladora* industry is being touted by proponents of the industry in both countries as a further benefit to Mexico for opening its border to the United States.

However, this assumption is not necessarily a valid one. First, it is not clear that this transformation is a clean break from the old-style *maquiladora* nor is it inevitable that the new *maquiladoras* will overtake or eclipse the former. It is more likely that the older type will continue to be widespread and that flexible combinations of the two types will grow alongside the new technologically advanced production facilities.[20] Furthermore, the integration approach does not fully take into account the strength of barriers to equal access to employment. For example, if we accept the socialist feminist assumption regarding the way in which women are incorporated into the export processing industry, then patriarchal norms and stereotypes of women's work and abilities would be a significant barrier for women trying to access better, higher-paying jobs. Thus, those following the exploitation thesis would argue that since women are hired in the old style *maquiladoras* based on gender stereotypes that fit with labour-intensive, repetitive tasks deemed unskilled, then it would not follow that jobs in the new *maquiladoras*, which conform more closely to what is traditionally perceived as male terrain, would be available to women. These new jobs call for technical ability, higher skill levels, and more decision-making power, which, according to conventional (patriarchal) "wisdom," are male traits. As well, this same line of reasoning would accord men a higher need for a liveable income because they are considered the main bread-winners of the family, whereas women work to earn 'pin' money; thus the former would have priority for these better-paying jobs over the latter. However, this is not necessarily true. In fact, 20 to 30 percent of the female labour force in Mexico are the main income earners of the household and many more are significant contributors without whom the family could not survive.[21]

As mentioned earlier, however, the gender composition of the *maquila* workforce is becoming increasingly more male. For example, while in 1975 approximately 27 percent of *maquila* employees in the border region

---

20 Kopinak, "Maquiladorization of the Mexican Economy."

21 Fuentes and Ehrenreich, "Life on the Global Assembly Line," p. 32.

were men, by 1986 this figure had risen to about 42 percent.[22] Within the exploitation camp, Pearson, Sklair, and Tiano address the phenomenon of increased male participation and provide some insight into the gender implications of the new *maquiladoras*. Sklair suggests that it is no longer necessary to hire exclusively women because the standard for the 'ideal' *maquila* worker has been sufficiently established through the historical progression of the industry. Moreover, due to the increasing strain of male unemployment and a supposed shortage of *maquila*-grade females, men are more likely to accept what he calls the "litany of docile, un-demanding, 'nimble-fingered' workers uninterested in joining unions or standing up for their rights."[23] Another explanation for the increase of male *maquila* employees is sectorial variations in *maquiladora* growth over the past ten years:

> Those sectors which have traditionally employed more male workers—metal products, furniture and wood products, and transport equip-ment—have steadily increased, so that employment opportunities have grown much faster than the overall growth in women's employment.[24]

Thus, according to this argument of sectoral growth, women's position within certain sectors (most notably the electronics, garment and food-processing industries which dominate the border region) is not being qualitatively changed. Rather, new types of capital-intensive *maquiladoras* are being established and hiring men for technical positions at higher status levels in the occupational structure. A third and related explana-tion is that traditionally feminized, labour-intensive industries have undergone a significant change in the nature and organization of the production process.[25] Following this line of thought, the proportion of line workers is falling relative to technical and administrative positions, and are thus incorporating more men based on patriarchal notions of the jobs to which women and men are suited.

Realistically, the explanation for increased male *maquila* employment is most likely a combination of the above reasons. Be that as it may, the fact remains that these changes are having a major impact on women workers. Thus far, the results of gender changes in the *maquiladora* sector workforce have generally not been positive for women. They continue to work in the most labour-intensive industries, such as garments and elec-

---

22 Sklair, *Assembling for Development*, p. 176.

23 Sklair, *Assembling for Development* (1989), pp. 171-2.

24 Pearson, "Male Bias and Women's Work," p. 155; see also Sklair, *Assembling for Development*, Ch. 8.

25 Ibid.

tronics, and in the least automated processes requiring the lowest skills. By contrast, within more capital-intensive industries, such as automobiles, women are concentrated in the less-skilled electronics jobs, and supervised with patriarchal management ideologies rather than with the newer work team or quality circle concepts.[26]

These patterns are probably not surprising to those in the exploitation camp given the history of women's integration in the assembly industry. However, it must also be stressed at this point that although there has recently been much growth in the newer type of *maquiladoras*, the old-style, labour-intensive operations are still by far the most prevalent. Even Japanese investment in Mexican *maquiladoras* has targeted primarily low-skilled and cheap labour.[27] As well, some firms are combining new, high-tech operations along with traditional assembly-line work organization within the same location. But in all of these cases, women are still most commonly found at the lower end of the job hierarchy.

FUTURE PROSPECTS FOR GENDER, WORK AND POLITICS

While the future, by definition, cannot be known scientifically, it is possible to imagine plausible scenarios on the basis of past and current trends. By studying the critical factors shaping such trends, the material conditions for future scenarios can also be identified. This exercise may be helpful both in developing research agendas and political action geared to favour the most desirable future.

With the passage of the NAFTA and its implementation beginning in 1994, *maquiladoras* as such cease to be justified. With tariff barriers gone (some after phase-out periods), all of Mexico's future manufacturing production could potentially be *maquiladora*-style. However, because the incentive for *maquiladoras* to use almost 100 percent U.S.-made inputs (except for labour) also disappears, and the possibility emerges for new backward and forward linkages between *maquiladoras* and the rest of the Mexican economy, the extent to which such linkages develop will have an important impact on prospects for women's employment in production.

The various pessimistic and optimistic scenarios we present in this section are thus based on how pervasive the *maquiladora* model of development will be and on what other economic and political conditions would be required to transcend such a model. These scenarios detail variations in the development of the industry and how these changes will

---

26 Kopinak, "Maquiladorization of the Mexican Economy."

27 Martin Kenney and Richard Flora, "Japanese Maquiladoras: Production Organization and Global Commodity Chains," *World Development*, 22, No. 1 (1993), pp. 27–44.

affect the lives of women through the sexual division of labour and the diverse possibilities for redressing class- and/or gender-based issues. After these scenarios have been analyzed, a conclusion will be made as to which scenario seems most likely to occur regarding democracy and the ability of the Mexican State to determine national economic affairs.

A fundamental question that should be raised in this analysis is this: "Do the relations through which women are being incorporated into economic development enhance or inhibit their capacity to shape and share values in the community process—that is, to be treated as equals with equal access to participation in decision making?"[28] In order to answer this question, all aspects of the relations of women's incorporation in the development process must be thoroughly examined. This would include an understanding of the dynamic interrelation of patriarchy and capitalism and how this manifests itself in the work place, in the home, and in the state.

Scenario I: Under this scenario, old-style *maquiladoras* would become generalized, in combination with more authoritarian and repressive state policies, controlling wages downwards. NAFTA gives more companies the opportunity to open up assembly industries resembling the old-style *maquiladoras* which hire mainly women for low-skill, low-technology, monotonous jobs. This type of industrialization is characterized by few linkages to the local economy, limited spread effects and a minimal redistribution of wealth, as much of the employment offers the lowest of wages and little or no job security. The *maquiladora* sector will remain qualitatively unchanged in this scenario, but will grow as more industries are able to take advantage of Mexico's supply of cheap, unorganized and politically repressed labour in their search for global competitiveness. With NAFTA, there will also be a further spatial diffusion of *maquiladora*-style production away from the border region and into the heart of Mexico, or indeed wherever unorganized labour is found. This would be building on an already existing trend in the industry—spatial relocation on the basis of labour force characteristics. For example, *maquiladora* firms are presently relocating from the eastern border region—the longest established *maquiladora* area where labour unions are beginning to pose a threat—to western regions, which are less problematic in this regard. In fact, as of October 1992, the 2,064 *maquiladoras* were distributed as follows along the northern border: 37.3 percent in the state of Baja California, 16.9 percent in Chihuahua, 13.4 percent in Tamaulipas (a traditional *maquiladora* zone where labour organization became a "problem"

---

28 Gay Young, "Women, Development and Human Rights: Issues in Integrated Transnational Production," *Journal of Applied Behavioral Science,* 20, No. 14 (1984), pp. 383–401.

for capital), 8.5 percent in Coahuila, and 8 percent in Sonora, with the remaining 15.9 percent distributed in the interior Mexican states.[29]

In this case, unless the sexual division of labour and existing gender relations evolve in both the public and private spheres, women will continue to be subordinated in both arenas. Within the public sphere of production, the division of labour by gender is carried over from the private sphere of reproduction. For example, women workers are relegated to low-paying, unstable positions that mimic and reinforce their role and position within the home. These positions draw on and resemble the jobs that women do within the home, and build on traditional female skills—or the perceived lack thereof. This guarantees the supposedly docile, subservient work force that is necessary for *maquila* work, which is highly supervised, tedious, physically demanding piecework. This type of exploitation in paid production coupled with the traditional forms found in the home, contribute to what has been termed women's double shift—a condition affecting women in both developed and developing countries (albeit much differently). Women caught in this double bind are responsible for all their traditional reproductive duties within the home, as well as a full day of labour in the factory. Thus, the life of a female *maquiladora* worker is often exhausting and stressful.

In sum, the overall character of this scenario is that poor economic and social conditions would be the primary motivation for collective organization. The struggle to meet practical needs would outweigh any concentrated efforts to address broader, gender-specific issues. However, while the increase in old-style *maquiladora* work would create a space for the unification of women under a common experience, the presence of an authoritarian and repressive state would stifle organizational attempts by women and workers generally. In light of the Mexican State's need to attract foreign investment in an increasingly competitive global environment, and the spatial mobility of capital, it is most likely that national and international economic processes would counteract most organizational efforts.

Scenario II: Under this scenario, "old" *maquiladoras* continue to operate, but "new" ones also become more prevalent as a result of NAFTA, while no significant political change occurs within the current semi-authoritarian regime.[30] These new *maquiladoras* offer higher-skilled, higher-paying, technical jobs which mainly go to men due to gender stereotypes that keep women out of technical positions and in more

---

29 BID 1993; Ernesto Quintanilla, "Tendencias recientes de la localización en la industria maquiladora," *Comercio Exterior* (Mexico City), 41, No. 9 (1991), pp. 861–68.

30 Ilán Semo, "Mexico's Democratic Pre-Transition: A Comparative Perspective," in Otero, *Neoliberalism Revisited* (forthcoming).

traditionally female jobs such as clerical positions and assembly jobs in the garment and electronics industries. Although these new *maquiladoras* are said to have a greater potential for domestic linkages and technology transfer, as long as these plants continue to operate in the interests of transnational capital, the goal of social and economic development in Mexico will be secondary to that of profit maximization. Thus, although the development of new *maquiladoras* may result in slight increases in local linkages and employment, to the extent that industrial location decisions continue to be made on the basis of cheap, unorganized labour, and favourable government incentives such as low tariff barriers, even this new style of *maquiladora* will not necessarily result in a significant improvement in the lives of Mexican women and men.

Under this scenario, the effects that the new *maquiladoras* promise to have on women's lives, combined with the above-mentioned effects of old-style *maquiladoras*, point to a dismal future for women in this sector of the economy—especially if they are largely excluded from employment in the new *maquiladoras*. With many new *maquiladora* positions going to men, women may be forced into homeworking or the informal sector— the lowest paying and least secure form of employment—sooner than if more old-style *maquiladoras* developed. In addition, this process of subproletarianization may be hastened if existing (old) *maquiladoras* are shifted to the Caribbean and Central America.

As with the old-style *maquiladoras* and perhaps to an even greater degree, women's duties and position in the sphere of industrial home-working and subcontracting are based on their role in the private realm of reproductive activities. In fact, with this type of employment, the public sphere of production and the private sphere of reproduction become one and the same. These positions are touted by the government as beneficial for women precisely because they enable women to tend to both spheres at the same time. As with other jobs in the unstable informal sector, these positions do not represent a significant improvement in women's lives because they are low-status, low-paying, and unregulated.[31] As well, work done in the informal sector and in the home does nothing to change the sexual division of labour within the private sphere. Owing to the flexible nature of this type of employment, women are expected to fulfill family obligations as well as contribute to the income pool. Thus, just as women who are involved in old-style *maquila* employment experience the rigours of the double shift, so too do informal workers and homeworkers, who do not even have the advantages of increased independence which comes from outside interaction with other workers.

---

31 Fiona Wilson, *Sweaters, Gender, Class, and Workshop-based Industry in Mexico* (London: Macmillan, 1991).

This scenario has a number of negative consequences for women's political organization. The "gendering" of the *maquiladora* will mean that only those low-paying, low-skill jobs associated with certain sectors such as garment and electronics assembly will be available for women. Like the previous scenario, this could mean a continuation of the exploitative practices found in the already existing *maquiladoras*. In terms of political participation, community-based movements will probably be more effective in meeting practical and strategic needs. However, it is possible that under this scenario there will be no quantitative or qualitative increase in women's paid employment. By hiring men for higher-skilled, higher-paid jobs, the gender stereotype of women's work will be reinforced. This would be especially true if women have no recourse but to work part-time in the informal sector for less pay and more unstable work. The time and energy constraints of this type of work could impede women's abilities to organize politically.[32]

An increase in male employment could also result in a reinforcement of male domination within the home. If wages increase, men will once again assume the role of the sole breadwinner, and strengthen the traditional role of women. Such reinforcement would tend to confine women's political participation to the reproductive and community spheres. Some positive possibilities for women's movements are opened by this scenario, however. For example, male migration to urban centres could result in women maintaining control over the domestic/community sphere free from the direct constraints of male authority. But, because this is often a very impoverished situation, organization would continue to be focused on subsistence needs rather than gender-specific goals. The main improvement here is that subsistence needs would be defined by women who are usually the caretakers within the private sphere.

Scenario III: In contrast to the previous two scenarios, the following one would constitute a significant improvement in the lives of women, along with a political liberalization which allows workers to organize independently and struggle for their rights. Under this scenario, old-style *maquiladoras* continue to grow and hire mainly women, and the newer forms are either insignificant in their proliferation and/or they continue to prefer men to women. Thus, in terms of access to *maquiladora* employment, women would remain mainly in the traditional labour-intensive, feminized industries such as the garment industry and electronics assembly. However, with political liberalization and a NAFTA that successfully enforces the side-agreement on labour standards and conditions, these types of assembly jobs would be more highly regulated, and conditions in the public sphere of production could improve for women.

---

32 Ibid.

In 1993, for example, Mexican workers and labour unionists from the United States have teamed up using the side-agreement to challenge union-busting efforts by General Electric and Honeywell. However, in both cases union organizers in the Mexican plants who became associated with the U.S. unionists were fired or forced to "voluntarily" accept severance packages. Therefore, it is evident that in order for this scenario to have a positive outcome for female workers, it is necessary for women to have a greater political voice so that labour standards are enforced and improvements in the industry are obtained.

Mexico would come to economically resemble the East Asian newly industrialized countries (NICs) while pursuing a model of outward-oriented development (as favoured by World Bank and International Monetary Fund) which includes increasing exports, economic growth and employment. Another possibility is that, like the East Asian NICs, Mexico moves from an export processing role to a commercial subcontractor role, which would necessitate or enable industrial upgrading and increased expenditures on research and development.

Maquila work, however, is contradictory in that it places severe limitations on women's political participation at the same time that it allows for a process of change in women's productive and reproductive roles. Although an increase in women's participation in the formal sector would continue to involve gender oppression and class exploitation, the patriarchal/capitalist structure of the *maquiladora* system would bring together larger numbers of women in the face of a common authority.[33] Within the factories, women can relate to each other as members of a specific class to demand improvements in the wages and working conditions. But *maquiladoras* also articulate the similarities between women outside the factory, in the private sphere. Issues of child care and fertility, sexual objectification, and the double shift are examples of these.

A positive aspect of this scenario is that an increase in the number of women workers in *maquiladoras* could result in a greater possibility for successful organization both within and outside the work force. It is possible that an increase in the sheer numbers of women who share common experiences could facilitate stronger national networks of women's organizations that address the problems associated with women's productive and reproductive work. Women's insertion into the paid work force has and can continue to have a positive influence on the effectiveness of their political participation. Women would become more visible through their role in the production process and, as the importance of their contributions to the home and community becomes increasingly recognized, their collective strength can also increase. Also, as community,

---

33 Young, "Women, Development and Human Rights."

labour, and gender-based organizations intersect, newer, more powerful forms can develop.

With the improved status of women's employment in paid labour, their position within the home may also improve. The double shift could then be eliminated or reduced as more equitable gender relations and division of labour begin to take hold in the area of reproductive duties. However, even if the private sphere does not evolve along with changes in production relations, at least oppression will have been reduced or eliminated in one realm, and women will be one step closer to achieving the goals of economic and social equality and emancipation. It must be emphasized that the goal is not equality with Mexican men (they are clearly not in a satisfactory economic or social position within North America); rather, it is the goals of economic self-sufficiency, equitable gender relations and human dignity for both women and men that must be pursued.

Scenario IV: Finally, a more optimistic scenario might develop out of North American integration. Two conditions are required for such a scenario. One is that sufficient job openings are obtained in both the old- and new-type *maquiladoras* in Mexico, in a path of equalization with its northern neighbours. If both men and women have an equal opportunity to be hired at the new type of higher-skilled, higher-paid *maquiladoras*, the possibilities for increased political participation might be enhanced. Thus, the second condition for obtaining this scenario is that democratic political transition develops quite substantially, so that workers and other subordinate groups and classes in society are able to find representation in the state. Such a political outcome would have to be gained by the tenacious struggle of these groups, for the ruling classes currently seem intent on imposing the old-*maquiladora*, cheap labour path of the first scenario.

A critical assumption of the fourth scenario is that women will have substantially improved opportunities for education and training. In this case, both women and men would reap the benefits of industrialization and economic integration with the North. Backward and forward linkages would also develop and produce added economic benefits for Mexico. Export growth would be matched by a similar expansion of wages and the internal market. As well, the Mexican State would increase its bargaining power *vis-à-vis* the U.S. and international capital, and therefore allow Mexico to set its own goals for national development. The result would be a more dynamic industrial base in Mexico and increased competitiveness in the world market for technologically advanced products. As these products command high prices in the world market, they would enable Mexico to accrue foreign exchange required for further industrialization.

Under a liberal feminist perspective, women would substantially improve their situation in this scenario. According to this logic, as women are integrated into higher-status employment positions in paid production, their status and role in the reproductive or private sphere would change to reflect the importance of these higher-paying, technical jobs that they occupy. Thus, the sexual division of labour within the home would evolve to a more equitable arrangement in which reproductive duties are shared according to the time available, rather than to gender stereotypes which assume that reproductive duties are women's exclusive domain. Economically, the lives of both women and men would be improved under this scenario, as both sexes would have the opportunity to find skill-enhancing jobs that are beneficial in terms of long-run employment opportunities.

Thus, the liberal feminist assumption is that once equitable access to employment is established, progressive developments in gender relations and the sexual division of labour in both the private and public spheres would naturally follow. This does not take into account the strength and power of patriarchal norms that run deep in Mexican society. The main weakness of the liberal feminist assumption is its economism.

An alternative and more realistic view would expect that women's role in society would change on the condition that a concerted political feminist struggle be waged around gender issues. Thus, women cannot be content with improved job opportunities; they must also struggle for social change in gender relations. To be sure, the new economic situation posited in this scenario becomes a much more favourable material condition for such a struggle which approaches a popular feminism.

If the economic situation proves to be as positive as the scenario suggests, an ease in the burden on the lives of both male and female workers could allow for a closer concentration on issues specific to gender equality. Also, equal opportunities to work will drastically alter the gender dynamic both within and outside the household. If women are no longer seen as supplementary wage earners, societal recognition of their economic importance can result in a positive change in the sexual division of labour. The eventual elimination of the double shift could allow women a greater degree of freedom to participate in political movements. Moreover, equal participation in the work force could lead to an increase in involvement in labour organizations that begin to address gender, as well as class-based, issues. A greater voice in the work place and community could also facilitate entrance into the more formal decision-making political structures which have traditionally excluded women. Such participation would ensure that gender-based issues are addressed and enforced in labour and social policies implemented by the state.

CONCLUSION

Because NAFTA is the culmination of capitalist economic restructuring in North America, in which the key concern has been reducing wage costs, it is unlikely that high wages, improved working conditions, and non-sexist attitudes in the work place will be a short- or a even mid-term outcome. If these changes are to occur for men and women, a strong, unified mass movement that addresses both gender and class issues is essential, both nationally and internationally.

Thus, the first challenge is to achieve a democratic transition in Mexico, which allows women and workers to organize independently to fight for their rights. This assumes strengthening organizations at both community and work, and linking them to regional and national organizations. A second level of struggle must be gauged at the transnational level. The fact is that there is a big gap between the globalization of the economy, on one hand, and the nationally-based civil societies in North America, on the other. Nevertheless, the debate over NAFTA encouraged the formation of transnational grassroots networks among women's organizations,[34] and has posited new challenges to labour internationalism.[35]

Assuming that a democratic transition will not prove to be an elusive goal of Mexican society in the mid-term, the NAFTA and eventually hemispheric economic integration will tend to create more common experiences for workers in all nations involved. Thus, the formation of international linkages will be critical for the future of women's political participation.

However, a sense of solidarity and equality does not come about spontaneously. In order for grass-roots collective organizations to develop and be successful, women must gain a deeper understanding of the broader ways in which capitalism and patriarchy interrelate. Development of class and gender organizations is a process and can only come about from an acknowledgement of common experience and interests. If a grass-roots organization is successful in providing women with a structure to voice their concerns, then this empowerment might extend to the broader establishment of women's right to self-respect and equal participation in the home, work and politics.

---

34 Teresa Carrillo, "Building Transnational Networks Among Grassroots Organizations: Recent Experiences from Mexican Women's Movements," Paper presented at the Latin American Studies Association meeting, Los Angeles, September, 1992.

35 Barry Carr, "Crossing Borders: Labor Internationalism in the Era of NAFTA," in Otero, *Neoliberalism Revisited* (forthcoming).

Pedro G. Marquez Perez
Department of Political Science
University of Calgary

13

The Mexican Automobile Industry

Given the intended transformation of the Mexican economy toward a model no longer based on import substitution and protectionism, the Salinas administration needed to develop the nonpetroleum industry in order to achieve successful economic development. In particular, the model promoted the development of the manufacturing sector as an important source of economic growth for the country. Moreover, among the various sectors of manufacturing, the automobile industry had particular characteristics that recommend it as a case study of the Mexican economic transformation. First, the auto industry—in general, not only the Mexican—has been historically considered as a pioneer industry in the development and application of modernization processes.[1] In other words, it has been characterized by its swift capability of adapting to new productive environments. Second, the Mexican automobile industry (MAI) offered a reliable example of how government regulations strongly influence industrial activity in a positive or negative manner.[2] That is, the MAI was an industry especially susceptible to any kind of change promoted by the government. In addition the automobile industry is an especially important component of North American industrial development in the context of NAFTA.

---

1 J. Womack, D. Jones, and D. Roos, *The Future of the Automobile: The Report of MIT's International Automobile Program* (Cambridge, MA: MIT Press, 1984), p. 12.

2 Douglas Bennet and Kenneth Sharpe, *Transnational Corporations versus the State: The Political Economy of the Mexican Auto Industry* (Princeton: Princeton University Press, 1985), pp. 4–5.

THE IMPORTANCE OF THE WORLD AUTOMOBILE INDUSTRY

Despite the economic protectionism practiced by the import substitution development model, the MAI belongs to a larger context, that is, the world automobile industry (WAI). The evolution experienced by the WAI has influenced the MAI's evolution regardless of protectionist policies. Therefore, any analysis of the MAI must begin with an overview of the international context and external dynamics influencing its development. After all, the MAI's auto assemblers are large transnational corporations with global operations. Ford, G.M and Chrysler—better known as the "big three"—along with Volkswagen and Nissan, are large transnational auto assemblers with central headquarters outside Mexico. The WAI has evolved in three major stages historically and is currently experiencing a fourth phase.[3] According to its analysts, each transformation has implied the development of new technologies, organizational procedures, and competitive strategies that reshape production decisions. Then, production relocation among different countries' auto industries seeks to explode those competitive advantages through research and development (R&D), new types of productive organization, access to raw materials, and reduced production costs—including cheap labour and government subsidies.[4]

Briefly, the first transformation occurred when the U.S. auto industry introduced lean production (1915) oriented to produce cheaper vehicles— better known as "Fordism"—contrasting with the European auto industry's objective to produce limited numbers of luxurious units for the top end of their market. The second transformation of the world's auto industry was characterized by diversification of European production, with the erection of commercial barriers against American producers. The result was a leaner European industry with special products developed to satisfy their own needs, separate from the rest of the world's automotive standards. The third transformation came with the end of the polarity between the U.S.-based industry and the European industry. The closer integration of European and American industry was triggered, at least in part, by the entrance in 1973 of the Japanese production philosophy of zero stocks, "just-in-time" and "total quality" control. Finally, the fourth transformation, supposedly still in progress, is characterized by

---

3   John Holmes and Predeep Kumar, *Divergent Paths: Restructuring Industrial Relations in the North American Automobile Industry.* Working Paper Series, School of Industrial Relations (Queens University, 1991).

4   J. Womack, D. Jones and D. Roos, *The Machine that Changed the World: Report on the MIT $5 Million and 5 Years Research Program* (Cambridge, MA: MIT Press, 1990), p. 46.

"computer-aided" production with reductions on the amount of labour work and large investments in capital.

Although apparently the WAI's current transformation has been mainly interested in factors such as better access to raw materials and reduced transportation and labour costs, experts highlight the use of advanced technology as the main axle of transformation. This trend is not convenient for partially industrialized countries—as Mexico—considering that its competitive advantage is low-wage, low-skilled labour. However, the fourth transformation is not yet a reality, and its final outcome will be determined by the new North American automobile industry.[5]

On balance then, the auto industry has been historically a pioneer industry in the development and practice of new design, production and assembly technologies, which have been copied by other industries. These characteristics have given the auto industry the high production efficiency and flexibility needed to adjust to sudden changes in its productive environment. Specifically, the auto industry has been efficient in adjusting and exploding those comparative advantages offered by different countries' auto industries, including Mexico's.

THE DEVELOPMENT OF THE MEXICAN AUTOMOBILE INDUSTRY

In the same way, the MAI's development provides an excellent example of how the geography of global industries, such as the auto sector, is constantly reshaped by government and firm interaction. As Bennet and Sharpe sustained, "production relocation is determined by the interaction among corporations with broader international strategic choices for organising production and marketing; and government policies toward economic development."[6] This interaction is exemplified by the history of the MAI. There were four main phases in the development of the Mexican industry: MAI's birth (1925–62); Import Substitution Industry (1962–77); Export Oriented Industry (1977–89); and Economic and Political Liberalization (1989–94). Each phase has been characterized by state intervention through legal decrees regulating the auto industry's participation in the country's development. These decrees have been the result of negotiations among the government, the transnational automobile corporations—that is, the "big three," Volkswagen (V.W.) and Nissan—and the Mexican auto parts industry.

---

5   Holmes and Kumar, *Divergent Paths*, p. 10.

6   Bennet and Sharpe, *Transnational Corporations*, p. 80.

The Birth of the Mexican Automobile Industry (1925–61). MAI began in 1925 when Ford established its first assembly plant in Mexico City. The Automotive Regulation of 1925 was the first antecedent of government interventionism towards its development, reducing 50 percent of taxes on imported parts. Until 1948, the free import of vehicles was allowed, but their prices were cheaper than those offered by the local industry. Therefore, the government established for the first time import quotas and licences. Like other partially-industrialized countries, the domestic market for automobiles in Mexico from the 1920s to the 1960s was served by finished imports or by assembling small imported vehicle kits in so-called "screw-driver plants," located virtually around Mexico City. However, the sector offered little solution to the nation's needs on job creation, raw materials consumption or technological development.

The Import Substitution Phase (1962–77). Significant change in Mexican state policy toward the auto industry occurred in the early 1960s, shaping the industry for the next twenty-five years. With the objective of promoting industrialization, the government passed the first Automotive Decree in 1962. It created a full-scale national automotive industry, forcing the international auto makers either to construct manufacturing plants in Mexico or to leave the country and forfeit the growing Mexican market to their competitors. In consequence, the industry experienced an intense substitution of import parts, providing a place for the Mexican auto parts industry (MAPI).

The Mexican state interest in promoting import substitution was reflected in the Automotive Decrees of 1962 and 1969 as the most appropriate path to develop the Mexican motor vehicle industry. The decrees ordered high levels of domestic content on a "product line" basis, and as much Mexican ownership of parts production as possible. "The 1962 Automotive Decree banned assembled vehicle imports at required high (60 percent) local content rules, for both vehicles and components manufactured in Mexico."[7] Transnational auto corporations established more sophisticated final assembly plants, but still significantly smaller and less integrated than those in the rest of North America. This assured the creation of an independent Mexican auto parts industry. The final assembly plants constructed during this period were geographically more decentralized, but still concentrated around Mexico City. During this period, there was virtually no trade in assembled vehicles either into or out of

---

7   J. Holmes, "From Three Industries to One: Towards an Integrated North American Automobile Industry," in M. Appel-Molot, ed., *Driving Continentally: National Policies and the North American Auto Industry* (Ottawa: Carleton University Press, 1993), p. 51.

Mexico (Table 1).[8] However, the increased oil export revenues of the late 1970s fuelled the domestic demand for vehicles, and domestic assembly grew with a substantial increase in imports of automotive components from the U.S. and Canada to feed the Mexican assembly plants.

For the Mexican government, the desire for an advanced auto industry has been always present but its policies have changed according to national economic perspectives. Until 1977, its policies imposed restrictions on imports and foreign investment. These policies opposed the Classical Liberalism ideology of free commerce. Nevertheless, a new perspective emerged in the late 1970s with changes in the strategies pursued by state policies.[9]

Export Oriented Production (1977–89). In response to the worsening trade balance of the whole economy, the Mexican government issued the Automotive Decree of 1977 requiring assemblers to achieve a better trade balance within four years. However, the collapse of the economy during the oil crisis and the severe debt in the early 1980s had two major effects on the auto industry. First, the urgent need to eliminate the chronic trade balance deficit forced the state to add new trade demands to the 1977 Auto Decree—notice that the trade deficit increased 550 percent from 1977 to 1981, thus forcing the parent companies in the United States to significantly increase investments in Mexico regardless of the economic instability. Most of the auto makers (with the exception of Renault) achieved these requirements by building world-scale engine plants, mainly in northern Mexico, to export to their plants in the United States and Canada, in the process "leading the country into a new era of export promotion . . . [ensuring it] as a major source location within the global strategies of the world auto industry."[10] The second consequence was a collapse of domestic automobile demand with the 1983 Automotive Decree. The objective of the decree was to rationalize the industry's structure, requiring assemblers to reduce their range of product offerings (a limit of five models; increased production of fewer models; and local content of 60 percent). Such efficient economies of scale were intended to reduce prices.

Until 1982, no vehicles were exported to the United States or Canada; however, this picture changed with rapid increases of exports in the following years to the North American market. This shift derived more

---

8 By 1977, only 4.2 percent of the total vehicle production was exported, with practically no imports of finished vehicles.

9 Helen Shapiro, "The Determinants of Trade and Investment Flow in LDC Auto Industries: The Cases of Brazil and Mexico," in M. Appel-Molot, ed., *Driving Continentally*, p. 128.

10 Holmes, *Driving Continentally*, p. 64.

Table 1. Motor Vehicle Production
and Exports: Mexico 1960–1994

	Production[a]	Total exports X	% of production	Exports to U.S.	to CAN	All exports X	Total M	Coef. M/X
1960	50	0	0.0	0	0	0%	0	0
1965	97	0	0.0	0	0	0%	0	0
1970	193	0	0.0	0	0	0%	0	0
1975	361	2,938	0.8	0	0	0%	0	0
1976	325	4,172	1.3	0	0	0%	0	0
1977	281	11,793	4.2	0	0	0%	0	0
1978	384	25,828	6.7	0	0	0%	0	0
1979	444	24,756	5.6	0	0	0%	0	0
1980	490	18,245	3.7	0	0	0%	0	0
1981	597	14,428	2.4	3	0	0%	0	0
1982	473	15,819	3.3	623	0	4%	0	0
1983	285	22,456	7.9	203	0	1%	0	0
1984	344	33,635	9.8	13,448	0	40%	0	0
1985	398	58,423	14.7	47,197	0	81%	0	0
1986	338	72,429	21.4	60,466	0	84%	0	0
1987	395	163,073	41.3	140,641	5,017	89%	0	0
1988	515	173,147	34.3	148,017	5,023	88%	0	0
1989	629	194,631	30.9	162,987	7,283	87%	0	0
1990	821	276,869	34.0	238,281	13,079	91%	5,376	0.02
1991	989	358,666	36.0	261,280	67,041	92%	9,371	0.03
1992	1,080	391,050	36.0	282,853	59,260	87%	11,487	0.03
1993	1,080	493,612	46.0	352,772	69,934	86%	10,027	0.02
1994	1,108	557,766	50.0	–	–	–	70,513	0.13

[a] Thousands of units. Sources: *Automotive News Data Book*, 1990; AMDA, *La Industria Automotriz de Mexico en Cifras* (The Mexican Auto Industry in Numbers), 1988; INEGI, *La Industria Automotriz en Mexico* (The Mexican Auto Industry), 1993; AMIA, *Boletin Anual* (Annual Bulletin), 1993; AMIA, *Boletin Noviembre* (November Bulletin), 1994; AMDA, *Cifras Diez Anos del Sector Automotor en Mexico* (Years of Numbers about the Auto Industry in Mexico), 1993.

from a reassessment by the Big Three of Mexico as a low-cost source of entry-level vehicles than to the government's Decree. For example, in 1986 the Ford Motor Company opened a new assembly plant at Hermosillo, Sonora, to assemble vehicles to sell in North American markets, using parts mainly from Japanese sources under advanced Japan-style production and management processes and work organization techniques. Under the provision of the 1983 Decree, this plant was allowed to assemble an extra model with only 30 percent domestic content on condition that at least 80 percent of the output was exported. The Ford plant achieved a quality product, ranked higher than the best volume assembly Japanese plants or the best North American automobile manufacturers in 1989. However, with the strengthening of the yen it became increasingly apparent that if the Mexican assembly industry wanted to be successful, it needed to switch components from "Japanese-made to North American-made." This explains, at least partly, the *maquiladora* and engine production investments made by a number of Japanese auto parts companies in Mexico and Canada (Table 2).

During the 1980s, Mexican workers suffered a disproportionate loss of income as a consequence of the collapse of the economy in the early part of the decade. For the auto industry, wages had declined during the same period below Korean wage levels, and were equal to Brazil's—the two main MAI competitors to supply the North American markets. In Mexico, "the *maquiladoras* had grown in number, employing more people and providing income to more Mexicans. But instead of initiating a process of development on their living standards, it seemed that Mexico was in a state of stagnation, where equilibrium was based on low wages, low Mexican value added, and unskilled labour."[11]

In the same period, Mexico became significantly more integrated in the North American auto industry, as a source of finished units and parts, with three important segments: a segment centred on Mexico City, consisting of relatively inefficient parts suppliers; a *maquiladora* segment along the northern border, taking advantage of the low-cost labour to produce high-quality parts for exports; and a group of export-oriented assembly and engine plants close to the United States–Mexico border, within rail or truck reach of "just-in-time" delivery.

Economic and Political Liberalization (1989–94). Two sets of circumstances converged by 1989. The first was continued intensification of world competition in the auto industry, particularly in the U.S. market.

---

11 Frances Hammond, "The Labour Impact of NAFTA," in Rafael Fernandez de Castro, Monica Verea Campos, and Sidney Weintraub, eds., *Sectoral Labor Effects of North American Free Trade* (Mexico: ITAM, 1993), p. 186.

TABLE 2. INVESTMENTS IN MEXICAN EXPORT
ENGINE PRODUCTION 1982–1988

COMPANY	PLANT LOCATION	START DATE	CAPACITY 1988	TARGET EXPORTS (1000s)	EXPORTS 1988 (%)	DESTINA-TION OF EXPORTS
GM	Ramos Arizpe	1982	450	90	20	US/ Canada, Europe, Australia
Ford	Chihuahua	1983	400	312	78	US/ Canada
Chrysler	Saltillo	1982	270	242	90	US/ Canada
Nissan	Aguascal.	1983	192	80	42	Japan, US
VW	Puebla	1980	440	211	48	Europe, US (until 1989)
Renault	Gomez Palacio	1984	350	133	38	US/ Canada, Europe
Other engine plants (for domestic market): GM (Toluca), Ford (Cuautitlan), Chrysler (Toluca), Nissan (Morelos)						

Source: B. Samuels, *Managing Risk in Developing Countries: National Demands and Multinational Response* (Princeton University Press, 1990); H. Shaiken and S. Herzenberg, *Automation and Global Production: Automobile Engine Production in Mexico, the U.S. and Canada* (University of California, San Diego, Center for U.S.–Mexican Studies, 1987).

New production and marketing strategies in recognition of the emerging trend of regional trading blocs led the international auto makers to re-evaluate the future role of Mexico within this industry, not only as a low-cost production location but also as an important element of the regional bloc, with potential for significant market growth over the next decades. Second, 1989's *Decreto para el Fomento y Modernizacion de la Industria Automotriz* (Automotive Industry Development and Modernization Decree [AIFMD]) and 1993's NAFTA reflected a state policy shift towards a radical reorientation of Mexico's approach to its industrial development strategy, which resulted in abandonment of the protectionism and import-substitution policies that dominated for almost 30 years. The policy shift favoured the promotion of an export-led, market-oriented automobile industry fully integrated into the world auto industry.

THE EVOLUTION OF THE MEXICAN AUTOMOBILE INDUSTRY

Even though the first steps towards the modernization of the Mexican automobile industry began with the establishment of auto-part *maquiladoras* along the border with the United States in 1979, its more significant technological and organizational transformations occurred under the AIFMD regulations in 1989 and NAFTA regulations in 1994. Although the MAI consisted of transnational assemblers, the auto-part industry and the auto-industry *maquiladoras*, in fact the Neo-liberal policy of President Salinas reoriented the role of the former two because the *maquiladoras* already operated under a free trade environment. Basically, for the new development model the auto industry would assume a pioneer role in Mexico's industrial transformation towards an open economy. Meanwhile, it would also assume an important role in the WAI's fourth transformation as key participant of the NAAI.

Table 3 shows the profile of both the *maquiladora* and automobile industries from 1984 to 1993. In general terms, the auto industry and the *maquiladora* industry followed a 1:10 ratio in number of plants, and a 1:3.5 ratio on value added and employment. Therefore, in general terms, the auto industry performed a significant role in promoting employment and economic output during the Salinas administration.

As suggested earlier, Social Neo-liberalism was conducted in three main forms: economic and political liberalization, and social reform. Obviously the transformation of the MAI was mainly conducted by the economic liberalization. However, the importance of Social Liberalism's political liberalization of the auto industry resided in the legal reforms developed to support the objectives of the economic reform. Finally, for the MAI the social reform was the least important of the three reforms; nonetheless, there were reforms of benefits provided by PRONASOL to the auto industry workers living next to assembly plants and auto-parts factories.

THE IMPACT OF POLITICAL LIBERALIZATION ON THE AUTO INDUSTRY

From the beginning of his administration, Salinas made it a major goal to achieve the modernization of Mexican industry within a legal framework capable of liberalizing economic activity. The industrial development and protective policies of former governments were abolished and replaced by the premise of Social Liberalism that the market should regulate industrial activity. However, due to the relevance of the

TABLE 3. PROFILE OF THE *MAQUILADORA* INDUSTRY
VS. AUTOMOBILE *MAQUILADORA* 1984–1993

MAQUILADORA INDUSTRY					
	1984	1986	1988	1993	Avg. Annual Growth %
Value added ($US mill.)	1,120	1,290	1,570	N/A	8.0
Employment	202,100	268,400	361,800	511,510	15.3
Plants	722	987	1,450	2,050	18.4
AUTOMOBILE INDUSTRY					
Value added ($US mill.)	194.9	304.4	486.7	N/A	30.0
Employment	29,378	49,048	77,502	210,925	25.9
Plants	51	78	129	183	25.0

Sources: INEGI, *Estadisticas Historicas de Mexico* (Historic Statistics of Mexico), 1993; INEGI, *La Industria Automotriz en Mexico* (The Mexican Auto Industry), 1993; AMIA, *Boletin Anual* (Annual Bulletin), 1993.

automobile industry for the Mexican economy, it continued to be subject to special legislation.

Initially, in consonance with the strategy implemented to reduce inflation, the government published in August of 1989 the "Decree of Tax Exemption for Compact Vehicles of Popular Consumption."[12] Its objective was to stimulate domestic demand and favour the production of those vehicles priced at $5,000 or less through tax exemptions for new "popular" vehicles and related imported parts. The decree demanded a minimum annual production of 40,000 units, adherence to the 1983 decree's local content regulation, and the fulfillment of tougher safety, pollution, and gas-consumption regulations.[13] Although only one model

---

12 SECOFI, *Decreto que Otorga Exenciones a los Automoviles Compactos de Consumo Popular* (Mexico, 1989).

13 Economic Commission for Latin American and the Caribbean, *Reestructuracion y desarrollo de la Industria Automotriz Mexicana en los Ochenta: Evolucion y Perspectivas* [Restructure and Development of the Mexican Auto Industry in the Eighties: Evolution and Perspectives] (Chile: United Nations Publications, 1992), p. 172.

fulfilled the definition as "popular"—the V.W. Beetle—the decree was successful in increasing its demand. In 1990, V.W. sold 84,245 Beetles, representing almost one fourth of the total sales of passenger vehicles, and 15 percent of the total vehicles sold in the domestic market.[14]

Although the "popular automobile" decree did not establish a new development policy for the MAI, it deserves to be mentioned because it reflects the priority of the price stabilization strategy and social concerns of Salinas's administration over its liberal initiatives. In other words, the AIFMD's publication (December 1988—just a few months after the "popular automobile" decree publication) shows the severe shift in industrial development policy, from the traditional strong, central regulation of industrial activity and market control to the liberalization of industrial activity and market forces.

Although the AIFMD continued with the old state practice of regulating the MAI via official decrees, it shifted the policy to promote MAI's development. The new policy was more consistent with the new conception of a modern Mexico: the WAI's globalization process and the gradual insertion of the MAI into international markets. In short, the 1989 decree was established to modernize the auto sector "to consolidate the economic liberalization in harmony with the current national and international circumstances, and objectives of the new industrial policy." Accordingly, "vehicles and auto parts must be manufactured on efficient scales, with the best quality and under internationally competitive prices affordable by the national consumer; but mainly capable of being exported."[15]

The AIFMD reduced the domestic content requirements from the previous level of 60 percent to 36 percent for assemblers and 30 percent for part producers. It also relaxed the restrictions on imported assembled vehicles with production facilities in the country, in order to supplement or complement their domestic production. The policy enabled the auto assemblers to expand their production lines marketable in Mexico, concentrate on the production of fewer models, improve economies of scale, and increase their exports. The decree provided the auto transnationals with a new perspective on the Mexican auto industry as part of the North American industry. Consequently, the auto assemblers announced significant expansion plans, designed to further increase the level of integration of auto production among Mexico, Canada and the U.S.

---

14 INEGI, *La Industria Automotriz en Cifras Mexico* [The Mexican Auto Industry] (Mexico, 1993), p. 54.

15 SECOFI, *Automotive Industry Foment and Modernization Decree* (Mexico, 1989).

The AIFMD in reality included two decrees: the first directed to the auto industry—considering passenger vehicles and trucks up to nine tons in weight—and the second towards the manufacture of transportation vehicles (TVMI)—vehicles over nine tons in weight. The decree involving TVMI was more radical in regard to deregulation and market liberalization, demonstrating the strategic importance of automobile transportation services for the modernization of the economy. The decree did not define the transportation services as a priority activity; its objective was to promote its efficiency and competitiveness. Overall, the TVMI decree's importance resided in the elimination, for the first time, of the requisite of 51 percent Mexican ownership established by the foreign investments law. Consequently, it made way for the creation of the first MAI's joint venture among Mexico's FAMSA and Germany's Daimler Benz.[16]

The decree for passenger vehicles established a more gradual liberalization. Its objective was to propose a middle point among the traditional state regulation system and the total liberalization demanded by the assembly transnationals. The decree eliminated the production restrictions considered fundamental by the 1983 decree to create economies of scale, granting total production freedom. In the same way, it allowed the assemblers, for the first time since 1962, to complete their product line offer through the importation of those vehicles not assembled in the country—that is, to rationalize the production of those vehicles produced more efficiently in Mexico, and import those produced more efficiently outside. However, this policy created a monopoly of auto imports, because the regulation only permitted the importation of vehicles to the assemblers. The main restriction established by the decree was to keep a positive trade balance compensated on a 2.5:1 ratio for 1991, 2:1 for 1992–93, and 1.75:1 after 1994. The decree also demanded a minimum of 36 percent of local value on assembled vehicles and limited imports volume up to 15 percent of the total units sold domestically for 1991–92, and 20 percent after 1993. The most noticeable consequence of the new regulations in 1991 was a sudden wave of luxury vehicle imports, highly demanded by the upper classes of society. Imports of luxury models such as Lincoln Town Car, Cadillac, Corvette, Maxima and Passat at considerably higher prices than those in the U.S. market reached the total of 3805, 5191 and 6048 units for 1990, 1991 and 1992 respectively.

Other significant regulations established by the AIFMD consisted of shifts from the 1983 decree's regulations on exchange currency budget and local value restrictions. The new decree unified both restrictions and defined local value in terms of trade balance by firm and not by product.

---

16 SECOFI and BANCOMEXT, *Industria de Autopartes. Study Elaborated by Booz-Allen & Hamilton and INFOTEC for the Mexican Government* (Mexico, 1992), p. 37.

The policy enabled the companies to transfer import costs to other items not included in balance of trade, such as financing, investments or profits. Therefore, the new system stopped further foreign investments in production, while supposedly it was one of the main objectives of the new development model. Moreover, the new regulations were incongruent with the new principles stated by the macroeconomic policy. Specifically, the strategy sustained the reduced importance of positive trade balances, if at the end of the year the balance of payments stayed positive upon foreign capital investments.

However, if one of the objectives of the decree was to free the MAPI from the restriction of Mexican ownership established by the *Ley de Inversiones Extranjeras* (Foreign Investments Law), without involving the political risk of intend to reform the law itself, then the continued protection to MAPI—that is, minimum 36 percent of local value—seems absurd. In other words, the legislation that promoted increased foreign participation in MAPI also limited the use of cheaper foreign parts on vehicle assembly. In the same way, the decree demanded that both vehicle and part producers offer international prices on the units and parts produced for the domestic market, under the threat of liberalizing the importation of all kinds of models if offered cheaper than theirs. However, in practice this clause proved to be illogical since automobile and auto parts prices had been under economic pact control since 1987.

Further liberalization of the MAI was regulated by NAFTA. Although it is expected that NAFTA will create significant benefits for the auto industry, its effects are yet too recent to be evaluated. Nevertheless, in general terms NAFTA was implemented in 1993 as part of a national strategy to consolidate economic development. That is, NAFTA was an agent designed to achieve industrialization, replacing the import-substitution and export-oriented protectionist policies practised in the past. However, prior to NAFTA, the auto industry was the most globalized of the manufacturing industries of North America.[17] Therefore, its transition towards full integration to the NAAI was shorter than those of other industries with a smaller degree of integration. Functionally, the key issues in the NAFTA automotive negotiation can be classified into four main groups:[18] the reduction of commerce barriers, the liberalization of investment laws and regulations, the elimination of performance

---

17 M. Appel-Molot, *Driving Continentally: National Policies and the North American Auto Industry* (Ottawa: Carleton University Press, 1993), p. 14.

18 Eduardo Andere and Georgina Kessel, eds., *Mexico y el Tratado Trilateral de Libre Comercio; Impacto Sectorial* [Mexico and the Free Trade Agreement: The Sectoral Impact] (Mexico: ITAM, 1992), pp. 62–4.

TABLE 4. NAFTA: AUTOMOBILE INDUSTRY INTEGRATION TIME SCHEDULE

YEAR	TARIFFS	RULES OF ORIGIN	AUTO PARTS (EXPORTS FROM)	FOREIGN INVESTMENT	USED CARS
1994		50%			
Mexico	10%		81%		
Canada	10%				
U.S.	0%		5%		
1998		56%			
1999				49%	
Mexico	5%		18%		
Canada	5%				
U.S.	0%		70%		
2003		62.5%			
2004				100%	
Mexico	0%		1%		
Canada	0%				
U.S.	0%		25%		
2010					100%

Source: C. Romero Jacobo, *Serra y el TLC: Si Habra Continudad Economica* (Serra and NAFTA: Economic Continuity Will Be Achieved), in *EPOCA Magazine*, No. 63, 17 August 1992.

requirements for the industry, and the rules of origin established during the negotiations.[19]

The reduction of commerce barriers on automobile products was established on a 25-year time schedule that included advantages to the MAI in consideration of its less developed status. Table 4 summarizes the terms of the agreement on rules of origin and foreign investment laws for the three countries. Notice that the relatively small requirement of "North

---

19 John Holmes, "From Three Industries to One: Towards an Integrated North American Automobile Industry," in M. Appel-Molot, ed., *Driving Continentally*, p. 25.

American" parts established by the rules of origin, increasing from 50 percent in 1994 to 62.5 percent in 2003, was considered by its analysts as beneficial for the MAI because it allowed the import of direct foreign parts from sources different than those from the United States and Canada into the MAI, especially from Asia, with the objective of guaranteeing future access of their products into the North American markets.

Finally, another important regulation respected by NAFTA was the "Corporate Average Fuel Economy Act" that regulates fuel consumption and pollution rates of the units imported to the U.S. and Canada automobile market. This act is important because it adds another variable to the production strategies of the transnational corporations assembling units in the three countries. That is, CAFE regulations are tougher on domestic units than on imported units. Therefore, the MAI's assembly industry could be used to produce those units that only fulfil the CAFE requirements as imported and not as local units.

Although NAFTA negotiations accorded respect to the AIFMD's terms for the Mexican industry, the agreement provided the three countries and the automobile transnational corporations with a long-term agreement useful to plan their future industrial activities. A cost and benefit analysis is helpful to evaluate the possible impact of NAFTA on the MAI. In accordance to Liberal theory, the benefits of an integrated NAAI would be the following:

1. International prices will allow better access to a larger number of consumers.
2. The increase in market competitiveness and efficiency will guarantee better offers for the consumers.
3. Increased market product variety of models will benefit consumers.

On the other hand, the costs would be:

1. The necessity of a quick consolidation of the national industry in order to achieve the efficiency levels required to compete. Consequently, those firms unable to achieve these adjustments will have to close and unemployment increase.
2. The imports of cheap used cars will damage the current used auto market.

For Liberalism, the integration of the NAAI would allow a more competitive market in the mid- to long-term, where the auto parts and assembler industries would have to review strategies:

1. Adjust their product mix, concentrate efforts on those with better probabilities of survival in an integrated market.

2. New production and distribution, considering the new markets.
3. Adjust into more flexible and efficient production processes.
4. Renew the products offered to the Mexican market and their strategic marketing plans to face the new competition.
5. Reduce costs and improve scale economies through better product designs and alliances with other firms.
6. Increase the technological capacity and quality control.
7. Consider vertical integration with raw materials and part suppliers.

Economic Liberalization

Although the Mexican automobile industry enjoyed significant prosperity from 1983 to 1987, it was from 1988 to 1994 that the industry experienced a fundamental shift in its economic activity. Despite the MAI continuing to be the subject of special legislation during this second period, its transformation gave place to an industry where the private sector became the motor of its development. The 1989 auto decree encouraged a better balance among the state's interest for a mature auto industry in active participation in Mexico's economy and the auto industry's interests for freer economic activity. The AIFMD again modifies MAI's activities, however; this time it did so by reducing the role of the state and promoting the participation of the private sector.

The new regulation for the MAI had an impact in both domestic markets and in production for export. Although this research mainly presents data regarding the assembly industry, the experience of the auto-parts industry was more or less similar because an increase in assembly production implied an increase in auto-part demand. The case of the auto-part export industry behaved similarly to the assembly industry because this industry not only exported in a direct way via joint ventures with foreign auto-part firms, but also exported via the parts supplied to the assembly industry to be incorporated into export production.[20]

With respect to impact on the domestic market, the domestic market share of the five transnationals changed between 1986 and 1990. In 1986 Nissan ranked number one in total unit sales with 28.5 percent and V.W. was second with 23 percent. However, from 1990 to 1994 V.W. jumped into first place with an average market share of 27 percent, while Nissan averaged 21 percent. The rest of the assemblers kept their share in the following order: G.M. in third, Chrysler in fourth and Ford in fifth. Although the change could be attributed to the "popular vehicle" decree of 1989—increased demand for the V.W. Beetle—this decree only lasted

---

20 Francisco Zapata, *La Reestructuracion Industria en Mexico: El Caso de la Industria de Autopartes* [Restructuring in Mexico: The Case of Auto Parts] (Mexico: El Colegio de Mexico, 1994), p. 73.

for a couple of months until the AIFMD was published in December of 1989. Consequently, some analysts argued that the key to V.W. success resulted from its better product mix. V.W. offered in 1990 a more complete line of vehicles from the "popular" Beetle to the imported luxurious Passat, while the product line of the other firms was limited or concentrated on market niches.[21] In summary, the new regulations of the AIFMD and NAFTA allowed the Mexican auto assemblers to restructure production and import strategies in order to maximize domestic market share. The production of vehicles could concentrate on the assembly of those units produced more efficiently in Mexico, and consequently upon economies of scale, to offer cheaper products to a more competitive market. The line of products could be complemented—with its legal limitations—with imported units, consistent with the premises of economic liberalism. The result is a more efficient auto industry where the main beneficiaries are the consumers.[22]

Economic liberalization increased MAI exports by the five companies that had started in 1982. In general terms, production and exports increased by 215 percent and 322 percent from 1988 to 1994, and 389 percent and 2,484 percent from 1983 to 1994. In 1994, V.W. and the Big Three exported close to half their production to North American markets. The firms with the highest and lowest rates of growth from 1987 to 1994 were V.W. with a dramatic increase of 1200 percent, and G.M. with a still important 140 percent.

The increase in exports not only provided MAI with a significant source of income, but also allowed it to learn about the international market, have access to modern technologies, and therefore improve its competitiveness. As shown by Francisco Zapata's research on MAI's international competitiveness, it adopted modern technologies to improve its "price, quality and punctuality."[23] The necessity to improve these parameters was demanded by the new market conditions, subject to international competition. Consequently, the MAI implemented technological improvements in productive and administrative processes. Some examples were the use of "just-in-time" production, statistical quality control, and robots to inspect assembly, on the one hand; and random supplier inspections and CAD-CAM (Computer Aided Design–Computer Aided

---

21 For example, Ford concentrated on mid-size and luxury vehicles such as the Topaz, Grand Marquis, and Lincoln Town Car. Nissan concentrated on "entry line" fuel-efficient vehicles and small trucks. See Katia Ostos Fulda, *Analisis de la Industria Automotriz ante el Tratado de Libre Comercio* (Mexico City: BA Thesis, ITAM, 1993), p. 27.

22 Mark Stevenson, "Mexico's Booming Auto Imports," in *Mexico Insight*, Special Supplement, *Excelsior* (29 May 1994), pp. 20–25.

23 Zapata, *La Reestructuracion Industria*, p. 53.

Manufacture) systems on the other. The introduction of computer systems to supervise the production systems allowed MAI to fulfill production and deliver to customers on time.

Another important consequence of the MAI's liberalization was its capacity to develop closer ties with their transnational matrix for the assembly industry, and create joint-ventures with foreign firms for the auto-part industry. According to *Expansion* magazine, the 35 most important firms of the Mexican auto-part industry in 1987 consisted of 17 firms of Mexican capital, 15 of foreign capital—that is, at the maximum 40 percent offering ownership allowed by the law—and three state-owned corporations. However, the same source for 1993 listed five firms of Mexican capital and 30 of foreign capital. Furthermore, some of the firms that were independent in 1987 merged or created joint-ventures with other new foreign firms, mainly from North America (80 percent) but also with Italian and Japanese capital (10 percent each).[24] The three state-owned corporations existing in 1987—Moto Diesel Mexicana, Motores Perkins and Rassini—were privatized in 1990 as part of Social Liberalism's privatization program.

The productive and industrial transformations promoted by Social Liberalism also challenged the old labour system which prevailed under the import substitution model. The alliance between the state and labour unions enabled the unions and workers to develop a strong negotiation capacity, which contributed to higher salaries, social benefits, and the participation of labour in decision-making. The modernization of the industry required a more flexible internal labour market, which in turn meant that labour lost many of its accumulated benefits.

The auto assembly and parts industries employed an average of 7 percent of the total employment of the manufacturing sector between 1987 and 1994, which in turn involved an average of 11 percent of the total official national employment (Table 5). Of the three major sub-industries—assembly, auto-parts and rubber industries—the assembly and auto-parts sectors employed, in the same period, 31 percent and 50 percent of the total employment of the MAI. However, the assembly industry's employment grew at a slightly higher rate than the auto-parts and rubber industries, as a result of investment in new plants.

On first impression, the data on foreign investments, exports and employment seem impressive, suggesting that automobile exportation is neither sporadic nor counter-cyclical in relation to reductions of domestic demand. Although the numbers seem to indicate that recent policies and

---

24 *Las Exportadoras e Importadoras mas Importantes de Mexico* [The Most Important Exporters and Importers of Mexico], *Expansion* (October 1988), pp. 1–10; (September 1994), pp. 54–69.

TABLE 5. LABOUR, MANUFACTURING AND AUTOMOBILE INDUSTRY
MEXICO 1987–1993 (YEAR AVERAGE)

YEAR	AUTOMOBILE INDUSTRY	MANUFACTURE INDUSTRY	NATIONAL TOTAL
1987	146,167	2,429,796	21,867,362
1988	156,793	2,431,904	22,051,203
1989	170,300	2,492,720	22,330,855
1990	180,742	2,510,276	22,536,351
1991	189,511	2,500,163	23,114,633
1992	200,881	2,510,610	N/A
1993	210,925	2,502,831	N/A

Source: INEGI, *La Industria Automotriz en Mexico* (The Mexican Auto Industry), 1993; AMIA, *Boletin Mensual, Diciembre* (December Bulletin), 1994.

automobile decrees promoted a significant structural reform and developed production capacity, in fact there were increasing trade deficits from 1990 to 1994.[25]

Commercial liberalization undermined the national integration process among both the finished-vehicles and auto-parts industries, which was further modified by technological modernization, in order to meet anti-pollution requirements of the United States and Mexico City. In other words, fuel-injection and catalytic-converter systems represent additional imports to those normally obligatory. In the same way, the luxury options imported from the United States increased the trade imbalance. Simultaneously, the domestic auto-part suppliers increased imports of cheaper raw materials both because of U.S. recession-reduced prices, as the pressure established by large purchasing firms upon selling firms to obtain internationally competitive prices, and finally to meet price regulations.

Another important factor explaining the growth of the trade deficit is that until 1991 Mexico was a consolidated motor engine exporter; however, after 1991 the WAI developed new high-performance motors not built in Mexico. Therefore, the MAI needed to invest in new technology to begin the production of the new motors, with its further impact on

---

25 Economic Commission for Latin American and the Caribbean, *Reestructuracion y desarrollo*, p. 176.

trade balance. Therefore, the sooner the modernization of the engine export production occurs, the sooner it will benefit MAI's trade balance.

In summary, the prosperity experienced from 1988 to 1994 presented—on a larger scale—similar characteristics to the growth that ended in the 1982 economic crisis, that is, large dependence on external and internal projects along with questionable solidity of industrial development. Although Social Liberalism was successful in transforming the automobile industry, this reorientation strongly depended upon circumstantial internal and external factors that raise doubts about the degree of development achieved.

Several external factors were important, including the U.S. trade deficit in auto products with Japan, dependence on foreign investments, and the capacity of the transnational corporations to modify their allocation of production in the most convenient way, regardless of national location. Internal factors also played a role, including dubious benefits from the price-stabilization program, reduced labour wages, easier access to credit, and incoherent projects such as the "popular automobile" decree; all expanded the demand for MAI's products. Therefore, if those internal and external factors change, then development of the Mexican automobile industry seems to lack long-term solidity. In other words, the auto-assembly industry and the auto-parts industry have acquired a dependent status, evolving from a developmental model that has not proven its efficiency, and influenced by such volatile external factors as the North American auto industry.

THE NEW AUTO INDUSTRY

The restructuring of the Mexican auto industry included the promotion of economic and social change. As suggested by Jorge Carrillo, the social changes were related to the management of human resources mainly characterized by the modification of social relations, training strategies, and the modernization of the administrative system and corporate structures.[26] There were three main objectives behind the restructuring of the industry: the development of its international competitiveness, the increase in exports, and consequently the creation of a solid auto industry participating in the economic development of the country. The conditions required to achieve these goals were basically the development of better quality, price and on-time delivery of its final products.

---

26 Jorge Carrillo did extensive research on industrial and social change in the Mexican automobile industry from its inception to 1993 in his PhD thesis, *La Ford en Mexico: Reestructuracion Industrial y Cambio en las Relaciones Sociales* [Ford in Mexico: Industrial Restructuring and Social Relations Change] (Mexico: El Colegio de Mexico, 1993), pp. 510–24.

In relation to quality, the new regulation of MAI's activities allowed it to have better access to modern technology via foreign investments, the creation of joint ventures with foreign firms and fewer restrictions on technology imports. In the same way, the macroeconomic stabilization program allowed the industry to have access to inexpensive credits, buy price-controlled raw materials, and import inexpensive parts upon the undervalued exchange rate policy. With regard to better prices, the AIFMD allowed the industry to adjust production lines, explode economies of scale and implement the use of modern production and organization technologies. Consequently, the industry increased productivity and became more efficient. Finally, to optimize on-time delivery of final products to foreign customers, the MAI opened commercial offices in the United States, reorganized its delivery logistics, created warehouses along the border, and implemented a computerized control system of production processes.

The common characteristics shared by the strategies pursued to achieve better quality, price and on-time delivery were their need for modern technology and large investments. The restructuring of the industry required important investments of capital in order to acquire expensive equipment, hire technical assistance, invest in research and development, train personnel, open new offices and implement "just-in-time" production. Before 1982 the government would have provided those needed resources, but for the new Neo-liberal model, the private sector had to finance these activities. Therefore, the AIFMD opened the possibility of increased domestic and foreign investments in the auto industry. Consequently, as sustained by Social Liberalism, private sectors became the motor of the MAI's development. However, the acquisition of such technologies strongly linked the MAI to foreign suppliers of advanced equipment and training for the MAI's workers, creating a Mexican auto industry severely dependent upon foreign sources of technology and investment.

In the same way, the MAI's exports were limited to a reduced number of clients in the U.S., giving place to possible future problems. The main problem is that the MAI could be easily affected by changes in its clients' activities, that is, if the U.S. assembly transnationals begin demanding vehicles and auto parts from a different country, such as Brazil or Argentina. In the same way, the rate of MAI's exports could be severely affected by fluctuations in the U.S. economy, or changes in its economic policy. In summary, although the restructuring could give place to significant benefits for those firms capable of developing international competitiveness—beside significant benefits to the nation's economy—the industry's success is highly limited by its significant dependence on external, uncontrollable, factors.

In conclusion, in 1985 some analysts expressed their opinion about economic liberalization in Mexico. They suggested that the Mexican economy was permanently subordinated to global forces. They expressed little hope that countries like Mexico would take any autonomous economic decisions capable of promoting their economic development. A study of the Mexican automobile industry by the same analysts maintained that "Mexican economic policies have always agreed with a relationship of dependency from the capitalist world; and its automobile industry has always assumed that same relationship towards the World's automobile industry. This complex structure has always limited its options and molded its actors' interests and decision-making capacity."[27] In 1995, this opinion could be advanced again. The Mexican auto industry is subordinated to external variables that limit its development and ability to make independent decisions. Therefore, the current strategy to develop its activities based on policies of economic and political liberalization has not been the most effective solution to MAI's problem of under-development signalled in 1985—at least not if it continues promoting economic dependence on one market.

---

27 Bennet and Sharpe, *Transnational Corporations*, pp. 4–5.

Morton Weinfeld
Department of Sociology
McGill University

14

North American Integration and the Issue of Immigration: Canadian Perspectives

INTRODUCTION

Debate continues about the likely implications for the signing parties of the North American Free Trade Agreement (NAFTA).[1] The parameters of most of these debates have been economic. But some observers report initial discussions—among academics rather than policy makers—of the idea of greater continental integration, moving beyond free trade.[2]

This paper explores the idea of continental integration from a Canadian perspective, with an emphasis on immigration. Such future integration could include freer (but not unrestricted) movement not only of goods, capital, and ideas, but of people. The integration would follow the model of the European Community in which freedom of movement is seen as a fundamental social right of workers from member states. NAFTA is just one instrument which will operate in a context where major external population pressures face Europe, Canada, Australia, and the United States, with a need for global responses.

---

1   Michael Hart, *A North American Free Trade Agreement: The Strategic Implications for Canada* (Ottawa: Institute for Research on Public Policy, 1990); Richard Lipsey, *Canada at the U.S.–Mexico Free Trade Dance: Wallflower or Partner?* (Toronto: C.D. Howe Institute, August 1990); Ronald J. Wonnacott, *U.S. Hub-and-spoke Bilaterals and the Multilateral Trading System* (Toronto: C.D. Howe Institute, October 1990); Richard Rothstein, "Continental Drift: NAFTA and its Aftershock," *American Prospect*, 12 (Winter 1993), pp. 68–84; Dolores Acevedo and Thomas J. Espenshade, "Implications of a North American Free Trade Agreeement for Mexican Migration into the United States," *Population and Development Review*, 18, No. 4 (1992), pp. 729–44.

2   Sylvia Ostry and Lawrence Taylor, remarks delivered at Facing North/Facing South Conference, University of Calgary, Calgary, Alberta, 3 May 1991.

Interestingly, the issue of possible continental integration will retain its topicality whatever the eventual outcome of Canada's incessant, internal constitutional debates. Factors pressing for a continental regional market of goods and labour, determined ultimately by geography, differing endowments of resources (both human and natural), and an emergence of competing regional trade blocs in the world community, would persist even in the case of full Quebec independence. For example, Hispanic immigrants to Quebec, whatever its relation to Canada, might well be seen as desirable "francophonisables" because of linguistic similarities between Spanish and French.

Not many years ago, the idea of Canada–United States free trade, or continental free trade, seemed unrealistic. But a trilateral North American free-trade agreement might well become "a building block towards an eventual hemispheric or even multilateral consensus on some of the most difficult issues on the global agenda,"[3] though one analyst suggests such a development might take several decades.[4]

In the case of population growth and immigration, a conventional view, articulated publicly by President Salinas, is that continental free trade will help stem the tide of illegal or undocumented Mexican immigration northward. According to the Mexican president, without free trade, "instead of seeing hundreds of thousands of Mexicans crossing the border looking for jobs in the north, you will see millions."[5] In Salinas's view, eventually there would have to be a free North American labour market. From this perspective, the United States and Canada could be faced with a choice between an increase in illegal Mexican immigration, in the short run, or an increase in legal immigration, in the long run. These issues should be considered within a broader international framework.

THE GLOBAL AND CONTINENTAL IMMIGRATION CONTEXT

What relation might there be, if any, between world population and immigration pressures, Canadian immigration and foreign policy, and continental integration?

The most dominant element of the world population context is that United Nations projections (medium growth variant) estimate that, by 2020, world population will have increased by an approximate 2.8 billion

---

3 Hart, *A North Amrican Free Trade Agreement*, p. 132.

4 Lipsey, *Free Trade Dance*, p. 4.

5 Michael Drohan and Peter Cook, "Trade or Face Immigrant Flood, Salinas Warns," *Globe and Mail* (5 April 1991).

from 1989 estimates.[6] While population in Canada and the United States is projected to grow by 19 and 21 percent, respectively, in that thirty-year period, that of Mexico will grow by 60 percent (55 million) and the rest of Central America by 70 percent (28 million), South America by 59 percent (175 million), Asia by 51 percent (1.58 billion), and Africa by 222 percent (795 million). Growth will be most rapid in the world's least-developed countries. One U.S. observer has called this growth a population time bomb.[7]

These demographic trends will place enormous pressures on Canada, the United States, and Australia, and to a lesser extent Europe, as immigrants and refugees are likely to seek ways, legal and illegal, of entering these countries. Considerations of Canadian immigration policy continue to be driven largely by *national* considerations, related to short-term economic costs and benefits, and absorptive capacity.[8] Yet the days of unilateral immigration policies, just like unilateral economic or environmental policies, may be numbered.

Political instability will compound these demographic pressures. Despite absolute progress made in some low- and middle-income countries, and the dramatic strides of the New Industrial Countries (NICs) of the Pacific Rim, the prognosis is not good. Absolute North-South gaps continue to grow for some countries, and even where substantial gains have been made, rising expectations may lead to political instability. These factors, as well as the fallout from the collapse of the Soviet empire, may lead to localized and civil wars which will create new waves of refugees.

Over the next thirty years, land—simple living space, as well as arable or potentially arable land—and potable water may become the most prized of national resources. To say that Canada and, to a lesser extent, the United States are richly endowed is an understatement. If the ten percent of Canada's land mass which is currently inhabited was to have the population density of Holland, Canada's population—in only that ten percent area of the country—would total over 400 million people.

In relative terms, Canada is also hugely endowed with arable land, despite the popular impression of Canada as largely inhospitable for agricultural production. Thus, Canada has roughly twice the arable land of Mexico, with less than one-third of Mexico's population. (This disparity

---

6   United Nations, Department of International, Economic, and Social Affairs, *World Population Prospects 1988*, Population Studies No. 106 (New York: United Nations, 1989).

7   Robert McNamara, "Time Bomb or Myth: The Population Problem," *Foreign Affairs*, 62, No. 5 (Summer 1984), pp. 1107–31.

8   Economic Council of Canada, *New Faces in the Crowd: Economic and Social Impacts of Immigration* (Ottawa: Economic Council of Canada, 1991).

does not further take into account the potentially offsetting differential agricultural productivity levels and the length of the growing season.) The U.S. advantaged position is comparable.

It is likely that, at some point in the future, the question may well be asked by the planetary community: according to what principles of natural justice do the citizens of Canada, the United States, and Australia enjoy their immense endowments of land, water, and natural resources? (Russia is comparably endowed, but there is, as yet, no evidence of tendencies for international migration to Russia!) Certainly, the answer cannot be that Canadians and Americans have earned their bounty, have created their land and resources. In fact, the answer is mainly luck in having been born in these countries, or for a few, in having the pluck and opportunity of choosing to immigrate.

In the future, it may be increasingly difficult to maintain the link between territory and national sovereignty. Indeed, large countries may well be seen as having an obligation to use their land mass not only for their own citizens but for the world community. A recent example would be the centrality of the Brazilian rain forests for the world's eco-system. A similar charge has been made concerning the planetary importance, and mismanagement, of British Columbia's forests.[9]

Without being overly futuristic, it seems that world population pressures will lead to increasing demands for immigration to Canada and the United States (the latter is only one-third as densely populated as Europe). How might Canada and the United States respond? Obviously, increasing immigration to North America—and Australia—cannot, alone, solve the problems of poverty in the developing nations. Dramatic increases in foreign aid will have to be considered. Even more desirable than aid (both for donor and recipient) would be economic integration through trade and investment, as is emerging within the European Community and with Japanese investment in Thailand, Indonesia, and Malaysia.[10] But, given these demographic contexts of the future, some new thinking, focused specifically on population and immigration and at least multilateral in nature, may be required.

The numbers of refugees and immigrants will likely swell, for conventional refugees and for immigrants/refugees fleeing conditions of chronic warfare, poverty, and violence. Recent refugee estimates hover around 18 million, with many more refugees found within their own countries. Who could have predicted the recent tragedy of Kurdish refugees or the outflows from Eastern Europe? Ironically, the greatest refugee

---

9 P. Lush, "Forest Industry Fearful of Boycott," *Globe and Mail* (8 April 1991).

10 Peter Cook, "Who Supports a Deal with Mexico?" *Globe and Mail* (9 April 1991).

burden in the world is being borne by the poorest countries: the twenty counties with the highest proportion of refugees have per capita incomes averaging $700.[11]

Population pressures on the northern African countries, fuelled by poverty and instability, will grow. National leaders like Julius Nyerere and Houari Boumedienne have, in the past, threatened the West with such population onslaughts.

Other political leaders of less developed countries have on occasion expressed similar sentiments.[12] And, as noted, President Salinas has reiterated similar views.

Canada's efforts to resolve its refugee backlog and to keep the new refugee determination system current have, to date, been relatively unsuccessful. Moreover, Canada has had little experience with mass illegal immigration compared to the United States, and is ill-prepared to cope with both a steady flow of refugee claimants, as well as sudden spurts of illegal immigrants, recent government legislation notwithstanding. In general, from the end of the 1980s, the increase in apprehension regarding immigration within the major immigrant-receiving nations parallels the increase in the number of immigrants.

MEXICO AND HISPANIC IMMIGRATION

By the late 1970s, the United States was apprehending one million illegal entrants annually, the vast majority crossing over the Mexican border.[13] This figure reached 1.8 million by 1986.[14] Of course, attitudes on both sides of the United States–Mexico border about undocumented Mexican immigration have been ambivalent. The passage of the Immigration Reform and Control Act in 1986 did not seem, by 1989, to have significantly reduced or deterred undocumented Mexican migration, but the final impact may not yet be known. Successful attempts by some American states to reduce benefits to families of undocumented migrants, *à la* California's controversial Proposition 187, may have an effect. In any event, since the

11 Jonas Widgren, "International Migration and Regional Stability," *International Affairs*, 66, No. 4 (1990), p. 751.

12 Widgren, "International Migration," p. 752, and cited in Michael Teitelbaum, "Right vs. Right: Immigration and Refugee Policy in the United States," *Foreign Affairs*, 59, No. 1 (Fall 1980), p. 47.

13 Vernon M. Briggs, Jr., "Employment Trends and Contemporary Immigration Policy," in Nathan Glazer, ed., *Clamor at the Gates* (San Francisco: Institute of Contemporary Studies, 1985), p. 143.

14 Robert Pastor and Jorge Castañeda, *Limits to Friendship: The United States and Mexico* (New York: Alfred A. Knopf, 1988), p. 344.

1980s, a new white-collar Mexican emigration to the United States has begun, in addition to traditional flows of unskilled immigrants.[15]

Preliminary results from the 1990 U.S. census reveal an increase in the total Hispanic population of 53 percent between 1980 and 1990, to a total of 22.4 million persons.[16] The U.S. Census Bureau reported 11.8 million Mexican-Americans in 1987, though that figure was probably far short of the actual total. To this amount must be added an unknown number of undocumented, or illegal, Mexicans (about 1.8 million such Mexicans claimed amnesty under the 1986 Immigration Act).

Mexican immigration to the United States, documented or not, enhances the degree of integration between the two countries. This is clear from the growing common border culture, the so-called Mexamerica, found in both societies. Mexican immigrants—and Canadians as well— are the least likely to claim U.S. citizenship[17] and more likely, because of proximity, to maintain extensive contacts with their country of origin. Thus, an interesting sociological contradiction ensues. The greater the failure of individual Mexicans and Canadians to integrate into the United States (as seen in low rates of naturalization), the greater the degree of societal integration of Mexico and Canada with the United States.[18]

Since the 1960s, one can say that, in general, European immigration to the United States has declined in absolute numbers of yearly immigrants and in proportions of total immigrants. European immigration averaged 124,000 per year in the 1960s, 80,000 per year in the 1970s, and 64,000 through 1988, but reaching 135,200 in 1991. Major increases have come from Asian immigration, which increased from 264,000 to 358,000.

Canadian immigration to the United States was about 28,600 per year throughout the 1960s, dropping to about 11,000 and 12,000 throughout the 1970s, but reaching 13,500 in 1991. Mexican legal, or documented, immigration to the United States has been more substantial, and has continued to grow. The flow averaged 44,300 per year through the 1960s, increasing to 63,700 through the 1970s, and 71,000 through the 1980s.

---

15 Pastor and Castañeda, *Limits to Friendship*, pp. 328–29; Katherine M. Donato, Jorge Durand, and Douglas S. Massey, "Stemming the Tide: Assessing the Deterrent Effects of the Immigration Reform and Control Act," *Demography*, 29, No. 2 (1992), pp. 139–57.

16 Felicity Barringer, "Census Shows Profound Change in Racial Make-up of the Nation," *New York Times* (11 March 1991), p. 1.

17 Alejandro Portes and Ruben G. Rumbaut, *Immigrant America: A Portrait* (Berkeley: University of California Press, 1990), pp. 119–20.

18 Jorge Castañeda, "Mexico's Coming Challenges," *Foreign Policy*, 64 (Fall 1986), p. 137.

Beginning in 1989, there is a major increase in Mexican immigration, reaching over 946,000 in 1991, out of a total 1.8 million immigrants.[19]

Immigration from the Americas to the United States has also increased, though not as dramatically as the Mexican rates. Central American immigration increased from an average of 9,700 yearly in the 1960s to 13,200 in the 1970s, to 26,000 in the 1980s, reaching 30,700 in 1988, but rising to 111,100 in 1991. For South America, the corresponding figures are 22,800 for the 1960s, 28,400 in the 1970s, and 38,800 in the 1980s, reaching 41,000 in 1988 and 79,900 in 1991. These increases in Hispanic immigration from the 1960s through the late 1980s were accompanied by even more dramatic increases in Asian migration. As a result, from the 1960s to the late 1980s, the Mexican proportion of the immigrant inflow ranged from 12 percent to 15 percent. But, from then, the Mexican and other Latin American proportions have increased dramatically.

The growth of the Hispanic population in the United States, not only from Mexico but from all South America, Central America, Cuba, Puerto Rico, and Europe, has added much to the U.S. race relations equation.[20] The sociological impacts have obviously been concentrated in select regions and urban centres, and tensions have arisen over the issue of bilingualism, notably in education. (Little quantitative socio-demographic research has been done on Canadian Hispanics, and Mata's 1988 unpublished report may be the most authoritative.[21])

Certainly, there are differences within the subgroups making up the Hispanic population in the United States, though Mexican-Americans remain the largest single group by far. Immigration plays an important indirect social role in pre-conditioning both societies—Mexico's and the United States'—not only to free trade agreements, but to possibly greater integration at some point in the future.

In 1991, the Canadian census recorded a total of 85,535 Canadians who claimed single origins and 34,445 who claimed multiple origins in Latin/Central/South America, with 16,450 specifically claiming Mexican origin. This is more than double 1986 levels. A total of 158,910 claimed Spanish origin, single or multiple, about 50 percent higher than in 1986. As many of these may have been born in South or Central America, there is a possible overlap in the two categories. Those claiming single ethnic

---

19 United States Department of Commerce, *Statistical Abstract of the United States* (Washington, D.C.: Bureau of the Census, 1990, 1993).

20 Alejandro Portes and Robert J. Bach, *Latin Journey: Cuban and Mexican Immigrants in the United States* (Berkeley: University of California Press, 1985).

21 F. Mata, "Immigrants from the Hispanic World in Canada: Demographic Profiles and Social Adaptation," report prepared for the multiculturalism sector, Secretary of State (Toronto: York University Centre for Research for Latin America and the Caribbean, 1988).

origins as Latin American (85,535) and as Spanish (82,675) totaled over 168,000; the comparable figure in 1986 was 89,000. Annual immigrant flows from South and Central America for 1991, 1992, and 1993 were 46,900, 37,900, and 38,800 (13.3 percent of the total), respectively.[22]

Therefore, one can speak of a Hispanic population in Canada in the mid-1990s of easily 250,000 to 300,000. Despite proposed cutbacks in Canadian immigration policies announced in 1994, which lower annual levels and de-emphasize family reunification, these numbers will be expected to grow through continuing immigration streams and due to a young age structure. From 1956 through 1987, Mata reports roughly 150,000 Hispanic immigrants to Canada, referring to countries of last permanent residence as either Spain or Latin America. By the 1970s, the proportion of Hispanic immigrants to Canada coming from Latin America, as opposed to Spain, was well over ninety percent. Between 1965 and 1987, a total of 10,853 immigrants arrived from Mexico specifically.[23]

Thus, the absolute and relative size of the Hispanic community in general in Canada is far smaller than that of the United States and is proportionally far more European in origin. But more important for the purpose of this paper is the fact that Hispanic immigration to Canada, as a proportion of total immigration to Canada, has been increasing steadily. The percentage moved from 0.2 percent for the years 1946 to 1955 to between 8 and 9 percent for 1985 to 1987.[24]

Of the 5,513 adult Hispanic immigrants to Canada in 1987, 34.9 percent were admitted as refugees, 31.6 percent as family class, and 33.5 percent as independent.

Within Canada's ethnic taxonomy, Canadians who are of Latin American, Central American, or South American origin are often defined for public policy purposes as visible minorities, while those of Spanish or Portuguese origin (and Greeks and Italians too, for that matter) are not. However, roughly 70 percent of Canadians of Latin American origin identify their racial origin as white.[25] Thus, the term "visible minority" does not denote race, as far as Canadians of Latin American origin are concerned. As long as Latin Americans are considered as visible minor-

22 Statistics Canada, "Ethnic Origin: The Nation," Catalogue 93-315 (Ottawa, 1993); Citizenship and Immigration Canada, "Facts and Figures: Overview of Immigration" (Ottawa: Strategic Research Analysis and Information Sector, November 1994).

23 Ibid., pp. 16–18.

24 Ibid., p. 16.

25 M. Mohan, *Labour Market Activity Survey, Part I: Analysis of Visible Minority Questions* (Ottawa: Statistics Canada, Employment Equity Data Program, 1990), p. 6.

ities, they are eligible to benefit from government employment equity programs.

In addition to the domestic impacts, on Canada and the United States, of immigration from and economic ties with Mexico, there are the geopolitical concerns. By and large, the interests in Latin America of U.S. and Canadian policy have been economic growth and development, democratization and social reform, control of illegal immigration and drug traffic, and the avoidance of or opposition to extreme socialist or communist regimes. A general concern for stability and a specific, if often unstated, worry over the possible destabilization of Mexico has underscored U.S. and Canadian policy. Canada–Mexico relations, specifically, have historically been minimal and nonconfrontational. The periodic role of Canadians as observers of Mexican elections, whether municipal elections in 1991 or the national elections of 1994, has been a source of friction.[26]

From a U.S. perspective, integrating Mexico into a free trade area may be one way of avoiding destabilization and meeting national security objectives, while enhancing Mexican prosperity and democracy. In turn, Mexican economic growth might dampen the flow of illegal Mexican immigrants. This is precisely one of the underlying consequences expected by U.S. and Mexican officials from economic integration. The hemispheric objective would be to encourage the progress towards democratization which occurred through the late 1970s and 1980s. Unfortunately, this paper cannot review the varying, often critical, interpretations of the Mexico–United States relationship historically and at present, including differing bilateral and general foreign-policy perspectives.[27]

Of course, there are many arguments which can be made against continental integration. Canadians and Mexicans might well fear the loss of national sovereignty in areas ranging from foreign policy to cultural specificity. Americans and Canadians might fear greater economic burdens resulting from Mexico's inferior economic status and increased immigration pressures. Pondering the European experience may be helpful in sorting through these various arguments.

THE EUROPEAN COMMUNITY

Many Canadians, particularly Quebeckers, have been interested in the political model of the European Community (EC) as a possible solution

---

26 J. Simon, "Mexican Officials Denounce Canadian Election Observers," *Globe and Mail* (14 March 1991); Damien Fraser, "Observers of the Mexican Vote Take Heat," *The Financial Post* (20 August 1994), p. 8.

27 Cuahtemoc Cardenas, "Misunderstanding Mexico," *Foreign Policy*, 78 (Spring 1990), pp. 113–30; and William Rogers, "Approaching Mexico," *Foreign Policy*, 72 (Fall 1988), pp. 196–209.

to Canada's constitutional problems. But the EC may also offer a model for the issues of continental sociopolitical integration and immigration. The ratification of the Treaty of Maastricht in late 1993 has added impetus to the dreams of European union, despite stumbling blocks on the way regarding extending the treaty to other European nations.

Certainly, on the issue of economic integration and, more specifically, free trade and the creation of a North American common market, the EC experience raises concerns which sound very familiar, such as fears that northern European firms might relocate plants to the lower-wage southern countries.[28]

The other side of the coin has been the concern about massive internal migration from low-wage to high-wage EC countries, under the principle of freedom of movement, which is far less controversial than the free movement of goods. Freedom of movement for workers within the European Community has been a specific policy objective since 1957. Progress is slowly being made in the area of recognition of diplomas, but exceptions persist in areas related to national security, though these too continue to be minimized through ongoing negotiations.[29] Some employment restrictions seem peculiar: "It will be some time . . . before a Spaniard born in Denmark and having studied Danish is allowed to work as a Danish teacher in a State school in his country of birth."[30]

The Canadian or American would ask, why not? Of course, to Canadians, the concept of a Spaniard born in Denmark is difficult to understand or accept. By and large, one would think Danes are born in Denmark. But is that so? We speak of Polish-Canadians, or Mexican-Americans, in a way that no one speaks of Spanish-Danes, or even Danes of Spanish origin. There are no hyphenated Danes, nor hyphenated EC nationals in general; the traditions of immigrant integration are far stronger in the New World. Moreover, the implied discrimination in employment described above would be illegal in the Canadian or U.S. case, where the guarantees of citizenship transcend issues of national or ancestral origin. Thus, freer movement in North America would quickly supersede the levels of equality and justice operative in the EC.

To be sure, the EC's freedom of movement does not imply that residents of member states are constantly on the move, or that access to

---

28 European Documentation, "1992—The Social Dimension," *Deadline, 92,* Periodical 2/1990 (Luxembourg: Office for Official Publications of the European Communities, 1990), p. 6.

29 International Labour Office, "Inter-regional Tripartite Round Table on Migration Workers from Non-EC Countries in the Internal Market," Informal summary record (Geneva: International Labour Office, 15–17 October 1990), pp. 57.

30 European Documentation, "1992—The Social Dimension," p. 33.

employment opportunities is as smooth as proponents might suggest. In general, we find that disputes among and within member states on agricultural and monetary policy, subsidies, foreign policy issues, as well as immigration and refugee policy towards potential non-EC migrants, and tensions between the priority of economic versus social integration continue to exist.[31]

The ultimate scope of EC population movements has not been enormous. As the EC has expanded southward to Greece, Spain, and Portugal, northward internal migration might have been expected to increase.[32] However, data on internal EC migration for the mid- to late-1980s do not reveal any upswing. For example, numbers of EC workers in Denmark and France have remained static, declining somewhat in the Netherlands and Belgium, and falling by up to 25 percent in West Germany.[33] The countries of southern Europe have not depopulated themselves.

Indeed, by 1988, the nationality breakdown of the twelve EC countries was 96.0 percent nationals, 1.5 percent EC foreigners, and 2.5 percent non-EC foreigners, with the latter group posing the major problems of integration. In the EC in 1991, a good deal of the migration process involved movement within EC countries, including returning nationals. Of all immigrants in the ten EC countries excluding Ireland and Portugal, 40 percent were EC citizens, 35 percent were non-EC Europeans, and 25 percent were non-Europeans.[34]

EC attitudes towards EC and non-EC migrants differ and, in turn, differ from U.S. or Canadian attitudes toward immigrants. The latter two countries have a more extensive history as immigrant-receiving countries and, thus, are more open to pluralism—despite periodic countermovements. There are no North American analogs (yet) to the anti-immigration Le Pen movement in France or the wave of German attacks on migrants and refugees. However, Mexicans have interpreted the passage of California's Proposition 187 as reflecting a not-so-latent anti-

---

31 Stanley Hoffmann, "The European Community and 1992," *Foreign Affairs*, 68, No. 4 (Fall 1989), pp. 27–47.

32 Thomas Straubhaar, "International Labour Migration within a Common Market: Some Aspects of EC Experience," *Journal of Common Market Studies*, 27, No. 1 (September 1988), pp. 45–62.

33 European Documentation, "1992—The Social Dimension," pp. 30–31.

34 Commission of the European Communities, "Policies on Immigration and the Social Integration of Migrants in the European Community," Sec (90) 1813, final report (Brussels: Commission of the European Communities, 1990), pp. 45–46; Eurostat, *Rapid Reports: Population and Social Conditions. International Migration Flows in Selected EC Countries, 1991*. Catalogue number CA_NK 93-012 (Luxembourg, 1993).

immigrant sentiment, and some may wonder if this may undermine the sentiments of cooperation which have underlain NAFTA.

For the moment, Canadian tensions refer mainly to clashes of values, rather than of fists. The recent Economic Council of Canada study on immigration speaks of a "moral contract" between hosts and immigrants. Thus, immigrants to Canada from traditional cultures would be expected to "relinquish at the door" those practices, such as mistreatment of women or religious intolerance, which conflict with Canadian norms.[35]

CONCLUDING OBSERVATIONS

Is it possible, or advisable, for North American economic integration to move beyond free-trade pacts? What, if anything, can Canadians, Americans, and Mexicans learn from the EC experience and organizational scheme which might be relevant to a North American Community (NAC) model? And to what extent ought increased freedom of movement be considered a part of that scenario?

Such a hypothetical model would entail giving priority to NAC member-states with regard to freedom of movement or migration. As in the EC, each member state would have control of its borders. Yet economic planners and workers themselves, in any country, might well begin to think of a continental labour and capital market.

Initially, this would put the greatest pressure on U.S. immigration policy, as both Mexicans and Canadians might want to migrate. But, in theory, economic integration between Mexico and the United States would eventually create more higher-wage jobs in Mexico, decreasing the Mexican migration flow northward. The process would entail reaching an equilibrium between these two forces. A NAC model would also allow for exceptions to freedom of movement, should Mexican demographic pressures outrace the U.S. economic absorptive capacity.

Economic integration would also resurrect and strengthen the fear of U.S. economic and cultural imperialism, strongly rooted in Canada, Mexico, and Latin America. In the EC case, while a united Germany may become a dominant force, the multilingual context and the size of the economies of France, Italy, and the United Kingdom lessen the centripetal pull of any one member state.[36]

Given the likely global population pressures on North America, the notion of a NAC model giving priority to Mexican and, indeed, Latin American immigrants, particularly refugee claimants, might be one

---

35 Economic Council of Canada, *New Faces in the Crowd*.

36 The United Kingdom is a special case with its historic Commonwealth connections to the Caribbean and Asia.

element in the process of devising a coherent international response. A sectoral arrangement might evolve, with North America offering *relative* priority and assuming major economic development responsibilities for Latin America, with the EC doing likewise for Eastern Europe, Africa, Japan, and the Pacific Rim and Gulf states, and Australia and New Zealand doing likewise for Asia. (This presupposes greater receptivity on the part of Mexico, and ultimately all of Latin America, to greater hemispheric integration.)

A worldwide hemispheric sectoral model would not have to be absolute or exclusive. Certainly, improvements in transportation and communication have led to population movements over greater distances, notably by Asian migrants to North America. But such a model might offer an initial way of prioritizing worldwide population and immigration responsibilities, pending evolution of a truly global solution.

This is not as far-fetched as it may appear. Indeed, we have evidence of international discussions on immigration matters reflecting this type of segmentation. For example, a recent meeting convened by the International Labor Organization (ILO) dealt with non-EC migrant workers to the EC. The exchange among participants at the round table was quite frank. But of equal interest was the roster of participants: six EC governments and six non-EC governments (Yugoslavia, Turkey, Morocco, Algeria, Tunisia, and Poland—i.e., North Africa and Eastern Europe).[37]

One subject which must be investigated is the degree to which any preferential treatment for NAC migrants, *à la* EC model, might violate Canadian and U.S. human rights considerations of equal treatment and nondiscriminatory immigration policies. Many existing laws, including the Canada–United States free-trade deal itself, discriminate in favour of citizens of one country over citizens of another, in trade as well as provisions for entry to Canada. Thus, a hypothetical immigration preference to citizens of Latin American countries, implemented through bilateral or multilateral arrangements, might pass constitutional muster.[38]

However, any greater labour mobility for Mexicans or Americans might lead to ethnic tensions within Canada's immigration queue. In recent years, 70 percent of immigrants to Canada have been from non-traditional (i.e., Third World) sources. This new source of immigration may now compete with expected outflows from Eastern Europe, which could exacerbate conflict in Canada between the older, European ethnic groups, and the newer, largely non-European, immigrant groups. The former group, largely middle class, has an agenda dominated by issues

---

37 International Labour Office, *Inter-Regional Tripartite.*

38 Interview with Professor Stephen Scott, Faculty of Law, McGill University, Montreal, 10 April 1991.

of cultural retention and status politics. The latter group, largely foreign born, is concerned primarily with the struggle against racism and bread-and-butter issues. These different priorities have been contained, with increasing difficulty, within Canada's multicultural umbrella.

But possible preferences for Latin American migrant workers might well be perceived as cutting back opportunities for other visible minority immigrants. In the United States, issues of politics and policy have at times placed African-Americans and Hispanics at odds over various issues, including immigration. While Hispanic organizations generally opposed the 1986 U.S. immigration law, African-American organizations were generally supportive. As global population pressures increase, one wonders whether similar tensions may emerge within the visible minority community in Canada—African-American, Asian, and Latin American—fuelled by competition over immigration, as well as other domestic policy issues.

To some, particularly in Canada and Mexico, continental integration means the subservience of Canadian resources and Mexican labour to the needs of primarily U.S. capital and markets. It seems impossible to dis-prove such fears by talk of access to one continental market for goods, capital, and labour. Not only are Canadian nationalists and labour leaders opposed to trilateral free trade—unlike the case with Mexican labour leaders, who seem supportive—it is doubtful whether substantial support exists among the Canadian public for trilateral free trade and more elaborate integration.[39] As indicated, similar sorts of fears have been present in the debates on European unity, past and present, regarding differences between the more prosperous northern Europe and the south-ern EC members. Those fears have not, as yet, been decisive.

From a strictly Canadian perspective, there are other factors to con-sider in any evolution of Canadian future development southward, not only to the United States, but to the rest of the Americas:

1. What impact might greater continental integration have on French-English relations and Canadian unity, if any? Conversely, what effects might Canadian fragmentation have on the prospects for continental integration? Would an independent Quebec have to re-negotiate a quadrilateral trade deal? What effect has European integration had regarding communal conflicts in EC states such as Belgium, and others? Might integration into larger political units defuse localistic antagonisms? Many Quebeckers see involvement in NAFTA as an alternative focus of political allegiance compared to

---

39 Peter Cook, "Who Supports a Deal," and Madeleine Drohan, "Labor Solidarity Lost," *Globe and Mail* (29 April 1991).

Canada. But in any case, the status of the French language might well
be weakened, as Spanish might emerge as a greater continental force.

2. Canadian history, and the fragility of Canadian union, has been, in
   part, a product of weak east-west linkages trying to resist the southern tug of the United States. Any continental integration might well
   exacerbate this difficulty, strengthening the southern pull even further.
   This was a fear concerning the Canada–United States trade deal. But,
   given the fact that Canada–United States free trade exists, greater
   Canada–Mexico ties (apart from being a defensive option), and subsequent Latin American links generally, might serve to dampen the
   feared U.S. dominance. From a Latin American perspective, Canada's
   lesser involvement in economic and cultural imperialism, real or perceived, might also take some of the edge off a Mexico–United States
   deal.

3. Parts of Canada and the United States are embracing Pacific Rim
   strategies of investment and immigration. This view is one of the
   factors fuelling a certain sense of alienation on the part of western
   Canada from central Canada. British Columbia and, perhaps, Alberta
   might see North American integration as conflicting with a Pacific
   Rim strategy. This vision is reflected in the name of British
   Columbia's newest political party—the Pacific Party. By contrast,
   central Canada might seem more amenable to a north-south (Latin
   American) configuration. Even here, regional differences exist; recall
   Quebec's greater enthusiasm for NAFTA than that expressed by the
   NDP government in Ontario.[40] Therefore, the possibility exists that
   Canadian immigration policies, or at least flows, will reflect and even
   shape provincial variation in long-term development goals. Of course,
   all provinces may welcome Hong Kong millionaires.

To conclude, this paper has approached the idea of a possible North
American integration beginning with free trade and including eventually
the freer movement of peoples. The EC model, for better or worse, is
before us. Free trade may start us down that path regardless of our
current intentions. Population pressures will likely also force Canada,
along with other developed western nations, to move towards inter-
dependent macro-immigration policies. Debate on these possible outcomes and linkages may be in order.

---

40 Glen Allen and Patricia Poirier, "Salinas Unswayed by Rae," *Globe and Mail* (10
   April 1991).

IV

Energy and the Environment

Alan Sweedler
Department of Physics
San Diego State University

15

Energy and Environment in the United States–Mexico Border Region[1]

INTRODUCTION: BORDERS AND BORDER REGIONS

This chapter analyzes energy and related environmental issues in the United States–Mexico border region, with a particular focus on the California–Baja California section of the border. Before discussing in detail the energy and environmental situation on the border, it will be helpful to give a brief discussion about borders and border regions in general.

The border region separating two states has traditionally served to demarcate the physical limits of the nation-state. The region was seen as politically, economically and socially peripheral to the main activities of the country, which generally took place far from the border zones. Border regions tended to be sparsely populated and for the most part undeveloped. Moreover, many border regions were militarized and seen as the first line of defense against would-be aggressors.

Since the end of World War II, however, some border regions have emerged as vibrant areas of economic growth and have served as constructive elements in relations between the nations that share the border region. A few examples of these areas are the border region between France and Germany, between the Nordic countries, and some portions of the borders separating the United States and Canada and the United States and Mexico.[2]

---

1 The author would like to acknowledge Patricia Bennett for assistance in obtaining energy-related information in Mexico and Baja California. Steve Sachs from SANDAG was also very helpful in developing much of the energy data for San Diego.

2 For a good description of border regions in the pre-1950 and 1950–1990 periods see Lawrence A. Herzog, "Changing Boundaries in the Americas," in Lawrence A. Herzog, ed., *Changing Boundaries in the Americas*, Center for U.S.–Mexican Studies, University of California, San Diego, 1992, pp. 4–7.

The end of the Cold War has given rise, on the one hand, to traditional border regions that serve as focal points of conflict between the states sharing the border and, on the other hand, to border regions that are better integrated and enhance cooperation between neighbouring states. Some cases of the former are the new borders between the regions of the former Yugoslavia, and the many new borders between the former republics of the Soviet Union. These new borders, which may be better characterized as frontiers or boundaries, are heavily militarized and in some cases are regions of violent conflict.

At the same time, however, other border regions have grown closer and become more integrated, and conflicting issues have been resolved. The United States–Mexico border region, the borders between the member states of the European Union, the border between Venezuela and Colombia, and the Russian–Finnish border are but a few examples. In the case of Germany, the border between East and West Germany has disappeared altogether.

COMPARING BORDER REGIONS

Several concepts have emerged that have proved helpful when comparing border regions. Kenichi Ohmae has recently introduced the notion of the "region-state," particularly useful when considering the economic aspects of border areas.

> On the global economic map the lines that now matter are those defining what may be called "region-states." The boundaries of the region-state are not imposed by political fiat. They are drawn by the deft but invisible hand of the global market for goods and services. They follow, rather than precede, real flows of human activity, creating nothing new but ratifying existing patterns manifest in countless individual decisions.[3]

Region-states tend to be linked to the global economy more strongly than with their host nations. Region-states tend to have between five million and 20 million people, must be small enough for its people to share common economic interests and large enough to justify adequate infrastructure for competition on the global scale. Clearly such a description could be applied to the U.S.–Mexico border region.

Another useful concept for comparing border regions is the idea of "periphery-centre" interactions.[4] In this framework, the border region is

3   Kenichi Ohmae, "Rise of the Region State," *Foreign Affairs* (Spring 1993), pp. 78–87.

4   Pertti Joenniemi, "Regionalization in the Baltic Sea Area: Actors and Policies," in Pertti Joenniemi, ed., *Cooperation in the Baltic Sea Region* (Taylor and Francis, 1993), pp. 161–177.

viewed as peripheral, both literally and figuratively, to the more central regions of the country. Many of the issues and problems in the border zone are seen as a consequence of the interaction between the border region and the centre of power. Complicating this dynamic is the fact that not only is there interaction between the border region (periphery) and the national capital (centre), but also with the border region of the neighbouring state which must also interact with its own national centre.

Globalization of the world economy has also changed the nature and role of borders and border regions in the international economy. Goods, capital, and in a few cases, labour, now freely flow around the world in a borderless global economy that has eroded the historic functions of borders and has created new options for development in border regions.[5] The relative oneness of borders has also created problems in the environmental arena, as transboundary transport of pollutants has increased because of rapid development in border regions.

Oscar Martinez has pointed out the evolutionary nature of borderland development. Over time, transboundary relations evolve from initial periods of alienation and hostility to situations of more or less peaceful coexistence. As cross-border interactions intensify, interdependence gradually takes place, leading ultimately to a fully integrated border region.[6]

UNITED STATES–MEXICO BORDER REGION

The United States and Mexico share a 2,000-mile border, stretching from the San Diego–Tijuana region on the Pacific Ocean to the Brownsville-Matamoros region on the Gulf of Mexico. The border zone is comprised of 25 counties found in the states of California, Arizona, New Mexico, and Texas and 35 municipalities in the Mexican states of Baja California, Sonora, Chihuahua, Nuevo Leon, Coahuila, and Tamaulipas. Approximately 10 million people live and work in the border region.

The region is one of the most dynamic border zones in the world. About 45 percent of the border population reside in the San Diego–Tijuana portion of the border and the number of crossings of the international border between these two cities is the largest in the world. For a complete description of the U.S.–Mexico border region, see the chapter by Paul Ganster.

5   Norris Clement, "The Changing Economics of International Border Regions," in James Scott, Alan Sweedler, Paul Ganster, and Wolf-Dieter Eberwein, eds., *Borders and Border Regions: New Roles in a Changing Global Context* (Berlin: Institute for Regional Studies, 1995).

6   Oscar Martinez, "Borderlands Entering New Stage," *Mexico Policy News*, No. 8 (Fall 1992), p. 22.

RELATION BETWEEN ENERGY AND THE ENVIRONMENT

The availability of energy supplies at reasonable cost is critical to the stability, well-being and economic development of any region. Since the use of energy invariably carries with it environmental consequences, energy-use practices and policies on one side of the border will inevitably impact the environment on the other side.

To examine more how energy use affects the environment, we need to look at the energy sector itself more closely. The energy sector may be divided into three areas. First, there is the *production* of the energy itself. This entails exploration and recovery of primary fuels, such as petroleum, natural gas, coal, and uranium. Following recovery, fuels like petroleum are refined to produce gasoline, diesel, jet fuel, heating oil, etc. Uranium is processed to produce enriched fuel for use in nuclear reactors. Coal and natural gas generally are used directly as recovered, without further processing. Each of the primary fuels can be used to generate electricity. In addition to the primary fuels, hydro-generated electricity is also a source of energy in Canada, the United States and, to a lesser extent, Mexico, and geothermal energy contributes to the U.S. and Mexican supply.

Second, a *distribution* system is required to transport the fuel or electricity to the point of use. This requires pipelines (under and over ground), electrical transmission lines, distribution centres, highways and rail systems. Third is the *consumption* sector, where energy is used for some purpose. Energy in the form of heat, obtained by the direct combustion of fossil fuels, is used mostly for industrial processes, space heating and cooking. In the form of electricity, energy is used for lighting, space heating, communications and for powering all electronic devices. Fuels in the transportation sector are, for the most part, derived from petroleum.

At each step in the energy cycle, there are impacts on the environment. Drilling for oil and gas obviously has consequences for the surrounding land, or water in the case of off-shore drilling. Extraction of coal impacts the land and may contaminate underground water tables. Mining and milling of uranium ore produce large quantities of radioactive materials which must be dealt with.

Useful work is obtained from energy resources by converting the energy from one form to another. Heat, for example, which is used to warm buildings or generate high-temperature steam to produce electricity, results from combustion of fossil fuels. The combustion process releases CO_2, NO_x, SO_2, particulates and other pollutants into the atmosphere, depending on the fuel.[7] Even when renewable energy resources are used,

---

7   Oil-fired boilers release 157 tons of SO_2, 5 tons of CO_2, 67 tons of NO_2, and 0.76 tons of volatile organic compounds per thousand gallons of oil consumed (EPA, Document No. AP-42).

such as wind, solar, and geothermal, there are consequences for the environment. For example, the manufacture of photovoltaic cells (solar cells) requires the use of potentially harmful chemicals and the exploitation of geothermal wells can have negative consequences for the surrounding land.

The main point to be made here is that any energy resource when used to produce useful work will invariably impact the physical and biological environment. The complex relation between energy use and the environment is even more complicated in international border regions. The physical environment does not respect political boundaries, and in most cases inhabitants of the border region share the same air shed and in many cases the same water supplies. In North America, transboundary transfer of pollutants is a continuing source of tension between neighbouring states and an important issue.[8]

ENERGY USE IN THE UNITED STATES AND MEXICO

To analyze the energy sector in the United States–Mexico border region it is necessary first to discuss briefly the energy sector in the United States and Mexico. The United States has a highly decentralized energy system, mostly owned and operated by the private sector. The coal, oil, gas and nuclear industries are dominated by large private corporations, regulated by various local, state, and federal agencies. The power generating sector consists mainly of investor-owned utilities which are regulated public monopolies.

Some of the relevant agencies that regulate the energy sector in the United States are the Federal Energy Regulatory Commission (FERC), the Department of Energy (DOE), the Nuclear Regulatory Commission (NRC), and individual state public utilities commissions that set electric and natural-gas rates. In California, the California Public Utilities Commission (CPUC) and the California Energy Commission (CEC) are the principal agencies charged with regulating the energy sector. At the local level, city and county jurisdictions may have to grant approval for energy-related construction such as gas pipelines and power transmission lines. In San Diego, planning agencies such as the San Diego Association of Governments (SANDAG) also play an important role in long-range energy planning.

The Mexican energy sector is structured very differently from that of the United States. The production, distribution and management of energy supplies in Mexico is under control of the federal government. The

---

8 See, for example, Stephen Mumme, "Importing Air Pollution," *New York Times* (23 July 1983), p. 17.

TABLE 1. U.S. ENERGY CONSUMPTION BY SOURCE, 1992

Oil	41%
Natural gas	25%
Coal	23%
Nuclear	8%
Hydro	3%

Source: EIA.

Secretaria de Energía, Minas y Industria Paraestatal (SEMIP) is the key government ministry responsible for formulating energy policies. SEMIP has direct oversight over the Comision Federal de Electricidad (CFE, the national electric utility), Petroleos Mexicanos (PEMEX, the state-run oil monopoly), the Comision Nacional Para el Ahorro de Energía (CONAE, the national energy conservation commission) and several energy-related research institutes. Currently, there are no large-scale energy-related activities within the private sector. This situation may change in the future with the implementation of NAFTA, as well as trends underway within Mexico to diminish the federal government's role in the energy sector.[9]

Energy consumption by source for the United States is shown in Table 1 for 1992. Fossil fuels (oil, natural gas and coal) dominate the energy mix, accounting for 88 percent of energy consumption; hydro- and nuclear-generated electricity plus a small amount of other sources (solar, geo-thermal, wind, and others) account for the rest.[10] The U.S. imported 40 percent of its oil, including 827 thousand barrels a day from Mexico, which accounted for 10.5 percent of total petroleum imports.[11] Almost 70 percent of petroleum was used in the transportation sector, and coal accounted for 55 percent of the electricity generated. Total energy consumption in 1992 was 82.36 quadrillion British Thermal Units (BTU), an increase of 1.5 percent from the previous year. Energy consumption per capita was 322 million BTU.[12] California had the second highest energy consumption, after Texas, but ranked 44th in energy use per capita, indicating that the California energy sector is quite efficient relative to other states.

---

9 Hiram Ordoñez, "Entra de lleno el sector privado a la generación de electricidad," *El Economista* (17 enero 1994), p. 32; Laura M. Ruis-Velasco and Miguel Badillo, "Independent Electricity Production Proposed," *El Financiero International* (1 February 1993), p. 26.

10 Energy Information Administration (EIA), *Annual Energy Review, 1992* (June 1993), p. 9.

11 *Annual Energy Review*, p. 131.

12 *Annual Energy Review*, p. 11.

TABLE 2. U.S. ELECTRIC GENERATION BY FUEL, 1992

Coal	55%
Nuclear	22%
Natural gas	10%
Hydro	9%
Oil	3%
Other	1%

Source: EIA.

Coal was the principal fuel used in the generation of electricity in 1992, accounting for 55 percent, followed by nuclear, natural gas, hydro, and oil, with geothermal and solar making a very small contribution. Nuclear power accounted for over one fifth of the U.S. electric supply and surpassed both hydro and natural gas as a source of electricity, as can be seen in Table 2. Total U.S. power generation in 1992 was 2,796 billion kilowatt hours, or 11,184 kilowatt hours per capita.[13]

Although a net importer of energy, the United States exported 103 million short tons of coal in 1992, mostly to Europe, Canada, Japan, and Brazil.[14] The United States is also a major supplier of petroleum products to Mexico, mostly unleaded gasoline.

Turning now to Mexico, Mexico is an energy-rich country, currently producing more energy than it consumes. Mexico's energy resources, however, are unevenly distributed, with most of the oil and gas producing regions located in the eastern, southeastern and Gulf of Mexico regions of the country. Baja California lacks any known fossil fuel reserves and the only presently exploited indigenous energy source is the geothermal fields located at Cerro Prieto, south of Mexicali.

Mexico's energy mix is much more dependent on petroleum than the United States'. In 1991, 73 percent of energy produced came from petroleum (about 50 percent of which was exported), 17 percent from natural gas, 4 percent from biomass, 3 percent from hydro, 2 percent from coal, and 1 percent from geothermal and nuclear energy.[15] Mexico is, of course, an oil exporter. During the first 7 months of 1993, PEMEX exported 1.33 million barrels per day of crude oil, about 64 percent of that to the U.S., 15.3 percent to Spain, 4.9 percent to the Far East, and 15.8

---

13 *Annual Energy Review*, p. 219.

14 *Annual Energy Review*, p. 201.

15 *Balance Nacional de Energia*, 1991, SEMIP.

percent to other markets.[16] For 1991 and 1992, Mexican exports averaged about 1.37 million barrels a day, representing about 50 percent of total production.[17]

In addition to petroleum, Mexico is a large producer and consumer of natural gas and is believed to have vast proven reserves, approximately 73 trillion cubic feet.[18] Mexico is both an exporter and importer of natural gas to and from the U.S. In the first three months of 1993, for example, Mexico imported more than 300 MMcfd (million cubic feet per day), but by August 1993, that amount dropped to about 70 MMcfd. By the end of 1993, Mexico had become a net exporter of gas to the U.S.[19]

In the electric sector, fuel input consists of oil, hydro, natural gas, coal, geothermal and nuclear power. In 1990, oil accounted for 54 percent, hydroelectric 20 percent, natural gas 12 percent, coal 6 percent, geothermal 4 percent and nuclear 3 percent.[20] In addition to the 25,2989 MW of installed capacity owned by CFE in 1990, Mexico also had about 3,000 MW of industrial cogeneration.[21]

The demand for electricity has been growing at a much higher rate in Mexico than in the U.S. From 1960 to 1990, installed capacity grew by a factor of 10, with an average growth rate of 8.3 percent per year. During the 1980s, however, the growth rate for installed capacity dropped to 5.6 percent, while the demand for electricity grew at close to 7 percent per year.[22] The northern border states experienced an annual growth rate 2.7 percent higher than the national rate, making it the region with the largest fraction of total electricity use.[23] This very high demand for electricity in the northern border states has a direct impact on the environment in the border region.

In terms of energy consumption by sector in Mexico, the transportation sector consumes the largest fraction of energy, 40 percent, followed by the industrial and residential/commercial sectors.[24] For the United States, in 1992, the largest consumer of energy was the industrial sector,

---

16 George Baker, "Challenges in Petroleum Policy for the Next President of Mexico," *Oil and Gas Journal*, 92, No. 3 (17 January 1994), pp. 33–40.

17 Ibid.

18 Carol Hewit, *Natural Gas Exports to Mexico*, California Energy Commission, Fuel Planning Office (2 June 1993).

19 *Oil and Gas Journal Newsletter* (20 December 1993).

20 CFE, 1991.

21 Ibid.

22 CFE, *Estadísticas for Entidad Federativa*, from 1982 to 1990, Mexico.

23 Ibid.

24 SEMIP.

which used 37 percent of total energy consumption. The residential/ commercial sectors used 35 percent and transportation 27 percent.[25]

CALIFORNIA–BAJA CALIFORNIA BORDER REGION

The California–Baja California border region consists of San Diego and Imperial counties on the U.S. side and the state of Baja California on the Mexican side. The population in this region was about 4.5 million people in 1992, equivalent to almost 45 percent of the population of the entire United States–Mexico border region.[26] Most of the population on the U.S. side is found in San Diego County and on the Mexican side in the municipalities of Tijuana and Mexicali.

The San Diego portion of the border region has a population of 2.5 million and covers an area of 4,261 square miles. Imperial county, with a population of only 124,300, has an area of 4,482 square miles.[27] The population of Baja California is close to 2 million. The growth figures for the area are indicated in Figure 1.

ENERGY USE IN SAN DIEGO AND BAJA CALIFORNIA

San Diego. Both San Diego and Baja California are heavily dependent on outside sources of energy, mostly petroleum products and natural gas. Figure 2 shows the regional energy supply for San Diego for 1991. It is clear that most of San Diego's energy originates from natural gas imported from Canada, the Rocky Mountain region, and the south-western United States; electricity imported from the northwest, southwest and Baja California; and refined petroleum products from other parts of California. If one includes the uranium that is used for fuel in the San Onofre nuclear reactor as originating from outside the region, then San Diego is *totally* dependent on out-of-region energy supplies.

Table 3 shows the end-use energy consumption in San Diego for 1991. Not surprisingly, transportation accounts for over 60 percent of end-use energy consumption, followed by the residential, commercial and industrial sectors. This end-use energy consumption pattern reflects the structure of the San Diego economy. Most San Diego residents commute to work in private automobiles with one or two occupants, accounting for the large fraction of end-use energy going into the transportation sector.

---

25 *Annual Energy Review*, p. 3.

26 Population figures from the Mexican National Census and projections by Consejo Estatal de Poblacion and the San Diego Association of Governments.

27 *California Statistical Abstract*, State of California, Department of Finance, 1993, p. 13 (estimate for 1992).

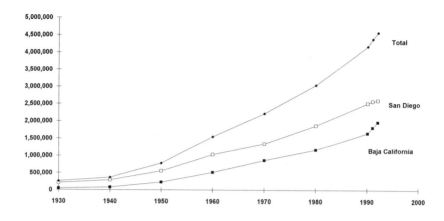

Figure 1. Population Growth of the San Diego–Baja California Region 1930–1992.

The San Diego economy is more heavily concentrated in the commercial and service sector than manufacturing, compared to other regions in California. Moreover, most of the rapid population growth during the last ten years has occurred in the northern regions of the county, resulting in longer commutes from home to work.

Figure 3 summarizes the energy sector for San Diego in the form of an energy flow diagram for 1990. The left side indicates energy input by fuel type, the centre portion shows end-use consumption by sector and the right side indicates the portion of energy that is productive and unproductive (losses).

One sees that the transportation and electric conversion sectors are the largest users of primary fuels. Forty-seven percent of San Diego energy supplies goes into the transportation sector and 38 percent into generating electricity. The efficiency of the transportation sector is only 32 percent and the conversion efficiency of primary fuels to electricity is 46 percent. Overall efficiency of the energy system, as measured by the ratio of productive to non-productive end-use, was 38 percent in 1990.

TABLE 3. SAN DIEGO ENERGY CONSUMPTION, 1991

Transportation	62%
Residential	21%
Commercial	19%
Industrial	4%

Source: San Diego Gas and Electric (SDG&E), CEC.

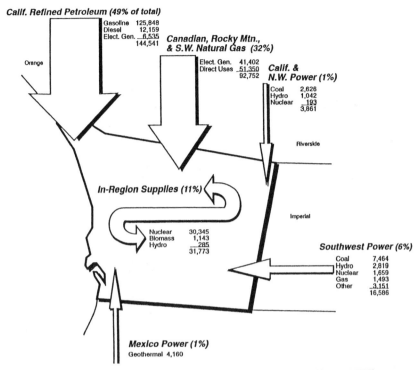

Calif. Refined Petroleum (49% of total)

Gasoline	125,848
Diesel	12,159
Elect. Gen.	6,535
	144,541

Canadian, Rocky Mtn., & S.W. Natural Gas (32%)

Elect. Gen.	41,402
Direct Uses	51,350
	92,752

Orange

Calif. & N.W. Power (1%)

Coal	2,626
Hydro	1,042
Nuclear	193
	3,861

Riverside

In-Region Supplies (11%)

Nuclear	30,345
Biomass	1,143
Hydro	285
	31,773

Imperial

Southwest Power (6%)

Coal	7,464
Hydro	2,819
Nuclear	1,659
Gas	1,493
Other	3,151
	16,586

Mexico Power (1%)

Geothermal 4,160

Figure 2. Regional Energy Supply Geography (1990 Billion BTU).
Sources: SDG&E, CEC, SANDAG.

The transportation needs of the region are met by gasoline and diesel fuel. Natural gas is used for direct use in the residential, commercial and industrial sectors as well as for the generation of electricity. Currently, almost no oil is burned in SDG&E's boilers, with most of the in-region power generation coming from nuclear power or natural gas-fired thermal plants.

San Diego has steadily increased its share of imported electricity over the years. San Diego now imports 56 percent of its electricity, and this trend is likely to grow. In addition to relying more heavily on buying power from outside the region, the fuel mix for in-region generation has changed significantly over the years. There has also been a switch from a heavy dependence on oil during the 1970s and early 1980s to a greater reliance on natural gas and nuclear power for in-region generation. This shift from oil to gas and nuclear power has resulted in a reduction in NO_x emissions.

Electric demand increased by 46 percent during the period 1980–1991, averaging about 4 percent per year. Natural gas use has tended to fluctuate over the same period. Because of its relatively clean burning

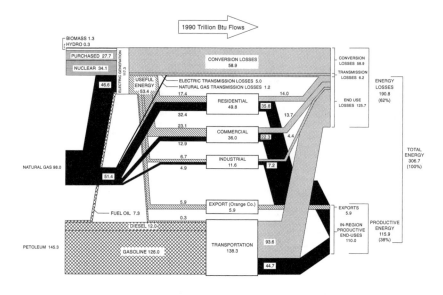

Figure 3. Regional Energy Flows. Sources: SDG&E, CEC.

properties, compared to oil or coal, it is expected that demand for natural gas will increase in the future.

Future Energy Needs and Planning in San Diego. Projecting future energy needs and planning to meet those needs for the San Diego region has been carried out by the San Diego Association of Governments (SANDAG).[28] Projected total energy demand to the year 2010 is expected to increase by 25 percent, even though the population is projected to grow by 41 percent. The fastest growing sector is the commercial sector, projected to grow by 56 percent, followed by the industrial sector with a growth of 43 percent and the residential sector at 35 percent. Energy demands for the transportation sector are projected to increase only by 12 percent owing to expected efficiency increases in the automobile fleet.

Fuel mix for the transportation sector is expected to change in the next 20 years. The use of gasoline and diesel fuels is predicted to remain constant with a mix of electric vehicles, methanol, compressed natural gas (CNG) and liquid propane gas (LPG) making up the increased demand. Should this scenario indeed be fulfilled, it will result in decreased air pollution caused by the transportation sector.

The Regional Energy Plan expects some of the future demand can be met by demand side management (energy efficiency programs) and renew-

---

28 San Diego Association of Governments, *Draft Regional Energy Plan*, 1994.

able energy sources. If fulfilled, this will also decrease air pollution in the region.

Per-capita energy demand is projected to decline. This is due to increased efficiency in the cars and trucks that make up the transportation fleet, increases in energy efficiencies of new buildings and demand-side management programs of SDG&E.

The future energy mix for San Diego will not be very different from what exists today. "New" sources of energy will consist of methanol, CNG, LPG and electric cars, but these will only account for 6.6 percent of supplies.

Total energy costs are projected to amount to about $5 billion (1994 $) per year by the year 2010. For 1991, total energy costs for the region were approximately $3 billion, which was about 5 percent of gross regional product.

Baja California. Baja California, with a land area of almost 28,000 square miles, is divided into four municipalities, which are roughly equivalent to U.S. counties. The name of each municipality is that of the largest community within it. There are four municipalities in Baja California: Tijuana, Mexicali, Ensenada and Tecate. Tijuana's population alone accounted for 45 percent of the total population of Baja California in 1990. Moreover, 98 percent of the population in the Tijuana municipality is urbanized, making it one of the most urbanized regions in all of Mexico.[29] At present growth rates, the population of Tijuana is expected to reach 1.2 million by the year 2000.[30]

Baja California is also home to 772 *maquiladora* factories, which is 38 percent of the all the *maqiladora* plants in Mexico.[31] Of these, 513 are located in Tijuana. The growth of the *maquiladora* industry in Tijuana in recent years is one factor that has contributed to the rapid growth in demand for energy, particularly electricity.

Energy sources and infrastructure in Baja California. Because Baja California is geographically isolated from the rest of Mexico, most of its energy supplies must be transported to the region from distant locations. In addition, Baja California is not connected to the Mexican national electric grid system or the natural gas pipeline system. This means that energy

---

29 Alejandro Canales, "Population Structure and Trends in Tijuana," in Norris Clement and Eduardo Zepeda Miramontes, eds., *San Diego–Tijuana in Transition: A Regional Analysis* (Institute for Regional Studies of the Californias, San Diego State University, 1993), p. 65.

30 Dr. John Weeks, San Diego State University, private communication.

31 *Twin Plant News*, 9, No. 4 (November 1993), p. 57.

needs must be met by in-region power generation using fuels imported from other regions in Mexico (with the exception of geothermal heat). The electric grid system is, however, connected to the U.S. grid system via its interconnections with the SDG&E system.

Baja California derives its energy from basically two sources: petroleum and petroleum products, and geothermally generated electricity. All of the petroleum products are imported to the region from other parts of Mexico or from other countries. For example, fuel oil used at the large (620 MW) Rosarito thermoelectric power plant, located 15 miles south of the border, is transported by tanker from PEMEX's Salina Cruz refinery 1,500 miles to the south as well as from foreign sources.[32] Geothermal energy used to power Baja California's other principal power station is derived from the geothermal fields at Cerro Prieto, located south of Mexicali.

The transportation sector uses diesel fuel, and leaded and unleaded gasoline. Liquid petroleum gas substitutes for natural gas, and is used mostly in the residential but also in the industrial and commercial sectors.

Baja California's electrical energy infrastructure consists of two large power-generating facilities (about 620 MW each), several smaller generating plants and appropriate transmission lines. The power grid is connected to San Diego via two 240 KV lines, one from Tijuana and the other from Mexicali. Generating facilities are shown in Table 4.

There are no oil refineries in Baja California and most petroleum products enter the region via a products terminal at Rosarito, brought to the region by tankers and barges. Between Rosarito and Mexicali there is a 10-inch pipeline to transport petroleum and a similar 8-inch pipeline between Rosarito and Ensenada.[33] Liquid petroleum gas (LPG) is brought into the region by truck or rail and distributed by truck.

Petroleum-based products (fuel oil, leaded and unleaded gasoline, diesel and LP gas) account for 87 percent of total energy supply for Baja California, geothermally generated electricity accounting for the rest. Like San Diego, all of the petroleum products come from outside the region, making both Baja California and San Diego heavily dependent of out-of-region supplies.

Electric sector of Baja California. The only indigenous energy source currently utilized on a large scale is the geothermal fields, located south of Mexicali at Cerro Prieto. The present installed capacity at Cerro Prieto

---

32 Baker, *op. cit.*

33 Margarito Quintero, *Fuentes Actuales y Potenciales de Energia en Baja California* (Mexicali, BC, Mexico: Instituto de Ingenieria, UABC, 1990).

TABLE 4. GENERATING FACILITIES:
BAJA CALIFORNIA

TYPE	LOCATION	CAPACITY (MW)
Geothermal	CP (Mexicali)	620.0
Thermoelectric	Rosarito	620.0
Gas turbine	Mexicali	62.0
Gas turbine	Tijuana	60.0
Gas turbine	Ensenada	55.0
Int. combustion	Mexicali	3.2
Total installed capacity		1420.2

Source: CFE.

is 620 MW with an additional 80 MW planned during the next ten years. About 35 percent of the power from Cerro Prieto is exported to Southern California under a contract with Southern California Edison (SCE) and SDG&E. San Diego's share of Mexico's geothermal power is 150 megawatts, which accounted for six percent of SDG&E's installed capacity in 1991.[34] In 1990, SDG&E imported over 1 billion Kwh and SCE 0.6 billion Kwh from Mexico. SDG&E also exported over 400 million Kwh to Mexico, accounting for most of the electric imports to Mexico. In 1992, electric exports from Cerro Prieto to California amounted to 1,406 Gwh and 614 Gwh to SDG&E and SCE, respectively.[35] For SDG&E this represented almost 10 percent of its supply. Electric exports from Baja California are given in Table 5 for the period 1983 to 1992.

In addition to the two large plants at Cerro Prieto and Rosarito, CFE operates several smaller plants in Ensenada, San Felipe and Mexicali that use diesel as a fuel. These accounted for less than 1 percent of electricity generation in 1991. Electric generation by fuel type from 1987 to 1991 for Baja California is given in Table 6.

Baja California Energy Consumption. Consumption of electricity by the residential, commercial, industrial, public facilities and irrigation sectors

---

34 United States/Mexico Electric Trade Study, U. S. Department of Energy and Secretaria de Energía, Minas e Industria Paraestatal, March 1991, p. 116.

35 CFE, private communication, April 27, 1993.

TABLE 5. ELECTRICITY IMPORTS
TO SAN DIEGO FROM MEXICO

YEAR	MWH	% OF SUPPLY
1983	33,636	0.3
1984	126,124	1.1
1985	203,021	1.9
1986	1,024,451	9.0
1987	1,429,304	12.0
1988	1,381,977	11.0
1989	1,318,455	10.0
1990	1,327,522	9.3
1991	1,394,923	10.0
1992	1,406,274	—

Source: CFE.

TABLE 6. ELECTRICAL GENERATION
BY FUEL TYPE (MWH):
BAJA CALIFORNIA

YEAR	FUEL OIL	GEOTHERMAL	DIESEL	TOTAL
1987	1,165,325	4,255,471	8,576	5,429,372
1988	1,190,388	4,447,894	17,220	5,655,502
1989	1,501,517	4,247,904	32,806	5,782,227
1990	1,925,632	4,679,242	89,448	6,694,322
1991	2,201,726	4,868,906	39,913	7,110,545

Source: CFE.

TABLE 7. ELECTRIC ENERGY USE BY
SECTOR (MWH): BAJA CALIFORNIA

1990						
	Domestic	Commerc.	Industrial	Pub. Light	Irrigation	Total
Ensenada	106,371	44,291	181,886	10,069	63,384	406,001
Mexicali	818,961	139,995	781,257	17,223	86,467	1,843,903
Tecate	20,706	8,593	46,360	1,709	3,046	80,414
Tijuana	227,667	111,252	604,783	18,174	1,065	962,941
Total	1,173,705	304,131	1,614,286	47,175	153,962	3,293,259
1991						
Ensenada	110,599	44,979	187,324	12,458	53,556	408,916
Mexicali	811,828	142,371	737,835	18,277	87,028	1,797,339
Tecate	23,042	9,226	51,888	2,188	2,844	89,188
Tijuana	390,745	158,780	662,064	20,796	1,973	1,234,358
Total	1,336,214	355,356	1,639,111	53,719	145,401	3,529,801

in Baja California for 1990 and 1991 is given in Table 7. Figure 4 shows electric consumption by municipality and sector for 1991. Some interesting features are evident. The industrial and residential sectors are the major users of electricity, followed by the commercial, irrigation and public lighting sectors. This is different from electric use patterns in San Diego, where the commercial and residential sectors use more electricity than the industrial sector. The difference in electric energy use patterns between Baja California and San Diego reflects the fact that manufacturing and assembly activities form a larger part of the Tijuana economy than they do in San Diego. This is primarily due to the *maquiladora* plant operations located in Tijuana.

In Mexicali, residential electric consumption is more than twice that of Tijuana, even though Mexicali's population is less than Tijuana's. Mexicali has some of the highest temperatures in Mexico, with daily average outdoor temperatures above 90°F for July and August. It also has a very inefficient air-conditioning infrastructure, mainly due to the poor shell characteristics of the housing stock and the low efficiency of the electric devices used for air-conditioning. In fact, Mexicali has the highest

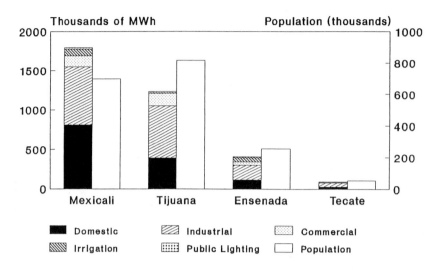

Figure 4. Electrical Use by City and Sector, Baja California 1991.

per capita residential energy use in Mexico.[36] The inefficient air-conditioning sector in Mexicali is an obvious area where improvements can be made. Reduced air-conditioning loads would result in a reduction in demand for electricity in Baja California.

Although per capita electric use in Baja California is greater than the Mexican average, it is still much less compared to San Diego. For Baja California as a whole, per capita electric use for 1991 was only 1,941 Kwh (2,579 and 1,514 Kwh for Mexicali and Tijuana, respectively), compared to 5,236 Kwh for San Diego.[37]

It is important to note, however, that demand for electricity in Mexico has increased at a much higher rate than in the U.S., as previously noted. During the 1980s, demand in Mexico grew at a rate of 6 percent per year, although the population growth rate was only 2.5 percent and the gross domestic product grew at a 1.4 percent rate.[38] In Baja California, electric

36 Odón de Buen, "Electricity Demand in Mexico in the Eighties and the Case of Mexicali," presented at the *IV Congresso Latino-Ibero-Americano de Investigacion de Operaciones Y Sistemas*, Mexico City, 9 October 1992.

37 Electric energy usage from CFE and SDG&E, population figures from SANDAG.

38 Emilio Lozoya Thalmann, Secretary of Energy, Mines and State Owned Industry (SEMIP), "Requirements of the electric sector in Mexico and cooperation opportunities between the public and private sectors," speech delivered to the *International Energy Conference*, Institute of the Americas, San Diego, California, 6 June 1993.

energy demand growth averaged about 6 percent per year between 1982 and 1990.[39] For the United States, demand growth during the 1980s averaged only about 2 percent per year, and in San Diego about 3 percent per year. It is quite likely that demand for electricity in Baja California will continue to grow faster than in San Diego. Meeting this future demand will have an impact on the entire San Diego–Tijuana region.

Transportation Fuels in Baja California. Like San Diego, the transportation sector in Baja California is the largest user of energy. The main fuels currently in use are leaded (Nova) and unleaded (Magna Sin) gasoline and diesel fuel.

Future Energy Needs of Baja California. The process of estimating future energy needs and planning to meet those needs is quite different in Mexico than in California. There are no counterpart agencies in Mexico or Baja California to the Public Utilities Commission, the California Energy Commission or SANDAG. Future electricity needs have been determined by CFE, based more or less on historical growth patterns. Demand for transportation fuels and LPG are met by increasing supplies from the interior of Mexico, or by importing fuels, such as unleaded gasoline, from the U.S. In 1992, for example, Baja California had to import one-quarter of its unleaded gasoline, up from only 4 percent the year before.[40]

CFE projections, made in 1990 for Baja California, indicate an expansion in generating capacity of 78 percent by the year 2000, compared to 1992.[41] Most of this new capacity would come from a major expansion of the existing 620 MW generating facility in Rosarito. According to these estimates, 340 MW would be added by 1995, another 350 MW in 1996 and another 350 MW in 2000. The plans also call for an additional 80 MW at the geothermal plant at Cerro Prieto. All the new generating capacity at Rosarito would use oil as fuel. If carried out to completion, the Rosarito plant could end up as the largest thermal power plant on the west coast of North America, with an installed capacity of 1,670 MW. Such a development would have a major impact on the San Diego region.

It should be emphasized, however, that the likelihood of these large additions actually being carried out in the time period indicated by the CFE projections is quite small. As of this writing (May 1994) no new

---

39 CFE, private communication, 27 April 1993.

40 Private communication from PEMEX, 5 May 1993.

41 U.S. Department of Energy and SEMIP, *United States/Mexico Electricity Trade Study* (March 1991), p. D-36.

construction has begun at the Rosarito plant and, as far as is known, no new construction plans have yet been authorized.

AIR QUALITY IN THE BORDER REGION

The most direct impact energy-related activities has on the environment in the United States–Mexico border region is on air quality. Energy use on both sides of the border has grown dramatically during the last 25 years as a result of the large population increase, the *maquiladora* program and the rapid industrialization that has taken place in the border region. In 1965, there were twelve *maquiladora* plants in the border area, employing only 3,000 people. By 1989, there were almost 1,300 plants in the border area employing approximately 360,000 people.[42]

In the larger border "sister cities," such as El Paso–Ciudad Juarez and San Diego–Tijuana, poor air quality is a reality. The Environmental Protection Agency (EPA) considers any area that fails to meet its National Ambient Air Quality Standard (NAAQS) to be a "nonattainment" area; the region must then work with the EPA to design a plan to meet the NAAQS. Failure to meet the standards in any one of six criteria pollutants (particulate matter, sulfur dioxide, carbon monoxide, nitrous oxides, ozone and lead) will place the area in the nonattainment category.

San Diego failed to meet the criteria for ozone emissions and carbon monoxide in 1989. El Paso's pollutants were above standards in three categories: particulate matter, carbon monoxide, and ozone.[43]

Air pollution generally originates from point and area sources. Point sources, such as power plants, industrial facilities and smelters, are sources that put over 100 tons per facility per year of pollutants into the atmosphere. Area sources are emissions spread out over a large area and come mostly from automobiles, trucks, light industrial operations and commercial and personal activities.

The EPA has collected data on both point and area emissions for the U.S. side of the border. Table 8 shows point and area emissions for five pollutants in San Diego County in 1985.

The volatile organic compound (VOC) emissions are a byproduct of plants that manufacture electronic and electric equipment, materials and supplies, transportation equipment and furniture. The manufacture of these items involves processes that use paint coatings and solvents that result in the emissions of VOC. Although VOCs are not a direct

---

42 Review of U.S–Mexico Environmental Issues, U.S. Trade Representative Report (February 1992), p. 75 (referred to as USTR Report).

43 Ibid., p. 77.

TABLE 8. AIR EMISSIONS FOR SAN DIEGO COUNTY (TONS/YEAR), 1985

Type	SO$_2$	TSP	VOC	NO$_x$	CO$_2$
Point	1,500	657	4,358	4,018	1,464
Area	8,860	77,527	115,386	68,350	325,761

Source: Adapted from *Review of U.S.–Mexico Environmental Issues*, U.S. Trade Representative, February 1992, p. 79.

consequence of energy-related activities, they are of concern because they are major precursors of ozone formation and contribute to air toxicity.[44]

According to a 1991 study for EPA by SECOFI, electronic and electric equipment, materials and supplies accounted for more than 40 percent of all products produced in Mexican border industries and transportation equipment and supplies made up almost 15 percent of all products.[45] There is concern that with the growth of these industries on the Mexican side of the border, VOCs could become a significant contributor to the region's air pollution. A U.S. General Accounting Office study conducted in the spring of 1991 reported that Mexico had not yet established air pollution standards for paint coatings and solvents in the border region.[46]

Air pollution more directly related to energy use originates from motor vehicle emissions. A joint SEDUE–EPA study done in 1990 in Ciudad Juarez showed that the combustion efficiency of the average vehicle was equivalent to the early-to mid-1970s American level.[47] Inefficient fuel combustion results in high emissions of VOC, nitrogen oxides, carbon monoxide and particulate matter. Although no similar data exist for Tijuana, it is likely that the situation is similar.

Other sources of air pollution arise from the burning of non-traditional fuels in the winter in many residences in the Mexican border area. Fuels such as wood scraps, cardboard and tires emit large quantities of particulate matter and carbon monoxide. This is a particularly severe problem in the El Paso-Juarez area.

Mexico and the United States are beginning to cooperate in dealing with transborder air pollution. The most extensive cooperation is in the

44 Ibid., p. 78.
45 Ibid., p. 78.
46 Ibid., p. 81.
47 Ibid., p. 81.

El Paso–Ciudad Juarez area where SEDUE and EPA have sponsored air quality studies and have established monitoring sites.

Air Quality Projections. The U.S. Trade Representative (USTR) has tried to estimate likely air pollution levels in the border region with and without a NAFTA agreement.[48] The claim was made during the NAFTA debate that NAFTA may lead to relatively more investment in the interior of Mexico compared to the border region, thereby reducing the rate of industrial growth in the border area from an annual rate of from 6–17 percent to 4–12 percent. Regardless of which scenario one accepts, the USTR also points out that "the number of Mexican pollutant-emitting facilities will increase [in the border area]; this will prompt Mexican commercial and residential pollutant increases that will affect the U.S. and will prompt concomitant increases in U.S. sister cities as well."[49]

Unless significant resolve is demonstrated on the part of both U.S. and Mexican authorities, air quality in the border region will continue to deteriorate. To halt this deterioration several things are needed: enhanced industrial inspections and enforcement, tighter new automobile emissions standards, vehicle inspection/maintenance programs and retrofitting, and retirement of existing highly polluting industries. Even if all these programs were to be implemented, the USTR analysis still shows increasing air pollution levels to 1996, with levels in the year 2000 the same as in 1992.[50] It seems unlikely, however, that all the above-mentioned programs would or could be put into practice, and therefore air quality in the twin-city areas of the border region will, in all probability, continue to decline.

Issues for the San Diego–Baja California Region. Having described the basic characteristics of the energy sector of San Diego and Baja California, it is now possible to address some of the main issues of importance to the region.

From the discussion above it is clear that the binational region is almost totally dependent on energy sources that originate from outside the area. The Mexican side of the border depends more on petroleum products than does the San Diego region, but both are heavily dependent on fossil fuels, all of which originate from outside the region.

As the population and economy of Baja California, particularly Tijuana and Mexicali, continue to grow, the demand for energy of all

---

48 Ibid., pp. 85–87.

49 Ibid., p. 85.

50 Ibid., p. 86.

types will increase. How this demand will be met could have a direct impact on San Diego's energy sector.

Rosarito Power Plant and Natural Gas. San Diego currently depends on Mexico to meet about 10 percent of its power needs. The contract between SDG&E and the CFE governing these power exchanges expires at the end of 1996. It is quite possible, indeed very probable, that owing to Baja California's growing demand for electricity, CFE will have to use currently exported electricity to meet domestic demand. SDG&E will then have to look elsewhere for this energy. At the present time, there seems to be sufficient power available in the southwest and northwest, but it is not known what the costs will be and for how long this power will be available.

Moreover, not only may SDG&E need to replace imported electricity from Mexico after 1996, but CFE itself may be looking to purchase power in the U.S. from the same markets that SDG&E also would be purchasing from. This could lead to a competitive situation between San Diego and Mexico, which might be exploited by those utilities selling power and could exert upward pressure on SDG&E's rates or cut into their profits.

Should Mexico decide to meet future electric needs by increasing capacity in Baja California, this could present both a problem as well as an opportunity for the region.

A significant problem would arise if the Rosarito power plant were expanded and oil or coal used for fuel. As noted earlier, an expansion of the 620 MW Rosarito power plant that uses oil or coal could have significant impact on the air quality of the San Diego–Tijuana basin. Currently, the plant produces 450,000 tons of CO_2, 870 tons of NO_x, 5,900 tons of SO_2, 800 tons of CO, 420 tons of particulates and 820 tons of hydrocarbons per year.[51] If the Rosarito plant were to add almost 1000 MW of oil-generated electricity over the next decade, it is clear that air quality would be significantly degraded in the San Diego–Tijuana region. It should be noted in this regard that CFE is expected to issue a tender for construction of a 700 MW coal- or oil-fired plant in Ensenada.[52]

If, however, natural gas could be provided to Baja California and used to fuel any expansion of Rosarito as well as replace the existing 620 MW of oil-generated power, one would expect to see significant reductions in air pollution.

---

51 M. Quintero-Núñez, C. Leon-Diez and R.I. Rojas-Caldela, "Environmental Impact of Two Energy Systems in the State of Baja California: Geothermoelectric and Thermoelectric Power Plants," *International Symposium on Heat and Mass Transfer in Energy Systems and Environmental Effects*, Cancun, Mexico, 22-25 August 1993.

52 CFE.

The possibility of supplying Baja California with natural gas has been under discussion for some time. Several proposals have been put forward. One, by SDG&E and Southern California Gas (SOCAL), known as Project Vecinos, would eventually supply Baja California with 500 MMcfd, an amount larger than is currently used in San Diego, via a 36-inch (the largest in Southern California) pipeline from Riverside county to the border crossing at Otay Mesa and then on to Rosarito.[53]

Another project has been proposed by Texas-based El Paso Natural Gas in which an east-west pipeline would be built connecting in Yuma, Arizona and continuing on to Rosarito. The total length of the El Paso line would be about 210 miles, compared to the SDG&E project of about 145 miles.[54]

SDG&E received approval for the project from the Federal Energy Regulatory Commission (FERC) on July 29, 1993. Before Vecinos can proceed, however, the Mexican government must agree to the project. The El Paso Natural Gas project has not yet received FERC approval.

If Mexico decides that natural gas is to be brought into Baja California and approves SDG&E's Project Vecinos, we would expect a significant and mostly positive impact on SDG&E and the San Diego region. Because natural gas is a cleaner-burning fuel than either oil or coal, pollutants from the Rosarito power plant will be reduced if existing oil-fueled boilers were replaced by natural gas. If future expansion of the plant also uses natural gas, reductions in pollutants can be expected, relative to what would be the case if oil or coal were to be used.

POLICY OPTIONS

The above discussion suggests some policy options that could mitigate the environmental impact of energy use in the border region.

1. Develop incentives to increase energy efficiency on both sides of the border. This may be the single most cost-effective approach for providing an adequate energy supply for the region while reducing negative impacts on the environment.

2. Develop policies that reward and encourage the use of cleaner-burning fuels in the transportation sector such as electric vehicles, methanol, CNG and LPG.

---

53 SDG&E.

54 Elliot Blair, "Power Plays," *San Diego Union Tribune* (20 June 1993), p. 3.

3. Initiate a vehicle inspection/maintenance program to reduce emissions from poorly tuned vehicles and to minimize tampering with smog-control devices. Consider developing similar emissions standards on both sides of the border.

4. Develop incentives to increase the use of natural gas in the border region. Wherever possible, natural gas should replace coal and oil.

5. Consider ways to reduce waiting time for vehicles at border crossing points in order to reduce emissions from idling vehicles.

6. Consider implementing demand-side management programs on the Mexican side of the border. The CPUC could play an important role in this.

7. Encourage the use of renewable energy resources, such as solar, wind, biomass and geothermal, in the border area.

8. Develop binational cooperative planning mechanisms between appropriate authorities on both sides of the border to rationalize energy and environmental policies in the border zone.

Bradly J. Condon
Director, Centre for North-American Business Studies
Simon Fraser University

The Impact of the NAFTA, the NAAEC, and Constitutional Law on Environmental Policy in Canada and Mexico

INTRODUCTION

There has been much debate over the constraints the North American Free Trade Agreement (NAFTA) and the North American Agreement on Environmental Cooperation (NAAEC) may place on the ability of Canada and Mexico to maintain independent environmental policies. The NAFTA prohibits the use of environmental measures to restrict trade. The NAAEC contains provisions aimed at ensuring that national and sub-national environmental measures are properly enforced in each country. However, both agreements affirm the freedom of each country to determine its own environmental policies and laws.

This article argues that constitutional law and political realities may do more to limit environmental policy options than either of these new North American agreements. Constitutional documents form the legal basis upon which national and sub-national governments are granted authority to make environmental laws. Without adequate constitutional jurisdiction over the environment, no government can give its environmental policies legal effect. Constitutional law may therefore place severe constraints on a government's ability to enact laws, and on its ability to enforce laws that lack a solid constitutional foundation.

This article first analyzes the legally binding environmental provisions of the NAFTA and the NAAEC. It then analyzes Canadian constitutional jurisdiction over environmental laws, and the relationship between the Canadian Constitution, the NAFTA the NAAEC, and the Canadian Environmental Protection Act. Next, it examines Mexican constitutional jurisdiction over the environment, as set out in the Mexican Constitution and federal environmental legislation. It concludes with comparisons between the degree of policy freedom available to Canada's and Mexico's federal governments under their respective constitutions, and considers the implications for implementation of the NAFTA and the NAAEC.

THE NORTH AMERICAN FREE TRADE AGREEMENT

There are essentially two sides to the trade-environment issue. From an environmentalist's perspective, the central issue is how to make trade environmentally friendly. From a free-trader's perspective, the primary focus is on making environmental regulations trade-friendly. The NAAEC addresses the environmental perspective, while the NAFTA deals with trade concerns.

The NAFTA limits the use of trade restrictions to implement environmental policy. Article 904(1) affirms the right of each Party to set standards *relating to* environmental protection. Similarly, Article 2101, which incorporates Article XX of the General Agreement on Tariffs and Trade (GATT), allows the use of trade-restrictive measures *relating to* the conservation of exhaustible natural resources. GATT and FTA panels have interpreted the words "relating to" in GATT Article XX(g) to mean that such measures must be "primarily aimed at" conservation.[1] The same analysis would apply to both NAFTA Article 2101 and Article 904(1) with respect to the meaning of the term "relating to." If a trade restriction is not primarily aimed at environmental protection or resource conservation, the implication is that its purpose is to protect domestic industry from competition and it will be ruled inconsistent with the NAFTA.

This is precisely what occurred in a case under the Canada–United States Free Trade Agreement (FTA) respecting Canada's requirement that all salmon and herring caught off the British Columbia coast be landed at B.C. fish stations. The United States challenged this measure as an export restriction that was designed to favour Canadian fish-processing plants. Canada said the measure was necessary to ensure accurate data collection for the purpose of managing the resource and could therefore be justified under FTA Article 1201, which incorporates GATT Article XX(g), as a measure relating to the conservation of an exhaustible natural resource. The FTA panel found it was necessary to land only 80 to 90 percent of the catch in Canada to ensure proper data collection, not 100 percent. The panel reasoned that, since there was a less trade-restrictive means of achieving the conservation goal, the measure in question did not qualify as one "relating to" conservation. Canada and the United

---

1 See *Canada—Measures Affecting Exports of Unprocessed Herring and Salmon*, Report of the GATT Panel (20 November 1987) BISD, 35th Supp. 98 and *In the Matter of Canada's Landing Requirement for Pacific Coast Salmon and Herring*, Final Report of the FTA Panel (16 October 1989), 2 C.T.C.T.C. (CCH) 7162.

States subsequently agreed to allow 20 to 25 percent of the catch to be landed outside Canada.[2]

Article 904(4) prohibits the implementation of environmental standards in ways that create *unnecessary* obstacles to trade. Similarly, Article 2101 allows the use of trade-restrictive measures *necessary* to protect human, animal or plant life or health. GATT panels have interpreted the word "necessary" to require governments to use the least trade-restrictive means to achieve environmental protection goals.[3]

Article 104 provides express permission to employ trade restrictions to achieve international environmental goals pursuant to specific international conservation and environmental agreements. Where there is a conflict between those agreements and the NAFTA, those agreements prevail to the extent of the inconsistency. In effect, Article 104 deems trade measures taken under the listed international environmental agreements to be measures relating to legitimate environmental objectives and deems them to be necessary. However, the least-trade-restrictive test is implicit in the Article 104 requirement that "where a Party has a choice among equally effective and reasonably available means of complying with such obligations, the Party chooses the alternative that is the least inconsistent with the other provisions of this Agreement."

In essence, if a country chooses the least trade-restrictive method of implementing its environmental policy, then its environmental laws will comply with the requirements of the NAFTA. However, if there is a less restrictive and equally effective method available, that method must replace one that is challenged. The NAFTA rules are not concerned with *what* environmental policies should be, but rather *how* they are to be achieved. Trade restrictions may only be used to achieve environmental goals where they are the most effective means available. Thus, from a legal perspective, the NAFTA does not limit a country's freedom to determine its own environmental policies.

---

2   See *In the Matter of Canada's Landing Requirement for Pacific Coast Salmon and Herring, supra,* note 4 and J. Anderson & J. Fried, "The Canada–U.S. Free Trade Agreement in Operation" (1991) 17 Can.–U.S. L.J. 397 at 403.

3   See *United States—Restrictions on Imports of Tuna,* Report of the GATT Panel (3 September 1991) DS21/R, 30 I.L.M. 1594; *Thailand—Restrictions on Importation of and Internal Taxes on Cigarettes,* Report of the GATT Panel (7 November 1990) BISD, 37th Supp. 200, DS10/R, 30 I.L.M. 1122 (1991); and *United States—Section 337 of the Tariff Act of 1930,* Report of the GATT Panel (7 November 1989) BISD 36th Supp. 345.

THE NORTH AMERICAN AGREEMENT
ON ENVIRONMENTAL COOPERATION

The North American Agreement on Environmental Cooperation (NAAEC) is the so-called "parallel environmental accord" that was promised by the Mulroney, Bush and Salinas administrations in response to environmental opposition to the NAFTA. The Clinton administration supported this side-agreement as a means to address perceived deficiencies in the environmental provisions of the NAFTA, particularly the non-binding nature of Article 1114, which discourages the lowering of environmental standards to attract foreign investment. However, negotiators had to seek to address these environmental concerns in a manner that would (1) be fully consistent with the NAFTA, (2) not supply new tools for disguised protectionism, and (3) respect the sovereignty of each nation. The NAAEC that was signed September 13, 1993 found innovative ways to enhance continental environmental protection without creating new non-tariff barriers to trade. It sets up a dispute-settlement mechanism through which complaints may be lodged against any NAFTA country that persistently fails to enforce its domestic environmental laws. However, each country remains free to set its own environmental policies and laws without interference from the others. The NAAEC focuses on enforcement of laws rather than their formulation.

The NAAEC establishes a Commission for Environmental Cooperation, comprised of a Council, a Secretariat and a Joint Public Advisory Committee.[4] The Council is charged with developing recommendations on a wide range of environmental issues, providing a forum for their discussion, and promoting trilateral environmental protection.[5] However, implementation of the Council's recommendations is not mandatory. Rather, the recommendations are to be made public, which will then give citizens an opportunity to put pressure on their governments to implement them.

The Secretariat, which is located in Montreal, will receive complaints that a NAFTA Party is failing to enforce its environmental laws. Notably, the Secretariat will receive submissions from persons or non-governmental organizations from all three countries, providing environmentalists from all three countries with a new forum in which to be heard.[6] This is particularly significant for Mexican environmentalists, who have complained that they do not have adequate access to their own government in such matters.

---

4   Article 8.
5   Article 10.
6   Article 14.

Under Part 5 of the NAAEC, where a Party alleges that another Party has persistently failed to effectively enforce its environmental laws in sectors of its economy that produce goods or services traded between the Parties or that compete with the goods or services of another Party, the Council administers a consultation and dispute resolution system to resolve the matter.[7] The process begins with consultations between governments. If the matter is not resolved within 60 days, then other dispute resolution methods are employed until the matter is resolved. First, the matter proceeds to an investigation, then to conciliation or mediation, and finally to arbitration before a panel of five experts in environmental law and international dispute resolution.[8]

The Panel hears arguments and issues a report determining whether there has been a persistent pattern of failure to enforce the environmental law.[9] If such is the case, the Panel recommends an action plan sufficient to remedy the pattern of non-enforcement. If the Party fails to fully implement the action plan, or another plan that is agreed to by the NAFTA Parties, the Panel may impose a fine of up to $20 million (U.S.).[10] In the case of Canada, Panel determinations will be enforced as orders of the Federal Court of Canada.[11] In the case of Mexico or the United States, failure to pay the fine may result in the re-imposition of tariffs sufficient to collect the fine.[12] Fines are paid into a fund that is then used to enhance the environment or environmental law enforcement in the Party complained against, in a manner consistent with its domestic law.[13]

The NAAEC contains two provisions that will be of concern to North American environmentalists, and Canadians in particular. First, laws regarding the management or exploitation of natural resources are excluded from the definition of "environmental law," making their enforcement immune to attack under the NAAEC.[14] This is, however, consistent with international legal principles that affirm each nation's sovereign right to exploit its own natural resources as it sees fit. Secondly, the NAAEC is not binding on any Canadian province that does not agree to abide by it and Canada cannot enforce the Agreement against Mexico or the United States unless the environmental law in question would fall under federal jurisdiction in Canada or, if not, a majority of the provinces

---

7 Articles 22, 23, and 24.
8 Articles 22–30.
9 Articles 31–33.
10 Article 34.
11 Annex 36A.
12 Article 36.
13 Annex 34.
14 Article 45.2(b). ·

have signed on to the Agreement.[15] From a Canadian constitutional perspective, these provisions were necessary to ensure that the federal government did not use the NAAEC to intrude upon provincial jurisdiction over the environment and natural resources.

Most of the remaining provisions of the NAAEC consist of non-binding political commitments that set out a framework for voluntary, trilateral cooperation on environmental protection. The creation of accompanying institutional structures enhances the likelihood that the three NAFTA countries will follow through on these commitments. However, the progress that is made will depend in large part on the political will of the governments in power, which in turn will depend on the priority the citizens of each country assign to environmental issues. In Canada, much will depend on the degree of co-operation that can be achieved among the federal and provincial governments regarding environmental jurisdiction.

THE CANADIAN CONSTITUTION

Both the NAFTA and the Canadian Constitution[16] subject laws to legal tests that determine their validity on the basis of their subject matter. Under the NAFTA, the issue is whether the true purpose and effect of an environmental law is to achieve a legitimate environmental objective or whether it is in fact a disguised barrier to trade. Similarly, the Canadian Constitution asks whether the true purpose and effect of a law is to address a valid Constitutional objective or whether it deals with a matter that is beyond the jurisdiction of the enacting government.

The federal government has the power to enter into treaty obligations, but their implementation as domestic law must be consistent with the division of powers between the federal and provincial governments under the Canadian Constitution.[17] As a result, Parliament may not have the constitutional authority to enact legislation implementing international agreements where the subject matter falls within provincial jurisdiction. While the federal government may have sufficient authority under its trade and commerce power[18] to fulfill its NAFTA obligations with respect to matters of international trade, the Canadian Constitution provides little guidance regarding the manner in which the federal government may implement its NAFTA and NAAEC environmental obligations.

---

15 See Annex 41.
16 *Constitution Act, 1867* (U.K.), 30 & 31 Vict., c. 3 [hereinafter the *Constitution*].
17 See *A.G. Can.* v. *A.G. Ont.*, [1937] A.C. 326, [1937] 1 W.W.R. 299, 1 D.L.R. 673 at 352 (P.C.) (the *Labour Conventions* case); *MacDonald* v. *Vapor Canada Ltd.*, [1977] 2 S.C.R. 134 at 167–72, 66 D.L.R. (3d) 1, 22 C.P.R. (2d) 1, 7 N.R. 477.
18 *Constitution*, s. 91(2).

With respect to matters affecting the environment or trade, in many cases, either level of government may legislate, one with respect to provincial aspects and the other, federal aspects.[19] Provincial authority over property and civil rights in the province enables each province to set environmental standards within the province.[20] Even where Parliament has validly enacted a single national standard, this will not preclude the provinces from establishing a variety of stricter standards. However, when provincial governments create trade barriers disguised as local environmental protection, the courts may view such legislation as an invalid attempt to regulate international trade.

Parliament has exclusive jurisdiction to regulate the importation of goods into Canada. In general, however, only the province may regulate the manufacture, possession and sale of products inside a province.[21] Thus, while Parliament has exclusive authority to impose or eliminate *tariff* barriers to trade, its authority to regulate non-tariff barriers to trade, such as environmental and consumer standards, remains ambiguous.

Because the Canadian Constitution does not explicitly grant authority over environmental matters to either level of government, environmental legislation must be linked to one or more heads of power in s. 91 (for federal legislation) or s. 92 (for provincial legislation).[22] For example, the residual legislative power of s. 91 "to make Laws for the Peace, Order, and Good Government of Canada" gives Parliament jurisdiction over environmental matters of national concern. Subsection 92(16) grants the provinces jurisdiction over matters "of a merely local or private nature in the Province."

The pith-and-substance doctrine is the constitutional equivalent of the "relating to" test of NAFTA Articles 2101 and 904(1). It classifies a law as "in relation to" a matter within federal jurisdiction or to a matter within provincial jurisdiction.[23] "Pith and substance" refers to the dominant or most important characteristic of the law in question. In this regard, it is remarkably similar to the "primarily aimed at" test of trade law.

---

19 P. Hogg, *Constitutional Law of Canada*, 2d ed. (Toronto: Carswell, 1985) at 317.

20 See Hogg, *supra*, note 11 at 737. See also, *A.G. Quebec* v. *Kellogg's Co. of Canada*, [1978] 2 S.C.R. 211; *Dominion Stores* v. *The Queen*, [1980] 1 S.C.R. 844; and *Labatt Breweries* v. *A.G. Canada*, [1980] 1 S.C.R. 914.

21 See *Citizens' Insurance Co. of Canada* v. *Parsons*(1881), 7 A.C. 96 (P.C.); *Caloil Inc.* v. *A.G. Can.*, [1971] S.C.R. 543, 20 D.L.R. (3d) 472 at 476–477, and *Reference Re Validity of Section 5(a) of the Dairy Industry Act* (The Margarine Reference) (1948), [1949] 1 D.L.R. 433 (S.C.C.); affirmed [1950] 4 D.L.R. 689 (P.C.).

22 *Friends of the Oldman River Society* v. *Canada (Minister of Transport)* [1992] 2 W.W.R. 196 (S.C.C.).

23 *General Motors of Canada Ltd.* v. *City National Leasing* [1989] 1 S.C.R. 641, 58 D.L.R. (4th) 255 at 275.

If a provincial environmental standard were found to be a disguised barrier to international trade, it could be ruled unconstitutional as a matter in relation to international trade. However, if the standard relates to local environmental regulation, is a necessary part of a valid legislative scheme, and is minimally intrusive on the federal trade power, it would likely be a valid exercise of provincial power. However, the courts have repeatedly expressed concern over constitutional interpretations that could upset the balance of power between Parliament and the provinces. Thus, while constitutional arguments against provincial disguised barriers to trade are likely to succeed in clear cases, where there is doubt regarding the true nature of the standard in question constitutional challenges may fail on the grounds that federal jurisdiction over environmental standards would be unduly enlarged.

THE RELATIONSHIP BETWEEN THE NAFTA, THE NAAEC, THE CANADIAN CONSTITUTION AND THE CANADIAN ENVIRONMENTAL PROTECTION ACT

Under both the NAFTA and the Canadian Constitution, environmental laws are judged by analyzing their subject matter and purpose. The NAFTA says a law must relate to environmental protection to be considered a legitimate environmental law. Similarly, the Canadian Constitution says a law must be in relation to a matter within the jurisdiction of the enacting government in order to be valid. The NAFTA requires a trade restriction to be a necessary and integral part of an environmental scheme before it can be justified under the environmental provisions. Similarly, the Canadian Constitution says a legislative provision that intrudes on the jurisdiction of another level of government must be a necessary and integral part of an otherwise constitutionally valid legislative scheme. The NAFTA requires environmental regulators to use the least trade-restrictive means available to achieve environmental goals. Similarly, the Canadian Constitution requires regulators to achieve constitutionally valid objectives by way of provisions that are the least intrusive on the jurisdiction of the other level of government. The result is that both the federal and provincial governments are obliged to avoid disguising trade barriers as environmental laws, the former under the NAFTA and the latter under the Canadian Constitution.

While the legal tests under the NAFTA and the Canadian Constitution are remarkably similar, there is one important difference between the two legal regimes. Genuine environmental laws are likely to withstand challenges brought under the NAFTA as long as they only restrict trade to the degree that is necessary to achieve the desired level of environmental protection. Unfortunately, the same cannot be said for constitutional challenges to either federal or provincial environmental laws. Even those environmental laws that have no impact on trade may be struck down as unconstitutional if they pursue aspects of environmental protection that may only be regulated by the other level of government. Viewed from this perspective, the NAFTA provides more protection for genuine environmental laws than does the Canadian Constitution.

Much of the Canadian Environmental Protection Act (CEPA) may be constitutionally unenforceable because it deals with many matters that fall under provincial jurisdiction. Part II of the CEPA regulates toxic substances. It is doubtful that federal jurisdiction over a subject as broad and all-encompassing as such would meet the Supreme Court's constitutional tests, particularly in light of the broad definition of toxic substances in s. 11, and the breadth of the subject matter with respect to which Cabinet may pass regulations under s. 34. Part III regulates the dispersal of nutrients in Canadian waters that promote excessive vegetation growth. Here, the Act can rely on federal jurisdiction regarding water pollution, the federal fisheries power (s. 91(12)) and the navigation and shipping power (s. 91(10)). However, it is doubtful that Part III could be validly applied to non-navigable waters that are wholly contained within a province. Part IV, which deals with federal departments, agencies, crown corporations, works, undertakings and lands, and Part V, regarding the fulfilment of Canada's international obligations with respect to international air pollution, would likely come within federal jurisdiction. So, too, would Part VI, which deals with ocean dumping.

An interesting legal issue arises regarding the NAAEC provisions requiring the enforcement of domestic environmental law. The federal government has been rather lax about enforcing CEPA by way of prosecutions for three reasons—one legal, one political and one cultural. Legally, some of the provisions would likely be challenged as unconstitutional were the federal authorities to seek enforcement in the courts. Politically, the government has been careful not to intrude on provincial jurisdiction in the interest of enhancing federal-provincial cooperation on environmental matters and maintaining good relations with provincial governments. From a cultural perspective, Canada is generally a less litigious society than the United States, and has traditionally preferred negotiated solutions to non-compliance rather than prosecutions and fines. The question is, in all of these circumstances, could Canada be subject to fines under the NAAEC for failing to prosecute environmental offenders under CEPA? Probably not.

First, it would be unreasonable to interpret the treaty as requiring Canada to intrude on provincial powers, particularly given the NAAEC provisions that implicitly recognize the limits of federal environmental jurisdiction. Second, it would be unreasonable to require Canada to enforce unenforceable laws. To do so would waste taxpayers' money pursuing a futile goal and do nothing to enhance environmental law enforcement in Canada, the underlying rationale of the NAAEC provisions. Finally, the NAAEC explicitly permits each country to determine its own environmental priorities given its unique circumstances, and one could argue that this allows the Canadian government leeway to determine what provisions to enforce and how and when. Nevertheless, the constitutional foundations of Canadian environmental law are not satisfactory. In contrast, Mexico has dealt with jurisdiction over the environment more effectively under its constitution.

ENVIRONMENTAL JURISDICTION AND THE MEXICAN CONSTITUTION

One of the most important aspects of the Mexican political system is the Presidential regime. The Mexican Constitution vests all executive power in the President and grants him the right to initiate laws. Members of Congress and state legislatures may also initiate legislation. However, the President controls Congress, the judiciary, state governors, the ruling party and the bureaucracy.[24] He also determines economic policy and foreign affairs. As a result, the Mexican President has more power over environmental policies and laws than either the federal or provincial governments of Canada.

The President's right to initiate laws has been amply exercised under the 1917 Mexican Constitution; approximately ninety percent of federal legislation is the work of presidential initiatives. The President also has the right to veto laws approved by Congress. The function of Congress is to critique, discuss, and sanction or modify the initiatives of the government. Congress does not have the power to directly order the publication of laws. The President has the power to promulgate laws, including the power to publish them, an indispensable requisite to their coming into force.

The President has the extraordinary power to legislate in times of national emergency, with respect to economic matters, and in relation to matters of health. In his capacity as chief of state, the President is the exclusive organ of the international relations of the country. He also has the power to interpret the laws and even constitutional provisions, although this is not expressly granted by the Mexican Constitution.

The President also has the power to pass regulations, a power that shapes the application of the law itself. The administration of the federal

---

24 The new President, Ernesto Zedillo Ponce de Leon, stated at his swearing-in that he will give greater independence to the Congress, the courts and local governments. While the 1994 election was the most credible in Mexican history, the President still wields tremendous power, as evidenced by this statement promising he will deliver what the Mexican Constitution has not.

government is freely determined by the President, independently of the legislative branch. Directly or indirectly, the chief executive also controls the nominations and general functioning of the federal public sector.

The key to understanding the Mexican political system and the role of the President is his power within the ruling political party, the Institutional Revolutionary Party (PRI). The party recognizes the President of the Republic, in the exercise of his office, as its supreme leader. This additional vesting of power in the individual who occupies the presidency greatly influences the constitutional system and the political process. In theory, Congress and the judiciary are independent of the executive branch and the Constitution guarantees the autonomy of the thirty-one states. The President nominates the ministers of the Supreme Court of Justice and the magistrates of the Superior Tribunal of Justice, with the ratification of the Senate and the Chamber of Deputies, respectively. But the Supreme Court has never overturned any key government decision, and despite the presence of opposition deputies, the PRI's majority has guaranteed the obedience of Congress. Moreover, the ban on immediate re-election to Congress prevents deputies from seeking independent parliamentary careers and forces them to depend on the bureaucracy for future employment. Following presidential initiatives, Congress amended the Constitution on 369 occasions between 1917 and 1984.

Because of the concentration of power in the President, one must look to the President for environmental policies and laws. President Miguel de la Madrid Hurtado (1982–1988) further laid the groundwork for President Carlos Salinas de Gortari's policies with his 1987 constitutional reforms and the enactment of the Ley General del Equilibrio Ecologico y la Proteccion al Ambiente (LGEEPA). Like the CEPA, the LGEEPA was enacted in 1988. Unlike Canada, the Mexican government was able to amend its constitution to accommodate the new legislation before it was enacted. The LGEEPA covers a similar range of matters as CEPA, with one notable exception: unlike CEPA, the LGEEPA sets out the constitutional basis for environmental legislation in Mexico.

The reforms of articles 27 and 73-XXIX-G of the Mexican Constitution established the underlying basis of the 1988 law. Since article 124 of the Mexican Constitution reserves to the States the areas of jurisdiction not explicitly given to the federal government, article 73 had to be amended in order to provide a more solid basis for federal environmental legislation. Article 27 was amended to give the state the right to impose public interest restrictions on the use of private property and the power to enact laws to "preserve and restore ecological balance." Article 73 now gives Congress jurisdiction to pass legislation to establish the concurrent jurisdiction of the federal Government, State governments and Municipalities in matters of environmental protection. Congress exercised this new power in the LGEEPA. In effect, the LGEEPA lays its own constitutional foundation.

The LGEEPA sets out the division of legislative authority between federal, state and municipal authorities and coordinates federal administrative agencies that deal with environmental matters. It establishes concurrent jurisdiction as the general rule, centralizes power within the federal government, and recognizes the need for inter-agency, state and municipal government participation at the implementation stage. The LGEEPA uses the same formula as the Mexican Constitution to allocate legislative jurisdiction. It reserves to the states and municipalities those matters that are not specifically granted to the federal government. It lists the subject matters that fall within federal jurisdiction and those that fall within state and municipal jurisdiction. These lists are the environmental equivalent of the Canadian Constitution's general division of legislative powers.

The LGEEPA sets out federal environmental jurisdiction in some detail. However, the question remains whether Congress may validly delineate its own legislative jurisdiction in a statute, even with the constitutional amendment that gives it that power under article 73-XXIX-G of the Mexican Constitution. The article 73 amendment has been criticized on the basis that mere legislation cannot establish the jurisdiction of the States. That must be specified in the Mexican Constitution itself, which reserves to the States the powers not expressly granted to the federal government. If a statute cannot establish constitutional jurisdiction in these circumstances, the issue then becomes whether the matters assigned to the federal government may be interpreted as falling under federal jurisdiction in any event. The new constitutional provisions have yet to be tested by the courts. However, in addition to the 1987 reforms, the statute may rely on other articles of the Mexican Constitution in which federal environmental jurisdiction might be implied. The LGEEPA touches on three basic aspects of environmental law: the use of natural resources, pollution prevention, and sustainable development.

Several articles of the Mexican Constitution grant legislative authority to the federal government over natural resources, human health, safety and pollution prevention and control, as well as the allocation of responsibilities regarding environmental protection and ecological balance between the federal, state and municipal governments.The LGEEPA division of environmental powers may thus be viewed as a codification of existing constitutional jurisdiction rather than an enactment thereof.

The combined effect of presidential power and the legislative and constitutional reforms permits Mexico to respond quickly to environmental crises. For example, in Mexico City, record levels of ozone in the winter of 1992 led the government to take drastic action. On March 24, 1992, President Salinas ordered the more than 30,000 industries in and around Mexico City to significantly cut pollution within eighteen months. Plants that do not install clean-air equipment will have to leave the valley. The government gave the 220 dirtiest factories two years to cut emissions by 70 percent, with the help of $1.1 billion in bank credits, or leave the city. In response to the government's ultimatum, General Motors announced it would move its truck plant out of the valley at a cost of $400 million. In the final week of March 1992, the air got so bad that the government decreed a state of emergency that closed schools, grounded 40 percent of the city's cars and ordered several industries to cut their activity by 30 percent until further notice.

The Mexican Constitution's divisions of branches of government and legislative powers must be viewed through the prism of the country's political reality. What counts most is the President's awesome power. It is the political will of the President that will determine the enforceability of Mexico's environmental law. In these circumstances, the interplay between Mexican environmental law, the Mexican Constitution, the NAFTA and the NAAEC is very different from the Canadian situation.

CONCLUSION

Both Canada and Mexico's Constitutions set up federal systems of government. Governmental power is thus distributed between a federal authority and several regional (or provincial or state) authorities so that every individual in the state is subject to the laws of two authorities, the central authority and a regional authority. The main difference between them with respect to the division of powers between federal and regional governments is that under article 124 of the Mexican Constitution the powers not expressly granted to the federal government are reserved for the states. In the Canadian Constitution, this is reversed, with the residual powers vested in the federal government.

A fundamental difference between the two Constitutions is that Canada has retained the British system of responsible government, under which the close link between the executive and legislative branches is inconsistent with any separation of the executive and legislative functions, while Mexico's presidential system follows the American pattern of making a separate distribution of the executive, legislative and judicial powers. The division of powers between federal and regional governments has posed a problem for environmental protection in Canada. The federal political system, with its division of powers between a central government and regional governments, was not designed with environmental laws in mind. Some environmental laws are more effectively designed and enforced locally, while others require a national or international effort in order to be effective.

The federal system complicates coordination and co-operation of federal and regional environmental authorities, adding to the cost of environmental regulation for both business and governments and leaving cracks in the system. Canada is all too familiar with the financial and environmental costs of federal-provincial battles over the division of constitutional powers. Over-burdened taxpayers foot the bill for all of the bureaucratic duplication.

In Canada, constitutional and political realities prevent the federal government from ensuring that provinces comply with the NAFTA requirement to use the least trade-restrictive means to implement environmental policy. The federal government does not even have juris-diction to enforce some of its own environmental legislation, leaving it open to criticism under the NAAEC.

The Mexican system differs from Canada's, and it is not without its advantages. Mexico has not suffered from constitutional infighting the way Canada has. The concentration of political and legal power in the office of the President allows constitutional reforms to pass quickly and efficiently. And concerns about the legal basis for action have not yet hampered presidential power in any significant way. Nevertheless, Mexico has had to amend its Constitution in an effort to accomodate the needs of an environmental regime within a federal constitutional system.

The Presidential system gives the Mexican President sufficient powers to carry out Mexico's obligations under both the NAFTA and the NAAEC. However, Mexico faces its own political and financial challenges that could make full compliance difficult. Corruption and poverty could make the implemention of Mexico's trade and environmental obligations problematic, impeding enforcement of environmental laws. While Mexico is making progress in both areas, it will likely take some time to resolve them.

In sum, neither system is perfect. There is much to be done in both Canada and Mexico to achieve the trade liberalization and environmental protection goals set out in the NAFTA and the NAAEC.

Michel Duquette
Department of Political Science
Université de Montréal

Domestic and International Factors Affecting Energy Trade

INTRODUCTION TO THE FREE TRADE DEBATE

The recent history of Canada's energy policy is particularly illustrative of attempts undertaken by the two layers of government—federal and provincial—to deal with territorial and economic cleavages. In the last ten years, the shift in policy from the National Energy Program (NEP) to the Free Trade Agreement (FTA) has been indicative of the difficulties encountered by policy makers in pursuit of goals. Policy makers have been overambitious, given the changing international environment and domestic arena.

Canadian public opinion is very divided on the issue of free trade. Many are concerned about the loss of the country's independence, while others hope for a bright future arising from an unbiased continental market economy, in which Canada would maximize its comparative economic advantages. In my view, most Canadian politicians and analysts had either unreasonable fears or unrealistic expectations about free trade. From a purely Québecois point of view, I suggest that defenders and opponents of free trade naïvely see the agreement as a way out of our endless domestic disputes and the relative decline of Canada in the world economy. Optimists foresee a booming economy, while pessimists foresee our eventual political assimilation into the United States.

Keeping a distance from political rhetoric, this article intends to suggest other, less dramatic, but nevertheless important, factors which may be affecting the context in which the energy provisions of the FTA are implemented. This paper can be seen as a rather impressionistic overview of some of the recent undertakings in the sector, illustrative of each set of factors, domestic, international, and continental, that are closely associated with the FTA between Canada and the United States. Data gathered through several years of research on the topic may prove useful and are indicative of long-term as well as short-term tendencies, some of which are favourable, others unfavourable to free trade. Obviously, many of these precede the application of the agreement. Hence, they deserve special treatment as domestic factors, either as federal-provincial or inter-provincial relations and conflict, or as traditional in-house bargaining between state and business. Otherwise, it is likely that new developments might indicate genuine consequences of the agreement in its early phase of implementation.

Comparing the FTA provisions to the General Agreement on Tariffs and Trade (GATT), it is quite true that the FTA constrains the use of energy export restrictions more than the relevant GATT provisions. In particular, export taxes are not allowed. The FTA also imposes additional constraints on the use of quantitative export restrictions. The most sensitive issue in Canadian public opinion is the proportional access clause, which may be a binding constraint in the future. If, as my hypotheses suggest, most developments, such as mergers, takeovers, privatizations, and new import-export patterns, occurred before free trade was implemented, it may indicate that other factors, both domestic and international, may be determinant. They may be either structurally rooted in the Canadian political system (one recalls the epic federal-provincial disputes of the 1970s over resources and income-sharing) or related to neoconservatism as a political philosophy in the changing world of the 1980s. Obviously, these conclusions may only be tentative. Free-trade policy brings about, as is generally acknowledged, mainly long-term effects. If short-term side-effects are not excluded, they are specifically understated.

THE PROVINCIAL COMMITMENT TO ENERGY DEVELOPMENT

The first factor, which is paramount to our analysis, is the proper organization of the energy industry, which, obviously, lies within provincial jurisdiction. As we know, things tend to be of a different nature in the United States. In Canada, up to the early 1970s, the major objective of the energy policy had been to foster a strong petroleum and gas industry, through pricing and tax incentives more generous than those available outside the resource sector. Both the provincial and federal bureaucracy promoted industry and encouraged economic growth in western Canada and elsewhere. However, such a policy imposed higher direct costs on other parts of the country, as prices varied considerably over regions. It also left the federal government with little income from the gas, petroleum, and power industries.

Under such conditions, the constitutional responsibilities of the provinces over natural resources were strengthened, allowing Alberta, Ontario, and Quebec to put forward their respective energy programs in oil extraction and refining, or hydroelectric and nuclear power. Thus, it is widely acknowledged that electricity generation and trade are greatly influenced by provincial and state governments. This may pose specific, sometimes difficult, problems for the implementation of a trade agreement on a national and international basis.

That may also be true, in some cases, as far as oil and natural gas are concerned. In Canada, resource development lies within provincial jurisdiction. Experience shows that the provinces invariably favour maximum resource extraction in the shortest possible time and on the largest possible scale, without particular concern for the nationality of the interests to whom these resources are conceded.

The case of Alberta is illustrative, in this regard, and pioneers the development of today's institutional arrangements between Canada and the United States. For instance, Alberta chose to adapt its economy to the main features of state-to-business relationships, which are found among entrepreneurs and bureaucrats in energy-producing U.S. states, such as Texas.[1] A generation ago, further regulations were put forward by Alberta's government with the Gas Resources Conservation Act of 1949, in order "to prevent federal encroachment over provincial resources."[2]

Alberta Gas Trunk Line (AGTL) was established as a consortium of private investors supported by public funds. AGTL was expected to facilitate gas distribution to consumers all over the province as well as to potential importers in the United States. Thus, the provincial capital gained control over a highly profitable activity in a rapidly expanding intercontinental market that eventually linked the province's gas and oil fields with customers located as far away as California. From 1971 onwards,

---

1 Limited permits allow the firm to undertake drilling in concessions. Such restricted leases leave remaining areas as Crown reserves, which may be sold by auction, through sealed bids, at a later time. Alberta receives three kinds of charges from the industry: initial payments from Crown reserves, annual rent payable on leases, and royalties which are levied as a percentage of the wellhead value of the resource when it is extracted. Other limits are imposed on drilling, in order to prevent waste. Finally, prorationing of the total output required among wells is another measure inspired from the Texas precedent, in such a way as to adjust the output to changes in total demand and prices on the international market.

2 S.M. Matheson, "The Evolution of Federal, State, and Provincial Energy Policy in the Western United States and Canada," in E.H. Fry, ed., *Energy Development in Canada, The Political, Economic, and Continental Dimensions* (Provo, Utah: Brigham Young University, Canadian Studies Program, Center for International and Area Studies, 1981), pp. 42ff.

Alberta's ambitions shifted to industrial diversification, a task to which the province devoted considerable money from their Heritage Fund.[3]

As a prime domestic factor, Alberta's economic policy in the postwar period bridged the gap that had widened between the United States and Canada during the so-called National Policy era and paved the way to the Free Trade Agreement of 1988.

FEDERAL JURISDICTION OVER DOMESTIC AND INTERNATIONAL TRADE

As a second domestic factor affecting the aims of energy policy and, eventually, the outcome of the FTA, one must consider the nature and characteristics of power at the federal level of government. As long as Ottawa was ruled by a political elite devoted to nation-building policies and strong state intervention (e.g., in the late Trudeau years), national energy policy was bound to clash with the provinces' own traditions—the NEP being a case in point. But, inasmuch as a new broadly based coalition of interests from the regions came into power, it gave rise to a new philosophy in resource management. This major shift occurred when the federal Conservatives won in 1984 and were confirmed for a second term in the 1988 election. Quite interestingly, the new regime looked back at lessons from earlier Conservative cabinets and found an example in Diefenbaker's 1961 policy, which it tried to follow.[4]

There is no question that the Constitution gives overriding responsibilities to Ottawa as far as interprovincial and international trade are concerned. It also entrusts the federal government with the responsibility of stimulating the industry in the name of "national development." Nevertheless, analysts agree that the 1961 national oil policy showed a preference for natural continental patterns of supply in which Canadian and U.S. crudes and other commodities could be freely used in the most economical markets.[5]

Such an energy policy was consistent with a high level of compatibility between the demands of the industry, the strategies pursued by the resource-producing provinces, and the federal bureaucracy. This policy

---

3   In 1979, the Alberta Heritage Fund, established to provide long-term benefit to the province from oil revenues, amounted to some $14 billion and was responsible for a spree of industrial initiatives in Alberta, as well as in neighbouring provinces.

4   Bruce G. Doern and G. Toner, *The Politics of Energy: The Development and Implementation of the NEP* (Toronto: Methuen, 1984), p. 79.

5   Ibid., p. 79.

coincided with an era of international wealth, from which Canada bene-fited through its open-door economic strategy.

It is generally admitted that the energy crisis changed all that, as it did in most western countries. It is no secret that Brian Mulroney's Conservatives harked back to those golden times, with their intention to revive continentalism. Popular support for Conservative policies, includ-ing free trade, which ran high for five years, has been desperately low since 1990, due to domestic political failures such as the ill-fated Meech Lake agreement, which antagonized Quebec and English Canada.

DEVELOPMENTS IN THE DOMESTIC ARENA BEFORE THE FTA

Not surprisingly, with the Conservatives, Canada entered, from 1985 onwards, into an entirely new approach to federal-provincial relations, as well as into a friendlier relationship with its southern neighbour. This resulted in an almost immediate expansion of trade and energy exports. Steps were taken to deregulate oil and gas exports to the United States. A gas pipeline section was built to northern Alberta to help producers increase cash flow with more exports, given a rather high price on the international market.[6]

However, deregulation of the domestic market was impeded by the existence of an array of federally funded programs for oil substitution. Ottawa simply put an end to most of them, over a two-year period.[7] Deregulation went ahead, albeit slowly.

There is no doubt that these long-expected measures had a definite effect on the rise in gas volumes flowing across the forty-ninth parallel, which increased 23 percent in one single-year period between November 1984 and August 1985. Nevertheless, given the new deregulated prices, which were highly advantageous for the U.S. market, this tendency was not reflected in royalties: $3,696 million by August 1985 as compared to $3,674 million for the previous year. This is all the more significant given the fact that natural gas sales were the most lucrative export market to the United States in the Canadian energy sector. Now, the question is about recent developments in such trade, as the pre-FTA period points to significant issues being raised and solved in a new fashion, quite foreign to NEP logic.

In its first years, the Conservative government still had to deal with the thorny "Canadianization" issue. The concept, in itself, was hardly

---

6   Michael Bliss, *Northern Enterprise: Five Centuries of Canadian Business* (Toronto: McClelland and Stewart, 1987), p. 557.

7   Yves Gingras and Jacques Rivard, "Energy R & D Policy in Canada," *Science and Public Policy*, 15, No. 1 (1988), pp. 35–42.

compatible with current practices in the United States or elsewhere in the West. Examples abound of a major shift in policy. In late 1985, Chevron of San Francisco, weakened by financial difficulties, was selling out Gulf Canada, among other assets. Informed of the opportunity, Sinclair Stevens, minister for regional economic expansion, designed a major take-over with bureaucrats and corporate friends.

On the one hand, Petro-Canada bought, at $1.2 billion, the whole retail network west of the Ottawa River, thus increasing the Crown's share. But the Toronto-based Reichmann brothers gained control of the reserves in the Beaufort Sea for an estimated $2.8 billion, after being given a fiscal exemption of $600 million from the federal treasury. Meanwhile, Toronto businessman Conrad Black gained control of the Gulf Edmonton refinery, the largest in Canada. This was clearly an indication of the government's commitment to the principle of national ownership.

On the other hand, foreign-owned Anglo-Kuwaiti Ultramar was allowed to expand its facilities out of Gulf's eastern distribution network and refinery in Montreal for $95 million, despite another bid for the refinery from Quebec-based Gaz Métropolitain. In this particular case, a foreign-owned oil company with strong roots in eastern Canada was preferred over a Canadian-owned firm. The new approach on investment could be spelled out as a general prohibition on the direct acquisition by foreign interests of financially healthy, Canadian-owned oil and gas firms with more than $5 million in assets. Smaller firms and financially unhealthy ones could be acquired by foreigners, subject to the outcome of discussions concerning planned future activities in Canada.[8]

In July 1986, Canadian Home Oil was sold to InterProvincial Pipelines for $1.1 billion, excluding holdings in the United States but including Sovereign Oil & Gas in the United Kingdom, a very profitable prospecting firm in the North Sea. Canadian-owned Nova sold its share in Husky Oil to Hong Kong investor Li Ka Shing, for $484 million. Smaller Canadian firms such as Sulpetro, of Calgary, or Ocelot, which had high expectations under the NEP but ended up crippled with debts, were auctioned, in 1987, to Imperial Oil (Exxon) and Mosbacher of Texas, respectively. Ottawa then issued a Salome-like judgment when the major player of the NEP era, heavily indebted Dome Petroleum, was offered to potential buyers. Canadian-owned TransCanada Pipelines (TCPL) offered $5 billion for the firm. American gas industry leader Amoco bid $5.4 billion and was the winner, despite nationalist lobbying and political pressures. The final offer of $5.8 billion was finally accepted in late 1987,

---

8   André Plourde, "Canadian Fiscal Systems for Oil and Gas: An Overview of the Last Two Decades," McMaster University Energy Studies Group, *Energy Studies Review*, 1, No. 4 (1990), p. 50.

but not without some resistance from all parties, including Canadian shareholders and foreign (Swiss) as well as domestic creditor banks. Yet Dome's Canadian subsidiary Encor was excluded from the Amoco deal and went to TCPL.

All these examples suggest the twilight of Canadianization as a principle in energy policy. Even more interesting was the magnitude of energy projects on the domestic field. They were, as we have seen, numerous and significant and aimed at attracting investors and money to the area, although short-term prospects were perceived as moderately grim. More than one observer noted that the Canadian attitude and the FTA were primarily intended to downplay mounting protectionism in the United States. Officials openly warned that the logging and energy industries could suffer the most if the FTA was not signed.

Although new parameters were designed to express clarity, the general philosophy was bound to be consistent with the basic principle. In all cases, Ottawa favoured criteria of financial health over nationalist preoccupations. So-called national treatment was applied to any firm operating in the sector. Petro-Canada, although still involved to some extent in Atlantic offshore drilling, went ahead with its retail market development program—an activity seen by Ottawa as more profitable than prospecting. Large Canadian firms received no special treatment. Heavily indebted ones were even sold, in whole or in part, to foreign investors. Otherwise financially sound corporations or co-operatives were protected from takeovers. Special tax exemptions were offered to smaller Canadian-owned firms faced with recession. Canadian investors from other provinces bought extra shares in these firms, an indication of continuity for the principle of national ownership.[9]

While deregulation was put forward and barriers to trade were lifted, data show that market forces swiftly re-organized the industry in a much more competitive way. The industry was allowed to feed on the consumer through higher prices for refined products (more than twice the U.S. prices) in order to gain financial strength. Therefore, permissive taxation from Ottawa was intended to facilitate the transition to free trade, with as little damage as possible to the industry. Intentions were good, but experience showed that the state, through its deepening deficit and global incapacity, and the Canadian people, subjected to cuts in services, were to suffer from such a policy.

In the grim overall picture, the FTA was the rainbow at which corporate expectations could stare, and from which could be built a new Canada, based upon regional sensitivities, community life, and market forces. Neoliberalism was at work; many believed in it and followed it.

---

9 Canada, *Energy Security in Canada* (Ottawa: Energy, Mines and Resources; document prepared for the Federal-Provincial Conference on Energy, 1987).

Relations between Canada and the United States had never been so good. What else could be left for an FTA to achieve?

Free Trade, an Alternative to International Competition

Given the federal government's initiatives on energy issues, relations between Canada and the United States were now on a much better footing for free-trade negotiations. During the winter of 1984–85, while Brian Mulroney was making overtures to the Americans for opening bilateral negotiations, his energy minister was operating as much in the provincial capitals as in Ottawa. These two simultaneous strategies were, in fact, complementary. The wish was to establish a climate of confidence between the two countries and to create a federal-provincial consensus through the harmonization of economic strategies and thereby stimulate a new wave of investment. In March 1985, the federal minister of energy announced an agreement in principle on oil and gas between Ottawa and the producing provinces: Alberta, Saskatchewan, and British Columbia.

In order to understand the different, and sometimes contradictory, perceptions that Canadians share on the FTA with the United States, one must take into consideration the question of regional disparities. Quebec, for its part, given its cultural and political uniqueness, feels locked into the central Canadian market and sees the agreement as an excellent opportunity to expand and diversify its manufacturing and service industry base. Ontario, the most affluent and populated of the provinces, was initially opposed to the deal, a position which many perceived to be an egotistical approach given its already privileged relations with its U.S. neighbours. A particular case in point is the Auto Pact, a sectoral free trade agreement signed in 1965, which had a significant economic impact on the Ontario economy. With some exceptions (i.e., Manitoba and Prince Edward Island), the primary resource-exporting provinces in western Canada and the Maritimes were much more favourable towards the deal. Having been hard hit by the recession and by U.S. protectionist measures, the FTA was seen by them as an opportunity to stimulate growth from trickle-down effects.[10]

Reciprocally, one may question the reasons that motivated the United States to enter into free-trade negotiations with Canada. First of all, it is important to recognize that global economic restructuring, since the mid-1970s, had weakened the dominant position of the United States on the international market. Furthermore, the growing trade deficit in the 1980s

---

10 Economic Council of Canada, *Open Borders: An Assessment of the Canada–U.S. Free Trade Agreement* (Ottawa: Supply and Services Canada, 1988), p. 44.

had forced the United States to implement protectionist measures in order to shore up its weakening manufacturing base. For example, increased competition had set off trade and tariff warfare between the United States and the European Community over grains, wines and spirits, and high-technology products.

ENERGY DEVELOPMENT UNDER THE FTA

Let us recall schematically the main features of the FTA. First, the partners agree to a complete phase-out of tariffs over a period of ten years. Second, most restrictions in the trade of agricultural goods, along with subsidies, are to be abolished, mainly on meat and grain. Third, the supply of energy resources would be more accessible for each of the partners. Prices of oil, gas, and power offered to the other partner would be the lowest on the market, allowing for an increase of energy trade among them. Fourth, there would be a gradual but significant liberalization of access to public markets and to commercial services, including finance. Finally, increasingly supple guidelines and bilateral institutions would be defined and implemented to settle conflicts on matters of foreign investment.

Energy trade must be considered as one of the primary ingredients of the FTA. Here again, a long-standing tradition of free movement of energy resources was bound to come up against protectionist measures, as was the case from 1976 to 1984, resulting in a maturing of unifying tendencies inherent to the North American continent. Canada, being the second largest energy producer of the OECD countries, and the largest per capita producer in the western world, has always been the primary supplier of natural gas to the United States. Both California and the Midwest have been major clients for Canadian natural gas since the 1950s. Canada supplies 13 percent of U.S. imports of oil and petroleum products as well as 100 percent of gas imports—this, within the long-term context of declining U.S. production, since 1969. Canadian gas exports must be able to meet the huge U.S. demand and, in this perspective, one can better understand the protectionist objectives of the NEP. It was imperative to the federal government that Canada not compromise its more vulnerable eastern Canadian market to the demands of the midwestern United States, and that resulting sales would benefit the national economy and not only the producing provinces.[11]

With growing U.S. demand for hydrocarbons and electricity (the latter being the object of restrictive measures by the United States), it seems that virtually all the bilateral obstacles for energy trade have been

---

11 Economic Council of Canada, *Open Borders*, p. 13.

lifted with the FTA. In the eventuality of world shortages, the United States is guaranteed more secure access to continental energy sources.

In his comprehensive and detailed discussion of the proportional access clause, introducing further constraints to the imposition of quantitative export restrictions, Plourde discusses this very controversial issue. The clause itself reads as follows:

> [T]he restriction does not reduce the proportion of the total export shipment of a specific energy good made available to the other Party relative to the total supply of that good of the Party maintaining the restriction as compared to the proportion prevailing in the most recent 36-month period for which data are available prior to the imposition of the measure, or in such other period on which the Parties agree.[12]

It is not unlikely that Mexico, with its immense oil and gas resources, may be called upon to play a major role in the setting up of a strategic energy supply system in the case of a worldwide market disruption.[13] In contrast with Mexico, the Canadian oil industry, with its limited resources, appears to be vulnerable to this clause, given that there are few safeguards in the text that would guarantee the protection of diminishing Canadian reserves. Worse, Ottawa is forbidden to look for a better return on its resources in other markets. Many fear the issue could become a sore point between the two partners. Such is not the case for natural gas and hydroelectricity, where Canada has extensive resources. In securing such a huge export market, the FTA renders possible the development of Canadian resources in need of huge investments, particularly in remote areas of Canada.[14]

Has the FTA, according to new data covering the years 1989 to 1991, contributed to changes in the patterns of supply, investment, and trade, that were established since the Conservatives came to power? Plourde tends to downplay the role of the FTA, mainly the binding character of some of its provisions, over the evolution of the energy sector in Canada. Although the whole issue remains a matter of simulation exercises, data may give at least an indication of future developments in the area.

---

12 Article 904(*a*), Canada–U.S. FTA, cited in Plourde, "Canadian Fiscal Systems."

13 In such a sensitive and controversial sector as mutual energy supply in a time of crisis, the architects of the FTA have proven to be more cunning than original. In effect, should Canada, in the event of shortage, claim its right to limit its energy exports to the United States, it must nevertheless guarantee its regular proportion of the reduced Canadian supply. In this sense, there could be no circumstances that would justify special rights over imports or exports.

14 Canada, *Energy and Free Trade* (Ottawa: Energy, Mines and Resources, Supply and Services, 1988), p. 9.

The main decision, in 1989, regarding energy was the approval, by the National Energy Board (NEB), of exports to the United States of ten exajoules of natural gas from the Northwest Territories. This decision was the first step toward the extension of the new northern Alberta gas line to the Mackenzie Delta. On the one hand, a slight expansion in the volume of exports of five percent was noticeable, although benefits did not increase, given lower prices on the market. Further increases are less likely to occur in the short term, as existing gas lines are operating at full capacity. Otherwise, the FTA does not seem to have shifted trade patterns between Canada and the United States, as each country had previously adjusted its energy regulations to market forces. This, along with the shift in energy policy previously implemented by Ottawa, is thus far more relevant to our argument than the FTA, as is openly admitted by the National Energy Board.[15]

On the other hand, electricity production and exports have been drastically reduced, due to unfavourable conditions for hydroelectric power in the last four years. While guaranteed volumes remained stable at around 8,000 Gwatts, interruptible power supplies to the United States fell 50 percent to a little more than 10,000 Gwatts. Quite consistent with the FTA provisions, guaranteed supplies were preserved. This is an accomplishment of the FTA *per se*. Shortages also pushed prices up, although not significantly, given this short-term crisis. Canadian electricity producers obviously chose to maintain the attractiveness of the market through competitive prices for their U.S. customers, having in mind the promising contracts under negotiation.

On 26 April 1989, Quebec Prime Minister Robert Bourassa concluded a very significant twenty-year contract for the supply of about $17 billion in power generation to the New York Power Authority, to begin in 1995. This agreement follows another $8 billion contract (signed earlier in December 1988) among the same parties. Directly related to the FTA, both arrangements are strong examples of Quebec's commitment to the agreement. However, implementation of the multibillion-dollar James Bay II project is still facing strong opposition from the Cree nation in northern Quebec, and even further delays were imposed by the federal government on environmental questions. There is no question that the whole issue will meet mounting demands from opponents, such as the Audubon Society and the Sierra Club (which have powerful entries as an environmental lobby in Washington) and from the Cree Indians. The latter are split into two political factions–a radical one around chief Matthew Coon-Come, who claims political autonomy for the whole James Bay area (as well as an end to hydroelectric projects), and a moderate one, possibly

15 Canada, National Energy Board, *Annual Report* (Ottawa: NEB, 1989).

around Abel Kitchen, president of the Cree Company. No one at this point ventures a prediction on the outcome of the conflict. The First Nations' claims over northern Quebec have become, along with the summer 1990 Mohawk uprising, issues of important magnitude and deep concern in Quebec.

More importantly, in the long term, the recession in the United States and in Canada, as well as growing concerns about the environment and the protection of wildlife, put into question the viability of major hydro-electric projects. It is no surprise that such preoccupations fuelled heated debates in communities in Vermont and other New England states in the last three years. As an example, in March 1989, and under heavy public pressures, the Maine Public Utility Commission even put an end to the $4 billion contract signed earlier by Hydro-Québec and the Central Maine Power Corporation (CMP). As far as energy is concerned, one must admit that the much expected trickle-down effects of the FTA have been rather disappointing for Quebec.

On the western scene, and after much delay, 1990 saw the approval, by the NEB, of a major construction project by TransCanada Pipelines, aimed at upgrading transport facilities across provinces, as well as south of the border. British Columbia, also plagued by low levels of hydro-electric power, partly shifted electricity generation from hydro to natural gas, in order to preserve guaranteed sales to the United States. The major event of 1990, a sudden rise in demand and production from September onwards, also illustrates the influence of international factors on the industry, namely the Persian Gulf crisis. Prices rose abruptly following Iraq's invasion of Kuwait. As an important producer, Canada was asked by the International Energy Agency to participate in a joint effort to expand strategic reserves in the event of war in the Middle East.

Short-term revenues helped increase cash flow for the industry, but no special drilling projects were undertaken. Rather, benefits were used to service the corporate debt.[16] This was obviously the consequence of the poor performance of domestic oil production in 1989, when Canadian exports of crude oil were slashed in half.[17] In 1990, exports to the United States did not increase because most new wells put into operation were emitting natural gas, and oil imports from the North Sea and the OPEC countries (other than Kuwait and Iraq) underwent a sharp rise. Given these conditions, the FTA is likely to remain a neutral factor for crude oil in the foreseeable future.

---

16 Canada, Energy, Mines and Resources, *Canadian Petroleum Market* (Ottawa: Energy, Mines and Resources, 1991).

17 Canada, External Affairs and International Trade, *Canadexport* (15 February 1990).

It must be noted that the growth of domestic oil and gas trade to the eastern provinces is structurally impeded by insufficient capacity, as well as high transport prices. Growing imports, in late 1990 and early 1991, were a result of this situation. This has forced the Quebec-based Gaz Métropolitain to look for arrangements with U.S. gas transportation firms from Houston, Texas, in order to maintain their level of supplies. Ontario also increased oil imports from the Midwest, partly in response to the partial destruction, and closure for repairs, of the Syncrude facilities in late 1989. At first glance, such developments point to strengthened north-south integration patterns in the energy sector and a stabilization of the coast-to-coast traditional axis. As a general conclusion, it can be asserted that structural changes in the energy industry, market forces, and strategic crises at the international level have increased market integration, not only between Canada and the United States, but also within the world market, OPEC as well as non-OPEC countries.

Other secondary factors, related to state and federal-provincial relations, may also be playing a role. Slow procedures on the part of the federal NEB to make a decision with regard to new projects, initially designed by the provinces—James Bay II or Soligaz[18] being a case in point—indicate that other, rather institutional, domestic constraints are challenging the FTA. This helps explain why particular initiatives are postponed and accounts for the genuine responses on the part of the provinces to maintain momentum, in the logic of the FTA, in a complex political environment.

Two Years of FTA: Conclusions and Perspectives

A first conclusion to be reached at this point is the potential internationalization of domestic political issues, previously dealt with at the provincial, interprovincial, and national levels of government. Such is the lesson, it seems to me, that can be gathered from the Cree lobbying in New York State and New England, and their alliance with U.S. environmentalists. Increasing demands in Congress of U.S. energy producers are not to be excluded, either. Hereafter, it is in New York City, Albany, Montpelier, and Boston, where the market lies, that sensitive issues of energy

---

18 Soligaz, originally designed in 1986 to allow for a stable supply of natural gas liquids from Alberta to Quebec, has been faced with strong opposition from Ontario's industry and doubts about profitability. It has been delayed several times at the NEB and does not appear, as late as April 1991, to be on the short-term agenda of this agency. This has prompted a prospecting spree in the Quebec lowlands from a consortium of Québécois, Australian, and the American Bow Valley prospecting firm, for a total investment of about $30 million. For more information, see *Magasine affaires plus* (April 1991).

development will be raised and decisions taken affecting the outcome of the FTA. This is, in the political arena, a significant consequence of global economic integration. Further limitations in trade may, and probably will, be imposed by the deficit that the United States experiences with Canada, mainly in the energy sector.

A second conclusion is that U.S. domestic factors, such as political pressures by minority groups and national lobbies, either in their respective constituency or in Congress, are relevant variables that may affect the outcome of the FTA in the short term. A third conclusion is that worldwide macro-economic trends such as recession, public indebtedness, or the U.S. deficit in the balance of trade with its neighbours, might have far more importance in the success (or failure) of the North American integration project than the much-feared binding provisions of the FTA, such as the proportional access clause.

Of great significance is the particular context of political life in each country. The United States showed strong national unity, even patriotism during the Persian Gulf crisis, while constitutional uncertainty in Canada is too important an issue at this point to be understated. Its influence upon the implementation of the FTA can be significant and should not be played down. To this day, it is quite true that no analysts have stressed major changes that may spring from the Pandora's box of a changing constitutional status for Quebec. Such an attitude is reassuring.

> It is doubtful the United States will be inclined to introduce elements of uncertainty in the application of the FTA, in case Canada would eventually split in two separate countries—English Canada and Quebec.[19]

In other words, the United States would not add further uncertainty to the rising uncertainties on its northern border. Otherwise, and from a strictly orthodox point of view, is it unlikely that the United States would turn down Quebec's future demands to resume the agreement. This may include genuine adaptations of some FTA clauses to the specificities of Quebec's economy. For instance, it may well be that structural economic weaknesses command a higher level of state involvement in local planning and business, or limited subsidies to help local industries in their effort to position themselves on the continental market. Such features should not deter locals from investing abroad, nor should they weaken, in any particular way, the network of relationships between entrepreneurs north and south of the border. This is specially true as far as energy development is concerned. Above all, it is for obvious reasons that

---

19 Denis Stairs, "Foreign Policy," in Stanley Beck and Ivan Bernier, eds., *Canada and the New Constitution: The Unfinished Agenda* (Montreal: Institute for Research on Public Policy, 1983), pp. 175–77.

neither the United States nor English Canada will favour an independent, isolated and impoverished Quebec seeking assistance and a special relationship with, or integration into, France and the mighty European Community.

It is quite certain that constitutional reforms, whatever changes they may foster in the east, will have little effect, if any, on energy development in the west. Continental oil and gas trade has little relationship with political issues. However, electricity trade does. One should keep in mind that, during the 1987–88 negotiations with Canada, one of the main objectives of the U.S. government was to gain easy access to Canadian energy resources. This was undoubtedly achieved, not only with regard to gas and oil, but also with regard to higher expectations from Quebec's hydro-electric potential. Given the present postponement of James Bay II, it may happen that only natural gas is of significant relevance to the FTA.

In a period where both the United States and Canada have committed themselves to expand the FTA to Mexico, one may even question the rationale of denying such arrangements to particular areas of North America, should Quebec achieve sovereignty. The almighty market forces, with their slide from expansion to recession and back to expansion, as well as the geographical proximity of neighbours, do more for the sharing of wealth and resources than does, on a domestic scale, the political agenda of states and provinces. International factors are paramount; domestic factors, as intricate as they may be, usually follow suit, and specific outcomes directly related to the accomplishments of the FTA remain to be seen. For the time being, only mere tendencies can be sorted out.

Dixon Thompson
Faculty of Environmental Science
University of Calgary

18

The NAFTA Parallel Accord on the Environment

INTRODUCTION

The entire backdrop against which trade and environment issues are discussed has changed dramatically since 1991. This revised paper will review the most important advances, which include international agreements, especially Brazil '92; increased attention to environmental issues by international organizations; the publication of a number of influential books; the evolution and application of a set of environmental management tools; and the signing of the parallel environmental accord to NAFTA and the appointments to the NAFTA Commission for Environmental Cooperation and the establishment of its Secretariat in Montreal.

RECAPITULATION

The links between the environment and the economy identified in the Brundtland Report,[1] and hence the links between trade and the environment, have been widely acknowledged by the international community. The global problems which require international approaches unfortunately are still with us: global warming, depletion of the ozone layer, trade in endangered species, hazardous waste, and contamination of the Arctic with volatile persistent toxic chemicals. At the regional level in North America, we still face problems with migratory species, acid rain and air pollution, and water quality and quantity. Domestic issues, especially related to fisheries and forestry, continue and will be influenced by the practices and attitudes established by NAFTA.

The nature of international environmental issues, and particularly those related to the NAFTA partners, has been summarized recently,

---

1   The World Commission on Environment and Development, *Our Common Future* (Oxford University Press, 1987).

which included concerns about migratory species and contamination of the Arctic.[2] Ongoing studies have increased the concerns about successful control of these two problems, both of which are typical of environmental matters requiring extensive and difficult international cooperation such as might be achievable under NAFTA and the parallel accord. Recently discovered migratory routes of raptors (hawks, owls, and eagles) between North and South America, along the east coast of Mexico, demonstrate the importance of trilateral cooperation in the protection of these socially and ecologically important birds.[3] In September 1992, researchers were recording up to 80,000 birds per day of 18 different raptor species. After bad weather stopped the migration temporarily, a flood of hawks appeared so that in one hour, 167,000 broadwings (hawks) were counted at one site. That one site recorded almost half a million hawks in less than eight hours. This did not include the many the nonraptor species which were also observed. The ecological approach to protection of migratory species dictates that they be protected in both summer and winter ranges and throughout the migratory routes between them. Hence, for the protection of these species, the NAFTA partners, and future partners in Central and Latin America, must be involved.

More detailed studies have also shown that contamination of the Canadian Arctic with volatile, persistent toxic substances is a threat to human health for those people who eat fish and wildlife.[4] Persistent toxic substances do not originate in the region, but evaporate all over the world and then are deposited in the Arctic after global atmospheric circulation brings them into contact with the extremely cold conditions there. Through bioaccumulation in lower trophic levels such as algae, and biomagnification up the predator-prey food webs, the concentrations of these persistent toxic substances increases and poses a health threat, especially through the potential to affect reproduction of people who eat fish and wildlife. This is a global environmental problem that has not yet received the attention of the international community the way global warming and ozone depletion have. However, NAFTA might provide a venue in which Canadian concerns could be raised.

Of the issues identified in the original article, the biggest difficulty remains the lack of political will to ensure that environmental issues are

2   D. Thompson, "Trade, Resources, and the International Environment," *International Journal*, 47, No. 4 (Autumn 1992), pp. 751–775.

3   S. Weidensaul, "Secret of the Hawks," *International Wildlife* (Nov/Dec 1994), pp. 38–41.

4   D. Thompson, "Trade, Resources, and the International Environment," *International Journal*, 47, No. 4 (Autumn 1992), p. 756.

given due consideration when the economic benefits, which trade is supposed to provide, are pursued. The need to move toward higher standards, rather than the lowest common denominator, is still paramount. The proposal that environmental problems can be solved through the extraterritorial application of laws of the United States continues to be resisted strongly by Canada and Mexico.[5] The control of trade in environmentally undesirable products and technologies continues to be resisted by commercial interests in the United States, although the banning of a product domestically but allowing international trade defies logic.[6]

INTERNATIONAL DEVELOPMENTS

The largest international event, if not the most significant advance, was the huge international congress at Rio De Janeiro on the 20th anniversary of the Stockholm '72 UN Conference on the Human Environment. The United Nations Conference on Environment and Development (UNCED) took place 3–14 June 1992 and was known as Brazil '92, "The Earth Summit," or "Rio." Participating were representatives of 178 nations, 8,000 delegates, 3,000 representatives from nongovernmental organizations, 9,000 members of the international media, which with the other interested parties totalled about 30,000 people. Given the number of nations with different "national interests"; the domination by bureaucrats, diplomats and politicians; and the fact that the United States and the Vatican tried to force their own particular ideologies on the entire proceedings, reaching an agreement on the final document, *Agenda 21*,[7] was a considerable accomplishment. That document has 40 chapters directed at forging a global partnership in sustainable development between developed and developing countries. Canada achieved considerable

---

5   J.O. Saunders, "Trade and Environment: The Fine Line between Environmental Protection and Environmental Protectionism," *International Journal*, 47, No. 4 (Autumn 1992), p. 742.

6   United Nations, *Consolidated List of Products Whose Consumption and/or Sale Have Been Banned, Withdrawn, Severely Restricted or not Approved by Governments* (New York: Department of International Economic and Social Affairs, 1991); International Institute for Sustainable Development, *GATT, the WTO and Sustainable Development: Positioning the Work Program on Trade and Environment* (Winnipeg: International Institute for Sustainable Development, nd), pp. 2 and 32.

7   United Nations Conference on Environment and Development, *Agenda 21*, adopted by the Plenary Session at Rio de Janeiro, 14 June 1992 and published by the UN for the General Assembly.

success as a major advocate for many of the initiatives such as those on fisheries, forestry, biodiversity, and global warming.[8]

A more focused event was the formation of the Business Council for Sustainable Development and the publication of *Changing Course: A Global Business Perspective on Development and the Environment*,[9] as parallels for the international business community to Rio and *Agenda 21*. The Council is composed of 50 business leaders, including two Canadians: Ken McCready, President and CEO of TransAlta Utilities, and Paul Stern, Chairman and CEO of Northern Telecom. The Declaration of the Business Council for Sustainable Development, which appears at the beginning of *Changing Course* and is followed by the names of the 50 members, states that the Council members are "committed to sustainable development, to meeting the needs of the present without compromising the welfare of future generations." The United Nations International Conference on Population and Development, held in September 1994, followed earlier UN conferences in Bucharest and Mexico City.[10]

Another very important event was the publication of the results of an international public opinion survey covering twenty-four nations, which showed that concerns about the environment were not restricted to the industrialized countries but that people in both rich and poor nations give priority to environmental protection over economic growth.[11] The International Chamber of Commerce has published its Business Charter for Sustainable Development,[12] and expects members to endorse and follow the sixteen principles for environmental management. The International Standards Organization (ISO) and the Canadian Standards Association (CSA) are developing a series of information bulletins, guidelines,

---

8   The Standing Committee on the Environment, *A Global Partnership: Canada and the Conventions of the UNCED*, House of Commons Canada, April 1993; G.V. Buxton, "Sustainable Development and the Summit: A Canadian Perspective on Progress," *International Journal*, 47, No. 4 (Autumn 1992), pp. 776–795.
9   S. Schmidheiny, with the Business Council for Sustainable Development, *Changing Course: A Global Business Perspective on Development and the Environment* (Cambridge, Mass.: MIT Press, 1992).
10   W. Roush, "Population: the View From Cairo," *Science*, 265, No. 26 (August 1994), pp. 1164–1167.
11   R.E. Dunalp, G.H. Gallup, Jr., and A.M. Gallup, *Health of the Planet* (Princeton, NJ: Gallup International Institute, 1993).
12   KPMG Environmental Services, "Environmental Risks and Opportunities: Advice for Boards of Directors," a booklet available at KPMG offices throughout Canada, nd.

and eventually international standards on environmental management.[13] The ISO has chosen Canada for the secretariat of the new ISO Technical Committee for Environmental Management.[14] The CSA has already published guidelines on environmental management, environmental audits, environmental labelling, life-cycle assessment, and phase I environmental site assessment.[15]

The International Institute for Sustainable Development (IISD) was established at Winnipeg as one of the few specific results of Canada's now-defunct Green Plan. The IISD has put out a number of very useful publications: *Business Strategy for Sustainable Development; Trade and Sustainable Development Principles; Coming Clean,* a report on environmental reporting by multinational corporations; *GATT, the WTO, and Sustainable Development;* and *Making Budgets Green: Leading Practices in Taxation and Subsidy Reform.*[16]

On the 20th anniversary of the publication of the very influential book *Limits to Growth,*[17] Meadows et al. updated their thesis and the global models used to assess global resource depletion, food production, industrial output, pollution, and population growth. In *Beyond the Limits: Confronting Global Collapse, Envisioning a Sustainable Future,* they conclude

---

13 The International Organization for Standardization (ISO) already certifies the quality assurance management systems of corporations under the ISO 9000 series Quality Management Standards. They are developing the ISO 14000 series Environmental Management Standards which should be out in 1996. One example is the working draft "Life Cycle Assessment—General principles and practices" (WD 14040) which was circulated for comment in Sept. 1994.

14 Canadian Standards Association, "Canada Gains Key International Environmental Role," *CSA Environmental Update,* 2, No. 1 (Spring 1993), p. 1.

15 Canadian Standards Association, *Guidelines for Environmental Auditing: Statement of Principles and General Practices,* Z751-94 (Rexdale, Toronto: Canadian Standards Association, 1994); *Life Cycle Assessment* Z760-94 (Rexdale: Canadian Standards Association, 1994; *User's Guide to Life Cycle Assessment: Conceptual LCA in Practice,* PLUS 1170 (Rexdale: Canadian Standards Association, 1994); Plus 1109, *Environmental Terminology for Canadian Business* (Rexdale: Canadian Standards Association, 1994); Z768-94 *Phase I Environmental Site Assessment* (Rexdale: Canadian Standards Association, 1994); Z750-94 *A Voluntary Environmental Management System* (Rexdale: Canadian Standards Association, 1994); Z754-94 *Guideline for Pollution Prevention* (Rexdale: Canadian Standards Association, 1994); Z761-93 *Guideline on Environmental Labelling* (Rexdale: Canadian Standards Association, 1993).

16 International Institute for Sustainable Development, 161 Portage Ave. E., Winnipeg, Man., R3B 0Y4. Fax (204) 958-7710.

17 D.H. Meadows, D.L. Meadows, J. Randers, and W.W. Behrens III, *The Limits to Growth* (New York: Universe Books, 1972).

that six specific sets of actions will move us toward sustainability: improve the signals, speed up response times, minimize use of non-renewable resources, prevent the erosion of renewable resources, use all resources to maximum efficiency, and slow and eventually stop exponential growth of population and physical capital.[18] Hawken published *The Ecology of Commerce*[19] which is short on specific solutions, but is leading many people in industry to rethink and revise approaches to environment and resource management issues.

Carroll's *International Environmental Diplomacy*[20] provides a broad perspective on the management and resolution of transfrontier environmental problems. In *Green Diplomacy*,[21] Bruce Doern has succinctly described how environmental policies are made in Canada, with a focus on international diplomacy.

The field of environmental management is changing so rapidly it is difficult to keep up. There are numerous newsletters available, but two which can be recommended are *Enviroline*,[22] which focuses on Canada and Western Canada in particular, and *Business and the Environment*, which has recently published *Trends in Corporate Environmental Management Vol. 1*,[23] in which recent information on the tools discussed below can be found.

Voluntarily changing business practices and introducing self-policing are necessary but not sufficient conditions for stopping resource depletion and protecting the environment.[24] Similarly, subscribing to international agreements to protect the environment for which there are few, if any, effective mechanisms for enforcement is also necessary but not sufficient. However, given the difficulties of establishing effective international legislation and enforcement, these efforts at changing the understanding of and response to international environmental issues are encouraging and have provided grounds for optimism. Overlapping, and extending beyond either end of the time frame for the above, the negotiations on

---

18 D.H. Meadows, D.L. Meadows, and J. Randers, *Beyond the Limits* (Toronto: McClelland and Stewart, 1992), p. 214.

19 Paul Hawken, *The Ecology of Commerce: A Declaration of Sustainability* (New York: Harper Business, 1993).

20 J.E. Carroll, (ed.), *International Environmental Diplomacy* (Cambridge: Cambridge University Press, 1990).

21 G.B. Doern, *Green Diplomacy: How Environmental Decisions Are Made* (Toronto: C.D. Howe Institute Policy Study 16, 1993).

22 *Enviroline*, published 20 times per year, 222 Riverfront Ave. S.W., Calgary, Alberta.

23 Cutter Information Corp., *Trends in Corporate Environmental Management Vol. 1*, Business and the Environment, 37 Broadway, Suite 1, Arlington, MA.

24 Cutter Information Corp, "Are Voluntary Environmental Charters Effective?" *Business and the Environment*, 5, No. 9 (September 1994), pp. 2–6.

the Uruguay Round of the General Agreement on Tariffs and Trade (GATT) sought to increase trade almost at any cost. GATT has so far resisted attempts to soften the very hard line against attempts to protect the environment which might interfere with international trade. Exceptions are made for those agreements which achieve broad international consensus, such as the Montreal convention for protection of the ozone layer, and the Convention on International Trade in Endangered Species. It is very important to note that while GATT forbids governments to restrict trade to protect the environment outside their borders, they have no control over the voluntary actions of corporations or consumers who take similar actions. That is, if corporations or consumers do not want to trade in products which are environmentally unacceptable, or which are produced by means which are environmentally unacceptable, then GATT cannot interfere.[25] GATT will likely establish a bureaucracy, the World Trade Organization (WTO), to start dealing with trade and environment issues in the next year or so.[26] The World Bank has also overhauled the mechanisms they use to address the environment and resource consumption aspects of the projects which their loans support. They will no longer provide funding for projects for which there is not an adequate Environmental Impact Assessment.[27]

The optimism which these developments encourage is offset by the very hard line taken against birth control and abortion by the Vatican at the United Nations Conference on Population in Cairo in 1994. The Vatican's somewhat successful efforts seriously slowed progress on one of the most pressing problems: the exponential growth in demand for space and resources, and production of pollution caused by the exponential growth in population. Population is not the only factor requiring control but it is a critical factor.

LITERATURE ON NAFTA AND TRADE ISSUES

It is clear, therefore, that the context within which, and the knowledge base upon which, discussions about trade and environment issues take place have changed radically. Kirton and Richardson published an

---

25 D. Thompson, "Trade, Resources, and the International Environment," *International Journal* 47, No. 4 (Autumn 1992), p. 764; P. Sorsa, "The General Agreement on Tariffs and Trade (GATT)," in J. Kirton and S. Richardson, eds., *Trade, Environment and Competitiveness*, National Round Table on the Environment and the Economy, Ottawa, 1992, pp. 181–207.
26 International Institute for Sustainable Development, *GATT, the WTO and Sustainable Development* (Winnipeg: IISD, nd).
27 B. Morse, T. Berger, D. Gamble, and H. Brody, *Sadar Sarovar: Report of the Independent Review* (Ottawa: Resource Futures International, 1992).

international perspective on *Trade, Environment and Competitiveness*[28] for the National Round Table on the Environment and the Economy. Hufbauer and Schott devote a chapter to environmental questions in *North American Free Trade*,[29] written for the Institute for International Economics. A clear and concise description of NAFTA is provided by Appleton in *Navigating NAFTA*,[30] which includes sections on environment and on water. Appleton notes that NAFTA does not have a specific section on environmental issues. It deals with those problems in six sections: the Preamble, the section on relationships with other agreements, the sanitary and phytosanitary (plants) measures subchapter, the chapter on technical barriers to trade, the chapter on investment, and in the dispute resolution provisions. The Preamble to NAFTA states that the partners are committed to sustainable development and to the strengthening of laws to protect the environment. It is particularly important to note that NAFTA states in the chapter on investment that the partners should not relax provisions for protection of the environment to attract investment.

TOOLS FOR ENVIRONMENTAL MANAGEMENT

Before moving to assess the environmental parallel accord to NAFTA, criteria for that review must be selected. I have chosen the evolving set of environmental management tools which improve accountability and accounting, which direct us toward sustainable development and which measure our progress.[31]

Space does not permit detailed definitions of the tools and their development and applications. As with other technical areas, they require detailed levels of expertise, skill and knowledge. Their effectiveness and efficiency will, in large part, be determined by the available data bases, the experience of the users, and the will to see them used effectively. The development and application of these tools as a set is of paramount importance, in spite of the fact that for the most part they started their development and application independently. The set of tools is not hypothetical, theoretical, or academic. In fact, most of the work on development and

---

28 J. Kirton and S. Richardson, *Trade, Environment and Competitiveness*, National Round Table on the Environment and the Economy, Ottawa, 1992.

29 G.C. Hufbauer and J.J. Schott, *North American Free Trade: Issues and Recommendations* (Washington, D.C.: Institute for International Economics, 1992).

30 B. Appleton, *Navigating NAFTA: A Concise User's Guide to the North American Free Trade Agreement* (Toronto: Carswell, 1994).

31 D. Thompson, "The North American Agreement of Environmental Cooperation: Tools for Improving Assessment and Accountability," International Association of Impact Assessment, 14th Annual Meeting, Quebec City, 15 June 1994.

application of the tools has been done by practitioners meeting needs for better accountability and accounting rather than by theoreticians or academics. Standards and guidelines for almost all of the tools have been or are being developed. Although all of them can be applied independently in highly specialized forms, they are broadly applicable and cut across the fragmentation caused by different levels of government, by spearate government departments, and by the independent activities of corporations and institutions.

When used as a set, these tools comprise an Environmental Management System (EMS). There is not yet a uniform international standard for EMSs, although the British Standards Association has published BS 7750 on EMS,[32] and the Canadian Standards Association has published drafts of the EMS guideline Z750.[33] It is anticipated that the International Standards Organization will publish their Environmental Management Standards, the ISO 14000 series, in 1996. Establishment of international EMS standards will resolve many of the problems of variations in terms and definitions.

The following set of tools is evolving and developing, but as of late 1994, it was comprised of (1) Strategic Environmental Planning or Strategic Environmental Assessment, (2) Environmental Management Structure, (3) Environmental Policy Statement or Code, (4) Environmental Impact Assessment, (5) Environmental Audits, (6) Environmental Reporting, (7) Environmental Indicators, (8) Product and Technology Assessment, (9) Life Cycle Assessment, (10) Life Cycle Costing, (11) New Systems of Accounting, and (12) Economic Instruments. This particular list has been selected because these tools have been developed or adapted specifically for environmental management. Other tools such as risk management, dispute avoidance and resolution, education and training, etc., are also important and are important subsets of or adjuncts to the tools listed.

1. *Strategic Environmental Planning* is the use of environmental protection and resource conservation skills and knowledge early in the corporate, institutional or government strategic planning processes, before individual projects are authorized. This helps to ensure that cost-effective decisions are made so that these concerns are dealt with in a proactive fashion, rather than as an expensive, reactive after-

---

32   British Standards Institution, *Specification for Environmental Management Systems*, Z7750, British Standards Institution, London, 1992.
33   Canadian Standards Association, *A Voluntary Environmental Management System*, CSA Z750, Canadian Standards Association, Rexdale (Toronto), 1994.

thought. It requires feedback and information from other tools in the
set: audits, reports, etc.[34]

2. The *Environmental Management Structure* is the formal and informal
    system for gathering and processing information, reporting, and
    making decisions. It must be fully integrated with the rest of the
    Management Structure and effectively linked to the external elements
    which affect the institution. No pure, single structure (centralized,
    decentralized, matrix) is always most appropriate, so hybrid struc-
    tures have evolved which seem to be more effective.[35]

3. The *Environmental Policy Statement* or *Code* likely includes a short
    vision or mission statement followed by specific topics such as water
    and energy conservation; the use of other tools such as audits,
    reports, assessments; waste minimization, hazardous wastes, etc. The
    policies must identify specific actions, specific outputs, and
    accountability where possible. For a large and complex organization,
    these statements can be fairly long and detailed. Each policy is
    backed by a detailed practice manual.[36] Many industry associations,
    such as the Mining Association of Canada and the Canadian Asso-
    ciation of Petroleum Producers, are updating their codes. The
    Responsible Care program of the Canadian Chemical Producer's
    Association has now been adopted by associations in at least 30 other
    countries. Japan's Keidanren (Federation of Economic Organizations)
    established an environmental code for the activities of Japanese
    corporations abroad. Many industry and corporation codes commit
    subsribers to meeting the same standards globally. *Business and the
    Environment* has reviewed over 40 selected industry codes.[37]

---

34 N. Lee and F. Walsh, "Strategic Environmental Assessment: An Overview,"
    in *Project Appraisal*, 7, No. 3 (September 1992), pp. 126–136; Task Force on
    Economic Instruments and Disincentives to Sound Environmental Practices,
    Economic Instruments and Disincentives to Sound Environmental Practices,
    Distribution Centre, Department of Finance and Inquiry Centre, Environment
    Canada, Ottawa, Nov. 1994, Annex D, "Description of Strategic Environ-
    mental Assessment Processes," pp. 72–81.

35 D. Thompson and L. McKay, *Management Problems in/of Environmental Science*,
    Report Alberta Environment Research Trust Grant No. T0518, Faculty of
    Environmental Design, University of Calgary, Calgary, 1984; C.A. Weaver,
    *The Design of an Environmental Management System for an Agricultural Organiza-
    tion*, unpublished Masters Degree Project, Faculty of Environmental Design,
    University of Calgary, Calgary, 1995.

36 C. Ryley, *Environmental Policy Statements*, Masters Degree Project in Progress,
    Faculty of Environmental Design, University of Calgary, Calgary, 1994.

37 Cutter Information Corp., "Are Voluntary Environmental Charters Effective?"
    Business and the Environment, 5, No. 9 (September 1994), pp. 2–6.

4. *Environmental Impact Assessment* is a systematic effort to predict and then mitigate and manage adverse environmental impacts of proposed projects, policies and programs. It must come before the fact and monitor results after implementation. The World Bank has set guidelines for international projects.[38] Post facto analyses are generally called environmental reviews.

5. *Environmental Audits* are regular, systematic reviews of the EMS, compliance with laws and regulations, conformance to policies, and development of an action plan to deal with deficiencies.[39]

6. *Environmental Reports* are systematic, objective reports of the state of the environment, or an institution's or corporation's impact on the environment and consumption of resources. They must show trends and be linked to goals and objectives.[40]

7. *Environmental Indicators* are specific measures of the quality of the environment, the stresses on it, or effectiveness of steps taken to reduce those stresses. They are used in preparation of environmental reports and to assist with managment.[41]

8. *Product and Technology Assessments* are efforts to predict and then reduce the adverse environmental, health, and safety impacts of products and technologies.[42] Variations of these assessments are

---

38 World Bank Environment Department, *Environmental Assessment Sourcebook, Vol. 1: Policies, Procedures, and Cross-Sectoral Issues, World Bank Technical Paper Number 139; Vol. 2: Sectoral Guidelines, World Bank Technical Paper Number 140, Vol. 3: Guidelines for Environmental Assessment of Energy and Industry Projects, World Bank Technical Paper Number 154* (Washington, D.C.: World Bank, 1991).

39 D. Thompson and M. J. Wilson, "Environmental Auditing, Theory and Practice," *Environmental Management*, 18, No. 4, pp. 605–615; Canadian Standards Association, *Guidelines for Environmental Auditing: Statement of Principles and General Practices* (Rexdale [Toronto]: Canadian Standards Association, 1993).

40 International Institute for Sustainable Development, *Coming Clean: Corporate Environmental Reporting* (Winnipeg: International Institute for Sustainable Development, 1993; A. Schipperus, *Environmental Reporting*, Master's Degree Project in progress, Faculty of Environmental Design, University of Calgary, Calgary, 1994; Ernst and Young Environmental Services, *Corporate Reporting on Environmental Performance* (Ernst and Young, 1994).

41 The State of the Environment Directorate of Environment Canada, Ottawa, Ontario K1A 0H3, publishes the *Environmental Indicator Bulletin;* Organization for Cooperation and Development, *Environmental Indicators: A Preliminary Set,* Paris, 1991.

42 G.S. Bridgewater, *The Environmental Impact Assessment of Policy in Canada,* Master's Degree Project, Faculty of Environmental Design, University of Calgary, 1992; M.K. Boroush, K. Chen, and A.N. Christakis, eds. *Technology Assessment: Creative Futures* (North Holland, NY: Oxford, 1980).

used to test drugs, pesticides, product safety, consumer products, and to determine standards for Canada's Ecologo.[43]

9. *Life Cycle Assessment* attempts to determine the environmental impacts of a product from sources of raw materials through manufacturing, marketing and use to final recycling or disposal. Efforts are then made to reduce the environmental impacts of all aspects of the product's life cycle.[44]

10. *Life Cycle Costing* attempts to determine amortized capital cost and the operation and maintenance costs of efforts to reduce environmental damage or to conserve resources. It is used to assess cost effectiveness of opportunities identified by Life Cycle Assessments. This is essential to identify where limited resources can be allocated most effectively and efficiently. Life Cycle Costing must necessarily include all currently quantifiable costs, which is somewhat different from full-cost accounting, which attempts to quantify and include hitherto external costs or nonquantifiable costs.[45]

11. New *Systems of Accounting* attempt to take into consideration those factors of environmental liability or degradation and resource depletion which have hitherto been considered as externalities. That is, they were costs which were not included in the corporate accounts or in gross-domestic-product calculations. Full-cost accounting will be achieved when costs for all adverse environmental impacts and depletion of resources can be effectively included in corporate or national accounting.[46]

12. *Economic Instruments* are incentives, disincentives, and other market adjustments to direct behaviour or to internalize costs that would

---

43 Environmental Choice Program, *Ecologo: The Environmental Choice Newsletter* (Ottawa).

44 Canadian Standards Association, *Life Cycle Assessment*, Z760-94, 1994; *User's Guide to Life Cycle Assessment: Conceptual LCA in Practice*, PLUS 1170, 1994; International Organization for Standardization, *Life Cycle Assessment—General Principles and Practices*, working draft submitted by ISO/TC 207 Working Group 1, WD 14040.

45 A. Willis, "Life Cycle Assessment and Full Cost Accounting," *Hazardous Material Management* (August 1994), pp. 31, 50.

46 D. Thomson and M. J. Wilson, "Environmental Auditing: Theory and Practice," *Environmental Management*, 18, No. 4, p. 613; Cutter Information Corp., *Business and the Environment, Trends in Corporate Environmental Management*, "Green Accounting," Vol. 1, Arlington, MA, 1994, pp. 79–84; Cutter Information Corp., "United Nations Releases Handbook on Greener National Accounting," *Business and the Environment*, 5, No. 1 (January 1994), p. 15.

otherwise be external and borne by the public rather than the party that caused the adverse impact.[47]

The accelerating development, standardization and application of these tools is rapidly improving the ability to set goals, to select appropriate options for attaining the goals, and to monitor (audit) and provide feedback (report) on progress.

NAFTA's Parallel Environmental Accord

The North American Agreement on Environmental Cooperation[48] (the parallel environmental accord), which was published in September 1993, clearly reflects the increased international concern about environmental matters. It was preceded in Canada by an "Environmental Review" published in October 1992, which concluded that with proper management practices and controls, any adverse environmental impacts would be within acceptable limits.[49] It is apparent that the Agreement was written by experts on environmental issues trying to deal with trade and environment issues, rather than by trade negotiators trying to understand and incorporate environmental matters in a trade agreement. Much of the "Advice on NAFTA and the North American Environmental Agreement" prepared by Canada's National Round Table on the Environment and the Economy in May 1993, appears to have been accepted.[50] The short accord document (42 pages in Canada's English version) is clear and easy to understand. It is composed of a Preamble, seven Parts made up of 51 Articles, and Annexes. Part III describing the Commission (12 pages) and

---

47 Task Force on Economic Instruments and Disincentives to Sound Environmental Practices, *Economic Instruments and Disincentives to Sound Environmental Practices* (Ottawa: Distribution Centre, Department of Finance and Inquiry Centre, Environment Canada, November 1994). See also International Institute for Sustainable Development, *Making Budgets Green: Leading Practices in Taxation and Subsidy Reform* (Winnipeg: International Institute for Sustainable Development, 1994), and A.M. Gillies, *Protecting the Environment and Reducing Canada's Deficit: Action Plan—Where to Start* (Winnipeg: International Institute for Sustainable Development, 1994).

48 Government of Canada, Government of the United Mexican States, and the Government of the United States of America, *North American Agreement on Environmental Cooperation*, Sept. 1993. This document is sometimes difficult to get, but can be obtained through Environment Canada or External Affairs.

49 Government of Canada, *Narth American Free Trade Agreement: Canadian Environmental Review* (Ottawa: October 1992).

50 The National Round Table on the Environment and the Economy, "Advice on NAFTA and the North American Environmental Agreement" (Ottawa: 28 May 1993).

Part V on Dispute Resolution (9 pages) make up half the document. The accord excludes extraterritorial application of any party's environmental laws (Article 37) while acknowledging the parties' rights and obligations under other international environmental agreements (Article 40), and national sovereignty is recognized in the Preamble.

International agreements generally reach consensus on what it is that the parties to the agreement want to achieve (protect endangered species, reduce or avert global warming, protect biodiversity, protect or restore the ozone layer, etc.). However, they frequently fall short on specifying actions which will help attain those goals, and in establishing the monitoring and feedback necessary for assessing and guiding progress. This is where the parallel accord is a significant step forward, because almost all the management tools identified above appear in the accord.

If management is defined as setting goals, organizing resources to achieve those goals, and providing feedback on progress, and if the tools listed above are important for environmental management, then the parallel accord establishes a very good foundation.

It would be stretching interpretation quite a bit to suggest that the accord includes Strategic Environmental Planning or Assessment. Presumably, this will be one of the principal activities of the Commission's Council, which is comprised of cabinet-level or equivalent representatives. Its functions are outlined in Article 10.

The Environmental Management Structure for the Agreement is outlined in Part III about the Commission for Environmental Cooperation, which is composed of a Council (Section A, especially Article 9), a Secretariat (Section B, especially Article 11), and Advisory Committees (Section C, especially Article 16 on the Joint Public Advisory Committee and Article 17 on the National Advisory Committees).

The Preamble is a broad environmental-philosophy or vision statement which, for example, reaffirms the sovereign rights of states to exploit their resources while also reaffirming the Stockholm '72 and Rio '92 Declarations. It reconfirms "the environmental goals and objectives of the NAFTA, including enhanced levels of environmental protection" (Article 1 (f)). Articles 1, 2, and 5 can be seen as Environmental Policy Statements for the three partners.

Environmental Impact Assessments are explicitly referred to in Articles 2 1(e), 10 6(d), and 10 7(a). In effectively enforcing environmental laws and regulations, the parties will take appropriate action to seek assurances of voluntary compliance, presumably through audits and reports (Article 5 1(c)), and will promote Environmental Audits (Article 5 1(f)). Articles 2 1(a), 5 1(g), 10 2(c), and 12 3 all refer to State of the Environment Reports. If it can be assumed that pollution prevention and control of trade in hazardous materials involves Product and Technology Assessment, then there are references to that tool in Articles 1 (j), 2 1(e),

2 3, and 10 2(b). And if products must be assessed before ecolabelling is possible, then there is another reference in Article 10 2(r). Environmental Indicators appear explicitly or implicitly in Articles 1 (i), 5 1(c), 5 1(g), and 10 2(c). The Council may make recommendations on "ecologically sensitive National Accounts" (Article 10 2(g)). Economic efficiency and effectiveness in environmental measures will require Life Cycle Assessment and Life Cycle Costing and the Council may make recommendations on "goods throughout their life cycles" (Article 10 2(m)). Articles 2 1(f) and 10 2(d) refer explicitly to promoting and making recommendations on Economic Instruments.

The set of tools is a very useful check-list to assess the willingness and the capability of a government, institution or corporation to make and abide by commitments to resource conservation and environmental protection. The Commission for Environmental Cooperation is very up-to-date with respect to environmental management for its own operations, and to what it is expected to promote and recommend to governments and the private sector. The Agreement is a good starting point for environmental management as it relates to NAFTA.

The North American Commission for Environmental Cooperation (NACEC) has been started with the establishment of the Secretariat in Montreal in the Fall of 1994. Victor Lichtinger is the Executive Director. NACEC held its first formal meeting in Washington, D.C. in July 1994.

The agreement is not binding and there is nothing to guarantee its effectiveness. It is, however, a very significant advance given the fact that the parallel accord is the first of its kind, so there was little experience, no precedents, and no models. The accord was drafted and agreed to very quickly—less than two years. The Agreement on Environmental Cooperation stresses cooperation and harmonization,[51] acknowledges national sovereignty and rejects extraterritorial application of environmental laws. It could have very significant impacts as NAFTA expands to SNAFTA (South and North American Free Trade Agreement). It is hoped that it will influence GATT's efforts to deal with environmental issues. It will promote improved environmental protection and accountability in the private sector by encouraging and eventually requiring the application of the twelve tools for environmental management. Processes for standardization at the national and international levels will likely accelerate the effective application of the tools.

What remains is the question of the political will to make the Agreement work. Off the record, some of those involved in the evolution

---

51 D. Thompson, "Mecanismos de cooperacion para la proteccion efectiva del medio ambiente y administracion de recursos," in T. Gutierrez and M. Verea, eds., *Canada en Transicion*, Centro de Investigaciones sobre America del Norte, Universidad Nacional Autónoma de Mexico, Mexico, 1994, pp. 563–591.

of the accord have expressed disappointment in the political nature of some of the appointments made to date. This suggests that effectiveness and efficiency may not be regarded as very important. It is likely that the clarity of the document, and its up-to-date content, are the result of its having been drafted by people with a good understanding of environmental issues and environmental management. That involvement, and what appears to have been a relatively small role played by lawyers and trade negotiators, may be a serious disadvantage if the process gets entangled in legal difficulties and the trade negotiators ignore it because it is someone else's creation. On the other hand, the recommendations are practical; the level of concern about international environmental problems have increased. The applications of the environmental management tools are also increasing in the private sector at the international level, with the result that grounds for optimism remain.

V

Public Policy and Culture

Neil Nevitte, Political Science, University of Calgary
Miguel Basañez, ITAM, Mexico, D.F.
Ronald Inglehart, Political Science, University of Michigan

19

Directions of Value Change in North America

INTRODUCTION

In our view, the prospects for continental integration hinge on both economics and values. Much of the analysis of values—judgements about the similarities and differences between and among Americans, Canadians, and Mexicans—as well as the speculation about the direction of value change, has relied heavily on impressionistic evidence. Such evidence is neither systematic nor reliable. For every brilliant insight, one can find scores of misperceptions; insights that were accurate generations ago may no longer hold true. Cultures change, but stereotypes live on long after they have ceased to describe reality.

This paper reports the initial findings from a collaborative research project that draws on a unique body of systematic evidence—the results of interviews with representative national samples from the United States, Canada, and Mexico. These surveys, undertaken first in 1981 and then again in 1990, were matched in design and content. All six surveys were part of a larger project—the World Values Surveys. With these data we ask several questions: Do the basic values of Mexicans, Canadians, and Americans differ in significant ways? Are the differences growing larger over time, or are the goals of North Americans converging?[1]

Our analysis begins by outlining one theoretical perspective on value change—the *post-materialist thesis*. We then turn to examine the survey data from the North American setting for the period 1981 to 1990 and

---

1 We are grateful to the Donner Canadian Foundation, whose assistance enabled us to collect and analyze the Canadian 1990 World Values Survey. We also thank Lori Davis and Johanna Vingerhoeds for their able research assistance. A more detailed analysis of these issues can be found in Ronald Inglehart, Neil Nevitte, and Miguel Basañez, *North American Dilemmas: Trade, Politics and Values* (Ann Arbor: I.S.R., 1991).

summarize some of the evidence indicating that significant value changes have indeed taken place in American, Canadian, and Mexican societies. We show that, in nearly every instance, the direction of value change is consistent with that predicted by the post-materialist thesis. This theme is illustrated in greater detail by drawing attention to shifts in the prevailing economic cultures of the three countries. The final part of the paper focuses on future-oriented evidence; it explores cross-national similarities and differences in those values that adults in all three countries want to pass on to their children.

Changing Values in Western Societies

A large body of evidence clearly demonstrates that the basic values and goals of the populace in advanced industrial states have been changing gradually over the past several decades. The possibility of intergenerational value change was first explored by Ronald Inglehart, who suggested that the basic value priorities of the Western populace have been shifting from a materialist emphasis toward a post-materialist one—from giving top priority to physical sustenance and safety, toward heavier emphasis on belonging, self-expression, and the quality of life.[2] That investigation was guided by two hypotheses: (a) the *scarcity hypothesis*, which holds that an individual's priorities reflect the socioeconomic environment (i.e., one places the greatest subjective value on those things that are in relatively short supply), and (b) the *socialization hypothesis*, which predicts that the relationship between the socioeconomic environment and value priorities is not one of immediate adjustment (i.e., a substantial time lag is involved because, to a large extent, one's basic values reflect the conditions that prevailed during one's pre-adult years).

The scarcity hypothesis is similar to the principle of diminishing marginal utility. It suggests that the recent economic history of advanced industrial societies is significant and unique in one important sense: the majority of their populations do not live under conditions of hunger and economic insecurity. Prolonged periods of prosperity appear to have encouraged the spread of post-materialist values in which needs for belonging, self-expression, and an autonomous role in society became more prominent.

This hypothesis does not specify a simple relationship between economic levels and the prevalence of post-materialist values. Instead, post-materialist values reflect one's *subjective* sense of security, not one's economic level *per se*. Wealthy people tend to feel more secure than poor

---

2 Ronald Inglehart, *The Silent Revolution* (Princeton: Princeton University Press, 1971).

people, but one's sense of security is also influenced by the cultural setting and social welfare institutions in which one is raised. For that reason, the scarcity hypothesis supplements the socialization hypothesis, which suggests that value priorities take shape by the time an individual reaches adulthood and undergo relatively little change thereafter.

Taken together, these two hypotheses generate a set of predictions concerning the direction and conditions for value change. First, while the scarcity hypothesis implies that prosperity is conducive to the spread of post-materialist values, the socialization hypothesis implies that neither an individual's values nor those of a society as a whole will change overnight. For the most part, fundamental value change takes place as younger age groups replace older ones in the adult population of a society. Consequently, after a period of sharply rising economic and physical security, one should find substantial differences between the value priorities of older and younger groups because they have been shaped by different experiences in their formative years.

The post-materialist thesis has been explored for over two decades. It was first tested in surveys carried out in 1970 with representative national cross-sections from Great Britain, France, West Germany, Italy, the Netherlands, and Belgium. Since then, the rise of post-materialism and its social, economic, and political consequences have been systematically tracked in more than twenty countries throughout the world.[3]

VALUE CHANGE IN NORTH AMERICA

If North Americans are undergoing a similar process of value change, we would expect to find: (1) that this materialist/post-materialist dimension works as a meaningful axis around which public attitudes are polarized in each country; and (2) that a gradual shift is taking place, with emphasis moving from materialist to post-materialist goals. An abundant body of evidence demonstrates that both propositions hold true for the United States.[4] But only fragmentary evidence is available for Mexico and Canada.[5] The Canadian socioeconomic situation is rather similar to that of the United States, and on those grounds it seems likely that the Canadian public may well be undergoing a similar shift. However, the

---

3   Ronald Inglehart, *Culture Shift* (Princeton: Princeton University Press, 1990); and Russell J. Dalton, *Citizen Politics in Western Democracies* (Chatham House, N.J.: Chatham House, 1988).

4   Inglehart, *Culture Shift.*

5   Neil Nevitte, *New Politics, The Charter and Political Participation* (Ottawa: Report to the Royal Commission on Electoral Reform and Party Financing, 1991), pp. 19–26.

Mexican situation is so different that it is uncertain whether the country would be undergoing the same process of cultural change.

Mexico enjoyed substantial economic expansion during the past fifty years, growing at an impressive mean rate of 6.5 percent annually from 1941 to 1981; however, it has experienced virtually no economic growth since 1982. Theoretically, the shift from materialist to post-materialist values results from rising levels of economic and physical security, which suggests that value change may be taking place in Mexico, though the economic stagnation of the past decade would tend to retard it. Other considerations also make it seem somewhat doubtful whether Mexico would be moving toward post-materialism at a rate comparable to other advanced industrial states. By most benchmarks, Mexico's economic level is much lower in absolute terms than that of either the United States or Canada: while the United States had a per capita Gross National Product of $19,840 in 1988, and Canada had one of $16,960, the Mexican level was only $1,760. This would lead us to expect fewer post-materialist values in Mexico than in the United States or Canada—if they are present at all. What does our evidence reveal?

Table 1 shows the results of factor analyses of the 1990 World Values Surveys data from the United States, Canada, and Mexico, and these results clearly demonstrate that the materialist/post-materialist value divide is a meaningful one for all three countries. In each case, the response patterns are strikingly similar: all six of the materialist items (i.e., fighting rising prices, strong defence forces, fighting against crime, maintaining order, economic growth, and stable economy) show a negative polarity in all three countries. And all the post-materialist items show a positive polarity in all three countries. However, a significant cross-national difference emerges. Though the basic pattern in Mexico is similar to what we find in the United States and Canada, it has crystallized less sharply. In Mexico, the average loading on the materialist/post-materialist dimension is weaker than in the other two countries and weaker than those that have been found in other advanced industrial states.

On the basis of these findings, one might surmise that the responses of the Mexican public resemble those of other Western societies but are at an earlier point on the trajectory. Post-materialism exists in Mexico, but it has emerged more recently, and it has had less time to crystallize than in economically more developed countries.

If this conjecture is correct, sustained prosperity, combined with the dynamics of intergenerational population replacement, should be producing a shift toward post-materialist values as younger (and more post-materialist) cohorts replace older (more materialist) ones in the adult population. Table 2 suggests that this trend has been taking place. In all three countries, we observe significant shifts in the balance between materialist and post-materialist orientations since 1981. By 1990, post-

TABLE 1. THE MATERIALIST/POST-MATERIALIST DIMENSION
IN THE UNITED STATES, CANADA, AND MEXICO, 1990
(FACTOR LOADINGS IN PRINCIPAL COMPONENT ANALYSIS)

United States		*Canada*	
More say on job	.64	More say on job	.64
Less impersonal society	.62	Less impersonal society	.59
Society where ideas count		More say in government	.50
more than money	.52	Society where ideas count	
More say in government	.45	more than money	.49
Protect freedom of speech	.33	Protect freedom of speech	.22
More beautiful cities and country	.26	More beautiful cities and country	.20
Fighting rising prices	−.28	Strong defence forces	−.29
Strong defence forces	−.31	Fighting against crime	−.29
Fighting against crime	−.35	Fighting rising prices	−.31
Maintaining order	−.49	Maintaining order	−.44
Economic growth	−.54	Economic growth	−.61
Stable economy	−.62	Stable economy	−.69

Mexico			
Less impersonal society	.62		
More say on job	.61	Fieldwork carried out by the Gallup Or-	
More say in government	.41	ganization (U.S.), N = 1,839; Gallup-	
Society where ideas count		Canada, N = 1,730; and by Centro de	
more than money	.32	Estudios de Opinion Publica (CEOP),	
Protect freedom of speech	.27	N = 1,531.	
More beautiful cities and country	.02		
Strong defence forces	−.11	*Source:* Representative national samples	
Fighting rising prices	−.12	from the three countries, interviewed in	
Fighting against crime	−.19	May and June, 1990, as part of the 1990	
Maintaining order	−.48	World Values Surveys.	
Economic growth	−.48		
Stable economy	−.69		

materialists had become more numerous than materialists in both the
United States and Canada. There was less of a shift in Mexico; even in
1990, materialists still outnumbered post-materialists there by two to one,
but a significant shift toward post-materialist values had taken place.
These changes are all in the predicted direction, but the shifts in the
United States and Canada are so large that they cannot be attributed to
intergenerational population replacement alone. In these two countries,
population replacement effects seem to have been compounded by period
effects: the impact of rising prosperity during the 1980s moved in the
same direction as the effects of population replacement from 1981 to 1990.
Closer analysis of the data shows that the speed of this value transformation varies from one country to the next. Mexico shows a correlation
between values and age that is only half as strong as that in the United

TABLE 2. MATERIALIST/POST-MATERIALIST VALUES IN NORTH AMERICA: CHANGES FROM 1981 TO 1990 (DISTRIBUTIONS BASED ON FOUR-ITEM INDEX)

	U.S.A.		Canada		Mexico	
Value Type	1980*	1990	1981	1990	1981	1990
Materialist	34%	16%	22%	12%	28%	25%
Mixed	56	61	62	63	63	63
Post-Materialist	10	23	16	26	9	12
Index[†]	−24	+7	−6	+14	−19	−13

* Note: Because this battery was not asked in the United States in the 1981 World Values Surveys, we used the results from the CPS 1980 National Election Study for the cross-time comparison in the United States. All other results are from the 1981 and 1990 World Values Surveys.

[†] % post-materialists − % materialists.

States. Post-materialist values have only begun to emerge in Mexico. Though a materialist/post-materialist axis of polarization is discernable in Mexico, it is less clearly crystallized than in other Western countries, and, in the 1981–90 decade, it provided a less important basis of socio-political cleavage. Because Mexico has a much lower per capita income than the United States or Canada, and in view of the economic stagnation that Mexico experienced during the 1980s, these findings suggest that the young are not automatically less materialistic than the old; these differences emerge in advanced industrial societies as a consequence of the different formative experiences that shape older and younger cohorts.

CHANGING VALUES IN NORTH AMERICA

It can be demonstrated that materialism/post-materialism is a meaningful value divide. However, have the value changes in North America (the shifts from materialism to post-materialism) had the same kinds of broad consequences that have been documented in western Europe? Most of the time, the answer is "yes." Space limitations prevent us from presenting all of the evidence, but Table 3 summarizes the broad outlines of an analysis of value change across thirteen attitude dimensions.

For example, North American post-materialists and the young are less sexually restrictive than their materialist and older counterparts. They are more likely to emphasize autonomy, and much more likely to value independence and imagination, rather than obedience. Post-materialists are less deferential to authority, more secular, and they are less likely to

TABLE 3. CHANGES PREDICTED FROM 1981 DATA
AND CHANGES OBSERVED, 1981–90

	Consistent Correlations*	Follows Predicted Shift[†]	Trajectory of Change
A. *Sexual restrictiveness*			
U.S.A.	Yes	Yes	
Canada	Yes	Yes	Converging
Mexico	Yes	Yes	
B. *Emphasis on independence, imagination over obedience and good manners for children*			
U.S.A.	Yes	Yes	
Canada	Yes	Yes	Converging
Mexico	Yes	Yes	
C. *Favour greater respect for authority*			
U.S.A.	Yes	Yes	
Canada	Yes	Yes	Converging
Mexico	Yes	Yes	
D. *Religious outlook*			
U.S.A.	Yes	Yes	
Canada	Yes	Yes	Diverging
Mexico	Yes	Yes	
E. *Church attendance*			
U.S.A.	Yes	(Yes)	
Canada	Yes	Yes	Converging
Mexico	Yes	Yes	
F. *Civil permissiveness*			
U.S.A.	No	–	
Canada	Yes	Yes	Diverging
Mexico	No	–	
G. *Emphasis on family duty*			
U.S.A.	Yes	No	
Canada	Yes	No	Converging
Mexico	Yes	No	
H. *Confidence in government institutions*			
U.S.A.	Yes	Yes	
Canada	Yes	Yes	Converging
Mexico	(Yes)	Yes	

(Table 3 continued)

I. Confidence in nongovernment institutions

U.S.A.	Yes	Yes	
Canada	Yes	Yes	Diverging
Mexico	Yes	(No)	

J. National pride

U.S.A.	Yes	Yes	
Canada	Yes	Yes	Diverging
Mexico	Yes	Yes	

K. Unconventional political participation

U.S.A.	Yes	Yes	
Canada	Yes	Yes	Converging
Mexico	Yes	Yes	

L. Support for employee participation in business

U.S.A.	Yes	Yes	
Canada	Yes	Yes	Converging
Mexico	No	–	

M. Following instructions at work

U.S.A.	Yes	Yes	
Canada	Yes	Yes	Converging
Mexico	No	–	

Total number of cases which generate predictions: 35
Correct predictions: 31 (89 percent)
Incorrect predictions: 4 (11 percent)

Notes: ( ) indicates weak relationship; – indicates no prediction
* Does this variable show consistent correlations with both age and value type (i.e., old = materialist; young = post-materialist)?
† Does the response to this variable shift in the predicted direction from 1981 to 1990?
Source: 1981 and 1990 World Values Surveys.

express confidence in government and nongovernment institutions. Post-materialists are less likely to score high on national pride; they are more cosmopolitan.

In most of these domains, there is striking evidence that substantial value convergence has taken place in the course of the last ten years; North Americans are becoming more alike in these respects. The findings are striking, and they are far more consistent than would be predicted by chance alone.

Continental free trade clearly implies that economies will become more open to global competition, higher levels of economic specialization, and greater economic integration. In that context, national attitudes toward economic matters (e.g., worker participation in management and state

TABLE 4. ATTITUDES TOWARD PRIVATE VS. PUBLIC VS.
EMPLOYEE MANAGEMENT OF BUSINESS AND INDUSTRY

	U.S.A.		Canada		Mexico*	
	1981	1990	1981	1990	1981	1990
1. Owners	59	56	58	53	28	51
2. Owners and Employees	32	35	32	37	46	46
3. State	2	1	2	1	9	3
4. Employees	7	8	8	9	17	0

Question: There is a lot of discussion about how business and industry should be managed. Which of these four statements comes closest to your opinion?

1. The owners should run their business or appoint the managers.
2. The owners and employees should participate in the selection of managers.
3. The state should be the owner and appoint the managers.
4. The employees should own the business and elect the managers.

* The value in Mexico's 65+ group is the same as that in the 55–64 age group because the Mexican sample contains fewer than thirty cases over 65 years of age.
Source: 1981 and 1990 World Values Surveys.

involvement in the economy) take on special significance. Canadians and Mexicans have traditionally assigned a much larger role than Americans do to public ownership and to state intervention in their economies. One might expect that those longstanding traditions would be reflected in attitudes of contemporary Canadians and Mexicans. Our evidence suggests otherwise. As Table 4 shows, Canadian and American attitudes toward state ownership of the economy are virtually identical, and there has been a substantial decline in public support for state ownership of the economy in Mexico in the 1981–90 decade. In this respect, the evidence points to a significant convergence of perspectives in the three North American countries.

The 1990 World Values Surveys also asked respondents from the three countries about general preferences toward private versus public ownership. The evidence points in the same direction as above. Again, the findings in the United States and Canada are strikingly similar; both indicate strong support for greater private ownership of business and industry. Support for increased privatization was somewhat lower in Mexico. About half (47 percent) of the Mexican respondents supported increased privatization, but those wanting more private ownership

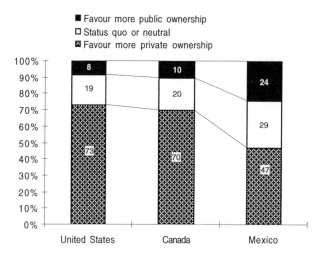

Figure 1. Support for public vs. private ownership, by nation.

Question: For each pair of contrasting issues, '1' means you agree completely with the statement on the left; '10' means you agree completely with the statement on the right; or you can choose any number in between. How would you place your views on this scale?

| 1 | 2 | 3 | 4 | 5 | 6 | 7 | 8 | 9 | 10 |

Private ownership of business and industry should be increased.

Government ownership of business and industry should be increased.

Favour more private ownership   (Choose 1, 2, 3, or 4)
Status quo or neutral   (Choose 5 or 6)
Favour more public ownership   (Choose 7, 8, 9, or 10)

Source: 1990 World Values Surveys.

outnumbered those favouring more public ownership by a ratio of two to one (see Figure 1).

How does the materialist/post-materialist value spectrum correlate with the age of the respondent? There is no linear relationship between age and support for public ownership in any of the three countries. In the United States, it is the young, and, in Canada, it is both the very young (18 to 24 years) and the old (65+ years)—mostly those outside of the work force—who support public ownership the most. In Mexico, the oldest are least likely to support public ownership. The impact of the materialist/post-materialist divide is similarly uneven. In the United States and Canada, post-materialists are slightly more likely to support public ownership, but in Mexico the post-materialist value divide has no effect whatsoever.

TABLE 5. CHANGING ATTITUDES TOWARD AUTHORITY AT WORK

	U.S.A.		Canada		Mexico	
	1981	1990	1981	1990	1981	1990
1. Follow instructions	68	61	55	52	33	39
2. Use own judgement	37	39	45	48	67	61

Question: People have different ideas about following instructions at work. Some say that one should follow the instructions of one's superiors, even when one does not fully agree with them; others say one should follow one's superior's instuctions only when one is convinced that they are right. With which of those two opinions do you agree?

Source: 1981 and 1990 World Values Surveys.

However, when it comes to employee participation, the evidence is very different and quite striking. In all three countries, the young are more supportive of employee participation in the workplace. And in the United States and Canada, post-materialists are significantly more supportive of employee participation in management of the workplace. The results are weaker for Mexico, but then, as we have said, the materialist/post-materialist divide works less powerfully in that setting.

Table 4 suggests a cross-national convergence in attitudes, whereas Figure 1 shows a preference for private ownership in all three countries. Table 4 also illustrates the broader shifts in public attitudes toward another economic domain: employee participation. In 1981, Mexicans shared the highest levels of support for employee participation, but, by 1990, these levels had dropped substantially. During the same period, U.S. and Canadian support for employee participation rose.

With respect to attitudes toward authority at work, another trend was evident (see Table 5). In 1981, Americans and Canadians were much more likely to agree that workers should follow instructions. By 1990, support for that idea dropped in the United States and Canada, while it increased in Mexico. Once again, the patterns point to convergence. Significant value changes clearly have taken place in the last decade and, with respect to a variety of attitudes toward economic matters, North Americans, it seems, are becoming more alike.

FUTURE DIRECTIONS

Speculating about future value change is always a risky business. It might be reasonable to suppose *ceteris paribus* (e.g., in the absence of changes like those that shaped the attitudes of the Depression generation) that we can expect the sustained rise of post-materialism. It is also likely

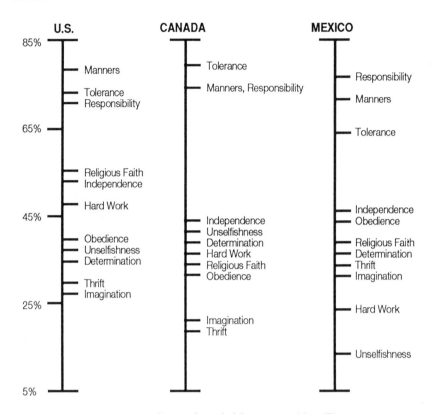

Figure 2. Important qualities for children in 1981. Figures represent percentages of respondents mentioning each quality.
Source: 1981 World Values Surveys.

that public values will continue to shift in the same direction as they have in the past decade.

Political socialization theory predicts that the priorities of future generations depend, among other things, on what kinds of values adults instill in their offspring. In this respect, our 1981 and 1990 U.S., Canadian, and Mexican surveys may provide some useful hints about what future directions value change may take; all surveys asked respondents about which values should be encouraged in children (see Figure 2). All respondents in the three countries were presented with the same question: "Here is a list of qualities which children can be encouraged to learn at home. Which, if any, do you consider to be especially important. Choose up to five."[6]

6   In 1981, the qualities used in the questionnaire were: manners, politeness and neatness, independence, hard work, honesty, responsibility, patience, imagination, tolerance, leadership, self-control, thrift, determination, religious faith, unselfishness, obedience, loyalty. The 1990 list was similar; however, the fol-

Respondents in all three countries ranked "manners," "tolerance," and "responsibility" as the three most important qualities for children. There are also cross-national similarities at the low end of the scale, where "thrift," "imagination," "determination," and "unselfishness" are found. We also detect some cross-national variations. American respondents assigned a higher priority to "independence," which was valued much less by Mexican respondents. And Canadian respondents gave a lower priority to "religious faith" than respondents in the other two countries. The cross-national stability, over time, of these results is particularly striking when the top priorities are considered. Americans gave "manners" the highest priority, while Canadians viewed "tolerance" as most important. Mexicans reserved the top spot for "responsibility." "Thrift" and "imagination" rated as low priorities in all three countries, but, after that, national variations clearly came into play. For Americans, "religious faith," "independence," and "hard work" ranked relatively high.

A number of significant shifts become evident when we compare the 1981 data with those collected in 1990 (see Figure 3). In 1981, Canadians mentioned "independence" about as frequently as "religious faith," but "independence" ranked higher in 1990. The same shift occurs in Mexico. In 1990, national differences in the importance attached to "hard work" also appear to have sharpened.

Does the materialist/post-materialist value divide have anything to do with the kinds of qualities respondents view as important for children? It would be surprising if it did not. In fact, there are systematic differences between materialist and post-materialist respondents—differences that consistently apply in each of the national settings. Materialists are always more likely to stress the importance of such traditional virtues as "manners," "hard work," "thrift," "religion," and "obedience," while post-materialists always give greater priority to "independence," "imagination," "tolerance," and "determination." Moreover, these results also hold when we take age differences into account. Where age is concerned, young North Americans value "independence," "determination," and "imagination," while their older counterparts placed greater emphasis on the same values as the materialists. However, unlike the materialists, older respondents add "responsibility" to the list of valued qualities. The point is that both the materialist/post-materialist and the age divisions have similar effects on valued qualities, but, as it turns out, the effects are independent of each other.

---

lowing qualities were not used: politeness and neatness, honesty, patience, leadership, self-control, and loyalty.

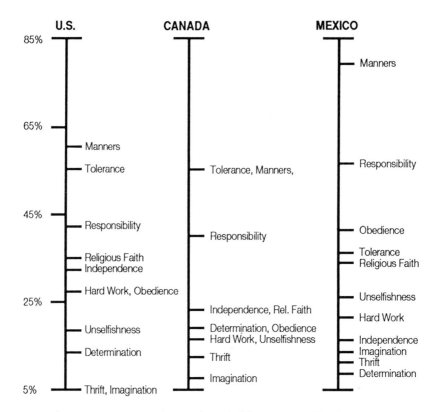

Figure 3. Important qualities for children in 1990. Percentages are generally higher than in Figure 2 since six fewer qualities were used. *Source*: 1990 World Values Surveys.

CONCLUSIONS

Our concern has been with broad themes of value change. We began by indicating that Ronald Inglehart has documented far-reaching value changes for over twenty years. These changes have had powerful effects on social mores, forms of political participation, attitudes toward authority, and perspectives on the family, children, the work place, and other domains. So far, these changes remain relatively unexplored in the North American setting, particularly in Canada and Mexico. We asked: Is there any evidence that these changes are taking hold in North America? If so, do they have the kinds of consequences that have been well documented in other settings? Our answer to both of these questions is "yes." We have not presented the detailed analyses that lie behind some of these broad conclusions; those are reported elsewhere.[7] But, the broad patterns are intriguing; the evidence clearly suggests attitudinal convergence in North America. It is worth emphasizing that this attitudinal convergence does not entail Canadian and Mexican conformity to U.S. norms. Rather, all three countries are experiencing changes that are linked to transformations that are similarly affecting all Western states; they have no national origin. One implication is that, should any policy convergences result from these changes (and elsewhere we have suggested that these changes are linked to policy convergence on such matters as health and environmental policies), greater North American economic integration would not necessarily imply policy harmonization with U.S. standards.

Our broad gauge of changing attitudes to the economy and the work place clearly suggests that U.S., Canadian, and Mexican attitudes toward private ownership, state management, worker participation, and authority in the work place are becoming more alike. Again, we do not find that Canadians and Mexicans are changing to become more similar to Americans—all are changing, and they are all changing in the same direction. Cross-national differences are eroding in what economists argue is the most significant attitudinal domain for a workable non-conflictual free trade arrangement.

Of course, any guesses about future changes are just that—guesses. But, to the extent that our evidence allows us to speculate in that direction, our findings are rather intriguing. They suggest a remarkable similarity in the kinds of qualities North Americans value for their children. They also suggest significant and cross-nationally stable similarities along the materialist/post-materialist value divide. According to these data, we might expect the next generations to place far more value on independence, determination, and imagination. Our 1981 to 1990 evidence indicates that post-materialist values make for much more sophisticated, articulate, and democratic societies. That is the good news. The bad news is that these same societies will place a much greater burden on public institutions; informed, vigorous, and outspoken societies are harder to govern. It remains to be seen how our institutions and political leaders will respond to that challenge.

---

7 Ronald Inglehart, Neil Nevitte, and Miguel Basañez, *North American Dilemmas* (Ann Arbor: I.S.R., 1991).

Gustavo del Castillo Vera
Director, Department of United States Studies
El Colegio de la Frontera Norte

The Cultural Dimension of a Free Trade Agreement: The Case of Mexico

INTRODUCTION

From the beginning of classical American anthropology, represented by Franz Boas and his students A.L. Kroeber, Ruth Benedict, and Margaret Mead, the main concern of the discipline has been culture and, especially, the process by which one culture spreads, penetrates, and assimilates others, thus arriving at the definition of so-called cultural areas.[1] This school (as well as the functionalist school, whose main spokesman was Malinowski) was never concerned with a problem that now seems critical to us, which is the control of those means which aid in the development of a culture and its survival within complex societies. To introduce the idea of control inevitably evokes images of power and of groups, or elites, that exercise power. This is of basic importance in the North American context, where such groups exist already, characterized by the symmetry of power and resources that make this concern over cultural diffusion and assimilation of strategic importance. Those individuals charged with negotiating a commercial agreement must also strive to maintain varied cultures present in contemporary Mexico and Canada.

CULTURE AND DOMINATION

In all societies that seem less complex, as well as in contemporary North American societies, cultural control is at issue, remaining in the hands of

---

Translated from the Spanish by the editor.—*Ed.*

1   The concept of a "cultural area" was originally developed by C. Wissler, but the more representative work reflecting Boas's influence is that of A.L. Kroeber, *Anthropology, Culture Patterns and Processes* (New York: Harcourt, Brace, 1923). Perhaps the best-known work among U.S. students of anthropology is Ruth Benedict's *Patterns of Culture* (Boston: Houghton, Mifflin, 1959).

shamans or other spiritual leaders, or in the collectivity of tribal chiefs, etc. Whenever there is a divergence from cultural norms, as defined at that moment, the traditional institutional mechanisms come into play in an effort to protect the old values. One has to ask who is responsible for maintaining cultural normalcy in our societies; but then one must also ask what the cultural norms are that are being defended and against whom.

In what way would a commercial accord affect cultural dimensions? If the main objective of such an accord is trade, in what way does culture enter the equation? There is no logical reason for there to be a linkage between foreign commerce and commercial policies, on the one hand, and culture, on the other. Yet, there is linkage because the agreement that is presently under consideration by the various parties involves creating conditions under which foreign investment can take place. It will also result in some limits on state action. In both instances, perforce, there are cultural implications.

The basis of a commercial agreement is the principle of national treatment for foreign investment. Without adoption of that principle, the large-scale foreign investment sought by the Mexican government will not materialize. Without that guarantee no government will be interested in signing an accord. National treatment means that foreign capital will receive equal treatment to that accorded national capital, thus eliminating the discrimination that has existed in the past. What does this have to do with culture? Everything. An admittedly extreme and improbable scenario nonetheless illustrates what is at stake. Suppose that one day a foreign capitalist buys (for better or worse) the Mexican daily *Excelsior*. The following day, the workers are dismissed (of course, with compensation), and the newspaper is closed. Under the majority of national laws and regulations, there is no legal restraint to prohibit such a development. In such a case, Mexico would have lost a good daily and a basic part of its heritage. More fundamentally, what is lost in this instance would be one instrument of cultural diffusion (and perhaps of cultural creation) of certain cultural values we consider "Mexican."

What will have been lost? In this particular case, one is dealing with an instrument of a dominant culture, commonly characterized as a national culture. Without elaborating on the scientific validity of the concept of a national culture, one has to consider other closely related concepts.

Few people would challenge the idea that Mexico is composed of a variety of regional cultures and that, in this sense, the idea of a national culture is a myth. That is to say, one might well ask what common values are there between a Tarahaumara Indian and a Yucatecan. However, one cannot dispute the fact that, after a half century of domination by one political party and the development of a dominant political system, certain values have been diffused throughout the system, which we might classify as comprising a common, overriding, national culture without regional barriers. But these cultural values are the result of domination, and they co-exist with the intrinsic values of different ethnic, racial, and caste groupings. Where these subnational cultures are sufficiently strong to retain the characteristics of a distinct culture, it is generally in the best interests of the dominant culture to maintain those other cultures. Of course, the other possibility is that these subnational cultures owe their survival to their very marginality or to the fact that some of them have successfully resisted the dominant culture.[2]

COMMERCIAL LIBERALIZATION AND CULTURE

So far, I have mentioned some of the problems associated with culture and the processes of hegemony. This same problem has to be placed in international terms in order to consider a free-trade agreement (FTA) among Canada, Mexico, and the United States. Again, it is assumed that any agreement concluded will be based on the principle of national treatment, as in the Canada–United States FTA (Article 502) and in the General Agreement on Tariffs and Trade (GATT) (Article III).

National treatment is not limited to the question of foreign investment but is also applicable to other aspects, such as standards for manufacturing, etc. The basic concern with this principle is that it brings about the harmonization of social policies that affect cultural aspects and that through these two mechanisms a process of acculturation is facilitated, with the transfer of values from one culture to another.

Since the process of acculturation was one of Mexico's main preoccupations with the negotiations, it is important to understand the specific terms of the Canada–United States FTA, their implications for the tripartite agreement, and the measures that might be introduced into an accord to minimize the impact of the principle of national treatment on Mexican culture.

It is important to indicate that the Canada–United States FTA contains provisions for limits on foreign investment which can affect some areas of culture. There are important exceptions to national treatment, such as limits on foreign investment. These limits are of two types. The first imposes limits on government purchases, financial services, and investment in the transportation sector (Article 2005). The second category of exclusions includes those services associated with child care, medical services, and educational services.

---

2 Aguirre Beltrán, *El proceso de aculturación* (Mexico: Center for Research and Higher Studies in Social Anthropology, 1982).

The questions that can be posed with respect to these restrictions are of two kinds. The first is to what point can the present negotiations incorporate the limits established by the bilateral agreement? The second is up to what point can one modify the bilateral accord to address Mexico's concerns? This question is especially important because there are demands by Canada, as well as the United States, for revision of the bilateral accord. Such revisions, within the negotiations with Mexico, do not involve any of the limits discussed earlier.

It is important to understand that negotiations concerning the service sector, which includes cultural industries, do not necessarily modify previous national laws pertaining to foreign investment. The Canada–United States agreement limits foreign investment and requires review, under certain circumstances, of foreign purchases of national industries. The accord permits such a review based on the level of investment. That review process was already part of Canadian legislation prior to the FTA, but, under the FTA, the level of investment required to trigger the review process has been substantially increased from $5 million ultimately to $150 million. Thus, in simple terms, there are more sectors of the Canadian economy now, than prior to the FTA, for which there will be no review of foreign investment. In practical terms, this means that the small firm is more vulnerable to pressure from foreign investment capital and, in Mexico's case, a similar course of action would threaten comparable Mexican industries.

Article 2005.2 of the FTA specifies that either country may enact retaliatory measures against the other country in the cultural sector, if it believes that discriminatory measures have been taken against that nation's interests. The retaliatory measures that are taken should have "similar commercial consequences." What does this mean, given the fact that Article 2005.1 exempts cultural industries? In short, Canada can take whatever internal measures desired to promote and to protect its cultural industries, as long as it is prepared to risk retaliatory measures by the United States.[3] This means that Canadian culture can be reinforced by such measures as subsidies, financial incentives, and restrictions on foreign investment, if it is prepared to entertain conflict with its neighbour.

CULTURE AND ACCULTURATION

It was noted earlier in this paper that, in addition to foreign investment, measures taken to achieve the harmonization of standards could affect cultural dimensions. Although the term "harmonization" normally applies

---

3   Richard G. Lipsey and Robert York, *Evaluating the Free Trade Deal: A Guided Tour through the Canada–U.S. Agreement* (Toronto: C.D. Howe Institute, 1988), pp. 106–7.

to production of goods, the question of standards is also applicable to the service sector, which includes cultural services. In this context, we need to ask how resilient a culture can be, and if the elements that comprise that culture are capable of withstanding the intrusive effects of another culture that monopolizes the means of cultural diffusion and penetration.

History is replete with examples of cultures that have disappeared, either as a result of the death of its adherents or by processes of acculturation so intense that features of the original culture are difficult to discern. Thus, with Mexico undergoing a commercial opening to the outside world, and with free-trade negotiations underway with the United States and Canada, the issue of acculturation might acquire significant proportions for Mexico. One obvious question is to what point might the harmonization of the service industry promote acculturation, recognizing that, although cultural diffusion may be symbiotic, in the final analysis, it is the dominant culture, in this case the United States, that will shape the final product. The critical questions are which service industries with social content will be subject to negotiation and what role those services play in Mexico's cultural fabric.

Canada's preoccupation in this respect was, and continues to be, the harmonization of medical services between two antagonistic systems, the one (United States) based on the capacity of the private sector to extract their profits from private individuals, the other (Canada) on transfer payments and state intervention. The public health system in Mexico conforms more to the Canadian than to the U.S. model in terms of the role of the state and involuntary transfer payments, although the quality and coverage of the services remain significantly lower than in Canada. The main concern has been that transfer payments are minimized and must be replaced by individual payments. Moreover, the quality of services available depends on the capacity of the patient to pay. This is not a dilemma for Mexico in the short or medium term; in a tripartite negotiation, the objective will not be the reduction of Mexican medical services but, rather, an increase in their quality and coverage. The problems (and cultural manifestations) in the short and long term have to be seen in a more subtle way.

One concern will involve educational issues, especially in relation to the problems of harmonization of standards and the accreditation of Mexican professionals and technicians seeking to establish some professional service or obtain temporary work permits for either the United States or Canada. The Canada–United States FTA establishes the right of professionals or technical specialists from one country to carry out services in the other on a temporary basis (Article 1501). Further, under Article 1402.3, the principle of national treatment is not required; that is, it is possible to have a different (but justified) treatment between nationals and foreign professionals.

According to some experts, in the agreements on services negotiated between Canada and the United States, the providers of such services do not require the harmonization of standards. In addition, Article 1403.3 anticipates the mutual recognition of the certification procedures for those who expect to require some services. In effect, this means a recognition of the legitimacy of national standards under which the necessary licences to offer services were authorized. Given this article, the discussion of harmonization would appear to be a moot point. But, not surprisingly, Article 1404 alludes to annexes that define the processes of harmonization in sectoral terms. The first sector mentioned in the appendices (Article 2) refers to the powers of the professional organizations of Canadian and American architects and states:

> They seek common professional standards . . . in the areas of *a*) education—and the mechanisms of accreditation of architectural schools; *b*) in the area of examinations required for professional practice; *c*) the experience necessary to practice; *d*) codes of professional ethics and conduct; *e*) the development of continuing education for their professionals.[4]

Although it could be argued that this sector represents an exception, I think that the future will be defined by this tendency. In this context, Mexico will have to be prepared to face up to the expectations of our other two commercial partners, with whom we are linking our future. That is, Mexico's educational practices will have to be modified and shaped in order to meet the requirements, not only of the needs of the national market, but also of the other two markets, and in order not to be subject to professional discrimination for lack of global competitive standards.

The pressures that this type of harmonization places on culture are difficult to foresee. History reveals that cultures disappear under the pressures of a dominant power, and, it is equally certain, not all cultures can develop the defence mechanisms required to survive without the assistance of the state. This is especially true when we witness the budding of an international commercial culture strictly linked to the interests of the contemporary states. There is little doubt that we are witnessing a convergence of ideologies in the three nations and, very possibly, a divergence of that commercial ideology from the popular culture. In this context, one could suggest that such popular cultures will experience difficulties gaining a public forum through political action, making their survival appear more difficult. Such cultures will be confronted not only by the existence of normative values external to their

---

4 John D. Richard and Richard Dearden, *The Canada–U.S. Free Trade Agreement: Final Text and Analysis* (Toronto: CCH Canadian Limited, 1988), p. 43.

society, originating in the dominant country's culture—including the so-called international business culture—but will also be under pressure from their own state, conceived as an instrument of their protection. That is, within a "solar system of cultures,"[5] those cultures that survive are those relegated to the periphery.

The processes of economic integration, whether in North America or in the European Community, are necessarily going to be accompanied by a surge of new normative values—or the bases that experience the cultural changes. In this sense, the decisions taken on economic integration assume a dialectic nature, forming part of the process of cultural change. What we consider culture thus includes an understanding of the decision-making process itself. This was perfectly evident to Alexis de Tocqueville, in the nineteenth century, in his classic study *Democracy in America*, in which he wrote:

> It is therefore necessary, if we would become acquainted with the legis-
> lation and manners of a nation, to begin by the study of its social
> condition. Many important observations suggest themselves upon the
> social condition of the Anglo-Americans, but there is one which takes
> precedence of all the rest. The social condition of the Americans is
> eminently democratic.[6]

In the same vein, it is necessary to ask what has been the form and content of the decision-making process in Mexico as it moves toward integration with the United States and Canada. What has been the level of popular participation (or of civic society, in general) within the decision-making process?

In Mexico, the consultative process on this theme has been characterized by the lack of openness and the centralization of decisions within a small bureaucracy, even when public hearings are held where representatives of industrial and other distinct interest groups and experts participate. Thus, in Mexico a free-trade agreement was conceived as an economic solution to the economic crisis of the 1980s; a North American commercial agreement has never been viewed as a social pact, one in which there was any identification and definition of those who would benefit and those who might lose over the short and long term.

Those definitions certainly exist within the premises and conclusions of particular econometric models; but the social subjects, first, have not been consulted and, second, have not been informed of the social or economic consequences of a free-trade agreement. Thus, the Mexican social

---

5 The term is used by Dr. Aguirre Beltrán.

6 Alexis de Tocqueville, *Democracy in America*. Trans. Henry Reeve, Francis Bowen, and Phillips Bradley, I (New York: Knopf, 1945), p. 53.

condition, as perceived by de Tocqueville, does not facilitate the openness in decision-making that is a basic requirement of a democratic process. It is legitimate to ask how far an agreement for economic integration can progress without a broad societal consensus, and, finally, whether any agreement that lacks such consensus can succeed, when a number of the social actors feel little obligation to play according to the rules of a new agreement. What future can a multicultural society like Mexico have within a half-closed negotiation characterized by obscurity and centralized decision-making?

Victor Konrad
Executive Director
Foundation for Educational Exchange
Between Canada and the United States

21

Higher Education Cooperation Among Canada, the United States, and Mexico

In reviewing the literature on higher education cooperation in North America—the numerous reports of conferences, the journal articles and the newsletters—I noticed that many of the items were keyed with a visual representation of the continent, usually an outline map of a borderless North America. A geographer by training and inclination, I was pleased if somewhat surprised by what appeared to be a pervasive coincidence. Further consideration suggests that the map of North America, the image of a continental relationship, is not in our consciousness, and that it needs to be reintroduced. Mexicans, Americans and Canadians need to be educated about each other, and to view the continent in its entirety and to see its potential.

When the European Community (EC) was configured as the pioneering trade agreement, culture and education were considered as integral dimensions. The North American Free Trade Agreement (NAFTA) has no provisions for education and culture.

> But closer economic ties will inevitably have cultural and educational implications. Now is the time to reflect on what North American economic integration will mean for other aspects of the complex set of relations between Mexico, the United States, and Canada—particularly for higher education. The universities in all three countries can play an important role in shaping a future in which there is not only better understanding of three diverse cultures, but a future in which the skills necessary for economic integration are available.[1]

Although NAFTA never was conceived as a comprehensive blueprint for a new political, economic and cultural order as in the case of the EC,

---

1   Philip G. Altbach, "NAFTA and Higher Education, The Cultural and Educational Dimensions of Trade," *Change* (July/August 1994), p. 48.

North American partners in trade, nevertheless, need to acknowledge that business relationships depend on mutual understanding and extensive integration of higher education approaches to promote more shared knowledge, coordinated skills and competitive outlooks. Contrary to widely held beliefs in political and economic circles throughout North America, education is not on the "soft" side of NAFTA. Indeed, the overall impact of NAFTA may fall short of its economic and political goals if educational and cultural dimensions are not adequately considered, integrated and funded.

In this brief chapter I aim to address both the status quo in higher education cooperation among the North American partner countries, and the initial steps which have been taken to enhance cooperation. Before steps were taken toward greater cooperation, the asymmetries in higher education among Canada, Mexico and the United States were great. Scholarly exchange was very uneven in all respects, research on broader North American topics was limited, and a tremendous news gap persisted in North American affairs, particularly in the United States. Now, in 1995, after three years of discussion, planning and reorientation, some consciousness-building has been achieved, and some structural realignment has occurred, but the substance of enhanced exchange and greater mutual understanding remains as a vision for the future. Following an overview of where we have been, this chapter will examine the move toward higher education cooperation, from its inauguration at the Wingspread Conference to the post-Vancouver conference actions to engage and link institutions across the continent.

BORDERS IN NORTH AMERICAN HIGHER EDUCATION COOPERATION

Although they are partners in NAFTA, the United States, Mexico and Canada display differences and inequalities in educational infrastructure, and related cultural presence and technological development. The asymmetries are most evident between the U.S. and Canada, on the one hand, and Mexico on the other. But substantial concerns about U.S. cultural domination worry both Canada and Mexico, and further complicate the trilateral relationship and stand in the way of mutual understanding.

> The United States, in terms of its higher education system, its [research and development] expenditures, and its technological infrastructure, not only dominates its NAFTA partners, but has the largest and most influential academic system in the world. Furthermore, U.S. cultural domination through film, television, and the print media is evident. The United

States is the center and the two other countries are, to a significant degree, peripheral.[2]

However, to be fair to Mexico and Canada, both of these countries, in their own way, have tried to level the asymmetries. Approximately 23,000 Canadians are studying in the United States this year whereas fewer than 5,000 Americans are studying in Canada. Only half as many Americans are studying in Mexico while the number of Mexican students in the U.S. is approaching 10,000.[3] Mexicans and Canadians, particularly those with leadership aspirations in their own countries, have drawn significantly more from American higher education than Americans have even attempted to learn from the internationally recognized intellectual and cultural institutions in Canada and Mexico.

The international emphasis in American colleges and universities is aimed at understanding cultures outside the continent of North America. Europe, Asia and Latin America south of Mexico receive considerably more emphasis in the curriculum and in research among scholars. Spanish is the most popular foreign language for U.S. students but Mexican culture and society is rarely associated with these linguistic studies.[4] Attention to Canada is even more limited. Approximately 1,000 scholars belong to the Association for Canadian Studies in the United States, but this number pales in comparison to the affiliation of interest groups focused on most individual European countries, and the rapidly growing associations for various sectors of Asian studies. Research and instructional agreements between U.S. institutions and counterparts in Mexico and Canada are extremely limited compared to similar agreements between U.S. institutions and their partners outside North America. A 1988 survey of a dozen major research universities in the midwest reported 515 agreements. Only twelve were with Mexican institutions and three with Canadian universities. Few of these agreements listed a high level of activity and four of the fifteen were listed as inactive.[5] With the announcement of NAFTA, and government encouragement and financial incentives for exchange, research and instructional agreements have increased in number among the three countries, and

---

2   Altbach, "NAFTA and Higher Education," p. 49.

3   Ibid.

4   Statistics on trilateral student exchange are woefully inadequate. Estimates for the current situation are based on figures reported by Roger G. Clark (Committee on Institutional Cooperation, U.S. Research Universities) at Wingspread in 1992, and revised with more recent figures provided by the Institute for International Education, New York.

5   Altbach, "NAFTA and Higher Education," p. 49.

particularly between Mexican and Canadian institutions. In the United States, active and effective educational exchange and linkage remains concentrated among institutions located in the states bordering Mexico and Canada.

The vast majority of American students and researchers, even those who work in the borderlands, remain uninformed about their North American neighbours. News about Canada and Mexico is rarely transmitted by the U.S. mass media, and this condition prevails in stark contrast to the information bombardment from the United States to Canada and Mexico. General knowledge about the United States abounds in both Mexico and Canada. However, systematic study of the United States is as underdeveloped in these countries as the study of Mexico and Canada is in the U.S. The Canadian Association for American Studies has only a few hundred members concentrated in the fields of literature and history. Americanists in the social sciences, and particularly those specializing in U.S. policy matters, are surprisingly few in number, and they generally communicate directly with their colleagues in American institutions rather than tackle the more difficult task and less acceptable orientation to establish a scholarly discourse about U.S. affairs in Canada. Mexican social scientists, concerned about U.S. domination, have long embraced socialist paradigms to establish a distance and a difference in their approach to the impact of powerful U.S. capitalism in North America. Before the 1980s few ventured across the border without this paradigmatic approach. Among the United States, Canada and Mexico there is a knowledge deficit but little acknowledgement of the deficiency. Given the tremendous potential of the proposed North American information highway, and the current access available through the Internet, this condition is almost beyond belief.[6]

Also difficult to understand is the meagre research effort devoted to North America in its continental scope, beyond the bilateral relationships between the United States and its neighbours. North America appears to be emerging from one continental relationship—coexistence, to another—effective cooperation. This emergence has been characterized by some North American specialists, and some of their work is represented in this book. Yet more assessments are required of why scholars of North America rarely established continental frameworks for their studies, and

6   Roger G. Clark, "The Mobility of Students and Scholars in North America," discussion paper prepared for the Wingspread Conference—North American Higher Education Cooperation: Identifying the Agenda (September 1992), p. 2.

why and how a realignment is emerging.[7] Some characteristics are evident. The continental economy, or at least the continental scope of North American economic activity, has captured the intellectual imagination, for it appears that North Americans are viewing the continental and hemispheric dimensions of their interrelationships for the first time. Obviously, continental perspectives are not new, but there appear to be new and vigorous reassessments, in part because North American academics are now viewing their continent in the mirror of European experience. Trade liberalization has moved Canada, Mexico and the United States toward a North American economic fundamentalism, and this fundamentalism is drawing in parallel movements toward cultural sharing, enhanced communication and scholarly linkage. Although there is a danger of incrementalism rather than true integration of interests, with a rapid and extensive move toward greater linkage, there is also a likelihood that limited resources from governments, and other traditional funders of higher education, can support only those efforts most certain to succeed. According to United States Information Agency (USIA) Director Joseph Duffey, the parallel developments on the softer side of NAFTA are more important long-term movements than the trade itself, for they promise to be the cement of international understanding.[8]

In Canada, understanding of North American issues, that is the rewards of intellectual capital invested in the academic exploration of continent-wide concerns, remains underdeveloped. A questionnaire requesting lists of current research and study on North America was sent to university and community college administrators in September 1994.[9] Almost 500 projects and courses were listed in the responses from institutions. Among these items, almost 300 projects and courses contained North American material but addressed mainly bilateral issues or multilateral issues extending beyond North America. A handful of projects and courses were designated as hemispheric in their scope. Exactly 100

---

7   Sam Lanfranco, "Exchange of Data Base Information Sources and Uses for Enhanced Networking," discussion paper prepared for the Wingspread Conference—North American Higher Education Cooperation: Identifying the Agenda (September 1992).

8   John Wirth and some colleagues in history recently explored such frameworks for their field. See John D. Wirth, ed., *History and National Identity* (Santa Fe: The North American Institute, 1994).

9   Pat Kern Schaefer, "Duffey Calls for Educational Integration Among 3 North American Countries," *USIA World*, 12, No. 6 (1993), pp. 2–3. See also Joseph Duffey, "The Converging Aspirations and Interest of Three Nations," Keynote Address, International Symposium on Higher Education and Strategic Partnerships: Mexico, Canada and the United States, Vancouver, 11 September 1993.

treated exclusively North American or trilateral content: 36 course offerings and 64 research projects. Both the courses and the research were concentrated in universities in Alberta, Ontario and Québec where almost 70 percent of the work was in the social sciences, most in economics, political science and anthropology.

Extensive North American interest may be found at the University of Calgary, Simon Fraser University, the University of Alberta, the University of British Columbia, and the University of Manitoba in western Canada. In Ontario, all research universities have developed some interest in trilateral work. The University of Toronto, York University, Queen's University, Carleton University, McMaster University, Guelph University, and the University of Waterloo are all active in this area. Québec's interest is concentrated at Université Laval, Université de Montréal, Université du Québec à Montréal (UQAM) and Université Sherbrooke. In Atlantic Canada, Dalhousie University leads in both courses and research on North America.

STEPS TOWARDS HIGHER EDUCATION COOPERATION: WINGSPREAD, VANCOUVER AND BEYOND

In September 1992, leaders from Mexico, Canada and the United States spent three historic days at the Wingspread Conference Center in Racine, Wisconsin, to chart a course of higher education cooperation in North America for the coming decades. While the three nations as an aggregate represent one of the world's highest per capita concentrations of centres of academic excellence and research and reflect a rich array of cultural diversity, Wingspread marked the first time that private and public sector representatives met to elaborate jointly a concrete plan of trilateral action to capitalize on the vast gamut of opportunities available in the region.[10]

Conference participants agreed on five basic guidelines to encourage cooperation:

• Culture and language studies are key to understanding diversity in North American identity and essential to increase mutual understanding;
• Information exchange to identify opportunities, and data base development and enhanced computer networking are central;

10 The questionnaire was prepared under the auspices of the North American Studies Working Group of the Canadian members of the North American Task Force on Higher Education, Research and Training. The working group is chaired by Victor Konrad (Canada–U.S. Fulbright) and includes Pierre Van der Donckt (Organization Universitaire Interamericaine) and James E. Cooke (Champlain Regional College).

- Mobility is crucial in cooperation and collaboration, and barriers must be reduced;
- Future relationships may be built on present cooperation;
- Asymmetries in resources and experience are not matched by asymmetry of interest in cooperation.

After three days of deliberation, including active debate and heated discussion, the fifty high-level representatives unanimously approved a statement of policies, objectives and recommendations for action. They agreed that priority areas should be the management of trade relations, sustainable development, public health, North American studies and language training. Wingspread was the first, essential step for the participants and the constituencies which they represented, the inaugural conference in setting the North American higher education cooperation agenda. The objectives of this agenda—a North American dimension in higher education, greater exchange of information, institutional collaboration, scholar mobility, removing barriers, engaging stakeholders, and exploiting emerging technologies.

Among the action initiatives defined in the agenda were the establishment of a task force on North American Higher Education Collaboration, and the commitment to implement a trilateral conference within a year if the task force reported sufficient progress. During the next twelve months, the task force, accompanied by additional representatives of higher education organizations and institutions in all three countries, met in Ixtapa, Mexico; Leesburg, Virginia; and Québec City. Progress reports were delivered on each occasion on the issues of strategic alliances, faculty and institutional development, information technology, scholar mobility and leveraging of resources.

On one front the task force surged ahead. In June 1993, the networking telecommunications subcommittee tabled a proposal for a North American Distance Education and Research Network (NADERN), an international consortium of educational, governmental and business institutions of Canada, the United States and Mexico.[11] The proposal was well developed, manageable, and supported by Northern Telecom. Meanwhile, USIA was finalizing a competition for trilateral university-to-university affiliation grants. Each grant of approximately US $100,000 was to be awarded to an American institution of higher education for explicit linkage development with partner institutions in Canada and Mexico. Trade and environmental concerns were identified as key issue areas. Research funding councils in all three countries were exploring trilateral

---

11 The Johnson Foundation, *North American Higher Education Cooperation: Identifying the Agenda* (Racine: Wingspread, The Johnson Foundation, 1993), p. 1.

cooperation, and the Mexican and Canadian Fulbright commissions were developing a cooperative plan aimed at including in their mandates research and study on trilateral topics.

Some good ideas, originated at Wingspread and in the task force meetings, did not catch on. Foremost among these was the notion of developing a North American educational commission. Although some guiding and coordinating body may yet emerge to replace the task force, many saw the establishment of a commission at the outset as affecting too much centralization and structure. Yet discussions of structure prevailed as the task force made plans for the conference in Vancouver.

From September 10 through 13, 1993, some 300 leaders in higher education from Mexico, the United States and Canada, and selected guests from abroad, met in Vancouver to implement the agenda established a year before at Wingspread. Keynote addresses by the Hon. Thomas E. Siddon, Minister of Defence, Canada, Joseph Duffey, Director of USIA, and Ernesto Zedillo Ponce de León, Minister of Public Education of Mexico, and now its President, stressed reaching out, looking at a common identity in North America, and reforming education.

> At the time of the Vancouver Symposium, profound forces affecting relationships between Canada, Mexico and the United States were at work. These included the North American Free Trade Agreement, the growing impact of new information management technologies in higher education and unprecedented international competition in the context of global knowledge-based economics. These forces were recognized as placing unprecedented demands on higher education, research and training, obliging business, government, labour and the academic community to develop new partnerships to respond to and shape developments.[12]

Symposium highlights included plenary sessions on the international context of strategic alliances and global changes, public policy context and strategies for North American higher education collaboration, implications of tomorrow's technological frontiers for business and higher education, and strategic partnerships between higher education and business to leverage resources. The outcome of the conference was defined in the Vancouver Communiqué. Six initiatives were listed for immediate action:

- establish NADERN;
- form an Enterprise/Education trilateral mechanism to examine issues of mobility, certification and applied education;

---

12 William H. Mobley, Robert V. Bloedon and Rafael Rangel Sostman, "Trilateral Task Force on North American Higher Education Collaboration, Networking Telecommunications Subcommittee, Interim Proposal," (ITESM, Northern Telecom and Texas A & M, 28 June 1993).

- bring faculty and administrators from the three countries together to chart collaboration;
- establish electronic information bases in each country to record trilateral cooperation;
- strengthen and expand North American studies;
- establish intensive trilateral exchange, research and training for students.

More than a year has passed since the higher education delegates met in Vancouver. The results of collaborative efforts are now becoming apparent, some in the new structures which have emerged, and others in the added value of exchange and collaboration. This substance of North American intellectual exchange is difficult to measure. It cannot be substantiated in number of students, courses, research projects and agreements alone. But as we look forward to the journal articles and books on North American studies, other evidence is emerging. Centres for the study of North America are developing, some in specialized fields like international relations (Carleton, Georgetown and ITAM), but others are more broadly based in the social sciences (UNAM, Calgary and Duke). At George Mason University a Center for the Study of the Americas offers graduate and undergraduate instruction on North America extending into the Caribbean. The University of Colorado's Center for the Study of the American West is extending its focus north into Canada and south into Mexico. Other examples of expansion and reorientation toward North American studies are accumulating in all three countries. The imperatives in Philip Altbach's recent eloquent call for action are being addressed.[13] Although they are not yet "primary foci for the Fulbright Program," the commissions in Canada and Mexico are growing and working to offer trilateral as well as bilateral exchange opportunities. Institution-to-institution exchanges and partnerships are growing according to recent appraisals by the Institute of International Education (IIE), the Association of Universities and Colleges of Canada (AUCC) and the Asociación Nacional de Universidades e Instituciones de Educación Superior (ANUIES). Trilateral student mobility is showing increases. Scholarly ties and conferences are growing in number and quality. Mexican, Canadian and American studies are growing, particularly Mexican studies in Canada and Canadian studies in Mexico. And language instruction in Spanish and French is seeing some growth.

---

13 Foreign Affairs and International Trade Canada, *North American Higher Education Cooperation: Implementing the Agenda,* Report on the International Symposium on Higher Education and Strategic Partnerships, Vancouver, 10–13 September 1993. (Ottawa: FAIT Canada, 1994), p. 6.

A Vision for North American
Higher Education Cooperation

An emerging vision for North American studies is propelled by the imperative to define and build scholarly linkages along the length of North America, yet the concept of North America remains ill defined and rarely embraced as a paradigm for intellectual pursuit by scholars across the continent. Indeed, colleagues from other continents operate with more highly developed notions of what North America is and how it works. In Mexico, the United States and Canada, concepts of nation and region frame critical enquiry, often to the detriment of a broader and more informed perspective from the continental vantage point. In a world where the "big picture," if you will, is increasingly required, North American scholars have been slow and reluctant to move beyond their well-chiselled niches of study.

This stance appears to be shifting as scholars pursue research on free trade, migration, multiculturalism, environmental impacts, and more, all in a North American context. USIA Director Joseph Duffey, speaking at the trilateral conference in Vancouver, called for "inquiries in the fields of North American studies," . . . "ideas for new research into values and identities that we North Americans share." He continued:

> Here in North America three nations share a favored quadrant of the globe. We inhabit what was once called the New World. We must begin to realize that our distinct national identities need not be sacrificed in order to forge a new regional community. So many quests for national identify today are being carried to the past. Our tradition in this hemisphere has always been to look to the future, to redefine, to reinvent, to forge our future by engaging it.[14]

This challenge, and the events which have occasioned it, invite extensive, new research on North American issues. Yet there remains the need for reviewing continental frameworks for this research, and for deriving a contemporary vision of what North America is and means. Bold and imaginary strokes are required to define North American studies, and encompass the diversity and richness and vitality of what is arguably the globe's vanguard continent. North American studies could become a locus for the exciting work now required to build and understand North American partnerships.

---

14 Altbach, "NAFTA and Higher Education," p. 49.

Herman W. Konrad
Departments of Anthropology and History
University of Calgary

22

Mexican Studies in Canadian Universities: The Canada–Mexico Academic Relationship, 1960s–1990s

INTRODUCTION

Mexican studies in Canadian universities developed in the context of a national university focus in area studies, specifically linked to Latin American and Caribbean studies. The national emergence of Latin American Studies with a professional identity took place in 1969 with the formation of the Canadian Association for Latin American and Caribbean Studies (CALACS). It, and its regional Ontario counterpart, the Ontario Co-operative Program in Latin and Caribbean Studies (OCPLACS), also established in 1969, represented benchmark events in that they resulted in professional networks to encourage communication, instruction, research and publication activities. Prior to 1969 the Latin American focus was restricted to the efforts of small groups of scholars in Canadian universities, or individual efforts despite the absence of formal institutional interests or support. Stock-taking efforts of interests and resources surrounding the emergence of professional associations resulted in a series of surveys which provided a profile of national activities.[1] Whereas in 1963 the 15 universities that offered Latin American courses focused

---

1 Herman W. Konrad, "A Preliminary Survey of the Status of Latin American Studies in Canadian Institutions," CALACS Working Paper (Calgary, 1970); Pedro Leon, "Los estudios sobre Iberoamericana en el Canada," *Historiografia y Bibliografia Americanistas*, 16, No. 1 (1972), pp. 71–98; Kurt Levy, "Latin American Studies in Canada: Some Recent Trends," Working paper No. 15, Fifteenth Seminar of the Acquisition of Latin American Library Materials (Toronto, 1970); J.C.M. Ogelsby, "Latin American Studies in Canada," Latin American *Research Review*, 2, No. 1 (1966), pp. 80–88; F.J. Tatlow, ed., *Directory of Scholars in Latin American Teaching and Research in Canada* (Ottawa, 1970).

primarily upon Hispanic literature, with a lesser focus upon history courses, by 1966 there were 35 institutions offering courses, now including offerings in anthropology, geography, and political science, in addition to the literature focus. By 1970 the majority of Canadian universities, 44 institutions, were offering courses in most of the social science disciplines. The formation of the Canadian Association of Hispanists in the early 1970s and the emergence of professional journals of the Hispanists and CALACS, clearly identified a critical mass of academic specialists and national distribution of Latin American interests. By the 1990s virtually all of Canada's 89 college and university programs included courses about Latin America.

The numbers of students enrolled in Latin American courses and members in the professional associations in the late 1960s were still modest. The majority were concentrated at universities in Calgary, Guelph, Laval, Manitoba, Montreal, Burnaby (Simon Fraser), Toronto and Waterloo. Course instruction was being provided by 150 professors who provided the base membership of the emerging professional associations. CALACS reported 200 non-student members in 1971 and OCPLACS a mailing list of 125 persons. The CALACS national distribution for that year showed 50 percent in Ontario, 24 percent in Quebec, 21 percent in the Western provinces and 4 percent in the Atlantic provinces. CALACS membership at the time was still dominated by professors in the Language and Literature fields (33 percent), Geography (20 percent) and History (18 percent), and lesser numbers in other social science disciplines.[2]

Teaching and research resources were still minimal, or as Kurt Levy concluded, "Latin American [library] holdings in Canadian universities . . . continue to be an 'underdeveloped' not to say a 'disaster' area."[3] A survey of CALACS members showed that most (81.4 percent) considered their library holdings as "fair to bad" with a minority indicating them to be in the "good to excellent" range.[4] The same survey, regarding national media (television, radio and newspapers) coverage of Latin America, was even less positive. The major complaints about the Canadian media coverage was that it relied almost exclusively upon United States sources, it lacked in comprehension of Latin American cultural and historical traditions and context, and was almost completely lacking in an infrastructure for collecting, reporting, and interpreting Latin American affairs.[5] Despite the minimal and inadequate library and media coverage

2 Newsletter/Bulletin: Canadian Association of Latin American Studies (Winter, 1971).
3 Levy, "Latin American Studies," p. 2.
4 Konrad, "A Preliminary Survey," p. 18.
5 Konrad, "A Preliminary Survey," pp. 15–17.

of Latin America, however, the Latin Americanists in Canadian universities were very confident of their ability to develop new programs and directions to overcome their resource deficiencies.

Such efforts were encouraged and strengthened by national developments. The 1960s had seen a great expansion of university programs, the establishment of new universities, and the hiring of significant numbers of new professors. Federal governmental pursuit of an international "third-option" strategy, to link national trade relations more directly with areas such as Latin America, and the creation of funded agencies such as the International Development Research Centre (IDRC) and the Canadian International Development Agency (CIDA), stimulated greater interest in Latin America. Area studies came to be seen by university administrators as important areas of teaching and research. At the same time a previously neglected development of graduate training capacities in the social sciences was being addressed. The results of the 1960s developments for Latin American studies was evident in the rapid expansion of undergraduate instruction and graduate training.

At the same time events in Latin America, especially in Cuba—Fidel Castro's success, the Bay of Pigs invasion, and the U.S.–Russia "missile crisis"—stimulated a Latin American interest. A rapid increase in graduate theses on Latin American topics, produced in the second half of the 1960s, was a byproduct of such these developments, from an annual average of 10 in the early 1960s to 40 by the end of the decade.[6]

LATIN AMERICAN AND MEXICAN STUDIES IN THE 1970S

The 1970s represented a decade of consolidation of activity in teaching and research and the emergence of Mexican studies as a visible factor. Throughout the 1970s, taking graduate thesis production as an indicator, one finds an annual output of 55 theses. At the beginning of this decade, according to Levy, there were some 150 Latin American specialists teaching in Canadian institutions.[7] This number increased rapidly, to almost 200 by 1972. A profile of these specialists in terms of national origin indicated that only a quarter of the total were Canadian, the others being from the United States (30 percent), Europe (30 percent) and Latin America and the Caribbean (15 percent). Taking the source of graduate degrees of academics involved in Latin American studies in Canadian universities showed that a minority were from Canada, over 50 percent from the United States, and 30 percent from European and Latin

---

6 Denise Brown and Herman W. Konrad, comps., *Directory of Canadian Theses on Latin American and Caribbean Topics, 1927–1980* (Calgary: CALACS, 1982), p. v.

7 Levy, "Latin American Studies," p. 7.

American institutions.[8] Thus foreign influences, in professional training and perspectives, still shaped choices of research topics and materials of instruction.

An examination of the 739 graduate theses listed in the *Directory of Theses on Latin American and Caribbean Topics* allows for an identification of the nature of interests prior to the 1980s.[9] This has particular relevance for Mexican studies' late emergence, as evident in Table 1, indicating less than 10 percent of professional degrees having a Mexican focus. The dominance of a Caribbean focus and the almost total lack of attention to Canadian relations with either the Caribbean or the rest of Latin America is also significant. The Caribbean focus was a byproduct of Canada's role in the British Commonwealth and colonial trade relations with the Caribbean area. The *Directory* data, at the same time, indicated that 75 percent of the graduate theses had been produced in the 1970s, the decade during which professional training within the social sciences as a whole in Canada can be said to have "come of age." A disciplinary breakdown of graduate research indicated an overwhelming dominance of the social sciences (70.8 percent), much lesser focus in the humanities (12.9 percent) and applied sciences (12.7 percent), and a minor attention to other science fields (3.6 percent).[10]

THE EMERGENCE OF MEXICAN STUDIES

Mexican studies as an identifiable area of study emerged out of both the developments in Canadian Social Sciences and the emergence of Latin American Studies programs. The shape and direction of the Mexican component, however, varied from national trends in Latin American and Caribbean studies. Here the influence of graduate training in the United States played even a stronger role and many of the scholars involved in these studies became located outside of Ontario whose professors and institutions had dominated earlier trends. The Western provinces and Quebec gradually emerged as important areas focusing upon Mexican studies. The 1970 survey of academics holding teaching posts in Canadian universities identified 14 percent as Mexican specialists.[11] Table 2 provides a profile of disciplinary identification, area of Canada located, with parallel data for the total number.

---

8 Herman W. Konrad, "The Development and Impact of Caribbean and Latin American Graduate Studies in Canadian Academic Institutions," *North/South* 7, No. 13 (1982), pp. 46–47.

9 Brown and Konrad, *Directory of Canadian Theses*.

10 Konrad, "The Development," p. 39.

11 Leon, "Los estudios sobre Iberoamericana."

TABLE 1. GRADUATE THESES ACCORDING TO GEOGRAPHICAL AREAS

AREA	NUMBER	PERCENTAGE
Mexico	68	9.2
Central America	27	3.7
Caribbean (including Belize & Guyana)	358	48.4
Northern South America (Colombia, Venezuela, Surinam, and French Guyana)	24	3.2
Andean South America (Bolivia, Ecuador, Peru)	31	4.2
Southern South America (Argentina, Chile, Paraguay, Uruguay)	45	6.1
Brazil	32	4.3
General: Latin America	68	9.2
Canada–Latin America	13	1.8
Canada-Caribbean	32	4.3
Europe–Latin America	14	1.9
Europe-Caribbean	1	0.1
Not specific	26	3.5
TOTAL	739	99.9

Source: Herman W. Konrad, "The Development and Impact of Caribbean and Latin American Graduate Studies in Canadian Academic Institutions," *North/South*, 7, No. 13 (1982), p. 49.

As indicated in Table 2, the Mexican interest had a strong western Canadian concentration at the beginning of the 1970s whereas the distribution of CALACS members, based on its mailing list, indicated greatest concentration in Ontario (50 percent) and Quebec (25 percent). At this time the Western provinces (21 percent) and Atlantic provinces (4 percent)

TABLE 2. MEXICAN SPECIALISTS COMPARED TO LATIN AMERICANISTS, 1970 (MEXICANISTS [N=20], LATIN AMERICANISTS [N=126])

DISCIPLINE	% MEXICANISTS	% LATIN AMERICANISTS
Language/Literature	15.0	29.4
History	25.0	11.0
Anthropology	40.0	14.3
Geography	10.0	17.5
Political Science	5.0	9.5
Economics	0.0	10.3
Sociology	5.0	5.5
Other	0.0	2.4
Area		
Atlantic Provinces	0.0	2.1
Quebec	10.0	12.3
Ontario	40.0	60.0
Western Provinces	50.0	25.3

Source: Herman W. Konrad, "Development and Impact of Caribbean and Latin American Studies."

represented a quarter of the 350 persons on CALACS' mailing lists. Also evident was a very narrow disciplinary base, with 80 percent of the Mexicanists representing the fields of anthropology, history and language/literature.

Formal institutional linkages with Mexican counterparts were initiated in 1971 when CALACS, along with three Mexican institutions (El Colegio de Mexico, Universidad Nacional Autonoma de Mexico, Instituto Nacional de Antropologia e Historia) co-sponsored a Canadian–Latin American Conference. This May meeting, held in Mexico's National Museum of Anthropology, included 80 representatives from 26 Canadian institutions, an equal number of Mexican participants, plus a small number of invited representatives from the Caribbean (Cuba, Dominican Republic) and South American (Colombia, Venezuela). The theme of the conference, "Development or Dependence: the Future of Canadian–Latin American Relations," resulted in a number of policy papers suggesting strategies for improving future relations. The meetings ended with the election of a four-person standing committee (two Canadians and two Mexicans) to pursue avenues for a formal organization of exchanges between academic institutions. The attempt to formalize a stable mechanism for enhancing inter-institutional exchanges and collaborative research and training activities, however, proved to be unsuccessful. The reasons for this failure in 1971 were three-fold. CIDA, which had generously supported the conference itself, was unwilling to provide further financial support, CALACS did not have its own funds for such developments, and almost half of the Mexicanists (45 percent) in Canada were recently hired United States scholars while 90 percent of the total had received their graduate training in U.S. institutions. Thus the existing U.S./Mexico networks were considered as normative, without a need to establish independent Canadian/Mexican bilateral alternatives. At the same time, within the Canadian social sciences as a whole, there was still a definite bias in favour of foreign criteria (publishing outlets, recognition) for acquiring academic status (tenure, promotion, salary increments) rather than a national one.

Within Canadian universities, however, there was a significant expansion of instruction and training in Mexican studies. While only one graduate thesis appeared on Mexican topics per year in the 1960s, the annual production was eight in the 1970s. This decade also saw a substantial increase in books and journal articles being published about Mexico, as well as papers given by Canadian academics in national and international conferences. The attention to Canadian–Mexican relations remained virtually absent, the exception being three chapters in Ogelsby's study of Canadian–Latin American relations and Sawatsky's excellent book on the Canadian Mennonite colonies in Mexico. One Master's thesis surveyed Canadian press opinion of the Mexican Revolution, while a few journal articles dealt with bilateral issues.[12]

The official governmental attention to Mexico also greatly increased in the 1970s, exemplified by the construction of a new Canadian embassy

---

12 On annual theses on Mexican topics, Eileen Delman and Herman W. Konrad, *Canadian Academic Publications on Mexican Topics: A Bibliographical Inventory, 1970–1987* (Calgary: University of Calgary, 1987). The works on Canada–Mexico relations include J.C.M. Ogelsby, *Gringos from the Far North: Essays in the History of Canadian–Latin American Relations, 1866–1968* (Toronto: Maclean-Hunter, 1976); Leonard H. Sawatzky, *They Sought a Country: Mennonite Colonization in Mexico* (Berkeley: University of California Press, 1971); Mona E. Browne, "Canadian Press Opinion of the Mexican Revolution, 1910–1920" (Master's Thesis, University of Western Ontario, 1975).

in Mexico City designed by one of the nation's leading architects. The diplomatic presence was upgraded by appointment of a cultural attaché—the only such Canadian post in Latin America—and the first meeting of the Canadian/Mexican Bilateral Trade Committee in Mexico City in November 1970. The Trudeau government actively pursued closer diplomatic and economic ties with Mexico, in part to offset the influence of the United States upon national trade patterns and economic structures, and to expand commercial ties with Latin America and other Pacific Rim countries. Canada and Mexico also found themselves in agreement on many international issues which opposed Washington policy and actions in Vietnam, Central and South America, and the Caribbean.[13] The coherence of Canadian–Mexican political, and to an extent domestic economic, policies, such as mixed-economy state-owned enterprises, however, did not translate into any significant academic research on bilateral issues. What did take place in the universities, nevertheless, was a strengthening of teaching and research programs about Mexico.

MEXICAN STUDIES IN THE 1980S

Comparing 1980s academic developments with federal governmental activities shows a reversal of trends. By the end of the 1970s the federal third-option policy was already seen as unproductive in achieving its goals. Despite Trudeau's re-election in 1980 and during the period up to the 1984 defeat of the Liberal government, the official Mexican card, if one can call it this, was no longer being played. The oil crisis of 1982 and Mexico's internal economic problems did not augur well for a strengthened Canada–Mexico relationship to offset regional hegemony by their powerful neighbour. Deference rather than opposition to Washington policy crept into the Ottawa strategy of managing its continental and hemisphere relationships. And when the Conservative Mulroney government took over in 1984 Mexico quickly lost any residual place of prominence in Ottawa's policy deliberations. The extent of this abandonment was clearly evident when serious negotiations were undertaken in pursuing a comprehensive trade agreement between Canada and the United States. Not only was Mexico completely ignored during the negotiations; the ambassador post was vacant for over a year while the agreement was being consummated. Tourist traffic increased, as did the exchange of auto engines and parts between the two countries; formal political relations remained in a holding pattern.

---

13 Omar Martínez-Legorreta, ed., *Relations Between Mexico and Canada* (México: El Colegio de México, 1990).

Academic research and training domestic Mexicanists, on the other hand, moved in the opposite direction. Two key factors played a significant role here, related to the development of programs allowing for increased graduate training and the beginning of new perspectives with a more relevant Canadian focus by Mexicanists in national universities. Although the expansion of the university system characteristic of the late 1960s and early 1970s, including the hiring of specialists in Area Studies, took the opposite trend resulting in financial cutbacks and lack of academic employment opportunities, there was a stabilization and maturing of existing programs. The assistant professors of the earlier expansion period whose research efforts were successful became associate and full professors. Their ability to supervise graduate programs increased, as did the number of students entering and completing such programs. In the social sciences as a whole the focus upon Canadian issues and national topics of interest deepened. Thus a new generation of scholars with a more firmly rooted Canadian perspective replaced the previous old-boy networks with their foreign orientation. This was not entirely an even process; taking full-time faculty in anthropology as an example, in Quebec the majority (77.0 percent) were Canadian as early as 1973–1974,[14] while in English Canada the nationalization of the social sciences was both slower and less complete. The Mexicanist specialists still were being strongly influenced by U.S. ideas and linkages.

A bibliographical inventory prepared as a supporting document for a national Mexican Colloquium held at the University of Windsor in October 1987 and the fifth edition of the *Directory of Canadian Scholars Interested in Latin American and Caribbean Studies* allowed for an assessment of the Mexicanist scholarly activities into the second half of the 1980s. Of the 260 individuals covered in the *Directory*, 42.3 percent (110 scholars) indicated Mexico as part of the area of their academic interest while 28.1 percent (73) identified Mexico as their country of research interest (79–97). Summer school programs that brought Canadian students to Mexico were being carried out by universities at Brandon, Calgary and Burnaby (Simon Fraser). In the same source 138 scholars indicated publication topics, of which 47.1 percent (65 individuals) included Mexico. Compared to the beginnings of the 1970s the Mexico interest had increased significantly, as had research and publication activities on Mexican topics.[15]

---

14 Thomas Symons, *The Symons Report*. Abridged version (Toronto, 1978).

15 Delman and Konrad, *Canadian Academic Publications*; Sam Lanfranco, ed., *Directory of Canadian Scholars Interested in Latin American and Caribbean Studies*, 5th ed. (Toronto: CALACS, 1987).

Information presented in the *Bibliographical Inventory* allows for a closer examination of disciplinary affiliation, topics of investigation, and location of Mexican specialists. Taking 63 books published by Canadian authors during the period between 1970 and 1985 one finds a clearly western-Canadian concentration of research. Not only were the largest number of authors from these provinces, they also produced roughly 60 percent of the total published. Continued reliance upon foreign publishing outlets is another notable aspect but with a shift away from U.S. presses (30.1 percent) to Mexican publishers. Including books previously published in English or French the percentage appearing in Spanish, in Mexico, was 52.4 percent.[16] Two aspects are notable: first, that Canadian authors were being successful in having their research about Mexico made available to a Mexican audience, and second, that Canadian university and commercial presses were still reluctant to publish materials about Mexico. The disciplines most heavily represented in these books were those of history and anthropology. The same history and anthropology emphasis is clearly evident in the graduate theses about Mexico produced between 1970 and 1985. A sample of 88 such works indicates 60.2 percent in these disciplines. The western Canada and Quebec concentration of graduate training relating to Mexican studies is also notable, with 82.5 percent of total degrees granted. In contrast, the more numerous Ontario universities granted only 16.3 percent of MA and PhD degrees in the field. The Atlantic provinces, as in the case of all previous data presented, continued to play an insignificant role in either the production of books or graduate theses.[17]

Intergenerational trends, between the faculty publishing interests and graduate thesis topics by the mid-1980s, showed a noticeable shift towards history and a noticeable decrease in the language/literature areas. Training of a new generation of economists, sociologists, and geographers with a Mexican focus was not a noticeable trend. Since graduate students tend to reflect the interests of their supervisors, the relatively high degree of concurrence between generations is not unexpected. The *Bibliographical Inventory* also included book chapters, journal articles and essays written by Canadian Mexicanists. Information from 250 such items published between 1970 and 1985 shows trends similar to that of the books and graduate theses, with anthropology leading the way (34.8 percent) followed by language/literature (26.4 percent), history (18.8 percent) and political science (10.0 percent). The geographical areas represented here shows the strong western influence (49.2 percent), followed by Ontario

---

16 Delman and Konrad, *Canadian Academic Publications.*

17 *Loc. cit.*

(31.6 percent), Quebec (15.2 percent) and the Atlantic provinces (4.0 percent).[18]

Particularly striking, and indicative of a minimal attention by Canadian Mexicanists to Canada–Mexico relations, was the almost total neglect of faculty and graduate research on binational affairs. Of the 63 books published only 2, or 3.2 percent, concerned themselves with Canadian–Mexican relationships. The same held true for the graduate theses of which only 2 of 88, or 2.3 percent, dealt with binational concerns. This failure to write on these issues was furthermore reflected in the faculty publications in journals where, of those that fall in the social science areas, only 6.5 percent dealt with Canada–Mexico issues. In view of these trends it is small wonder that there existed a significant information gap relative to the nature of binational relationships. Canadians, it seemed—at least by the mid-1980s—had not even begun to take a serious interest in exploring and explaining how and why two nations occupying the North American continent, and sharing borders with the same superpower, utterly failed to view their continental role in a comparative perspective. For despite the maturation of Mexican studies within national institutions and the existence of a considerable cadre of specialized faculty, they were not producing basic information that governmental officials, businessmen, or other sectors of the Canadian society might utilize in strategic planning.

By the end of the 1980s the patterns already identified had not changed in any significant way. Production of graduate theses increased, as have the numbers of book and articles about Mexico. By the end of the 1980s there were well over 200 MA and PhD theses produced in Canadian universities. Adding this number of domestically-trained professionals to those holding teaching and research position in universities, one comes up with a figure of roughly 400 Mexicanists nationally in the academic arena.[19] What was still lacking, relative to Canadian interactions with Mexico—past, present, and future—was a focus on the nature of that relationship.

MEXICAN STUDIES IN THE 1900S: TRENDS AND PROSPECTS

Although Canadian official attention to Mexico was largely absent during negotiations with the United States resulting in the Canada–United States trade agreement, the Mexican decision to begin similar negotiations

---

18 *Loc. cit.*

19 Herman W. Konrad, "Canadian Research Capacities and Achievements Concerning Mexico: A Preliminary Overview," paper prepared for FOCAL Canadian–Latin American Capacities Project, 1993.

dramatically changed both attitudes and activities. The result can be clearly seen in the academic activities that have taken place during 1990–95. Mexican and continental studies very quickly became a "hot" topic, particularly in disciplines such as economics and political science. Outside the universities, in the governmental and business sectors, the sudden need to have more information about Mexico, now dramatically reshaping economic and political strategies both domestically and internationally, further stimulated research activities. Even the public media, traditionally content to feed off U.S. channels of information about Mexico and Latin America in general, began to take a more active and direct interest in Mexican affairs. Labour unions, church groups, human rights groups, ecology lobbyists, and political parties in Canada had now "discovered" Mexico.

Partly due to what has been seen as a negative byproduct of the U.S.–Canada Trade Agreement, especially in Ontario, and partly due to greatly enhanced trade opportunities in Mexico by the Canadian business sector, Mexican affairs became a significant factor in Canadian awareness. The decision by Ottawa to join the Organization of American States, in 1990, symbolized for many a recognition that Canada's future lay in the Americas. Sorting out that role, however, turned out to be a complicated and frequently acrimonious process in the domestic context. Direct interactions with Mexico, to the contrary, became a significant priority at many levels. Taking the number of direct contacts and meetings between Canadian and Mexican counterparts—Non-governmental Organizations (NGOs), official government delegations, academic groups—in the 1990s, the amount of activity has been spectacular. And this leaves out the over half million Canadians who visit Mexico as tourists annually to enjoy the pleasures of sea, sand, sun, and winter climate not available in Canada.

The combination of domestic, regional and international developments, at the same time, reshaped the academic profile of research about Mexico in Canadian institutions. In Ontario universities, where relatively few Latin American specialists had been previously concerned with Mexican affairs, there has rapidly been developing significant and serious research projects focusing upon binational economic and political issues. To a large extent this trend took place across the country, evident by the increasing number of conferences, colloquia, and other gatherings of established specialists. What was equally significant was the mix of persons involved in such meetings, involving not only academics but also government officials, businessmen, and representatives from a wide variety of NGOs. This combination was new as academics, in earlier decades, had been reluctant to be closely associated with the Canadian business sectors. Equally important were the changes within Latin America, with the elimination of many of the military dictatorships and the painful peace process in Central America. Since the Mulroney government was seen by many academics as being less than forthright in its opposition to Washington's interventionist policies and practices in Latin America, while academics strongly opposed U.S. policies, this irritant also diminished. With the elimination of the Cold War and the lessening of ideological tensions in this hemisphere conditions have arisen that allow for a more realistic evaluation of economic, social and political issues within Latin America and domestically.

The implications for Canadian–Mexican relations and Mexicanists studies were revolutionary relative to what took place in the 1960–90 period. This was particularly the case in Canada since the 1994 implementation of the NAFTA, with the rapid development of a serious interest, across a broad spectrum of academic, governmental, and private sectors, to understand the role of Mexico in North American affairs and what this might mean for Canada. External Affairs Academic Relations Division's inclusion of Mexico as an important area of concern, and initiatives taken to support Canadian Studies programs in Mexico, became a clear sign of change. Federal and even provincial governmental support of workshops and conferences within Canada about issues involving Mexico became part of the "discovery" of the importance of Mexico as a continental neighbour and potential market for increased economic exchange.

THE RESEARCH FOCUS

As indicated by Christon I. Archer, in his paper "The View from the North: Canada's Historians of Mexico," prepared for the Universidad Iberoamericano–hosted 1992 symposium on Canadian Social Science research on Mexican themes, there is a definite Canadian perspective emerging.[20] Following pioneering research begun by Ogelsby in the 1960s, the 1970s saw a number of national scholars gaining international recognition with the publication of major studies. Mexico's colonial history became a focus by Timothy Anna (Manitoba), Archer (Calgary), Richard Boyer (Simon Fraser), Konrad (Calgary), and Claude Morin (Montreal).[21] The major books of these scholars have all been published

---

20 This 1992 conference represented the first binational attempt to assess the nature and direction of Canadian research perspectives about Mexico.

21 Including the following works: Timothy Anna, *The Fall of the Royal Government in Mexico City* (Lincoln: University of Nebraska Press, 1978); Christon I. Archer, *The Army in Bourbon Mexico, 1760–1810* (Albuquerque: University of New Mexico Press, 1977); Richard Boyer, *La gran inundación: vida y sociedad en la ciudad de México, 1629–1638* (México: Fondo de Cultura Económica, 1975) and *The New World of Bigamists: Marriage and Domestic Life in Colonial Mexico*

in Spanish in Mexico, either as translations or in original editions. This type of access to readers in Mexico rather than only in the English reading world, in contrast to much of the United States Mexicanist scholarship—and this trend is common in Canadian scholarship—sets our scholars apart. As pointed out by Archer :

> Whatever the reasons, Mexican historians often comment that Canadian researchers have special affinities for their history and that they are unencumbered either by the official or nationalist interpretations expected of Mexicans or the indelible cultural baggage of having been born, brought up, and educated in the United States. . . . Canadians on the other hand tend to experience fewer problems with Mexican history or with the modern state. They possess few if any heroic expectations of a nation; they have no background of imperial pretensions; they under-stand fully the boom and bust economic cycles experienced in their own regions and provinces; and they comprehend the chaotic forces driving multiculturalism, regionalism, provincialism, and nationalism.[22]

The topics pursued by Canadian historians cover a broad range of areas and themes. Timothy Anna's (Manitoba) books focused upon the transition from colonial to independence periods. And aside from his many articles, he has supervised half-a-dozen doctoral theses dealing with regional Mexican issues. Archer (Calgary) has become a recognized expert on the military aspects of the same period, with his 1977 book winning the prestigious Herbert E. Bolton Prize of the Conference of Latin American History (1978) and Pacific Coast Branch, American Historical Association Prize (1979). Konrad's (Calgary) book (1980), also a winner of the Bolton Prize (1981), dealt with the evolution of the great landed estates over a two-century period. His later research has focused on tropical forest transformations on the Yucatan Peninsula, forest extraction industries, and ecological issues. Richard Boyer (Simon Fraser) examined the impact of floods on Mexico City during the 1629–38 period and marriage and domestic life in Colonial Mexico. Claude Morin's (Montreal) major emphasis has been on historical demography and economics. Such studies of Mexican colonial history by Canadian scholars,

---

(Lincoln: University of Nebraska Press, 1992); Herman W. Konrad, *A Jesuit Hacienda in Colonial Mexico: Santa Lucía, 1576–1767* (Stanford: Stanford University Press, 1980); Claude Morin, *Santa Inés Zacatelco, 1646-1812: contribución a la demografía historica del México colonial* (México: INAH, 1973), and *Michoacán en la Nueva España del siglo xviii: crecimiento y disigualdad en una economía colonial* (México: Fondo de Cultura Económica, 1979).

22 Christon I. Archer, "The View from the North: Canada's Historians of Mexico," paper presented at Canada–Mexico Symposium, Universidad Ibero-americana, Mexico City, February, 1992, p. 2.

although well known in Mexico and internationally, received much less attention in Canada.[23]

Historical research has not been limited to colonial themes. Marie Lapointe (Laval) examined the foreign influences in indigenous separatist activities on the Yucatan Peninsula in the second half of the nineteenth century. David Raby (Toronto) looked at education and social revolution in the 1921–40 period. Russell Chace (York) and William French (U.B.C.) have produced papers (also French's 1981 MA thesis) on Canadian involvement in the development of Mexican industrial infrastructures during the Porfiriato (1876–1910). French's doctoral thesis (University of Texas) on Chihuahua mining developments won a dissertation prize and later research examines the work ethic of northern Mexican miners. Other important historical studies, although written by specialists of other disciplines, also need mention. Frans Schreyer (Guelph) introduced new insights and significant scholarly attention with his revisionist study of the role of small ranchers in the Mexican Revolution (1980). This is one of the few books published by a Canadian press (University of Toronto Press) although the Spanish Mexican edition is better known. Leonard Sawatzky's (Manitoba) study of the Mennonite colonies in Mexico represents the only detailed study of migration from Canada to Mexico. Ross Crumrine (Victoria) published a study of the Mayo society in Sonora. And Alfred Siemens (U.B.C.), who recently received the Carl O. Sauer Distinguished Scholarship Award of the Conference of Latin American Geographers, examined the foreign travelers' accounts of the nineteenth century in Veracruz.[24]

The anthropological sciences have played a key role in the Canadian research endeavour regarding Mexico. Mexico's pre-Hispanic cultures and its rich mosaic of indigenous societies have been a magnet for international attention for well over a century. In this area, as was the case in historical studies, it was foreign scholars primarily from the United States

---

23 Timothy Anna's most recent book is *The Mexican Empire of Iturbide* (Lincoln: University of Nebraska Press, 1990).

24 Marie Lapointe, *Los mayas rebeldes de Yucatán* (Zamora, Michoacán: El Colegio de Michoacán, 1987); David L. Raby, *Educación y revolución social en México, 1921–1940* (México: SEP/SETENTA, 1974); William E. French, "The Nature of Canadian Investment in Mexico, 1902-1915" (MA thesis, University of Calgary); Frans Schreyer, *The Ranchers of Pisaflores: The Case History of a Peasant Bourgeoisie in Twentieth Century Mexico* (Toronto: University of Toronto Press, 1980); Sawatzky, *They Sought a Country*; Ross Crumrine, *El ceremonial de pascua y la identidad de los Mayos de Sonora* (Mexico: INI, 1974), and *The Mayo Indians of Sonora, Mexico: A People who Refuse to Die* (Tucson: University of Arizona Press, 1977); Alfred H. Siemens, *Between the Summit and the Sea: Central Veracruz in the Nineteenth Century* (Vancouver: University of British Columbia Press, 1990).

who provided the initial presence and institutional teaching and research programs. And here, as well as in the social sciences in general, the domestication process has become evident in recent years. While eminent international scholars such as Franz Boas worked extensively in both Canada and Mexico early in this century, the identity of a Canadian presence in archaeological endeavours starts with R.S. "Scottie" MacNeish, who joined the National Museum in 1949 and founded the Department of Archaeology at the University of Calgary in the 1960s. MacNeish's pioneering studies on the origin of maize, and the students and faculty he attracted, left a lasting mark on the training and research activities in Canadian universities. Other key figures consolidating the university presence were W. Meyer-Oakes (Toronto and Manitoba) and Paul Tolstoy (Montreal). David and Jane Kelley, who came to the University of Calgary in the late 1960s, played a key role in training national doctoral students who later became instrumental in setting up teaching and research programs in other universities in Canada. The beginning of a national awareness of the Canadian pre-Hispanic attention and its international recognition is evident in review articles by David Pendergast and James Langley.[25]

The international recognition is particularly applicable to the breaking of the ancient Maya code, or the decipherment of this spectacular civilization's writing system. And as Michael Coe's recent history of this process indicates, David Kelley's persistence in the phonetic basis of Maya writing and his book on the decipherment of Maya script became benchmarks in developments resulting in the current ability of an expanding group of epigraphers to read the Maya codices and inscriptions.[26] Prominent among them is Peter Matthews, first an undergraduate student of Kelley, now his replacement at Calgary. Matthews' brilliance already gained him an international reputation as an undergraduate, who after doctoral studies at Yale University was awarded the MacArthur Fellowship, considered by the U.S. public media as a "genius prize."[27] Matthews now teaches at Calgary, and aside from a very busy international conference schedule is codirector of Maya research project along with Mario Aliphat, another Mexican former student of David Kelley, at El Cayo, Chiapas. Other Maya area scholars making important contributions to scholarship include Michael Blake (U.B.C.), Laura Finsten

---

25 James Langley provides a detailed overview in his 1992 Mexico City Canada–Mexico Symposium paper, "Canada, Mexico and the Archeaology of Mesoamerica."

26 Michael D. Coe, *Breaking the Maya Code* (London: Thames and Hudson, 1992). David H. Kelley's major contribution is *Deciphering the Maya Script* (Austin: University of Texas Press, 1976).

27 Coe, *Breaking the Maya Code.*

(McMaster), Elizabeth Graham (York), David Pendergast at the Royal Ontario Museum, and Olivier de Montmollin. Working in other regions of Mexico are Jane Kelley (Calgary) in a large-scale survey project in Chihuahua, Louise Paradis (Montreal) on Olmec cultures in Guerrero, and Michael Spence (Western Ontario) on the Teotihuacan site in the Valley of Mexico. In 1992 a number of archaeologists, after discussions at meetings of Canadian Mexicanists at Calgary (1990) and Mexico City (1992), formalized the creation of a new professional association, the Canadian Association for Mesoamerican Studies. Its objectives are to promote, in Canada, the study of the area of ancient Aztec and Maya culture areas and to address the public interest in these cultures.[28]

The social side of anthropology, in terms of courses offered and faculty engaged in research, is more numerous. The Quebec universities (Montreal and Laval) have been particularly active. They have also attracted a considerable number of Mexican students for professional training. At Laval, Marie-France Labrecque and Ivan Breton codirected a team research project studying peasant adaptations to modernization in Yucatan, resulting in a book published both in French (1981) and Spanish.[29] Breton also researched the transformation of the Gulf of Mexico coastal fishing industry, while Labrecque studied economic conditions of the women's workforce in the Yucatan. Pierre Beaucage, with groups of students from the University of Montreal, has been engaged in a series of studies of contemporary issues of ethnic identity in the mountainous regions of Puebla as well as the ethnohistory of indigenous communities. The ethnic question was also examined in depth by Frans Schryer (Guelph) in the Huasteca regions of Veracruz, resulting in a major reinterpretation of rural agrarian conflicts in the 1970s and 1980s. His recent book on ethnicity and class conflict and a series of journal articles in important journals place him the forefront of researchers on rural Mexico.[30] Ross Crumrine (Victoria) has become an important interpreter of Sonora indigenous religious practices and rituals.[31] Jane Kelley (Calgary), apart from her archaeological activities, has produced two books on Yaqui life histories, initially published in English and later

---

28 Langley, "Canada, Mexico."

29 Yvan Breton and Marie-France Labrecque, *L'Agriculture, la Peche et l'Artisanat: Proleterisation de la Paysannerie au Mexique* (St. Foy: Laval University Press, 1981), with the Spanish version published by INI.

30 Frans Schreyer, *Ethnicity and Class Conflict in Rural Mexico* (Princeton: Princeton University Press, 1990).

31 Compare footnote 24 and Ross Crumrine and Alan Morinis, eds., *Pilgrimage in Latin America* (New York: Greenwood Press, 1991).

appearing in Spanish editions in Mexico.[32] Modernization issues have been studied by Jacques Chevalier (Carleton) in terms of conflicts between fishermen and a petro-chemical complex, while Marilyn Gates (Simon Fraser) has a long trajectory of research on development projects and peasant adaptations to change in the humid tropics with a focus on Campeche.[33] Also in the Maya lowlands Konrad (Calgary) and a number of graduate students, and students from York University have been involved in peasant and environmental studies. Elinor Melville (York) has produced a detailed study of the environmental impact of sheep-raising in the sixteenth-century highlands of Mexico.[34] And Raymond Weist (Manitoba), in addition to his work on Michoacan migrants to California, has recently turned his attention to Mexican migrant worker experiences in Canada.[35]

Of the some 200 graduate theses produced on Mexican topics by the end of the 1980s the largest percentage were in the anthropological disciplines. This is a trend that is continuing into the 1990s, due to the continuing interest in Mexican society, the good access that Canadian academics have to Mexico and heightened interest resulting from current economic integration of the North American continent. Alfred Siemens (Geography, U.B.C.), for example, was one of the pioneers in uncovering evidence of intensive agricultural practices in the Mexican lowlands by the pre-Columbian Maya. Such discoveries have reshaped current understanding of subsistence strategies in the Classical Maya period. Mexican graduates of professional training in Canada have, upon returning to Mexico, become important links in bilateral academic relations and research activities. Canadians working in Mexico reinforce such links.[36] Canadians and Mexicans are in the process of developing binational collaborative activities. This is being reinforced by the increased number of Government of Mexico scholarships being offered to Canadian students

32 Jane Kelley, *The Tall Candle* (Lincoln: University of Nebraska Press, 1971), and *Yaqui Women: Contemporary Life Histories* (Lincoln: University of Nebraska Press, 1978).

33 Marilyn Gates, *In Default: Peasants, the Debt Crisis and the Agricultural Challenge in Mexico* (Boulder: Westview Press, 1993).

34 Elinor G.K. Melville, *A Plague of Sheep: Environmental Consequences of the Conquest of Mexico* (Cambridge: Cambridge University Press, 1994).

35 Raymond Weist, *Mexican Farm Laborers in California* (San Francisco: R&E Associates, 1986).

36 For example, Dr. Denise Brown, at the Universidad Iberoamericana (Mexico City), Dr. Mario Aliphat-Fernandez, at La Universidad de las Americas (Cholula), Dr Lawrence Taylor, at the Colegio de la Frontera Norte (Tijuana), Dr. Gabriela Vargas-Cetina and Dr. Igor Ayora-Diaz (San Cristobal de las Casas).

and the inclusion of a Canada–Mexico Agreement on Museums and Archaeology in the 1991 Canada–Mexico Cultural Relations Agreement.

In the literature field Mexico has had a long-standing Canadian interest, both in the language and literature fields of instruction and research activities in Canadian universities. Books published in this area include: Manuel A. Arango (Laurentian) on the Mexican novel in the revolutionary period; Candelaria Arceo (Calgary) on the romantic short stories of Justo Sierra Mendez; Ross Larson (Carleton) on the Mexican narrative tradition; and Rodney Williamson (Ottawa) on the Spanish in Tabasco.[37] Special mention needs to be made of one Canadian scholar considered a major figure in Mexican letters. This is Serge Zaitzeff (Calgary) who has produced no fewer than twenty books published in Mexico, dealing with a wide range of Mexican literary figures. These include studies of the works of Rafael López, Roberto Arquellas Bringas, Julio Torri, Ricardo Gómez Robelo, Carlos Díaz Dufoo Jr., Ruben Campos, Francisco Gonzalez Guerrero, Mariano Silva y Aceves, and Alfonso Reyes. Zaitzeff's accomplishments have been recognized in Mexico by his winning the prestigious Villarutia Prize and becoming a member of the Mexican Academy of Letters. The publication activities of these Canadian scholars, however, are more widely known in Mexico than in Canada.

Research in other social science areas includes the disciplines of political science, sociology, and to a lesser extent geography and economics. Judith Adler Hellman's (York) work on economic and political issues, Judith Teichman's (Toronto) focus on Mexican political decision-making processes, and Teodore Cohn's (Simon Fraser) work on patterns of trade with the United States and food security issues affecting both Canada and Mexico have resulted in important political science contributions.[38] In the mid-1980s a small working group at the Université de Québec à Montréal (UQAM), in collaboration with researchers at Mexico's national university (UNAM), began an important joint project to examine the transformation of continental economic relations. The Montreal team,

---

37 Miguel A. Arango, *Tema y estructura en la novela de la revolución mexicana* (Bogotà, 1984); Candelaria Arceo de Konrad, *Justo Sierra Mendez: sus cuentos romanticos y la influencia francesa* (México: UNAM, 1985); Ross Larson, *Fantasy and Imagination in the Mexican Narrative* (Tempe, Arizona, 1977); Rodney Williamson, *El Español en Tabasco* (Mexico, 1986).

38 Judith Adler Hellman, *Mexico in Crisis* (New York: Holmes and Meier, 1983); Judith Teichman, *Policy Making in Mexico: From Boom to Crisis* (Boston: Allen and Unwin, 1980), and *Privatization and Political Transition in Mexico* (Pittsburgh: University of Pittsburgh Press, 1995); Teodore Cohn, "Canadian and Mexican Trade Policies Towards the United States: A Perspective from Canada," in John Curtis and David Haglund, eds., *Canada and International Trade*, Vol. 1 (Montreal: Institute for Research on Public Policy, 1985), pp. 3–61.

including Dorval Brunelle, Christian Deblock and Cary Hector, organized a series of conferences and published pioneer studies on Canada/Mexico issues linked to continental trade developments.[39] Their work is not widely known in English-speaking Canada as their publications have appeared either in French or Spanish. André Corten (UQAM) represents another Quebec scholar working on political ideology issues concerning Mexico.

Few Canadian sociologists, other than Richard Roman (Toronto), have focused upon Mexico as their primary area of research. Roman's book on revolutionary Mexico's political ideology is well known in Mexico, and he has also published on questions of nationality and class issues.[40] Jean Louis De Lannoy, also at Toronto, has published articles on educational and indigenous issues; Merlin Brinkerhoff (Calgary) on women's work in Mexico and Canada; and Gerardo Otero (Simon Fraser), one of the very few Mexican scholars holding positions in Canadian universities, has published numerous articles on agricultural issues and the impact of new trade relations upon Mexico's rural sectors.[41]

Geographical research about Mexico, which had a higher profile in the 1970s, has a limited number of Canadian scholars, such as Jean Pierre Thouez (Montreal) whose emphasis has been on demography, Sawatzky's work on agricultural settlements at Manitoba, and Siemen's pre- and post-conquest analysis of agrarian systems of production. Economists, until the NAFTA negotiations, had been notable by their absence in Mexicanist studies. Here mention needs to be made of Sam Lanfranco's (York) interest in relations between oil and food supplies, and Mark Thompson (U.B.C.), who has worked on labour unions and paid some attention to Canadian investment in Mexico during the Porfiriato period early this century.[42] Numerous studies by a new generation of Canadian economists, however, have been initiated in the 1990s.

The research focus overview presented above does not pretend to cover all scholarship; rather, it concentrates upon the work of scholars

---

39 Dorval Brunelle and Christian Deblock, *Le libre-échange par défault* (Montreal: VLB Éditeur, 1989); Cary Hector et al., *Le Canada et le Mexique: Autonomie et interdépendance dans les années 1980* (Montréal: Université de Quebec à Montréal, 1989).

40 Richard Roman, *Ideologia y clase en la revolución mexicana* (Mexico: SEP/ SEPSENTA, 1976).

41 Gerardo Otero, ed., *Mexico's Future(s): Economic Restructuring and Democratization?* (Wisconsin: Wisconsin University Press, 1995).

42 Sam Lanfranco, "Mexican Oil, Export-led Development and Agricultural Neglect," *Journal of Economic Development*, 6, No. 1 (1981), pp. 125–55, and "Technology, Trade and Transnational Corporations in the Food Processing Sector of Mexico: A Case Study," UN/UNCTAD, Doc TD/B/C.6/AC 6.2, Geneva.

that entered the Canadian university system prior to the 1980s. The younger generation of scholars who completed their graduate training in the 1980s, and in the early 1990s, had the disadvantage of not finding positions open for them in universities faced with declining resources and position cutbacks. Available data, however, suggest that over 20 graduate theses will be produced annually about Mexico in the 1990s. If one adds the continental emphasis linked to trade and related issues that number will likely increase.

THE IMPACT OF THE NORTH AMERICAN FREE TRADE AGREEMENT

While Canada's formal entry into the Organization of American States (OAS) increased governmental and research focus upon Latin America as a whole, the NAFTA negotiations provided a "jump-start" for research related to trade and strategic decision-making covering a wide variety of areas. The location of research also shifted, with Mexico becoming a key area for private sector, governmental, NGO, and academic intensification of activities. If one takes the three countries involved in the NAFTA negotiations there has been a seminar, conference, or workshop active during most weeks during the 1992–94 period, and the majority had at least some Canadian participation. One result has been the involvement of a new and growing number of Canadian academic researchers focusing on Mexico and the Canada–Mexico relationship. A second result has been the appearance of volumes of collected essays and conference proceedings. A third has been the establishment of formal working linkages with Mexican colleagues and institutions. The net result has been the strengthening of infrastructures for research and exchange purposes.

Much of the research stimulated by the NAFTA negotiations has a very recent or forward-looking focus. And as the strength of Canada's industrial output resides in Ontario, scholars there are taking a more prominent part in this research. Max Cameron (International Affairs, Carleton) has co-edited a recent book and published articles on the process of negotiation. Lorraine Eden and Maureen Appel Molot, also from Carleton, have been investigating the automobile industry. Michael Hart, from Carleton's Institute for Research on Public Policy, has looked at the strategic implications for Canada of the NAFTA.[43] The Wilfrid Laurier University Trade Development Centre produced a guide for

43 Maxwell Cameron and Ricardo Grinspun, eds., *The Political Economy of North American Free Trade* (Montreal, 1993); Michael Hart, *A North American Free Trade Agreement: The Strategic Implications for Canada* (Ottawa: Carleton University, 1990).

doing business in Mexico.[44] Canada's Department of External Affairs commissioned a wide variety of market studies relevant to trade with Mexico. Numerous articles and books have also appeared in Mexico and the United States dealing with Canada–Mexico issues from a Canadian perspective.

Investigative reporting on Mexico by the Canadian public media, virtually absent other than when internationally relevant events or major disasters were being covered, has become a regular occurrence. The amount of activity by NGOs and special interest groups, now based on actual on-site investigation rather than merely using copy from U.S. media sources, has been very substantial. Canada's national media voice, the Canadian Broadcasting Corporation (CBC), established an office in Mexico City in 1994 to improve Mexican reporting. A new era of Canadian research about Mexico has clearly begun, no longer restricted to academic concerns within university disciplines, and involving a great number of individuals. This same process is also taking place in Mexico, where interest in that country's relations with Canada has become a focus of significant attention and research activity. The net result is that Canadian and Mexican researchers are in closer communication and a mutual binational awareness is now very much of a reality.

From a research perspective the impact of the NAFTA has been very positive. The continental focus and preoccupation with the ramifications of the NAFTA, however, may result in overlooking a perspective with more historical depth. This is both a byproduct of contemporary pre-occupations and the nature of area studies as they have developed since the 1960s. Observing the content of national and international conferences dealing with continental trade–concerns suggests that there are two sets of scholars. On the one hand, both in Canada and the United States, there exist a critical mass of scholars expert in this set of binational issues. On the other hand, regarding Mexico and the United States are another criti-cal mass of scholars. Virtually no expertise exists, however, that has equal command of both sets of relations, while the Canada–Mexico expertise is just barely developing. What is still lacking and in serious need of atten-tion is a research focus that helps to clarify the nature of Canadian–Mexican interactions, and the role of the United States in managing them before and after 1944, when formal diplomatic relations were established.

A series of cultural and academic events in Mexico and Canada in 1994, celebrating 50 years of Canada–Mexico formal diplomatic relations, provided a stimulus for intensified research. The results of many of these projects were presented in a series of conferences held in Mexico and Canada. Three conferences in 1994, with proceedings in preparation for

---

44 *Doing Business in Mexico* (Laurier Trade Development Centre: Wilfrid Laurier University, 1992).

publication, are worth noting. The Mexican Association for Canadian Studies organized an international conference, "Canada–Mexico: 50 Years of Diplomatic Relations" (27–29 April) at UNAM, with 80 Canadian and Mexican program participants. Quebec's Laval University hosted a conference assessing the events of 1988–94, with 30 Canadian and Mexican participants (2–4 November). The Canadian Association of Mexican Studies' inaugural public event, at the University of Calgary, attracted 100 Canadian and Mexican program participants, focusing upon the conference theme "Canada–Mexico Relations: Past, Present and Future" (10–13 November).[45] Such conferences have brought to light the current state of Mexican Studies in Canada and corresponding Canadian studies in Mexico. Questions that still require in-depth analysis include the nature of Mexican–Canadian relations while Canadian foreign policy was still being made or significantly shaped in England after the passing of the British North America (BNA) Act, and the nature of Canadian–Mexican economic relations during the early decades of this century when Canadian-based companies played a major role in building Mexican industrial infrastructures.

RESEARCH FUNDING

Federal governmental agencies, established early in the Liberal Trudeau governments, have been and remain the principal source of research funding. The IDRC provided funds that allowed associations such as CALACS to stabilize its administrative structures and enhance exchanges and links with Latin America, including Mexico, from the early 1970s till the early 1980s. In the six years covering 1985–90 IDRC has provided an average of roughly $1 million a year for development projects that had a Mexican component. Most of these funds went directly to scholars and investigators in other countries, but Canadian universities and scholars have also been included. IDRC's role in fostering communications links between Canadian and Mexican institutions and scholars has received and still receives funding support. The principal source of funds for Mexican research has been SSHRCC. Most of the scholars who produced the publications referred to in this overview have received either Canada Council or SSHRCC funding. Information available for the years covering 1983–92 indicates funding for 68 research years by Canadian scholars on

---

45 Dr. Jorge Carpizo, then Secretario de Gobernación, gave the opening address and was given an Honorary Doctorate in Laws from the University of Calgary at the conference. Themes covered included Canada-Mexico relations, historical and anthropological case studies, health issues, environment, continentalism, NAFTA, indigenous issues, and Salinas reforms.

Mexican topics. Included were 37 grants going to 29 scholars representing 17 universities. A breakdown of this funding, according to research-years-funded/number-of-scholars/number-of-institutions results in the following: Atlantic provinces (3/1/1), Quebec (19/9/2), Ontario (23/15/9), Western provinces (23/10/5). Over 80 percent of the SSHRCC funds have gone to the anthropological sciences, much less funding for history and political science, and none to research in economics or geography. This distribution cannot be blamed on SSHRCC but on the quality and number of applications received. This funding profile underscores the lack of attention in important areas of research and the type of Mexicanist research that has attracted the greatest interest. Distribution of this funding support, by area, also provides a rough indicator of the location of much of the more popular activities in archaeology and anthropology. Scholars in the Western provinces have received 54 percent of the archaeological and 22 percent of the anthropological research funds; those in Quebec 14 percent of the archaeological and 61 percent of the anthropological funds; and in Ontario 32 percent of the archaeological and 17 percent of the anthropological funds.[46]

SSHRCC funding has also played a key role in supporting the annual conferences of professional organizations, special conferences and symposiums, journals and other publications in Canada. The international reputation of the foremost of the Canadian specialists in Mexican studies has been significantly enhanced by SSHRCC financial support. It has also played an important role in allowing graduate student research to take place in Mexico. This is especially the case in archaeology, where most of the projects funded have included a team of graduate students and their professors. Funds provided directly by universities, via departments or special research funds, have also been substantial. This includes support for graduate student research of MA and PhD theses; research funds utilized by scholars during sabbatical leave periods; travel funds for attending conferences and getting to research sites; and conferences, symposiums and workshops held on university campuses. International Development funds spent or committed for Mexico-related research projects, for the period April 1984 to March 1998, are slightly above $8.6 million. Seven million dollars of these funds have originated from CIDA and IDRC, Canada's primary foreign assistance agencies.[47]

Upon Canada's entry as a full member of the OAS and the beginning of the NAFTA negotiations, the Academic Relations Division (ARD) of the Federal External Affairs and International Trade Ministry has

---

46 Information supplied by the International Division, Association of Universities and Colleges of Canada (AUCC), Ottawa.

47 *Loc. cit.*, CUPID—Rollup Report #13.

provided increased funding support for developing infrastructures between Canada and Mexico. The creation of the Canadian Forum for Latin America (FOCAL), linked to the North-South Institute for the purpose of improving relations with Latin America, has resulted in initiatives that impact upon Mexican research. FOCAL is currently supporting the creation of directories and communication systems linking Canadian and Mexican scholars. It sponsored a November 1991 Canada–Mexico Symposium on Science and Technology held in Mexico City as well as exchanges and conferences in Canada. The ARD assisted in funding a specialists' workshop at the University of Calgary (March 1990) resulting in the appearance of the *Canadian Mexicanists Network Newsletter*, also receiving support from the same source. A binational symposium, hosted by Mexico's Universidad Iberoamericana (February 1992) and focusing upon Canadian social science research concerning Mexico, was partially funded by ARD. Byproducts of 1990 and 1992 events included the formation of the Canadian Association for Mesoamerican Studies, focusing upon archaeological research, and initial organizational steps for the formation of a Canadian Association for Mexican Studies.[48] ARD has also played a significant role in assisting the increased number of conference activities in the 1993–94 period. Mention needs also to be made of the increasing participation of Inter-American Organization for Higher Education (IOHE), which has substantial CIDA funding, in support of conferences and other academic activities directed towards enhancing academic linkages with Mexican institutions. Recent funding trends show a pronounced increase in areas related to infrastructure building rather than basic research. Private sector support for university-based academic research has still to be developed.

CANADA–MEXICO UNIVERSITY LINKAGES

Formal university linkages between the two countries are recent while individual scholars have established ongoing contacts as the result of research activities. Early attempts at establishing inter-institutional linkages, in the 1960s and 1970s, were largely pioneering efforts with limited follow-through. This was the case in the CALACS attempt to foster a professional linkage as a follow-up of the 1971 meetings in Mexico City.[49] An even earlier effort by El Colegio de Mexico and the Canadian

---

48 For objectives and activities see *Canadian Mexicanists Network Newsletter*, vols. 4–5.

49 Herman W. Konrad, "Experiences and Strategies in International Institutional Collaboration: Reunion Latinoamericano-Canadiense, May 24–27, 1971," report prepared for CIDA on behalf of CALACS (Calgary: University of Calgary, 1971); and Konrad, "Canadian Research Capacities."

Institute of International Relations resulted in two colloquiums, the first in Oaxtepec, Mexico, in 1967, and the second in Toronto, in 1969. The objective of this joint endeavour was to bring together specialists in international relations, economics, political science, history, sociology and other disciplines to examine current issues and future binational relations. A third colloquium, involving York University and El Colegio de Mexico, after two years of planning was held at El Colegio de Mexico in 1983. The results of this meeting were finally published in 1990 in a volume titled *Relations Between Mexico and Canada*.[50] The first sentence in this book written by the editor, a former Secretary of Academic Relations of a prestigious Mexican graduate studies university, identifies the central problem: "Despite their apparent geographical proximity, Mexico and Canada have remained peculiarly ignorant of one another."[51] In retrospect these early efforts represented good intentions without a supporting infrastructure to build upon.

Since study and research in another country provides an effective basis for long-term associations, this factor represents a key element in constructing personal or institutional linkages. Taking the university context as a case in point, between the 1960s and the end of the 1980s one finds some 400 Canadians in the academic context with this type of Mexican linkage. This would include the individuals who have produced the 200 theses on Mexican topics and roughly 200 university-based academics identifiable as Mexican specialists. The number of Canadians who have studied in Mexican institutions is not great, although a number of universities have conducted summer field schools in Mexico. The University of Calgary, for example, has been conducting summer programs in Mexico for over two decades with the involvement of 20–50 students in individual programs. Simon Fraser University has conducted semester-abroad programs in Mexico. Architecture students from the University of Ottawa have been in programs located in the Yucatan. Such study-abroad programs introduce university students to Mexico early in their careers and these participants are more likely to focus upon Mexico if they continue to graduate studies. Mention needs also to be made of perhaps a greater number of students who have gone to Mexico to take part in specialized language training and summer courses offered by a wide number of private and institutional agencies. One example of such a program is UNAM's Escuela para Extranjeros. University administrators in a number of Canadian institutions are now contemplating the development of semester-abroad programs in Mexico.

---

50 Martínez-Legorreta, *Relations Between Mexico and Canada*.
51 Martínez-Legorreta, *Relations Between Mexico and Canada*, p. 9.

Mexican students in Canadian institutions provide another important linkage. In 1990 there were 1,380 Mexican students studying in Canada compared to 6,621 from the United States. The greatest number went to Ontario (42.1 percent), followed by British Columbia (28.9 percent), Quebec (19.9 percent), with lesser numbers in the prairie provinces (Alberta, 4.3 percent; Manitoba, 2.2 percent; Saskatchewan, 1.1 percent). Other Canadian provinces attracted insignificant numbers of Mexican students.[52] The distribution pattern of Mexican students in 1990 indicates parallels to choice of location for newly arrived immigrants, i.e., in areas around Vancouver, Toronto, and Montreal. According to Sandra Fuentes, Mexico's ambassador to Canada, over 6,000 young Mexicans came to Canada in 1992 to participate in recreational camps for children. This early association might have long-term impacts on the linkages between the two countries. Compared to the number of Mexican undergraduate and graduate students who annually go to U.S. institutions, the Canadian numbers are very insignificant. Mexican students studying in Canada for less than three months do not require visas. Recent information indicates slightly fewer than 1,000 Mexican visa students coming to Canada in 1993 and 1,200 in 1994. Canadian universities have not been active in recruiting Mexican students in comparison to a wide variety of U.S. institutions, which annually send recruiting teams to Mexico.

But there are signs, both within Canadian universities and by the federal government, of developing a more organized strategy of enhancing institutional linkages. Part of that interest is being stimulated by recognition that undergraduate students should have the opportunity to include study in another country as part of their education. The ERASMUS program of the European Community has been identified as a model. The IOHE has organized and funded a number of trinational meetings of university officials to look into mechanisms for facilitating such educational exchanges. Individual universities in Canada and Mexico are beginning to negotiate agreements that allow exchange of students, faculty and research information. These agreements will allow graduate students in identified fields to register in the home university and take part of their training on the partner's campus. Credit will be transferred and costs associated will be carried by the sender institution. A variety of such binational university agreements are in place and others are being negotiated.

Information published in the *Canadian Mexicanist Network Newsletter* (Vol. 4, No. 2, December 1993, and Vol. 5, No. 1, May 1994) documents the accelerated trend in bilateral Canada–Mexico university agreements. Forty academic linkage and exchange agreements, involving 17 Canadian

---

52 *Canadian Mexicanists Network Newsletter*, 4, No. 1 (July 1993), p. 13.

and 22 Mexican universities, were identified. Specific programs involved have a greater focus on the professional and science faculties than upon the humanities and social sciences. At the same time there has been an upsurge of collaborative research projects between Canadian and Mexican universities, with 40 projects involving 20 Canadian and 17 Mexican institutions.[53] And as a byproduct of the NAFTA initiatives, trilateral agreements involving Canadian, Mexican and United States universities have been rapidly taking shape involving 30 universities from the three countries.[54] Exchange visits by university presidents and rectors in 1994 will, at the same time, soon increase the number and variety of binational formal agreements. These very recent activities point to a rapid development of infrastructure mechanisms to enhance both the research activities and capacities of both countries relative to each other, and the strengthening of the Mexican studies emphasis in Canada.

Another developing trend is that of visiting professor exchanges. An increasing number of Canadian academics annually spend periods of from two weeks to a sabbatical leave period in Mexican universities. They either teach specialized seminars and/or short courses in areas of research. Besides the sharing of research information, such activities allow individual scholars to become familiar with the programs and administrative realities in the other country. It would be useful for administrative officials of universities in both countries to spend up to a term in one or more universities in the other country. This would create greater knowledge of differences and similarities in administrative structures and subsequently more realistic planning within Canadian and Mexican universities.

CONCLUSION

Mexican studies in Canada and binational university interactions have significantly advanced in the past two decades but are still in need of improved infrastructures and funding support. Current trends suggest there is important movement in this direction as Canadian academic, governmental, private and NGO sectors are increasingly becoming aware of Mexico as Canada's nearest and most important Latin American neighbour. From a continental trade perspective the Canada–Mexico portion of trade, although increasing, has remained minimal. If this hub-and-spokes

---

53 Based on information from *Report on the Inventory of Canadian University Linkages with Mexico and the United States* (Ottawa: AUCC, 1993); *International Agreements of Mexican Institutions of Higher Learning with Universities in Canada and the United States of America* (Mexico: ANUIES, 1993); *An Inventory of U.S.–Canada and U.S.–Mexico Academic Linkages* (New York: International Educational Exchange, 1993); and a survey of Canadian universities by the author.

54 *Loc. cit.*

pattern of trade—with the hub being the United States and the spokes Canada and Mexico—is to be transformed, the direct interactions of Canada and Mexico need to be dramatically enhanced. The research and training capacities linking Canada and Mexico have had a rather striking parallel with the trade patterns, being dominated by institutions and influences from Canada and Mexico's most proximate neighbour. This is the principal reason why so little has been investigated and published about the nature of Canada–Mexico relations.

Whether the economic adjustments and restructuring implemented in Canada by two terms of the Mulroney government and the two *sexenios* represented by the De la Madrid and Salinas governments, and the NAFTA, alter the continental trade patterns remains an open question. Developments in Canadian and Mexican academic circles, however, suggest that the capacity to eliminate the information deficit between Canada and Mexico has been significantly altered since the 1960s. At present there is a positive conjunction of private-sector, governmental and academic interests in enhancing knowledge about current and future binational linkages. Past history and recent events in Mexico nevertheless clearly indicates that political and economic priorities undergo shifts and dramatic turnabouts. The political and economic events in Mexico after the inauguration of president Ernesto Zedillo in December 1994 indicate such abrupt changes can escape political decision-makers. This places even greater weight upon the Canadian and Mexican research communities to move forward, with energy and systematic planning, to increase research endeavours, and expand linkages and binational communication.

One way of measuring Canadian developments is to compare national professional training of specialists with other jurisdictions. The annual production of graduate theses (MAs and PhDs) provides one such measuring stick. Taking the annual production of such degrees in the United Kingdom over a five-year period (1981–86), for example, indicates a yearly average of 77 Latin America theses of which 21.2 percent (average of 16.4 yearly) focused upon Mexican topics. For Latin America as a whole the U.K. figure corresponds very closely with Canadian national output in the 1980s. The Canadian output about Mexico in the 1990s will have exceeded that from the 29 United Kingdom universities listed in *Theses in Latin American Studies at British Universities in Progress or Recently Completed*.[55] Another similarity between Canadian and British professional training concerning Mexico is the overwhelming concentration in the social sciences, with greatest numbers in the anthropological sciences and history.

---

55 Institute of Latin American Studies, *Theses in Latin American Studies at British Universities in Progress or Recently Completed* (London: University of London, 1984).

Important differences are in a greater number of theses in political science and economics in the United Kingdom and the fact that 85 percent have been at the doctoral level. In Canada, the percentage at the Master's level approximates that at the doctoral level in the British institutions. Another important difference is that the U.K. institutions attract a greater number of Latin American students into their graduate programs than do their Canadian counterparts.

Compared to the United States, however, the Canadian picture takes on an entirely different perspective. Here, and particularly in California and Texas, major centres of Latin American and Mexican studies have existed since early in this century. The Latin American Studies Program at the University of Texas (Austin), in the late 1960s when Mexican studies in Canada was just starting to be visible, already had an annual output comparable to the Canadian national production at the end of the 1980s. The Austin campus, during the four-year period 1966–69, produced an annual average of 17 theses about Mexico, 66 percent as MAs and 34 percent doctoral dissertations.[56] This breakdown is close to the Canadian current pattern, as is the prominence of anthropology, history and language/literature fields. The Texas data (1971) concern only one university in one state, while Mexican studies has a dominant role in many institutions in a great number of U.S. universities.

Canadian capacities are at a very early stage of infrastructure development. Graduate training in Canadian universities, particularly at the doctoral level, needs to be strengthened. Collaborative research involving both Mexican and Canadian investigators needs to be encouraged. Faculty and student exchanges between Canadian and Mexican universities in all parts of both countries require serious attention. Scholarships supporting professional training and research funding need to be increased, both in existing areas of strength and in a wide ranges of areas where little or no attention has been given thus far. Information about the work already accomplished and in progress needs to be more readily known nationally and binationally so that the existing base can be more effectively taken advantage of. To make most effective use of scarce resources it might be more effective to develop a limited number of centres for Mexican studies, building upon programs with a critical mass of scholarship. This should not discourage institutions without strong programs from expanding their expertise, identifying and actively supporting a type of Centres of Excellence Program for study and research. The shape and direction of Canada–Mexico relations in the twenty-first century will hinge on the development of such expertise, both in Canada and in Mexico.

---

56 Institute of Latin American Studies, *Latin American Research and Publications at the University of Texas, 1893–1969* (Austin: University of Texas Press, 1971).

John Herd Thompson
Department of History
Duke University

Canada's Quest for Cultural Sovereignty: Protection, Promotion, and Popular Culture

In his polemic *Why We Act Like Canadians*, Pierre Berton lectures Sam, his fictitious American correspondent, on the definition of the enigmatic word "culture":

> As for culture we [Canadians and Americans] don't even speak the same language. You think of culture in terms of opera, ballet, and classical music. To us it covers everything from Stompin' Tom Connors to Hockey Night in Canada. What is merely "industry" to you is culture to us. Books, magazines, movies, radio, television—all culture. Anne Murray is culture. . . . *Maclean's Magazine* is culture. The government subsidizes them all, in one way or another, because all are genuine Canadian artifacts, distinct and unique, something that nobody else has—the ingredients of our national mucilage.[1]

Sam should be forgiven any confusion. Culture, writes Raymond Williams, "is one of the two or three most complicated words in the English language."[2] Nowhere is the word more complicated than in the cultural relationship between Canada and the United States. "Culture" has a number of distinct and incompatible meanings, and those of us who presume to talk about it should define how we are using it. For Berton, his fictitious Sam, and myself, the word is not being used in its anthropological sense—meaning "a given people's particular set of preferences, predispositions, attitudes, goals, their particular way of perceiving,

---

1   Pierre Berton, "The Puzzle of Free Trade," in *Why We Act Like Canadians: A Personal Exploration of Our National Character* (Markham, Ontario: McClelland and Stewart, 1987), p. 9.

2   Raymond Williams, *Keywords: A Vocabulary of Culture and Society* (London: Fontana, 1983), p. 87.

394 / John Herd Thompson

feeling, thinking, and reacting to objective reality."[3] "Culture" in the quotation, and in this paper, means "the works and practices of intellectual and especially artistic activity."[4] Berton is accusing his character Sam of seeing culture only in terms of *culchah*, the so-called high culture of painting, sculpture, literature, music, opera, and ballet of Europe, adopted by the bourgeoisie of North America to differentiate itself from the masses. What Berton is celebrating as Canada's "national mucilage" is the mass or popular culture that Canadians consume as the product of their subsidized cultural industries.[5] In this context, cultural sovereignty is the power of a sovereign government to control the operation of cultural industries.[6]

LEGISLATING CULTURE IN CANADA

For almost a century, Canadian governments have attempted to assert this cultural sovereignty, and to control the allegedly deleterious effects of U.S. newspapers, popular fiction, magazines, comic books, motion pictures (and now videotapes), radio, and eventually television and the associated recording industry. Canadians now routinely use the term "cultural imperialism" to describe these effects; however, an American sociologist has recently suggested that "cultural diffusion" would be more appropriate.[7] However we choose to describe it, no one would deny the widespread presence of U.S. popular culture in Canada. Although every nation state on the planet is penetrated by U.S. mass media to some degree, Canada's situation has been, and remains, unique. The explanations for this situation are familiar, and may be quickly summarized.

---

3   Raymond Gagné, "French Canada: The Interrelationship Between Culture, Language, and Personality," in Bruce Hodgins and Robert Page, eds., *Canadian History since Confederation* (Georgetown, Ontario: Irwin-Dorsey, 1972), p. 526.

4   Williams, *Keywords*, p. 90.

5   "Mass" culture is the better descriptive term because, again, as Raymond Williams notes, "popular" culture is not a culture created by the people, and the term itself was not bestowed upon this form of culture "by *the people*, but by others, and it still carries two older senses: inferior kinds of work; and work deliberately setting out to win favour." Williams, *Keywords*, p. 237.

6   Given an anthropological definition of culture, cultural sovereignty would be absurd: "a nation doesn't possess a culture as one possesses property, a nation *is* its culture." Michael Bergman, "Free Trade: Trick-or-Treaty?" *Cinema Canada*, 149 (February 1988), pp. 14–15, cited in Barbara Fairbairn, "The Implications of Free Trade for Television Broadcasting in Canada," *Canadian Issues/Themes canadiens*, 12 (1989), p. 80.

7   Joel Smith, *Canada's Television, Entertainment, and National Culture Dilemma Reconsidered—Real or Spurious* (unpublished manuscript).

First, Canada's exposure to American mass culture is not mediated by language: seventy percent of its population shares a language with Americans. Second, English Canadians have no long history of national existence upon which to build a national identity: like Americans, they trace their ideological roots back to seventeenth-century Britain. The critical difference is that Canadian exposure to U.S. mass culture is not mediated by distance. Eighty percent of the Canadian population lives within 100 km of the U.S. border, with the result that both U.S. print and electronic media are immediately available.

Canadian cultural nationalists have long had statistics at their fingertips to demonstrate the consequences of this proximity. Rick Salutin's litany in the anti-free-trade anthology *If You Love This Country* can serve to illustrate their case:

> Only 3 to 5 per cent of all theatrical screen time in Canada goes to Canadian films; 97 per cent of profits from films shown in Canada go out of the country, 95 per cent to the U.S.; 95 per cent of English-language TV drama is non-Canadian; Canadian-owned publishers have only 20 per cent of the book market, though they publish 80 per cent of Canadian titles; 77 per cent of the magazines sold here are foreign; 85 per cent of record and tape sales are non-Canadian. . . . Canadian plays are the *alternative* theatre here.[8]

Allowing for the appearance of new technologies, similar figures could be provided for any decade back to the 1920s. To a Canadian cultural nationalist, these numbers add up to the conclusion that "the overall extent of Canadian cultural domination [by the United States] is effectively unparalleled."[9]

This explains why Canada has been searching for cultural sovereignty for almost as long as the United States has been exporting popular culture. Prodded by a nationalist intelligentsia concerned with creating a Canadian national identity, and by Canadian cultural industries seeking the same sheltered market enjoyed by other Canadian manufacturers, successive governments have groped for policies to cope with U.S. mass culture. The invariable first step has been investigation. From Aird to Massey-Lévesque to Applebaum-Hébert, royal commissions, task forces, and special committees have filled library shelves with weighty reports. The legislation which sometimes followed falls into two broad categories:

---

8   Rick Salutin, "Keep Canadian Culture Off the Table—Who's Kidding Who," in Laurier LaPierre, ed., *If You Love This Country* (Toronto: McClelland and Stewart, 1987), pp. 205–06.

9   Ian Parker, "The Free Trade Challenge," *Canadian Forum* (February–March 1988), p. 34.

attempts to *protect* Canadian cultural industries with regulatory or tariff barriers, and attempts to *promote* indigenous Canadian mass culture through subsidies to individual artists, or government-sponsored creation of cultural infrastructures. Policies were not always clear-cut; protectionist and promotional solutions were sometimes applied alternately or even simultaneously.

The most unambiguously protective cultural legislation has been Canada's policy toward U.S. periodicals. The protracted battle between the Canadian government and *Time* is the most intensively studied case,[10] but magazines were first identified as a problem during the 1920s. In 1925, four U.S. magazines had larger circulations than the leading Canadian title—then, as now, *Maclean's*—and *Saturday Evening Post* rubbed salt into the circulatory wounds of its Canadian competitors by (truthfully) billing itself as "Canada's best-selling magazine."

The subsequent campaign against U.S. magazines illustrates the typical alignment of forces behind campaigns for cultural sovereignty. It combined publishing entrepreneurs seeking an advantage against their U.S. competitors with a nationalist intelligentsia which argued that U.S. mass culture was "a menace to Canadian ideals and to the moral development of the youth of this country." It was difficult to accuse *Saturday Evening Post* or *Ladies Home Journal* of immoral influence, so the target became pulp magazines imported from the United States, with titles like *Black Mask*, *Dime Detective*, and *Spicy Adventure*, "the off-scourings of the moral sewers of human life . . . a putrid flood of undisguised filth." Aroused Canadians demanded that something be done "to dam this trash flowing over the border." In 1930, Bennett's Conservative government obliged with a tariff which quickly had the desired effect: by the mid-1930s, Canadian circulation rose 65 percent and that of U.S. magazines fell an equal amount.[11]

Legislation to promote alternative Canadian mass-cultural industries has been a more typical response than legislating protectionist measures. The first direct subsidy to a mass-cultural industry was made in 1903. The Canadian government provided Canadian Associated Press with an annual grant of $60,000 to distribute news from Britain, which had been overlooked by the U.S.–based Associated Press, from whose wires all

---

10 See Isaiah A. Litvak and Christopher J. Maule, *Cultural Sovereignty: The "Time" and "Reader's Digest" Case in Canada* (New York, 1974), and "Bill C-58 and the Regulation of Periodicals in Canada," *International Journal*, 36 (1980), pp. 70–90; and Roger Frank Swanson, "Canadian Cultural Nationalism and the U.S. Public Interest," in Janice L. Murray, ed., *Canadian Cultural Nationalism* (New York: Council on Foreign Relations, 1977), pp. 54–79.

11 Mary Vipond, "Canadian Nationalism and the Plight of Canadian Magazines in the 1920s," *Canadian Historical Review*, 58, No. 1 (March 1977), pp. 43–63.

Canadian dailies received their European news.[12] King's Liberal government evaded demands for a magazine tariff in the 1920s by offering Canadian publishers a tax incentive, a drawback on the import duties they paid on special grades of papers.

But what became the most characteristic Canadian promotional response to the conundrum of cultural sovereignty was the creation of a publicly financed infrastructure, the approach adopted in film-making and broadcasting during the 1930s.[13] After competition from Hollywood suffocated the infant Canadian film industry in its cradle, the Canadian government rejected the quota solution used in Britain and Australia in favour of the Canadian Government Motion Picture Bureau (later, the National Film Board), charged with the production of documentaries rather than feature films.[14] The Canadian Radio Broadcasting Commission, which became the Canadian Broadcasting Corporation (CBC) in 1936, marks the most visible difference between the cultural industries of Canada and the United States: Canada has a publicly owned and publicly financed radio and television broadcasting system, and the United States does not. The creation of the CBC was an outspoken assertion of cultural sovereignty. "Britannia rules the waves—shall Columbia rule the wavelengths?" was the slogan of the Canadian Radio League, a national lobby group of the early 1930s, which rallied more extensive popular support for public broadcasting than any other cultural sovereignty cause, before or since. As Graham Spry, a League spokesperson, put it to one of those ubiquitous parliamentary committees, "the question is, the State or the United States!"[15] The Broadcasting Act of 1968 requires all radio and television stations, public and private, to "safeguard, enrich and strengthen the cultural, political, social and economic framework of Canada"—to be an ingredient, in other words, of Berton's "national mucilage."

---

12 John A. Schultz, "Whose News: The Struggle for Wire Service Distribution, 1900–1920," *ARCS*, 10 (1980), pp. 27–35. The subsidy failed to accomplish its purpose: according to Schultz, "CAP cables consisted mainly of society news and rarely averaged more than 500 or 600 words daily." The experiment was ended in 1910.

13 See Allan Smith, "Canadian Culture, the Canadian State, and the New Continentalism," *Canadian-American Public Policy*, 3 (October 1990), pp. 10–20.

14 Peter Morris, *Embattled Shadows: A History of Canadian Cinema, 1895–1939* (Montreal: McGill-Queen's, 1978), pp. 175–95. The governments of Ontario and British Columbia had short-lived and less successful civil service movie companies. British Columbia went so far as to require theatre owners to show these documentaries; however, the government was unable to persuade moviegoers to actually watch them!

15 Plaunt, quoted in Margaret Prang, "The Origins of Public Broadcasting in Canada," *Canadian Historical Review*, 46, No. 1 (1965), pp. 9–31.

Cultural promotion has given Canada cultural industries that are substantially nonmarket driven, whereas in the United States, for the most part, the market rules. Even with the severe budget cutbacks imposed on the CBC in recent years, Ottawa spends more on culture, broadly defined, than Washington does, to serve a Canadian population one-tenth that of the United States.[16]

Because they do not speak the same language with regard to culture, Americans have never taken Canadian complaints of U.S. cultural domination seriously. There has never been any conscious government-business conspiracy to push the products of U.S. popular culture northward. Therefore, any cultural influence exerted upon Canada is understood as passive and probably benevolent. Thus, there is no understanding of, let alone sympathy for, Canadian policies to achieve cultural sovereignty. When Parliament first discussed restricting the circulation of U.S. magazines in 1923, the *New York Times* held up Holland, Switzerland, and Belgium as small nations that had survived next to large ones: "these examples from Europe ought to convince the Canadians that they are not in danger of cultural extinction."[17]

Americans have also viewed Canada's cultural policies through what Roger Frank Swanson has called a "first amendment optic," the belief that any interference with the free flow of ideas is inherently wrong.[18] "We have learned better," said the same *New York Times* editorial, and "the Canadians, too, may learn that they will gain nothing by giving their own publications virtual freedom from competition." If Canada went ahead with its plan to ban the importation of U.S. magazines, the *Times* suggested "an agreeable form of reciprocity. As Canada bootlegs rum to us, we could bootleg literature to Canada."

CULTURE AND ECONOMIC REALITIES

These American beliefs are not simply rationalizations, but "well entrenched and held largely without cynicism."[19] However, John Meisel

---

16 The budget President Bush presented to Congress for the 1991–92 fiscal year allotted US$833 million to "culture, arts, and humanities." *New York Times* (4 February 1991), p. 8. Note that U.S. high culture is not governed entirely by market forces, but most patronage comes from private philanthropists, not the state.

17 "Canadian Culture," *New York Times* (7 March 1923), p. 14.

18 Roger Frank Swanson, "Canadian Cultural Nationalism and the U.S. Public Interest," in Janice L. Murray, ed., *Canadian Cultural Nationalism* (New York: Council on Foreign Relations, 1977), p. 56.

19 Barbara Fairbairn, "The Implications of Free Trade for Television Broadcasting in Canada," *Canadian Issues/Themes canadiens*, 12 (1989), pp. 80–81.

has observed "that this ideological position often miraculously coincides with crass self-serving economic interests."[20] The historical and contemporary importance of this economic interest is easily calculated. Although Canada has a much smaller population than the other trading partners of the United States, it has been and remains the most important single export market for U.S. popular culture. These products are not unsaleable surpluses being dumped at fire-sale prices; prices are in fact traditionally "slightly higher in Canada." The most recent figures reflect long-standing trends, again allowing for technological change in the cultural industries. In 1989, Canadians bought 39.9 percent of all the U.S. books and 78 percent of all the U.S. magazines sold abroad—more than US$1.4 billion worth.[21]

Canada is the second largest absolute consumer of U.S. movies, and by far the largest per capita consumer, returning 1989 rental fees of US$152.5 million.[22] Recorded music sales return about US$80 million, but the Department of Commerce notes that this neglects the "large proportion of pre-recorded music sold [which] is manufactured by subsidiaries of U.S. companies."[23] Sales of television programs earn an estimated $125 million.[24] These are figures for gross earnings from cultural industry exports, but there has traditionally been a very large percentage profit on cultural exports to Canada; once a cultural product has been produced, the cost of exporting it to Canada is minimal, for the linguistic and geographic reasons discussed above. Asked, in 1975, why his magazine was struggling to preserve its Canadian operation, a *Time* executive replied that "they don't call Canada the candy store for nothing."[25]

Neither U.S. cultural industries nor the U.S. government has been prepared to see the so-called candy store close. However, not all of Canada's cultural sovereignty policies are perceived as equally threatening. The pattern of U.S. reactions may be summarized as follows: Canadian cultural protectionism has usually drawn an immediate response, but Canadian attempts to promote domestic, mass, and high culture have

---

20 John Meisel, "Escaping Extinction: Cultural Defence of an Undefended Border," in D.H. Flaherty, ed., *Southern Exposure: Canadian Perspectives on the United States* (Toronto: McGraw-Hill Ryerson, 1986), p. 165.

21 U.S. Department of Commerce, International Trade Administration, *U.S. Industrial Outlook*, 26–2; 26–9 (Washington, 1991). The next largest customer for both is Britain, which purchases eight percent of U.S. book exports and five percent of U.S. magazine exports.

22 Ibid., Article 32–2.

23 Ibid., Article 32–4.

24 Fairbairn, "Implications of Free Trade," p. 76.

25 *Business Week* (20 October 1975), p. 52.

usually been ignored because these attempts have never seriously threatened the profits of U.S. firms exporting cultural products, as with the
documentary niche chosen by the National Film Board (NFB). Nor was
the demonstration effect of Canada's cultural public enterprise feared by
U.S. private business. Corporate America showed a great deal more hostility to Ontario's system of public electric power generation than it did
to public film production or broadcasting. Cultural promotion, in its
public enterprise form, was not only nonthreatening, its effects could
even be positive. For example, CBC television has spent millions to buy
programs from U.S. networks: in the supreme example of this irony, U.S.
football first came to Canadian screens via the CBC.[26]

If the general pattern of the U.S. response has been predictable, the
precise stratagems employed by business, government, or the two acting
in concert have not. U.S. entertainment companies have not always
needed Washington to help them counter Canadian cultural sovereignty
policies that threatened their interests. If they have a Canadian subsidiary, U.S. cultural exporters would make their case directly, as *Time*
did to dissuade the Diefenbaker government from discriminatory tax
changes.[27] Even if they didn't, they could lobby the Canadian government. In 1947, faced with an impending quota law and the possibility that
the NFB would begin feature film production, the Motion Picture Association of America sold the Canadian government on the Canadian Cooperation Project, a transparent flim-flam which promised to display
Canada to the world through the work of Hollywood studios. Producers
were to be encouraged to use Canadian locations whenever appropriate,
Canadian news in the newsreels was to be increased, and scriptwriters
promised that Canada would be mentioned as frequently as possible in
the dialogue of features made in Hollywood. The wonder is not that the
plan achieved no results—for Hollywood did not intend it to—but that
this bizarre scheme took in such otherwise hard-headed Canadians as
C.D. Howe and Donald Gordon.[28]

When the U.S. government intercedes on behalf of a U.S. cultural
industry, it is for the same reasons that it acts when any U.S. economic
interest is threatened: because the firms concerned are domestically
important, and can bring pressure to bear on Washington. This is not
calculated subversion on the part of the United States; the goal is to

---

26 Paul Rutherford, *When Television was Young: Primetime Canada, 1952–1967*
(Toronto: University of Toronto Press, 1990), p. 131.

27 John G. Diefenbaker, *One Canada: Memoirs of the Rt. Hon. John G. Diefenbaker*,
Vol. 2 (Toronto: Macmillan, 1976), pp. 308–10.

28 The project is described in "Canadian Co-operation, Hollywood Style," Ch. 4
of Pierre Berton's *Hollywood's Canada: The Americanization of Our National Image*
(Toronto: McClelland and Stewart, 1975), pp. 167–200.

enhance export earnings, just as it would be with any other industry. In addition, as Roger Swanson points out, "Washington is not a monolith." Aggrieved U.S. cultural industries can work through the White House, the legislative branches, or through the state or commerce departments.[29] The balance of trade in the products of mass culture industries is so heavily in favour of the United States that it is impossible for them to retaliate by cutting off mass culture imports from Canada. When the Canadian Bill C-58 devastated the advertising income of U.S. border television stations, a proposal to block Canadian exports of film, videotapes, and sound recordings was quickly discarded as useless. Threatened (or actual) retaliation takes place in another trading sector. The twenty-year campaign to defend *Time* and *Reader's Digest* featured alleged threats by the department of defence to cancel aircraft purchasing contracts, to block the 1965 Auto Pact, and to impose quotas on oil imports from western Canada.[30]

CANADIAN PROTECTIONIST POLICIES

The pace and intensity of Canada's action and, thus, of U.S. reaction quickened in the mid-1960s. Standing guard against foreign direct investment and the snares of NATO and NORAD was no longer sufficient, as John Kenneth Galbraith warned the 1968 Couchiching conference that the critical issues in sovereignty were not economic but cultural. Galbraith urged that it was essential to defend Canadian broadcasting, the publishing industry, and the film industry. "These are the things that count," he added.[31]

Canadian governments accepted Galbraith's advice. There was a flurry of investigation with findings similar to those of previous investigations. And, when action followed, it became more difficult to distinguish, in policy terms, where promotion left off and protection began. The Broadcast Act of 1968 not only demanded that "programming should be of a high standard" and be "predominantly Canadian in content and character," it also required that the programming be produced "using predominantly Canadian creative and other resources." The legislative record is too long to describe in detail, but the most important parts must be summarized briefly.

---

29 Swanson, "Canadian Cultural Nationalism," p. 64.

30 Litvak and Maule, *Cultural Sovereignty*, passim.

31 Galbraith's remarks, reprinted in R.P. Bowles et al., *Canada and the U.S.: Continental Partners or Wary Neighbours* (Scarborough, Ontario: Prentice-Hall, 1973), pp. 88–89.

First came quotas for Canadian content on both radio and television, and the creation of the Canadian Radio and Television Commission (CRTC) to enforce them. When cable transmission systems were established, Canadian cable companies were allowed to retransmit U.S. signals without paying royalties to the originating stations. In the spirit of *Catch-22*, Canadian stations have the privilege of simultaneous substitution; they can bump from cable distribution U.S. stations that are carrying the same program at the same time. The government also created the Canadian Film Development Corporation (now Telefilm), which granted public funds for film (and now television) production, and, through a capital cost allowance program, permitted a 100 percent tax credit for investment in a Canadian feature film.

In all cultural industries, Trudeau's Liberal government applied the regulations restricting foreign investment with particular rigour, but within this already restricted cultural sector, book publishing companies received special care. Canadian magazines were protected by tariffs prohibiting the entry of U.S. competitors with more than five percent Canadian advertising, and promoted through postal subsidies. The most dramatic of the new policies, as far as the Canada–United States relationship was concerned, was Bill C-58, a 1976 amendment to the Income Tax Act which denied deductions for advertising costs to Canadian advertisers who attempted to reach their domestic market via U.S. radio and television stations or periodicals. It was this Maclean-Hunter monopoly bill that eliminated *Time Canada*, and launched *Maclean's* as English Canada's newsweekly.

Have these policies worked? Canadian cultural sovereignists grumble that, for radio and television, "Canadian content . . . continues to be very loosely defined."[32] But if not strictly defined, the content regulations are strictly enforced, so that in terms of the quantity of Canadian mass cultural production, the record is uneven, but on the whole impressive. The most obvious broadcasting failure is English-Canadian television drama, which is almost non-existent. The best example of success is recorded music. The combination of a protective tariff on imported tapes and albums and the promotion of Canadian content regulations for air play have launched both a domestic industry and a number of individual careers. There is room for scepticism about the quality of the popular culture that government policy is promoting and protecting. Critics sniff haughtily at "filling the airwaves with undistinguished rock 'n' roll— acceptable as long as it is played by a band from Sudbury or Winnipeg,

---

32 Paul Audley, *Canada's Cultural Industries: Broadcasting, Publishing, Records and Film* (Toronto: Canadian Institute for Economic Policy, 1983), p. 257.

but not if it comes from Des Moines."[33] The cultural sovereignist responses to such comments range from denial to a defensive "Sure, it's junk—but at least it's *our* junk."

Arguing that these policies have established cultural sovereignty would require a leap of faith that not even a cultural bureaucrat from the department of the Canadian Secretary of State could make. But the fact that the ultimate goal remains elusive is never accepted by their supporters as a reason for eliminating the policies. As John Hutcheson puts it, "Canadian production holds only a minor share of the market, but what little there is [is] a consequence of some form of government support, whether subsidy, regulation or tax incentive."[34]

U.S. response to these new cultural policies of the 1970s had evolved a long way from the bemused paternalism with which the *New York Times* lectured Canada in the 1920s. As an academic commentator observed in 1976, "there are indications that U.S. tolerance levels are not as high as they were a few years ago."[35] This puts the case in the mildest terms possible; what are referred to as "irritants" by professional trade negotiators are festering sores to the members of Congress who speak for the U.S. cultural exporters afflicted by them.

CULTURE AND THE FREE TRADE AGREEMENT

The Canada–United States Free Trade Agreement (FTA) removed few of these irritants. Canada's negotiators claimed that culture had been kept off the negotiating table and had been formally exempted from the final agreement; Canadian critics of the FTA denied both these contentions.[36] In fact, the FTA is ambiguous. Article 2005, paragraph 1, states that "cultural industries are exempt from the provisions of this agreement" with the exception of certain specifically enumerated concessions by Canada: the recording industry was not exempt, and the 11.8 percent Canadian tariff had to be eliminated; Canadian cable television companies

---

33 Dave Chenoweth, "Does the Quantity Equal the Quality?" *Montreal Gazette* (21 March 1980); and Charles Pullen, "Culture, Free Trade, and Two Nations," *Queen's Quarterly*, 95, No. 4 (Winter 1988), p. 888.

34 John Hutcheson, "Culture and Free Trade," in Michael D. Henderson, ed., *The Future on the Table: Canada and the Free Trade Issue* (Toronto: Masterpress, 1987), pp. 109, 111.

35 Swanson, "Canadian Cultural Nationalism," p. 63.

36 The best argued example is Susan Crean's "Reading Between the Lies: Culture and the Free Trade Agreement," *This Magazine*, 22, No. 2 (May 1988), pp. 29–33.

were required to pay royalties to American broadcasters for signals that they retransmitted on Canadian cable systems. However, this general exemption in paragraph 1 is followed by paragraph 2 which says that "notwithstanding any other provision of the agreement, a Party may take measures of equivalent commercial effect in response to action that would have been inconsistent with this agreement but for paragraph 1." In other words, if Canadian cultural sovereignty legislation is exempted from the FTA, the American right to retaliate is also exempted.

The Canadian government's claim that Canada's cultural legislation has any privileged position in the FTA was specious. A more realistic interpretation would be that the FTA maintained the cultural *status quo ante bellum*: Canada can keep the policies it already has, but the United States has the power to retaliate against them in any sector it wishes. Testifying before the House Ways and Means Committee in March 1991, U.S. Trade Representative Carla Hills said exactly that. "We didn't give it up in the Canadian agreement. . . . What we did was agree to disagree. We maintain our rights to bring cases against Canada. . . . Canada has maintained its right to disagree with us."[37]

After negotiating the FTA, however, Canada made significant cultural concessions not formally required by the agreement. When Canadian cultural sovereignists charged that secret undertakings had been reached to water down old policies and shelve proposed new ones, Secretary of State Flora MacDonald dismissed their charges as nonsense. "Canada's right to determine its own culture has been respected in every way," she promised in *Quill & Quire*, the trade magazine of the Canadian publishing industry.[38] MacDonald's promises didn't survive the November 1988 Canadian federal election—nor did MacDonald, for that matter. Three of the specific promises she made in her *Quill & Quire* article were immediately broken by the Mulroney government: on postal rates for Canadian periodicals, on foreign ownership in the publishing industry, and on film distribution policy.

A preliminary version of the FTA had called for Canada to equalize postal rates for U.S. magazines. This clause was removed, but the Canadian government in effect carried out what the FTA had not required it to do. A $220 million indirect subsidy was first translated into a vaguely defined $110 million program to begin in March 1991, but the new program was cut by $45 million before it was even introduced.[39]

---

37 Reuter Transcripts (12 March 1991).

38 Flora MacDonald, *Quill & Quire*, 54, No. 9 (September 1988), p. 82.

39 Stephen Godfrey, "Is Culture Truly Excluded from Free Trade?" *Globe and Mail* (20 January 1990), pp. C1, C3.

The second major Conservative cultural casualty was the Film Products Importation Act, a film distribution policy proposed by Secretary of State Flora MacDonald, a policy that went beyond promoting the creation of feature films to require that Canadian companies control the means to disseminate what they created. But once the legislation had been reworked by cabinet, it was, in Jeffrey Simpson's words, "lights, camera, *in*action" in Ottawa.[40] "The minister has gone in with a tiger of a policy," wrote Susan Crean, "and come out with kitty litter."[41]

The U.S. lobbying campaign against the bill was carried out by Jack Valenti, President of the Motion Picture Association of America. *Maclean's* columnist Allan Fotheringham described Valenti as "the most important person in the Canadian film industry . . . the rich lobbyist for the Hollywood interests who has R. Reagan's ear . . . Through Washington-via-Sussex Drive pressures [he] has emasculated Flora MacDonald's brave but futile attempt to guard Canadian film interests."[42] Valenti appeared on CBC radio, and before the Empire Club, to defend his point of view: if a traditionally co-operative country like Canada challenged the distribution systems of major studios, he argued, it would have what he called a "viral contagion" effect in the European Economic Community, where France was leading resistance to U.S. film and video exports. Valenti contained the virus. The redrafted film distribution bill was "a feeble shadow of what was recommended," protested Daniel Weinsweig of the National Association of Canadian Distributors.[43]

In book publishing, the Mulroney government backed off from its so-called Baie Comeau policy against foreign takeovers, a policy which required that companies up for sale be offered to Canadian purchasers, and which used the traditional device of state ownership of the company as a final alternative to a takeover. The government maintained that the policy remained in force, but "actions speak louder than words," complained publisher Malcolm Lester after New American Library of Canada vanished into the maw of the Penguin publishing house. "If cultural matters are exempt from the free-trade agreement," Lester asked, "why does the government appear to be caving in to U.S. pressure?"[44]

---

40 Simpson, "Lights, Camera, Inaction," *Globe and Mail* (11 May 1988), p. A7.

41 Crean, "Reading Between the Lies," p. 31.

42 Allan Fotheringham, "The Trouble with Thinking Aloud," *Maclean's* (11 July 1988), p. 52.

43 Stephen Godfrey, "Is Culture Truly Excluded from Free Trade?" *Globe and Mail* (20 January 1991), p. C1.

44 Lester quoted in "Fine Print in Trade Pact Turns Good News to Bad," *Globe and Mail* (16 September 1988).

Fifteen months later, a representative of the Association of Canadian Publishers wrote a requiem on the demise of Lester & Orpen Dennys, Malcolm Lester's publishing house: "The government's Baie Comeau policy to expand Canadian control of the industry has been timorously and inconsistently applied," concluded Roy MacSkimming.[45]

The government's change of course on film distribution and book publishing are examples of the sort of dispute-avoidance strategies that will be necessary to make the FTA work as intended. The real significance of the FTA for Canada's cultural industries is that the United States was once indifferent to cultural promotion and, accordingly, left cultural promotion activities alone; today, all is negotiable. However much it protests the opposite, Canada conceded in the FTA the U.S. definition of culture; that culture is a business like any other, and that any action to restrain it calls for retaliation or compensation.[46]

"From here on in, the business definition of culture will prevail in Canada too,"[47] argued Susan Cream, and the Mulroney Conservative government made no secret of its distaste for state enterprise in general. The FTA was part of their attempt (similar to that of President Salinas in Mexico) to make Canada a more market-driven society. The severe cuts in the budget for public broadcasting and the quiet retreat from the cultural policies just described were evidence that the Conservatives intended Canada to move toward the market-driven model of mass culture industries which prevails in the United States.

This is not, however, to say that the Conservatives used the FTA as a way to deliberately sabotage Canada's cultural industries and undermine the nationalist intelligentsia that so heartily opposed them and their trade policy. Even if they watered down Baie Comeau, Tory policies like that on investment in the book-publishing industry still infuriated Americans such as Representative John Dingell, a Michigan Democrat who pressed the administration to "urge the Canadian government to do away with the policy altogether."[48]

---

45 Roy MacSkimming, "Does the Political Will Exist to Save the Publishing Industry?" *Globe and Mail* (16 January 1991), p. A11.

46 Vincent Mosco, "Free Trade in Communication: Building a World Business Order," in Kaarle Nordenstreng and Herbert I. Schiller, eds., *Beyond National Sovereignty: International Communication in the 1990s* (Norwood, N.J.: Ablex Publishing, 1993), pp. 195–197.

47 Crean, "Reading Between the Lies," p. 31.

48 Dingell speaks for Gulf and Western Inc., which ran afoul of the policy through its acquisition of Ginn & Co. See Jennifer Lewington, "Ottawa Book Policy Target of Attack by Quiet Congress Veteran," *Globe and Mail* (18 March 1989).

As negotiations to create a trilateral North American Free Trade Agreement began, the Mulroney government steadfastly insisted that the NAFTA would have no effect on Canadian cultural industries. There was no significant cultural industry trade between Mexico and Canada, with the result that "Mexican cultural imperialism is hardly a credible threat," a columnist noted.[49] Even between Mexico and the United States, trade in the products of cultural industries is small, much smaller than that between the U.S. and Canada.[50]

Thus, if the Canadian negotiators had hoped that Mexico would cooperate with Canada to press the United States for more explicit exemptions for cultural industries, they were disappointed. Although there were some Mexicans who worried about the NAFTA's implications for Mexico's cultural sovereignty, most Mexicans neither understood the Canadian point of view on cultural industries nor sympathized with Canada on it.[51] "Canada should be the 51st U.S. state," a young Mexican told a *Globe* reporter in February 1991. "Canada is so lacking in its own culture that it had to steal hockey and the Stanley Cup from the U.S. to have something to call its own[!]"[52] During his 1990 visit to Ottawa, President Salinas dismissed out of hand the suggestion that cultural issues could be a serious concern for Mexico. On the contrary, increased cultural trade offered Mexican cultural industries the prospect of increased sales in the large Spanish-speaking market in the United States.

NAFTA negotiations in fact threatened to rip the bandages off the festering sores left from the Canada–U.S. FTA. Senators and representatives have good job security and long memories; as *Globe* correspondent Jennifer Lewington put it, "some irritants, especially in the cultural area, are political time bombs with an uncertain fuse."[53] In its successful attempt to persuade the Senate and the House to grant it "fast track" negotiating authority for the NAFTA, Carla Hill's most consistently effective sales pitch was the argument that renewed negotiations would mean new opportunities to resolve the question of Canadian cultural

---

49 Jeffrey Simpson, "A Deal Most People Oppose, Offered by an Unpopular Government," *Globe and Mail* (13 August 1993), p. A16.

50 Using magazines as an (admittedly language and education biased) example, Canada takes in 78 percent of U.S. magazine exports and Mexico 3 percent. U.S. Department of Commerce, *Industrial Outlook* (1991), Article 26-6.

51 Katherine Ellison, "Free-Trade Pact Raises Cultural Concerns," Raleigh *News and Observer* (7 April 1991), p. 22A.

52 Madelaine Drohan, "Here We Go Again," *Globe and Mail* (9 February 1991), p. D1.

53 "Ottawa Book Policy," *Globe and Mail* (18 March 1989).

sovereignty legislation in favour of the United States.[54] The promise to deal severely with "offensive" Canadian legislation like Bill C-58 was offered to a wary Congress as an inducement to get involved with negotiations with Mexico. Congress also considered, but did not pass, an amendment to the law which implemented the NAFTA that would have expedited the process of retaliation against Canadian cultural policies judged injurious to U.S. cultural exporters.[55]

The NAFTA negotiations continued the stalemate on cultural industries. The eventual NAFTA accord left the provisions of the Canada–U.S. FTA—the agreement to disagree about Canada's cultural policies— unchanged. By the time the NAFTA was inaugurated in January 1994, the Republicans and Conservatives who had devised it were both out of office.

In Ottawa, the new Liberal government of Jean Chrétien denounced the "Conservative regime [which] has deliberately undermined our national cultural institutions," and promised "to commit itself to cultural development." Its first year in office, however, offered little evidence that the new Canadian government took these promises seriously. In March 1994, over the protests of the Association of Canadian Publishers, the new government approved the sale of Ginn Publishing Canada to the U.S. entertainment conglomerate Paramount Communications Inc., rather than insist that it go to a Canadian buyer.[56]

When Paramount itself was immediately swallowed by still larger U.S. entertainment conglomerate Viacom Inc., cultural nationalists demanded that Ottawa block the takeover until Viacom agreed to divest some of its Canadian holdings in publishing and film distribution. Despite the protests, the takeover was approved by the Chrétien government without conditions. To sugar-coat the Cabinet's capitulation, Viacom asssured them that it would re-invest some of its Canadian profits in Canada's cultural industries. In a gesture eerily reminiscent of the "Canadian Co-Operation Project" of 1947, Viacom promised that Famous Players, its cinema chain, would "undertake to exhibit more Canadian films," and that its subsidiary Blockbuster Videos would "promote Canadian films in its U.S. home video stores." Viacom also promised to invest $23.8 million CDN in Canada's Wonderland, an Ontario amuse-

---

54 See her testimony before the Senate Finance Committee, February 21, 1991 and before the House Ways and Means Committee, March 12, 1991.

55 John Saunders, "U.S. Congress Eyes Ways to Hem Canada in on Culture," *Globe and Mail* (21 October 1993), p. B7.

56 *Creating Opportunity: The Liberal Plan for Canada* (Ottawa: The Liberal Party of Canada, 1993), p. 88; Hugh Winsor, "Ginn Fizzle," *Globe and Mail* (19 March 1994), p. D5.

ment park.[57] A *Toronto Star* editorialist searched for appropriate denunciations for the Liberal cabinet: "Cowards? Hypocrites? Or Canadian puppets on American strings?"[58]

Perhaps stung by such reproach, the Chrétien government made sudden nationalist advances on two cultural fronts in January 1995. In April 1993 *Sports Illustrated* had discovered a technological loophole in Canada's restriction on split-run editions of foreign magazines. The magazine simply beamed its U.S. edition to a Canadian printing plant by satellite, added a couple of Canadian stories, and became in the process a "Canadian" magazine in which Canadian advertisers were permitted tax deductions for the cost of their ads. To the cheers of Canadian magazines, Ottawa responded with an 80 percent excise tax.[59]

The second case involved cable-television regulation. In 1994 the CRTC had ruled, as Canadian law required it to, that Nashville-based Country Music Television be removed from Canadian cable systems in favour of the New Country Network, a Canadian competitor. In this case Ottawa acted by not acting: the Cabinet refused to override the CRTC decision. Heritage Minister Michel Dupuy specifically cited the cultural exemption under the NAFTA as the basis of Canada's right to protect its cultural industries. "We intend to take a strong line when Canadian cultural interests are threatened," he announced.[60]

Democratic President Bill Clinton kept silent about these U.S.–Canada cultural differences, unlike his predecessors. But his trade representative Mickey Kantor yielded nothing to any Republican in his zealous defence of U.S. cultural exporters. Lampooning the lyrics of country music, *The Financial Post* reported that Kantor was "mighty fussed and he took to making threats about retaliating against a passel of Canadian entertainment industries." Trade-war over television regulation was resolved by a merger: Country Music Television absorbed the New Country Network, and suddenly "the hurtin' is over and the lovin' has started between the country music broadcasters."[61] The excise tax on split-run magazines remains, however; the *Sports Illustrated* case may become the first to provoke the United States to exercise its right to retaliate against Canadian cultural protectionism.

---

57 Hugh Winsor and Val Ross, "Viacom Deal to Net Culture $400 Million," *Globe and Mail* (17 December 1994), pp. B1, B7.

58 "The Viacom Mirror" (20 December 1994).

59 Valross, "Split Decision on Split-Run Invader," *Globe and Mail* (24 September 1994), p. A20.

60 Shawn McCarthy, "New Face-off Looms with U.S. on Trade," *Toronto Star* (26 June 1995).

61 "Back Off Mickey," *The Financial Post* (27 June 1995).

Conclusion

No matter how the United States responds to the magazine tax, the brief flurry of cultural nationalism directed at Country Music Television and at *Sports Illustrated* cannot obscure the continuation under the Chrétien Liberal government of the trend initiated by the Mulroney Conservatives. Canada continues to move toward the market-driven, U.S.–style cultural policies.[62] The 1995 Canadian federal budget made substantial cuts to the budget of the CBC, the National Film Board, Telefilm, and to subsidy programs for the magazine- and book-publishing industries. Finance Minister Paul Martin promised further cuts in future budgets. Canada's provincial governments show similar inclinations.[63] This convergence of U.S. and Canadian understandings of "culture" may hold greater peril for Canada's cultural sovereignty than any threatened U.S. retaliation to specific Canadian policies of cultural protection and promotion.

62 Charlotte Grey, "Donna in the Lion's Den," *Saturday Night* (July/August 1995), p. 20.

63 Diane Turbide, "Assessing the Damage," *Maclean's* (20 March 1995), pp. 78–79.

Colin Hoskins, Stuart McFayden, and Dorothy Zolf
Department of Marketing and Economic Analysis
Faculty of Business, University of Alberta

24

Canada–Mexico Co-production Agreement on Film and Television Programming

INTRODUCTION

The United States has dominated world trade in feature films and television programming. This is a consequence of enjoying a competitive advantage in the form of the largest domestic market due to its unique combination of population and wealth.[1] U.S. dominance has posed particular problems for audio-visual producers in the adjacent countries, Canada and Mexico.

One strategy that is increasingly being used to compete in producing feature films and television programming for the global market is the formation of international joint ventures. Governments have facilitated and promoted this strategy by negotiating international co-production agreements. In 1991 the Canada-Mexico Co-production Agreement on Film and Television Programming was signed. This paper examines the rationale for, the terms of, and the early experience with this agreement. The treatment of the cultural industries under the NAFTA trade agreement between Canada, Mexico and the U.S. is also considered and the implications for the Canadian and Mexican industries and the operation of the co-production treaty studied.

CANADIAN BACKGROUND

Canada has a population of over 27 million, with 15.6 million TV sets in 9.7 million households. Cable is connected to 7.7 million of these households, a penetration rate approaching 80 percent. Annual television

---

1 See C. Hoskins and R. Mirus, "Reasons for the U.S. Dominance of the International Trade in Television Programmes," *Media, Culture and Society*, 10 (1988), pp. 499–515.

advertising is around US$1.4 billion.[2] However, these numbers are misleading indicators of market size insofar as Canada is divided into an English-language market and a French-language market, the former being about four times larger than the latter.

U.S. off-air signals were available in Canadian border areas, where most of the population lives, even before the establishment of the Canadian television broadcasting system. In the late 1960s and early 1970s extensive cabling was undertaken. Canada thus became one of the first countries to be cabled due to the attraction of bringing in U.S. signals unavailable, or available only with poor reception, off-air. Today, Canadian off-air signals typically received include the Canadian Broadcasting Corporation's (the public broadcaster) English and French-language networks, private networks (CTV in English Canada and TVA in Quebec) and independent broadcasters. U.S. entertainment programming features prominently in the offerings of the Canadian private broadcasters. In addition to these services, the basic cable package includes three or four U.S. commercial network signals, a PBS signal and several Canadian and U.S. cable specialty channels. Further offerings include more cable specialty channels and Canadian pay channels. Only 25 percent of viewing is of Canadian programming, mainly informational, with U.S. entertainment accounting for almost all the remainder.[3]

In feature films, Canadian English-language productions have not been successful in attracting large box office in competition with U.S. movies with their huge promotion budgets and established star system. In fact only 3 percent of theatrical viewing is of Canadian films, with about 95 percent of viewing being of U.S. films. Obtaining distribution has been a problem for Canadian English-language films. Canadian French-language films in Quebec have, until recently, been more popular.

In 1983, a Broadcast Fund was established to provide public support for the development of television production independent of broadcasting networks and stations. The fund is now administered by Telefilm Canada, an agency of the federal government. The budget for the fund was $65 million in 1993–94. The fund has been instrumental in the development of one of the most vibrant independent production sectors outside the United States. In 1988, a Feature Film Distribution Fund was added with a budget, in 1993–94, of nearly $25 million. The objective of this fund is to assist the film industry in Canada to produce, promote and market Canadian films by providing resources to more effectively compete in the international marketplace. In some provinces of Canada,

---

2 BIB, *World Guide to Television and Film, 1994.*

3 D. Ellis, *Networking*, report commissioned by the Friends of Canadian Broadcasting, 1991.

provincial agencies have been established to provide further sources of funding.

With a relatively small domestic market split into two language groups, Canadian producers have actively sought international co-production partners in order to broaden the market and maximize funding opportunities. The federal government has encouraged this approach by negotiating international co-production treaties with Algeria, Argentina, Australia, Belgium, China, Czech Republic and Slovakia, France, Germany, Hong Kong, Hungary, Japan, Ireland, Israel, Italy, Mexico, Morocco, the Netherlands, New Zealand, Romania, Spain, Switzerland, and the United Kingdom. Projects under such agreements are administered by Telefilm Canada. Official co-productions are recognized as national productions, thus being counted as Canadian content for quota purposes and permitting Canadian private investors to be eligible for tax incentives. A majority of treaty co-productions have been undertaken with France, a surprising number being shot in English. The United Kingdom has been the next most important co-production partner.[4]

Mexican Background[5]

Although at 92 million Mexico has a much larger population than Canada and more TV households, estimates of the number of TV sets (15 million) and annual television advertising (nearly US $1 billion) are lower. Cable penetration is only 7 percent of television households. However, the Mexican market is growing rapidly—the number of television sets was estimated to be only 9 million four years ago—and is overwhelmingly Spanish speaking.

Privately-owned Televisa dominates off-air television with three national networks and a local station serving Mexico City. Nearly 80 percent of the programming broadcast off-air is Mexican (Televisa produces at least 45,000 hours of programming annually) with the remainder

---

4 See C. Hoskins and S. McFadyen, "Canadian Participation in International Co-productions and Co-ventures in Television Programming," *Canadian Journal of Communication*, 18 (1993), pp. 219–36.

5 This section is based in part on material supplied to the authors by the Department of Communications, Ottawa. Statistical material on the size of the television market is from BIB, *World Guide to Television and Film, 1994*. Information on recent trends in the Mexican film industry is drawn in part from the Mexico section of *Variety International Film Guide 1992* and *1993*. Information on recent trends in television is drawn from the *TBI Yearbook 94* and from *The Production Guide: Film-Television-Video, Mexico 1994*. Information on Mexico's co-production treaties is also from the latter source.

largely from the United States. Televisa's main off-air broadcasting rival is Television Azteca, with two national networks and a local station serving Chihuahua. Television Azteca had been publicly owned but was part of a US$641 privatization package in 1993.

Cabelevision, a Televisa subsidiary, is the largest cable operator, with nearly 250,000 subscribers to its Mexico City franchise. It offers twenty channels in its basic package, including transmission of the U.S. networks in English. Nearly 100,000 also subscribe to at least one of the two pay-per-view channels. Televisa's main rival in the new delivery field is Multivision. Since 1989 Multivision has offered a basic 16-channel package by microwave in Mexico City and by direct-to-home satellite elsewhere. In addition up to three pay-per-view channels and HBO Olé are now available. Multivision has acquired rights to distribute NBC's Spanish-language news channel Canal de Noticias and the Fox Latin American Channel (FLACS).

The flow is not all one way, however, as Galavision, Televisa's subsidiary in the United States, transmits Televisa programs to the U.S. Hispanic market. Televisa also has a part-interest in Univision, another Spanish-language network in the United States.

During the 1940s and 1950s Mexican films received wide international distribution. However, for the last two decades film production has been dominated by low-budget movies (averaging US$160,000) featuring violence, sex-comedy and other cheap exploitation fare. Of the 340 films shown in Mexico City in 1991, 170 (50 percent) were American, 92 (27 percent) were Mexican with the remainder from other countries including Canada. The State has tried to stimulate productions of cultural value and to incorporate new talent from Mexican film schools. Nevertheless, production has fallen from 112 films in 1988, the largest number since 1958, to only 34 in 1993. The low production budgets and low production levels are a reflection of existing market realities. Since the 1970s Mexican film production has been directed to the domestic market, the "Hispanic" market of the United States, and to some Central American countries. Each of these markets is weak. Only limited revenues are achievable on the export of audiovisual products to Central American countries. Cinemas have been closing down and the government exhibition company has been sold.

However, there is some good news. Independent production has been promoted by incentives and support provided by IMCINE (The Mexican Film Institute) and the Fund to Promote Quality in Cinema, while the film *Como agua para chocolate* (*Like Water for Chocolate*) was a spectacular international success.

Co-production with Latin America is being promoted primarily through the Latin American Agreement on the Co-production of Motion Pictures. Mexico's partners in this agreement are Argentina, Brazil,

Colombia, Cuba, Dominican Republic, Ecuador, Nicaragua, Panama, Peru and Venezuela. Despite its title, the treaty covers television and video as well as feature films. The co-producing countries must contribute at least 20 percent of the production costs and be involved technically and artistically. This agreement is complemented by two common-market-type agreements, one involving the same countries and the other the same countries plus Spain. The only other co-production agreement is the one with Canada. Televisa's feature film production division, Televicine, is targeting co-productions, linking up with both Mexican and foreign companies to produce about a half-dozen pictures annually.

TERMS OF THE CANADA-MEXICO CO-PRODUCTION AGREEMENT

The final agreement was signed on 8 April 1991, following a Telefilm Canada delegation to Mexico which resulted in an exchange of proposals. Officials from Telefilm expressed a desire to include television productions in an agreement because of the expanding market expected for programs for broadcast, cable and satellite channels. These proposals were received favourably not only by IMCINE, but by Mexican private producers, including Televisa.

The treaty signed governs co-productions in film, television and video and covers the following:

1. Co-productions are to be accorded national status under quota regulations. Accordingly, each co-producer may take advantage of all (tax and incentive) benefits available in its own country.
2. The minority participant must make at least a 20 percent contribution to the budget.
3. The technical and creative contribution shall reflect the financial contribution.
4. Original sound tracks shall be in either English, French or Spanish. Dubbing or sub-titling shall normally be carried out in Canada or Mexico.
5. Foreign performers may be employed if approved by both Canada and Mexico.
6. While location shooting may take place in any country if authorized, live action, animation, voice recording and laboratory work shall be done in one or the other of the producing countries.
7. Third-country participation is encouraged as long as the minority contribution still meets 20 percent and as long as the third country has a co-production treaty with either Canada or Mexico.
8. The sharing of receipts by the co-producers should, in principle, be proportional to their respective contributions to the production financing.

9. A Joint Commission is established to ensure that the agreement is implemented so as to attain the overall balance of financial, creative, and technical participation of the two countries.

Motivation for a Canada-Mexico Co-production Treaty

For Canadian producers Mexico provides an attractive, low-cost environment. The weakness of the peso is a key factor in an industry where "there is never quite enough money to do what you want to do, so you're always looking for a place that will enable you to take what you have and make it look like much more. One of the great advantages of shooting in Mexico is that each dollar seems to act like three."[6] Skilled craftsmen, a good technical infrastructure, and desirable shooting locations make Mexico an attractive co-production partner. But a negative factor is the "history of corruption cited by a number of film makers. One producer said he had to make a 'six-figure payment' to a provincial military commander to secure official co-operation. Others complained of customs delays in sending film to the United States for processing and of difficult dealings with unions."[7]

Co-production with Mexico permits Canadian producers to participate in projects with Latin American countries which are signatories to the Latin American Agreement on the Co-production of Motion Pictures.

In the Mexican case, a treaty has the potential to strengthen the production industry, especially on the film side, and lessen the dependency on foreign productions. "If it were not for foreign films the majority of Mexican film industry workers would be out of jobs!"[8] Increased co-production is attractive because, unlike purely foreign productions, it stimulates the Mexican production industry while permitting some control over content.

Co-production with Canada provides Mexican producers with the capability of producing in the English language and hence greatly improving the chances of selling to the U.S. market. Canadian locations can provide an American urban look.

Canada's large web of co-production treaties provides Mexican producers with the opportunity to participate in multi-country productions

6 Jon Denny, the producer of *Trying Times*, a PBS comedy series that filmed six episodes in Mexico, *New York Times* (1 January 1990), pp. 31, 35.

7 Héctor López, former director of the Mexican government's National Film Council who is now a consultant to foreign studios filming in Mexico, *New York Times* (1 January 1990), p. 35.

8 Ibid.

involving partners in, for example, France or the United Kingdom. Perhaps most importantly, it opens up the possibility of Spanish-language co-productions with Spain.

An important motive generally for co-productions is that they permit the pooling of finances necessary to accumulate the budget necessary to produce internationally competitive programming. It is reported that multinational financing is indispensable for any project in Mexico with a budget in excess of US $500,000.[9]

It is more difficult to evaluate the importance of cultural goals in motivating an agreement. The extensive array of regulatory agencies, funding agencies, and public broadcasting facilities in both Mexico and Canada provides abundant evidence of the extent to which domestic cultural considerations are primary. In Canada, for example, Telefilm Canada states:

> In all cases, the Canadian producer must be in complete control of all matters related to the Canadian side of the production, and also must be actively involved in the non-Canadian side of the production until the project is completed. The producer is also expected to look after Canadian interests in the promotion and distribution of the production.
>
> These cooperative ventures are not intended as substitutes for national productions. They can, however, provide useful ways of supplementing indigenous film and television production.[10]

THE EARLY EXPERIENCE WITH THE CO-PRODUCTION TREATY

Three co-production projects have been undertaken so far. As two are multi-episode television series there has been an impressive volume of shooting and large budget expenditures.

The first co-production under the agreement, *Sweating Bullets,* partnered Accent Entertainment and Florest-Roffiel-Senyal. Twenty-two one-hour episodes of this action drama have been produced. The project was shot in Mexico but was of Canadian origination and majority. The program has aired on the late night slot on the CBS network in the United States.[11]

Tarzan is a Canada-France-Mexico co-production. Seventy-five half-hour episodes of this French majority project have been shot so far in Mexico. This drama series, with an ecological theme, is targeted at children.

---

9 P. Cowie, ed., *Variety International Film Guide 1992* (1992).

10 Telefilm Canada, *Co-production: Policies and Procedures* (Montreal: Telefilm Canada, 1989), p. 1.

11 C. Brown, ed., *Co-production International 1994* (London: TBI, 1994), p. 198.

The third co-production underway, *Garden of Eden*, is a feature film set in Mexico, of Mexican origination and majority, and is a U.S./Mexican border story.

This is an impressive level of activity, especially when one considers that a number of Canada's co-production treaties have yet to generate a project. An examination of the elements of the projects is revealing. The suitability of Mexican locations is important to all three: no tropical jungle is available for *Tarzan* in Canada. The two television series are shot in English and aimed at international, particularly U.S., sales. One of the projects involves France, through Canada's co-production treaty with that country, hence facilitating additional financial pooling and an enhanced budget. An element of balance has been struck early with one project of Canadian origin and majority, one Mexican, and the third a French majority.

NAFTA and its Implications

Canada managed to exempt cultural industries from the FTA with the United States although a "notwithstanding" clause was included which permits the United States to take counter-measures of equivalent commercial effect if Canada introduces a cultural measure that would (but for the exemption) be inconsistent with the provisions of the FTA. This FTA exemption is maintained under the NAFTA and extended to apply to trade with Mexico. When the counter-measures can be used is open to interpretation. Adam Ostry, Director General of Cultural Industries Policy, Department of Canadian Heritage, claims that "the U.S. right to retaliate is limited to measures inconsistent with the FTA, not the NAFTA, and therefore cannot be exercised with respect to new areas covered by the NAFTA such as intellectual property."[12]

There is no blanket exemption governing trade in cultural products between Mexico and the United States. However, Acheson and Maule argue that the difference is not as great as it appears, as there are specific exemptions. These include requirements to use Spanish for television programs (except when authorized to the contrary) and advertising (subtitles are an alternative to spoken Spanish), the requirement that the original advertising be removed from re-transmission of cross-border signals, and various Mexican nationality requirements. Furthermore, Acheson and Maule point out that "all three countries' ownership restrictions in broadcasting and cable have been preserved by exempting them

---

12 A. Ostry, "Cultural Policy in the Age of Liberalized Trade," paper presented to the International Conference on Communication in the Americas, University of Calgary, 5 June 1994.

from the national treatment requirements of the investment chapter of NAFTA."[13]

Deborah Drisdell, Manager–Coproductions for Telefilm Canada, suggests the direct effect of the NAFTA in the audiovisual sector has been minimal but that the indirect effect has been significant. NAFTA has raised the profile of Mexico in Canada and vice versa, and resulted in Canada-Mexico relations, trade and co-operation, such as through the co-production agreement, becoming a mutual priority for both governments.[14]

CONCLUSION

Previously, domestic production with export sales abroad was the dominant mode in film and television. In the more negotiated, circumscribed, competitive world of the 1990s the independent production industry can better be seen as "a condition of inter-locked, quasi-arms-length relationships. Its strategic degrees of freedom are at once increased by the globalization of markets and decreased by the need to negotiate cooperative arrangements with other firms and governments."[15] In linking up with another firm, one or both partners may enjoy options otherwise unavailable to them, such as "better access to markets, pooling or swapping of technologies, enjoying larger economies of scale, and benefiting from economies of scope."[16] At the same time each partner in a co-production encounters constraints on creative freedom, pricing and territorial scope as part of the venture.

Although they do not share a common language, Canada and Mexico both share a border with the most successful audiovideo producer in the world and in many ways are natural partners bringing complementary attributes to co-production. Canada can provide the North American English that facilitates international sales especially to the United States, financing, and a web of treaties permitting Mexican producers to participate in multi-partner co-productions with countries such as France and the United Kingdom. Canada's co-production treaty with Spain provides interesting opportunities for Spanish-language productions targeted at

---

13 K. Acheson and C. Maule, "International Regimes for Trade, Investment and Labour Mobility in the Cultural Industries," *Canadian Journal of Communication* (forthcoming).

14 Interview with Deborah Drisdell in Montreal on 22 November 1994.

15 T. Levitt , "The Globalization of Markets," *Harvard Business Review*, 61, No. 3 (1983), pp. 91–102.

16 F.T. Contractor and P. Lorange, "Competition vs. Co-operation: A Benefit/Cost Framework for Choosing Between Fully-Owned Investments and Cooperative Relationships," *Management International Review*, 28, Special Issue (1988), p. 5.

one of the larger international linguistic groups. Mexico brings desirable shooting and climatic locations, low shooting costs, multi-country co-production opportunities with additional Latin American countries, and Spanish-language market access opportunities.

The Canada-Mexico co-production treaty also has implications for the United States. Both Mexican and Canadian production companies have been producing for the U.S. market for a number of years. Narrow-casting and more targeted scheduling by the networks may create a demand for greater diversity and more specialty programs in the U.S. market. Mexican-Canadian co-productions may find a niche in segments appealing to different language and ethnic groups, different age groups, and high culture as well as relatively low-cost action drama targeted at U.S. networks' late-night time slots, a period when the (now fragmented) network audience cannot support higher-cost U.S.–produced drama.

The level of activity in the first years of the co-production treaty is very encouraging. However, if this is to be built on it is important that the early experience be a good one. Potential co-production partners are easily scared off by reports of unusual difficulties in joint production. Industry sources report there still seem to be problems with Mexican immigration and customs.

Notes on Contributors

Adamache, Robyn. Ms. Adamache is completing an M.A. in Geography at Simon Fraser University. Her thesis is entitled "Discourse and Regional Development: Selling the Mexican *maquiladora* industry in the U.S. popular press." Her current research interests include regional development, gender and development, the social impacts of restructuring in the Americas, and media representations of development issues.

Alarcón Gonzalez, Diana. Diana Alarcón received her Ph.D. in economics from the University of California, Riverside. Her area of specialization is economic development. She has been a research associate at El Colegio de la Frontera Norte in Tijuana, Mexico, since 1988, and is currently on sabbatical working at the World Employment Report Office at the International Labour Organization in Geneva, Switzerland. She has published several articles on different aspects of trade liberalization, the distribution of income, and poverty in Mexico. She is the author of the book *Changes in the Distribution of Income in Mexico and Trade Liberalization* (El Colegio de la Frontera Norte, 1994).

Basañez, Miguel. Mr. Basañez is president of Perspectiva Estratégica, a major polling firm in Mexico, and editor of *Este País*. He is joint author with Neil Nevitte and Ronald Inglehart of *North American Dilemmas* (Ann Arbor: I.S.R., 1991).

Condon, Bradly J. Professor Condon is the director of the Council for North American Business Studies, programme director of the Canadian Institute of International Affairs, a member of the Board of Directors of the Canadian Foundation for the Americas, and teaches international trade policy at Simon Fraser University. He is a trilingual lawyer and international speaker with expertise in issues involving international trade and environmental law. He has published numerous articles on constitutional law, the North American Free Trade Agreement, and the environment, both in Canada and in Mexico. Professor Condon was selected by the U.S. government to take part in the 1995 Congressional International Visitor Program on International Trade. He has also been chosen by the Canadian Bar Association and the Commonwealth Bar Association to design a program on international trade for the 1996 Commonwealth meeting of lawyers and judges in Vancouver, British Columbia.

Culos, Claudia. Ms. Culos graduated from Simon Fraser University in 1993 with a joint major in Sociology and Latin American Studies, and is currently working in Japan. Her research interests include women and grassroots political movements in Latin America.

del Castillo Vera, Gustavo. A political scientist, Dr. del Castillo is director of the department of United States studies at El Colegio de la Frontera Norte. He has received a Canadian International Development Research Council fellowship in support of his study of North American integration. Among his publications is *Ventajas y desventajas de Mexico en el GATT* (1985).

Duquette, Michel. Professor Duquette is a member of the department of political science at the University of Montreal and is a researcher at the Centre for the Study of Industrial Development and Technology at the University of Quebec at Montreal. Among other works, he is the author of *Grands seigneurs et multinationales: l'économie politique de l'éthanol au Brésil* (1989).

Ganster, Paul. Professor Ganster is director of the Institute for Regional Studies of the Californias at San Diego State University. Trained as a specialist in Latin America with a Ph.D. in history from the University of California, Los Angeles, for the past decade his research and publication efforts have been directed towards policy questions of the United States–Mexican border regions. His current research interests include environmental issues of the border region and other aspects of transborder interactions as well as comparative border regions. Professor Ganster has been a faculty member at the Universidad de Costa Rica, the Universidad de las Américas in Mexico, and the Universidad Autónoma de Baja California.

Gerber, James. Professor Gerber teaches economics at San Diego State University and is a member of the adjunct faculty of Universidad

Autónoma de Baja California in Tijuana, Mexico. He holds a Ph.D. in economics from the University of California, Davis. His most recent publications include "The Origins of California's Export Surplus in Cereals" in *Agricultural History*, and "The North American Free Trade Agreement: Its Impact on California" in *Frontera Norte.*

Gutiérrez Háces, Maria Teresa. Dr. Gutiérrez Háces is a member of the Center for Research on the United States at the National Autonomous University in Mexico City. Since the mid-1980s, she has been part of a joint research project with the University of Quebec at Montreal on trilateral relations. She is the author of, among other works, *The Commercial Integration of Mexico, the United States and Canada* (1990), and *Old Ways, New Perspectives in Mexico–United States Relations* (1989). She was invited by the senate of Mexico to participate in the March 1991 debate on the free trade agreement with Mexico and was the organizer, in 1990, of the National Action Party conference on the Canadian experience with the free trade agreement.

Hoskins, Colin. Professor Hoskins teaches marketing and economic analysis in the faculty of business at the University of Alberta, Edmonton. With Stuart McFayden, he is studying international joint ventures in the production of television programming.

Inglehart, Ronald. Ronald Inglehart is a professor of political science at the University of Michigan, Ann Arbor. He is the author of, among other works, *Culture Shift* (Princeton, 1990), and *The Silent Revolution* (Princeton, 1971), as well as co-author with Neil Nevitte and Miguel Basañez of *Convergence in North America* (forthcoming).

Kerr, William A. Professor Kerr teaches economics at the University of Calgary. His research interests are international trade and commercial policy. He has done work on the CUSTA, NAFTA, Canadian trade with the Pacific Rim and Canadian trade disputes with the European Union. Recent publications include *The Economics of International Business* (Chapman and Hill, 1995), co-authored with N. Perdikis.

Konrad, Herman W. Professor Konrad teaches anthropology and history at the University of Calgary. A founder and past president of the Canadian Association of Caribbean and Latin American Studies (1985–87), he is the editor of the *Canadian Mexicanist Network Newsletter*. He has held several visiting professorships in Mexican universities and, for three years, was director of the Instituto Interuniversitario para Investigaciones en Ciencias Sociales en Yucatan. His book, *A Jesuit Hacienda in Colonial Mexico: Santa Lucia,*

1576–1767 (1980), won the Bolton Prize in 1981. He has published extensively on Mexican agrarian systems, economic history, and Canadian-Mexican relations.

Konrad, Victor. Dr. Konrad is presently on leave from the University of Maine, Orono, to serve as the first executive director of the Foundation for Educational Exchange Between the United States and Canada (a Fulbright program). He is an editor of the Borderlands Project at the University of Maine at Orono Center for United States–Canada Relations.

Marquez Perez, Pedro. Mr. Marquez Perez at the time this paper was completed was a graduate student in Political Science at the University of Calgary. He is a graduate of the Mexican Technological Institute, and worked in the Mexican civil service during the Salinas presidency.

McRae, Robert N. Professor McRae is Head, Department of Economics at the University of Calgary. Until recently his research has focused on Canada; now he is estimating energy consumption behaviour of developing countries in Asia. He has published extensively in the area of energy economics, and has presented his research to numerous national and international conferences, university seminars, business organizations, and government agencies.

McFayden, Stuart. Professor McFayden teaches marketing and economic analysis in the faculty of business at the University of Alberta, Edmonton. He has studied the Canadian broadcasting industry and the implications of market globalization for television programming.

Nevitte, Neil. Until 1995 Professor Nevitte was a member of the Political Science Department at the University of Calgary. He recently joined the Department of Political Science at the University of Toronto. Professor Nevitte is co-author, with Ronald Inglehart and Miguel Basañez, of *Convergence in North America* (forthcoming).

Otero, Gerardo. Professor Otero teaches Latin American studies and sociology at Simon Fraser University. He is the editor of *Neoliberalism Revisited: Economic Restructuring and Mexico's Political Future* (Westview Press, forthcoming). His recent research is on the globalization of capitalism and the biotechnology revolution as it affects Latin American agriculture, and on the transformation of the Mexican state and the agrarian structure under neoliberalism.

Randall, Stephen J. Dr. Randall holds the Imperial Oil–Lincoln McKay Chair in American Studies and is Dean, Social Sciences, at the

University of Calgary. He is author of a number of books and articles in the area of United States' foreign economic policy and inter-American relations, including *The Diplomacy of Modernization* (1977), *United States Foreign Oil Policy* (1985), (with Mark Dickerson) *Canada and Latin America* (1991), *Hegemony and Interdependence* (1992), and *Canada and the United States: Ambivalent Allies* (1994). He is co-editor of *The Canadian Review of American Studies* and, from 1991 to 1995, of the *International Journal*.

Sweedler, Alan. Professor Sweedler teacher physics and is director of the Center for Energy Studies at San Diego State University. He has been an advisor to UNESCO, the California Energy Commission and the San Diego Association of Governments on matters of energy policy and planning. He was a Congressional Science Fellow in the U.S. Senate, where he worked on energy and United States–Mexico relations. His most recent publication is *Energy and Environment in the California-Baja California Border Region* (1995).

Thompson, Dixon. Professor Thompson teaches in the faculty of environmental science at the University of Calgary. Among his previous assignments, Professor Thompson worked with Maurice Strong on international environmental issues.

Thompson, John Herd. A graduate of the University of Winnipeg and Queen's University (Ph.D.), John Thompson is a professor of history at Duke University in Durham, North Carolina. Previously, he taught for almost twenty years at McGill University in Montreal. Professor Thompson is author of *Decades of Discord* (1985), which was a finalist in the Governor General's awards for nonfiction, and *Harvests of War* (1978). He is co-author, with Stephen Randall, of *The United States and Canada: Ambivalent Allies* (1994). His particular interests are in western Canadian history, the history of North American agriculture, and Canadian-American relations.

Weinfeld, Morton. Chairman of the department of sociology at McGill University, Professor Weinfeld is author of a number of works on Canadian immigration policy and ethnic relations, including *Immigration and Canada's Population Future: A Nation-building Vision* (1988).

Zolf, Dorothy. Professor Zolf is a visiting assistant professor of marketing in the faculty of business at the University of Alberta. Until 1989, she was an associate professor in the graduate program in communication studies at the University of Calgary. Her research has focused on regulatory issues in broadcasting.

Index

Hydro-electric development, 63, 165, 258, 261, 262, 264, 266, 268, 269, 270, 271, 272, 273, 274, 278, 296, 303, 304, 305, 306, 308

Immigration, 9; 42, 46, 111, 139, 144, 145, 153, 156, 158, 159, 170, 171, 172, 179, 237–251. *See also* Labour
Import substitution, 215, 216, 217, 218, 232
Income distribution: in Mexico, 1, 24, 127–138, 170, 194, 195, 196, 200, 203, 208
Intellectual property rights, 118
International Development ResearchCentre (IDRC), 365, 385, 386
International Monetary Fund (IMF), 4, 96, 116
International Trade Commission (US), 94, 99,119
Investment: foreign, 38, 41, 46, 47, 48; in Canada, 42, 43, 303; in Mexico, 37, 41, 57–76 *passim*, 118, 119, 123

Japan, 5, 42, 106, 119, 205, 240, 249
Joint Trade Commission, 120

Labour, 2, 6, 7, 10, 37, 46; labour standards, 43, 45; in Mexico, 1, 2, 9 19, 24, 30, 127, 131, 133, 137, 138, 142, 144, 145, 146, 172, 193–213, 216, 217, 221, 232, 233, 234, 235, 238, 248, 249, 250; migration, 42, 108, 209
Latin America, 20, 22, 25, 26, 38, 39, 43, 46, 60, 61, 62, 63, 66, 68, 70, 116, 117, 122; migration from, 239, 243, 244, 245, 248, 249, 250, 251
Liberalism, 47–55, 215–235

Manufactured goods, 119, 129, 193–213
Maquiladora industries, 1, 130, 131, 146, 148, 149, 150, 167, 177, 193–213, 221, 223, 224, 268, 272, 275. *See also* Labour: in Mexico

Mazda: in Mexico, 216
Mennonites in Mexico, 367
Mexican Film Institute (IMCINE), 414–418
Mexican Power and Light Company, 26
Mexican studies, 361, 365–392
Mexico City Tramways Company, 26
Modernization: of Mexico, 215, 222, 223, 226, 232, 233, 234
Mulroney, Prime Minister Brian, 2, 5, 284, 298, 302

Narcotics: illegal traffic in, 42
National Energy Board (Canada), 85, 87, 88
National Energy Policy (Canada), 42, 85, 86
National Film Board (Canada), 400
National Action Party (PAN), 4, 6, 56
New Brunswick, 188, 189
North American Agreement on Environmental Cooperation, 281, 282, 284, 285, 286, 288, 289, 293, 294
North American Commission for Environmental Co-operation, 46, 311–326
Nissan: in Mexico, 216, 217, 222, 230
Nuclear energy, 66, 75, 258, 259, 260, 261, 262, 263, 266

Oil and natural gas, 79–91, 119, 124, 129, 130, 163, 168, 215, 221, 296, 287, 299, 300, 302, 303, 304, 306, 308
Ontario: energy development in, 296, 302, 306

Pacific Rim, 239, 249, 251
Party of the Institutional Revolution (PRI), 3, 4, 37, 48, 49, 54, 58, 290, 291
PEMEX, 59, 89, 90, 91 , 260, 261, 268
Perot, Ross, 2
Petro-Canada Limited, 86, 300, 301
Petroleum industry, 3, 42, 67, 69, 73, 74, 79–91. *See also* oil
Political culture, 329–343, 398–401